MW00813191

Received by Christ

Re-envisioning Reformed Dogmatics

*R*e-envisioning Reformed Dogmatics is a series that explores afresh the rich and diverse dogmatic heritage of the contemporary Reformed tradition. The series will plumb the depths of the riches of the Reformed tradition by engaging in constructive and interdisciplinary study while also challenging assumptions that are sometimes expressed as the Reformed tradition's contemporary consensus. There are in current discussions, contrary trends at work in Reformed Theology. Some are eager to expand Reformed orthodoxy to include all Protestants while others narrow the definition of what is "Reformed" to what characterizes the teachings of, say, the Dutch Reformed Church or the Church in Scotland. *Re-envisioning Reformed Dogmatics* is a series that will explore the rich and complex plurality of thinking in Reformed tradition. The monographs in this series will invite readers to think in fresh ways about various theological loci while exploring constructive developments within this dynamic tradition. They will include subject matter that has been hitherto neglected or excluded from conversations about Reformed theology in an effort to recover the intellectual treasures that once made up the full dogmatic deposit of the confessional era. In this way, the *Re-envisioning Reformed Dogmatics* series is marked by that self-same spirit that once motivated the Reformer's clarion call: *Ad fontes* ("to the sources"). Now, with five hundred years of theological development since this first call was uttered, the authors in this series renew that clarion call. This time, however, the sources to which the authors in this series turn include those of the Reformers and their theological heirs.

Received by Christ

A Biblical Reworking of the
Reformed Theology of the Lord's Supper

Celine S. Yeung

CASCADE *Books* · Eugene, Oregon

RECEIVED BY CHRIST
A Biblical Reworking of the Reformed Theology of the Lord's Supper

Re-envisioning Reformed Dogmatics

Cascade Books
An Imprint of Wipf and Stock Publishers
199 W. 8th Ave., Suite 3
Eugene, OR 97401

www.wipfandstock.com

PAPERBACK ISBN: 978-1-6667-4827-7
HARDCOVER ISBN: 978-1-6667-4828-4
EBOOK ISBN: 978-1-6667-4829-1

Cataloguing-in-Publication data:

Names: Yeung, Celine S. [author]

Title: Received by Christ : a biblical reworking of the Reformed theology of the Lord's Supper / Celine S. Yeung.

Description: Eugene, OR: Cascade Books, 2023 | Series: Re-envisioning Reformed Dogmatics | Includes bibliographical references and index.

Identifiers: ISBN 978-1-6667-4827-7 (paperback) | ISBN 978-1-6667-4828-4 (hardcover) | ISBN 978-1-6667-4829-1 (ebook)

Subjects: LCSH: Lord's Supper—Reformed Church. | Reformed Church—Doctrines—History. | Lord's Supper—History of doctrines. | Lord's Supper.

Classification: BV825 Y48 2023 (print) | BV825 (ebook)

Table of Contents

Acknowledgments

WORDS CANNOT EXPRESS MY gratitude for the theologians who have guided me throughout my academic journey, especially Drs. Paul T. Nimmo, Bruce L. McCormack, Dirk J. Smit, and Dennis T. Olson. I am deeply indebted to Dr. Nimmo, my MTh supervisor at the University of Aberdeen, for his friendship and for inspiring me to venture into the topic of sacraments in the first place. Dr. McCormack helped me immensely during my days at Princeton Theological Seminary, from the time I was first settling down as a foreign student, to the overseeing of my final stages of dissertating. His theology offered me brand-new perspectives and helped me concretize my own. His advice for me, most memorably "follow your gut," gave me affirmation I needed to sustain through my PhD journey. Dr. Smit constantly offered me encouragement, and has taught me to be charitable to figures I do not agree with and to appreciate their contributions in their own contexts. Dr. Olson, an expert on the book of Exodus, gave me most helpful insights on this text, especially concerning the Sinai covenant and its renewal. I am grateful to many of my peers at PTS for their friendship and patience. The list is indeed long. Special mention goes to my international cohort, in addition to Cambria Kaltwasser, Bonnie Lin, and Megan and Rory Misiewicz, for being there for me. I must mention my alma mater China Graduate School of Theology in Hong Kong, whose all-rounded support for their alumni is basically unheard of. I am indebted to so many people at CGST, especially President Emeritus Dr. Stephen Lee, Dr. Daniel Lee, and colleagues whom I worked with as a member of staff, who offered me support even when I was abroad. I always remember my home church Emmanuel Chinese Church, which gave me a non-denominational upbringing that encouraged fresh engagement with traditions. I must thank my pastor Rev. Chan Ka Leung for encouraging me and reminding me that "theology is done for the church." I must also thank my peers at ECC whose lives convince me that theology must be down to earth and always stay relevant. My heartfelt thanks go to my very good friend Cheng On Yin for being there all the time. Last but not least, I am forever grateful to my parents Stella and Philip Yeung and identical twin sister Joanie for their unswaying love and support, and for inspiring a lifelong pursuit of biblical and theological inquiry.

List of Abbreviations

Ap	Apology of the Augsburg Confession
c. Faust	Augustine. *Answer to Faustus, a Manichaean.* Translated with notes by Roland Teske. Vol. I/20 of *The Works of Saint Augustine.* Edited by Boniface Ramsey. 50 vols. Hyde Park, NY: New City, 2007.
cat. rud.	Augustine, *On the Catechising of the Uninstructed*
CD	*Church Dogmatics.* 4 volumes in 13 parts. Edited by G. W. Bromiley and T. F. Torrance. Edinburgh: T. & T. Clark, 1956–75.
civ. Dei	Augustine. *St. Augustin's City of God and Christian Doctrine.* Vol. 2 of *A Select Library of the Nicene and Post-Nicene Fathers of the Christian Church, First Series.* Edited by Philip Schaff. Grand Rapids, MI: Eerdmans, 1956.
CO	*Ioannis Calvini opera quae supersunt omnia.* Edited by Wilhelm Baum et al. 59 vols. *Corpus Reformatorum* 29–87. Brunswick, CA: Schwetschke Bruhn, 1863–1900.
doctr. chr.	Augustine. *Teaching Christianity.* Introduction, translation, and notes by Edmund Hill. Vol. I/11 of *The Works of Saint Augustine.* Edited by John E. Rotelle. 50 vols. Hyde Park, NY: New City, 1996.
en. Ps.	Augustine. *Expositions on the Psalms.* Translated by Maria Boulding. Vol. III/15 of *The Works of Saint Augustine.* Edited by John E. Rotelle. 50 vols. Hyde Park, NY: New City, 2000.
Ep.	Augustine. *Letters.* Translated with notes by Roland Teske. Vol. II/1 of *The Works of Saint Augustine.* Edited by John E. Rotelle. 50 vols. Hyde Park, NY: New City, 2001.
FC	Luther, Martin. *Formula of Concord.* In *The Book of Concord: The Confessions of the Evangelical Lutheran Church,* edited by Robert Kolb and Timothy J. Wengert, 481–660. Minneapolis: Fortress, 2000.

Inst.	Calvin, John. *Institutes of the Christian Religion*. Edited by John T. McNeill. Translated by Ford Lewis Battles. Philadelphia: Westminster, 1960.
Io. eu. tr.	Augustine. *Homilies to John's Gospel*. Translated with notes by Boniface Ramsey. Vol. III/15 of *The Works of Saint Augustine*. Edited by Daniel E. Doyle and Thomas Martin. 50 vols. Hyde Park, NY: New City, 2008.
LC	Luther, Martin. *The Large Catechism*. In *The Book of Concord: The Confessions of the Evangelical Lutheran Church*, edited by Robert Kolb and Timothy J. Wengert, 377–480. Minneapolis: Fortress, 2000.
LW	Luther, Martin. *Luther's Works*. Edited by Jaroslav Pelikan and Hartmut T. Lehmann. 55 vols. American ed. St. Louis, MO: Concordia; Philadelphia: Muhlenberg, 1955–86.
Op. Ox.	Scotus, *Opus Oxoniense*
Quaest. in IV Sent.	Ockham, *Quaestiones in librum quartum sententiarum*
SCL	Beekenkamp, W. H., ed. *Berengarii Turonensis De Sacra Coena Adversus Lanfrancum*. Kerkhistorische Studien Behoorende Bij Het Nederlandscharchief Voor Kerkgeschiedenis 2. Hagae Comitis: M. Nijhoff, 1941.
STh	Thomas Aquinas. *Summa Theologiae*. Translated by Fathers of the English Dominican Province. http://www.newadvent.org/summa/.
TDNT	*Theological Dictionary of the New Testament*. Edited by Gerhard Kittel and Gerhard Friedrich. Translated by Geoffrey W. Bromiley. 10 vols. Grand Rapids: Eerdmans, 1964–76.
TT	Calvin, Jean. *Tracts Containing Treatise on the Sacraments*. 3 vols. Translated by Henry Beveridge. Edinburgh: Wentworth, 2009.

Introduction

I

WHY DOES THE CHURCH need a reworking of the theology of the Lord's Supper? The Reformed motto *ecclesia semper reformanda* means that the church needs to ever reexamine its theology. Much of Protestant Eucharistic theology today, for example, Lutheran, Reformed, and Baptist, is built on the foundations of theological giants of the Reformation. Yet their theologies took shape in historical contexts that are vastly different from that in which we find ourselves today. The Protestant Reformers lived in Christendom, in which Christianity was largely taken for granted by society. In response to long-held practices of the Roman Catholic institution, they focused on condemning idolatry and consoling weak consciences. For them the main problem of sin that sacraments must address was a lack of assurance in our conscience and knowledge of salvation.[1] Today, however, the concerns of Protestant churches are no longer that members of their congregations grew up venerating the Eucharistic elements, or mistaking the rite to be an expiatory sacrifice. In the modern secular society, not only is the Christian faith no longer the default worldview, religion is generally held to be *irrelevant* in public discourse. The challenge of the church is actually to show that faith is relevant to human society at all. Further, if today theologians still presuppose the traditional outlook of sin that predominantly locates sin in the individual, our broken world cries for attention to political oppression,

---

1. See, e.g., Luther's *The Blessed Sacrament*, LW 35:53; *Treatise on the New Testament*, LW 35:85–86; *Against the Fanatics*, LW 36:351–52; *Still Stand Firm Against the Fanatics*, LW 37:101–2; Calvin, *Inst.* 4.14.1, 3, 6–11, 16; 4.17.1; Calvin, "Short Treatise," in *TT* 2:164, 167, 173, 179.

1

economic exploitation, inequality, racism, sexism, etc. In other words, sin manifests in more than just individuals' weak conscience or lack of virtues, but systemically in our political structures. The church must fundamentally rethink its theology of the Lord's Supper in today's context. Is the Eucharist commonly understood to be a private affair between an individual and Christ, about the individual's gaining of "benefits"? Is the church echoing the secular idea that religion is simply a private, inner matter and therefore irrelevant to public life and world issues?[2]

Compounded with this is the fact that the lay Christian typically finds sacramental theology obscure, loaded with language such as distinctions between sign and reality, substance and accidents, not to mention *ex opere operato* and *ex opere operantis*. While concise, technical doctrinal articulations are important to clarify particular issues when controversies arise, they often reserve important theological reflections to those in the church who have resources and indeed the leisure to be trained in theology. In some "higher" sacramental theologies which impose a clear distinction between ordained clergy and the lay congregation, the lay believer is often kept at a distance from the altar and expected to play only a passive role. It is possible for a Eucharistic theology to alienate not only the secular public but even the lay believer within church walls.[3] This is not to mention that Eucharistic discourses all too often presuppose Western conceptual frameworks such as the neo-Platonist dichotomy between sign and reality, as well as the Aristotelian notion of "substance" and "accidents," which are rather alien to the non-Western world. Yet the church in the twenty-first century is no longer dominantly Western, but becomes more and more Asian, African, and South American. A fresh look at the Lord's Supper that is not burdened by Greek metaphysics is much needed.

Another important observation about traditional Eucharistic theologies that prompted this study is that these traditions, whether Roman Catholic, Lutheran, or Reformed, have typically overlooked the Jewish

2. In this light, I especially appreciate authors who have chosen to build their Eucharistic theology afresh from reflecting on Scripture (particularly Jesus's table ministry) instead of seeking to build on prominent traditions and theological giants whose theologies were formed under very different historical contexts. The church always needs such a fresh eye. Examples include Cochrane, *Eating and Drinking with Jesus*; Barth, *Das Mahl des Herrn* (abridged English: *Rediscovering the Lord's Supper*); Blomberg, *Contagious Holiness*; Chester, *Meal with Jesus*; Eberhart, *What a Difference a Meal Makes*.

3. See, e.g., Barth, *Rediscovering the Lord's Supper*, 2.

roots of the rite. The Last Supper, during which Jesus Christ instituted his Supper, took place explicitly in a Passover context according to *all four* Gospel accounts (Matt 26:17; Mark 14:12; Luke 22:1, 7; John 13:1). Jews had been celebrating and interpreting the Passover for hundreds of years before Christianity even came to the scene. Yet in understanding the New Testament, theologians have too often made obsolete what God has done and said in the history of Israel. As a result, Eucharistic theologies typically speculate out of context what Jesus's words at the Last Supper meant, presupposing certain metaphysical questions that Scripture does *not* pose. Following Augustine, different traditions fundamentally construe the bread and wine as "symbols" that stand for something invisible. Some traditions also attempt to explain the manner of Christ's presence in the food. Yet it is hardly asked as to what Jesus's words would have implied in the context of the Jewish Passover. In addition, traditional Eucharistic theologies also fail to pay respect to the fact that, at the Last Supper, Christ specifically referenced a (new) *covenant* (Matt 26:28; Mark 14:24; Luke 22:20). What has evaded theologians is the meaning of his words specifically in the context of a covenant meal. In particular, it is clear that Jesus's words alluded to Moses's on Mount Sinai at the inauguration of a covenant between YHWH and Israel, "Behold the blood of the covenant" (Exod 24:8; Heb 9:20). The church should fundamentally ask new questions that respect the Old Testament background of the Last Supper.

Undoubtedly, more and more modern authors appreciate the importance of the Jewish Passover in our understanding of the Lord's Supper.[4] But few authors would bring a detailed recounting of the Passover narrative to bear on the theology of the Supper. For those who make reference to the Passover at all, it is common to simply compare the Last Supper to the Jewish Passover seder, as codified in m. Pesaḥ. 10 (the rabbinic form of the ritual retelling of God's deliverance of the ancient Israelites out of

---

4. Joachim Jeremias may be the most influential in positioning the Last Supper and its meaning in the context of the Jewish Passover. Joachim Jeremias, *Die Abendmahlsworte Jesu* (English: *The Eucharistic Words of Jesus*). Other notable examples include Warfield, "Fundamental Significance of the Lord's Supper"; Thurian, *Eucharistic Memorial*; Torrance, "Paschal Mystery of Christ and the Eucharist"; Feeley-Harnik, *Lord's Table*; Heron, *Table and Tradition*; Mathison, *Given for You*; Barth, *Rediscovering the Lord's Supper*; Hunsinger, *Eucharist and Ecumenism*; Pitre, *Jesus and the Jewish Roots of the Eucharist* and *Jesus and the Last Supper* (interestingly, in Pitre's works he concluded that the bread at the Last Supper was not primarily the bread on the Passover table but the bread of presence in the tabernacle, which was accessible only to priests, and was never mentioned in any of the Last Supper accounts); Scotland, *New Passover*; and Billings, *Remembrance, Communion, and Hope*.

slavery in Egypt that accompanied the Passover meal).[5] Similarly, while there are theologians who mention the Sinaitic context of the cup of the Last Supper, few study the detailed narrative in Exodus and bring it to bear on our understanding of the cup.[6] In fact, many simply assume that the cup of the Last Supper was one of the four cups of wine instructed in the Jewish seder.[7] The main problem with this assumption is that the seder was in fact established only *after* AD 70, when the Jerusalem temple was destroyed, specifically in reaction to this crisis that rendered divinely commanded Passover sacrifices (central to the festival) impossible.[8] According to Jewish commentary on the *haggadah*, available history began only at the end of the Second Temple period.[9] Little is known about the customary liturgy of the Passover meal at Jesus's time, *except* what God commanded Israel in the book of Exodus. As the commentary on the *haggadah* assures us, "we may assume that the rules prescribed by the Torah for this ritual were observed, as they were understood at those times."[10] This seems to be supported by the Second Temple literature of the book of Jubilees too.[11] If one takes seriously Jesus's saying that he did not abolish but fulfilled the Old Testament (Matt 5:17), it is definitely

5. E.g., Jeremias, *Eucharistic Words of Jesus*, 84–88; Heron, *Table and Tradition*, 19–22; Mathison, *Given for You*, 211–14; Feeley-Harnik, *Lord's Table*, 120–27.

6. An exception is Pitre, *Jesus and the Last Supper*, 90–95. Pitre discussed the Sinaitic narrative substantially to show that Jesus, the new Moses, saw his own death as a covenant sacrifice.

7. E.g., Jeremias, *Eucharistic Words of Jesus*, 84–88; Heron, *Table and Tradition*, 21–22; Mathison, *Given for You*, 213; Pitre, *Jesus and Jewish Roots of Eucharist*, 158–60.

8. This is the main thesis of Baruch M. Bokser's *The Origins of the Seder*. However, Joel Marcus laid out evidence that Second Temple Jews already had the seder as prescribed in m. Pesaḥ. 10. See Marcus, "Passover and Last Supper Revisited," 303–24. Yet his arguments only show that Second Temple Jews had some form of order in their celebration of the Passover meal, one that may be very similar to the later established seder. But there is still no evidence that the order they had was the one codified in m. Pesaḥ. 10.

9. Tabory, *JPS Commentary on the Haggadah*, 3–4. Tabory explained that writings dated from the Second Temple period, including Jubilees, Wisdom of Solomon, Philo's writings, scrolls from Qumran, and Josephus, all gave details about Passover sacrifices but not details of actual rituals. "Therefore," Tabory stated, "when I talk about the paschal ritual before the first century C.E., I cannot go beyond generalizations and there is no evidence that the texts used in the haggadah today antedate the end of the Second Temple period." Tabory, *JPS Commentary on Haggadah*, 5.

10. Tabory, *JPS Commentary on Haggadah*, 3.

11. "And do thou, Moses, command the children of Israel to observe the ordinances of the passover, as it was commanded unto thee" (Jubilees 49:22).

warranted to understand the Lord's Supper through Israel's history as narrated in the OT, especially the Passover prescribed in the Torah, as well as Israel's covenant with God.

This study was also prompted by political unrest. Since 2014, my hometown Hong Kong has been going through the most turbulent times in its history. There was the 2014 Umbrella Movement that called for universal suffrage, but ended in the arrests and imprisonment of its leaders. The months-long protests since June 2019 were originally sparked by an extradition bill, but were since then fueled by unprecedented police crackdown. In some of the protests, as many as one to two million people took to the streets (the population of the city is only between seven to eight million). Many in the city decried the lack of reasonable response on the part of the government. Despite the fact that Hong Kong was promised at least fifty years of autonomy at its handover to China in 1997, Beijing has been exerting more and more control on this former British colony. In June 2020, Beijing imposed a national security law in Hong Kong, which bans even dissident speech. As a Hongkonger working on the theology of the Lord's Supper, I cannot help but ask: why does the Supper matter? In the world at large, there have long been reports of persecution of ethnic and religious minorities.[12] In such a context, what is the message of the Lord's Supper for the powerless? Traditional Reformed Eucharistic theologies that emphasize "nourishment" of the soul, assurance of faith, or what metaphysically happens in the bread and wine on the table, seem to be utterly out of touch with those who are oppressed. Yet precisely the history of the Passover, the very backdrop of the Last Supper, speaks of God's hearing the cries of Israelites who were suffering and triumphantly delivering them out of bondage, making them his people (Exod 2:23–25; 3:7–10). In ignoring the Passover context of the Lord's Supper, so much is lost. The meal no longer speaks to the oppressed, but has instead become a private, spiritual matter for the individual believer to contemplate. A fresh look at the Supper that brings liberation to the forefront is desperately called for.

Lastly, the whole world was swept off its feet by the COVID-19 pandemic since 2020. A simple internet search reveals an array of articles,

---

12. For example, in December 2020, the European Parliament passed a resolution entitled *Forced Labour and the Situation of the Uyghurs in the Xinjiang Uyghur Autonomous Region*; and in October 2021, in response to the military coup and persecution of Rohingya Muslims in Myanmar, the resolution *On the Human Rights Situation in Myanmar, Including the Situation of Religious and Ethnic Groups* was also adopted.

blog posts, and debates concerning keeping the Lord's Supper (or not keeping it) during lockdowns. The question of whether online communion is permissible flooded the internet. I observed, and many people also remarked to me, that there has been a sparked interest in the theology of the Lord's Supper among pastors and lay Christians alike, not to mention a growing interest in Huldrych Zwingli's simplistic approach to the Supper that does not require consecration of elements by clergy, a clear advantage during a pandemic. While mere convenience does not entail truth in doctrine—and it is not the aim of this project to treat the issue of online communion—the pandemic nevertheless uncovers the need to revisit Zwingli's Eucharistic theology, which this project will do.

II

A theology of the Lord's Supper aims to explain *what* Jesus's words at the Last Supper meant and mean. While different traditions have been focusing on this *what* question, a more fundamental question should be *where*—where to look for the answer to the *what* question. A fresh look at the Lord's Supper that pays heed to the OT narrative of the Passover and covenant-making may be just what is needed. Among the major theologians who expounded a theology of the Supper, only Zwingli attempted to delve into the Exodus narrative of the Passover and bring it to bear on our understanding of the Supper.[13] I will follow Zwingli's lead in looking for the answer specifically in the book of Exodus. The first chapter will be a presentation of his Eucharistic theology, highlighting his later emphasis on the Passover connection of the Last Supper in a subsidiary essay written in 1525, which has been overlooked by many commentators.[14] I will show how this approach is promising, in particular how Jesus's words, "This is my body," echoed closely a climactic phrase said at the institution

13. Zwingli was not the first to make the connection, of course. The early church, including Paul, did so. See Hunsinger, *Eucharist and Ecumenism*, 130. Catholic theology has always acknowledged that the Last Supper was a Passover meal. Aquinas, for example, noted that, in the New Law, the Eucharist corresponds to the banquet of the paschal lamb (*STh* II.I q. 102, a. 5; also III q. 46, a. 9 and III q. 74, a. 4.). Yet what is stressed is more discontinuity than continuity between the two testaments.

14. The few exceptions include renowned Zwinglian scholar Gottfried W. Locher, who however only briefly noted Zwingli's new idea. See Locher, *Die Zwinglische Reformation*, 222; also Locher, *Zwingli's Thought*, 221. Bruce Gordon referenced Zwingli's dream from which he got his inspiration, yet his main focus was about the reception of dreams during Zwingli's time. Gordon, "Huldrych Zwingli's Dream," 302–8.

of the first Passover. Unfortunately, even Zwingli's contemporaries have failed to pick up this promising approach of his as they critiqued him. It is time to revive this lost foundation of Reformed Eucharistic theology. I will also explain how Zwingli's attention to the first Passover shines new light on the controversial discrepancy between the Synoptics and the Gospel of John concerning the date of the Last Supper.

Zwingli's approach that pays attention to the book of Exodus will be used as a springboard, in chapter 2, to delineate a fuller account of the Supper in light of its connection not only to the details of the first Passover, but also to Israel's covenant meal at Sinai, both of which Jesus's words, and the Last Supper narratives, clearly referenced. The text I will focus on will be Exod 12 (institution of the first Passover) and Exod 19–24 (covenant meal at Sinai). It will be demonstrated that Jesus's life and death fulfilled the salvation typified by the two monumental events of Jewish history: the Passover and Sinaitic covenant. Jesus's body was offered as the ultimate Passover lamb, and his blood once and for all made possible a divine-human covenant relationship. At the Last Supper, he precisely instituted a new Passover meal to remember him and inaugurated the new covenant. Jesus's words—the imperatives to "take" and "eat" "in remembrance"—precisely repeated divine commands for the first Passover; his presentation of the "blood of the covenant" in the presence of the "twelve" were also already prefigured at Sinai. The key phrases—"This is my body" and "This is my blood of the covenant"— were in fact Jesus's rewording of the two climactic phrases said during these two events to point to himself. He *is* the true Passover and the new covenant. In sum, the significance of the Supper lies in the absence of the Passover lamb and blood in future celebrations, signaling the *fulfillment* of the age-old Passover and divine-human covenant in Jesus Christ. My new perspective offers a new, historical paradigm to look at the Supper, one in which God acts throughout history to make possible sinners' way back in his divine presence again.

Chapter 3 will contrast such a historical approach to traditional, metaphysical accounts of the Lord's Supper. Because the doctrine spans two thousand years, the focus will be on three major Eucharistic controversies in the West (Radbertus *versus* Ratramnus in the ninth century, the Berengarian controversy in the eleventh century, and the Reformation). The chapter will present these as persistent conflicts between two metaphysical approaches to the Supper: a symbolic approach that originated from Augustine, and a realist approach that rejects mere symbolism by affirming a real presence of Christ. The former presupposes a neo-Platonic dichotomy between visible sign and invisible reality, emphasizing that reality lies in the invisible and spiritual realm. The tendency, however, is anti-materialism.[15] Just as in the history of intellectual thought Platonism had attracted Aristotle's critique, Augustine's highly Platonic approach to the Supper eventually invited an Aristotelian correction that affirms and even explicates a material presence of Christ using the Aristotelian notion of substance. In the Catholic tradition, the Aristotelian track always prevailed. I want to show that, while the Aristotelian track is right to safeguard against the Platonic/Augustinian tendency to turn the meal into mere symbol, it nevertheless fails on its own terms—in the end it has to emphasize an insensible, appearance-less substance that has no analogy with the bodies that Christ is supposed to redeem. I will show that Luther's and Calvin's approaches, in rejecting Zwingli's mere symbolism, also failed to materialize Christ's "bodily" relation with the believer. I will argue for a third alternative to these approaches: rediscovering the temporal, historical character of the Supper, and understanding it in terms of Jewish categories of Passover and covenant, instead of metaphysics. It takes *both* the incarnation and the ascension of Christ seriously. It is precisely in history that Christ's body is a real body, in full analogy with ours, and has real bodily fellowship with us as a subject, not a sheer substance or a metaphysically (un)analyzable object. At the same time, theology must take seriously the fact that he has sent his Holy Spirit to be with us before his physical return. Especially in this light, the Supper does not only celebrate the past but calls us to be covenant partners of God, and anticipates the future return of Christ.

Locating the Supper in history opens the way to see it dynamically. Chapter 4 aims to present an important and even shocking aspect of the Supper that traditional Eucharistic theologies have bypassed, namely the restored table fellowship between God and sinners—the unholy in the presence of the holy. Traditionally, the focus of the Supper has always been the partaking of Christ's body and blood by the individual believer, whether it is physical (Catholic/Luther), spiritual (Calvin) or symbolic (Zwingli). Traditionally, the presupposed outlook is that in the Supper we receive Christ. Yet the historical narrative of God's salvation and covenant-making with his people presents a very different picture: we are once driven away from divine presence because of sin, yet because of

15. On this point, therefore, I will depart from Zwingli, who out of the fear of idolatry attempted to undermine the significance of anything physical.

Christ we are forgiven and may come to the Lord's table again. In other words, we are received *by* Christ. I will discuss the theological problems with the traditional notion of "eating" Christ for nourishment, particularly using Calvin's organic notion of engrafting and nourishment as an example. In a nutshell, it sees salvation in mostly static and impersonal terms. Such a notion of nourishment of the soul reinforces individualism and is ethically unhelpful in a community called to love *as* Christ loves us. Most devastatingly, it reduces Christ to a means of some "benefits" for the believer rather than an end in himself. Instead I want to stress the significance of the Supper in light of the restored God-sinner table fellowship. We are not only allowed to come to the Lord's table and proclaim his forgiveness, but we are restored as covenant partners with God again. In this sense, the Supper is never a mere symbol for invisible grace. It is the *direct* antithesis of alienation from God which is the result of sin. God in Christ has overcome this alienation. The Christ-sinner table fellowship *is* the reality of salvation. Without this table fellowship, reconciliation is abstract.

Table fellowship, and indeed a covenant relationship, is always two-way. While salvation is purely divine grace, it calls for active human response. Precisely by the blood of Christ we are restored as covenant partners of God again. Chapter 5 aims to take seriously Jesus's reference to a new *covenant* and inquire as to its content. As is clear in the Sinaitic covenant, to which the cup alludes, a vertical covenant relationship with God has to do with one's horizontal relationship with others. Coming to the Lord's table necessarily encompasses our fellowship with others. Jesus at the Last Supper precisely set an example of love and gave a new commandment to love as he has loved us (John 13). Ethics should then be at the very core of a theology of the Supper. The chapter will first explain how traditional Eucharistic theologies, preoccupied with metaphysical inquiry, have been unhelpful in bringing interpersonal dynamics to the forefront of inquiry. While symbolic theologies tend to focus on a reality in an otherworldly realm, realist theologies tend to focus on the miracle in the elements. At the outset, Western theology locates the *imago Dei* in the human soul, and thereby frames the problem of sin fundamentally in subjective and noetic terms, instead of sociopolitical terms. By contrast, this project pays close attention to Jesus's new commandment to love one another. Instead of a metaphysical riddle to be explained, the Supper above all poses an ethical challenge to the faith community. The focus is in fact the neighbor, and broken social reality that need to be addressed. A case will be made against Calvin's notion of the Supper as a sensory "aid" that assures weak faith—it is in fact a difficult command. A case will also be made against the Reformed rejection of the Lutheran *manducatio impiorum*, especially Calvin's categorizing and exclusion of the "unworthy" from communion with the Lord. In fact, *all four* Gospel accounts highlight the presence of Judas at the Last Supper (I will coin this the "real presence of Judas"). The significance of the Supper precisely lies in the gracious and undeserved divine-human table fellowship that is restored by Christ. Again, the physical table fellowship *is* the reality of salvation, the direct antithesis of alienation—sinners who once were God's enemies have come together to the Lord's table proclaiming his forgiveness, and responding to Christ's new commandment to love. I will close by exploring the political implications of the Supper in light of the Passover, an undeniably political event, which speaks of God's ultimate victory over oppression.

III

In sum, the new approach aims to bring in the narrative of the Passover and Israel's covenant meal at Sinai to bear on our understanding of the Lord's Supper. It locates the meal in the *history* of God's redemptive work. Instead of asking what the elements symbolize, whether they have any objective effect, or how they are related to the body and blood of Christ, a historical approach focuses on dynamic table fellowship. If sin alienated the human race from God, then salvation restores them in his presence again. God himself became a human in Christ, died as the ultimate Passover lamb, whose blood brought forgiveness and allowed sinners to be covenant partners of God again. If sin brought alienation in the most concrete way, then salvation should also bring fellowship in the most concrete way. The new Passover and covenant meal is therefore hardly a sign for some otherworldly reality. Christ himself, in full flesh and blood, sat and ate with sinners, in celebration and inauguration of a new covenant. Sinners are not only forgiven, but are given a new commandment again. The meal therefore calls sinners to respond as covenant partners of God. In place of the traditional Augustinian framework that fundamentally sees the meal as visible word, as if its significance lies in some static visible-*vs.*-invisible contrast, a more helpful reformulation is to see it dynamically as *acted word*, and *obeyed word*. The Word is active and effective in reconciling sinners to divine presence, and once again calling them in obedience to a renewed covenant relationship.[16]

This study will deviate from traditional Eucharistic theologies in significant ways in terms of method. Instead of adopting neo-Platonist or Aristotelian metaphysical categories, my approach seeks to respect and use Jewish categories, such as the OT understanding of Passover celebrations, "blood of the covenant," divine presence, the prohibition against consumption of blood, and even the significance of the ceremonial presence of the "twelve" according to Jewish culture. In turning a predominantly metaphysical inquiry into a historical inquiry, this work will not assume at the outset the general notion of "sacrament."[17] "Sacrament" is the Vulgate translation for the Greek word *mysterion* in the NT.[18] Traditionally, both Roman Catholic and Protestant Eucharistic theologies categorize the Lord's Supper as an instance of "sacrament." While official Catholic teaching acknowledges seven sacraments, Protestant teaching acknowledges mainly two. Both typically give a general treatment of sacraments, and *then* fit the Supper into the given generalized notion.[19] Most commonly, following Augustine, a sacrament is held to be a visible sign of invisible grace. Yet, paying attention to the historical context of the Last Supper exposes the unsuitability of a general philosophical notion of signs, but instead sees the occasion as part of the historical fulfillment of the Passover and covenant typified in the Old Testament. NT scholar Markus Barth also challenged the use of the general and non-biblical notion of "sacraments." As he noted, the notion of *mysterion* in the Pauline New Testament, which is often used to define sacraments, in fact applies to Christ alone.[20]

In addition, diverse Eucharistic traditions, in discussing the Lord's Supper, always focus on Paul's liturgical text in 1 Cor 10–11 as well as

16. My historical approach that emphasizes Christ as a *subject* active in *history* in lieu of impersonal metaphysical categories such as "substance" also echoes the turn in modern theology to historicize the being of God. See, e.g., McCormack, *Orthodox and Modern*, 10–12; also his introduction to *Mapping Modern Theology*, 10–13.

17. Hence this study will not include a discussion of baptism.

18. See, e.g., discussion in Cutrone, "Sacraments," 741; Ayres and Humphries, "Augustine and the West," 156. Cutrone noted that *sacramentum* was the translation of *mysterion* in African Latin translations of the Epistles to Ephesians and Colossians.

19. E.g., Lombard's *Sentences*, Book IV; Aquinas's *Summa Theologiae*, III. qq. 60–90; Zwingli's *Commentary on True and False Religion*; Calvin's *Institutes* 4.14.

20. Barth, *Rediscovering the Lord's Supper*, 100–101. See also Karl Barth's Preface in *CD* 4/4, x.

debates on the Bread of Life discourse in John 6. This study, by contrast, aims to highlight the historical narrative given by the four Gospels, and especially rediscover the centrality of the covenant and hence the new commandment given by Christ in John 13 as fundamental to our understanding of the Supper. Traditionally, as the focus is on the timeless liturgical text in 1 Corinthians and Jesus's difficult sayings to Jews in John 6, questions concerning the Supper are often posed as relating to two items—the bread and wine—and their corresponding relationship (whether symbolic or realistic) to the body and blood of Christ. For too long, theology sees the Supper in terms of these bread-wine and body-blood conceptual pairs.[21] Yet in the Last Supper accounts, "blood" is never simply blood but always explicitly "blood *of the covenant*" (or "*new covenant* in my blood"). As Alasdair Heron noted, while the elements are commonly held to be denoting the pair body/blood, the conceptual pair presented in the Gospel texts is more likely body/covenant.[22] This latter pair certainly gives a more dynamic and interpersonal picture, and indeed a more biblical one, than body/blood. I will show that an even more appropriate pair is Passover/covenant, the two monumental events in Jewish history.

In this light, several more significant deviations from traditions are worth mentioning. Apart from not assuming the notion of "sacrament" at the outset, my method takes note of the fact that the bread and the wine allude to *different* historical events (the Passover and covenant-making respectively), and therefore challenges the long-held assumption that the bread and wine are essentially two parts of the same rite with the same meaning. In my study they will be given separate treatments in light of the old Passover and of the Sinaitic covenant inauguration respectively. Also, this fresh look at the Supper through the lens of history instead of metaphysics that concerns the body-blood pair does not only give a fresh answer to the question of real presence of Christ. It reevaluates the very question itself. The problem with the body-blood pair as well as the question of real presence is that they assume a static and impersonal outlook

21. For example, Augustine named the Supper the "sacrament of the body and blood of Christ." See his *Homilies on the First Epistle of John*, 7.6; *Sermon 131*. Many followed suit: the first treatise on the Lord's Supper is said to be Radbertus's *De corpore et sanguine Domini* ("The Lord's Body and Blood") from the ninth century together with his opponent Ratramnus's with the same title. Another example is Luther's rebuttal of Zwingli, *Sacrament of the Body and Blood of Christ* (*LW* 36).

22. Heron, *Table and Tradition*, 14.

that focuses on the elements on the table and their possible relation to the flesh and blood of Christ. In trying to make sense of such relations, impersonal philosophical categories are often imported for explanation. The body-blood conceptual pair also frames the traditional outlook that sees the Supper as fundamentally about us receiving Christ's flesh and blood, instead of us being received *by* Christ at his table. In such an outlook that is preoccupied with our "reception" of Christ's body and blood instead of the covenant, there always exists an unexplainable gap between one's reception of Christ and one's moral formation—presumably, it is possible that a person can faithfully come to the Eucharist without there ever being any improvement in his/her moral life.[23] As Peter Leithart complained, traditional Eucharistic theology has mostly conducted its investigation through a "zoom lens" that zooms in onto what is on the table. As is typical of Western theology, Eucharistic theology has been dominantly about seeing (visible signs) and knowing (invisible reality), instead of actions of people.[24] It is time, Leithart contended, that Eucharistic theology uses a wide-angle lens, and gives weight to the faith community along with their culture, history, and dynamics. Precisely by focusing on history instead of bread/wine and body/blood, we may bring to focus the *actions* of God in Jesus the Nazarene, and the actions of those called to this new covenant relationship. Sinners are received *by* Christ who renewed their covenant relationship, and this opens a paradigm for new questions.

Despite these deviations from traditions including major Reformed theologians, my work may be situated within the Reformed tradition. My approach builds on Zwingli's attention to the Old Testament. I am committed to the *sola scriptura* principle, that theology must be faithful to Scripture, including *both* NT and OT. My study will take insights from biblical studies seriously. I understand that the body of Christ, before his return, is at the right hand of the Father in heaven. It is his office as high priest to intercede for us at the mercy seat. My work will also accentuate in the work of Holy Spirit. In addition, I stand within the Reformed tradition in its distinction between expiatory and thanksgiving sacrifices, and recognize the Lord's Supper as a non-expiatory thanksgiving sacrifice.

23. Some theologians have pointed out that sacraments could be used by the privileged as tools to reinforce unjust hierarchy and abuse. See, e.g., Grimes, "Breaking the Body of Christ"; Winner, *Dangers of Christian Practice*; also Cavanaugh, *Torture and Eucharist*, 207–21.

24. Leithart, "Way Things Really Ought to Be," 159–63.

My emphasis on human obedient response to God would also align with the Reformed emphasis on the importance of sanctified works and the covenant basis of reconciliation. Last but not least, my work affirms *ecclesia semper reformanda*, that even long-held theological beliefs can be reevaluated. While the Reformed theology of the Lord's Supper is diverse and the literature is vast, I will mainly focus on Zwingli and Calvin in my discussion and critique.

1

Zwingli's Dream

I wish to go into the matter of the passover somewhat deeply.
—Zwingli[1]

HULDRYCH ZWINGLI (1484–1531) IS often known as the "third man"
of the Reformation.[2] His reform commenced the Swiss Reformation.
He wrote polemically against idolatry in the church. He oversaw the
publication of the first German Bible in Zurich. Yet interestingly, as a
Reformer he managed to make himself a bitter opponent of virtually all
the main players of the Reformation, including Luther, Calvin, and the
Anabaptists. He is typically known for his "memorialism," and his denial
of the real presence of Christ in the Eucharist. To Luther, he had turned
the words of Christ at the Last Supper, "This is my body," into nothing.
As Luther put it, "they say that it is merely a useless commemoration,
which can be of no advantage to you or to anyone else. Be on guard!"[3] To
Calvin, who also denied a physical presence of Christ in the Eucharistic
elements, he had nevertheless repudiated any communion with Christ
and thereby turned the sacrament into an empty sign. The Anabaptists,
who were his early followers, later distanced themselves from him when

1. Zwingli, "Subsidiary Essay," in *Huldrych Zwingli: Writings*, 2:210.

2. For helpful overviews of Zwingli's life and context of his works, especially his
reformation, see Jackson, *Huldreich Zwingli*; Farner, *Huldrych Zwingli*; Courvoisier,
Zwingli; Locher, *Zwingli's Thought*; Stephens, *Theology of Huldrych Zwingli*; Opitz, *Ulrich Zwingli*; and Gordon, "Huldrych Zwingli."

3. Luther, *Against the Fanatics*, LW 36:351.

15

he supported infant baptism. Even his friends who agreed with him theologically disagreed with him politically. He chose the sword, and died in a battle against his theological opponents—hardly a saint. In his short life, no reconciliation between him and the other Protestant leaders was accomplished successfully. His successor Heinrich Bullinger had to deal with the deep rifts that he left on the Protestant scene. As noted by Bruce Gordon, Zwingli's unexpected death in 1531 did not only mean that he was unlike Luther, Calvin, and Melanchthon, who lived to develop their ideas over many decades, but also that many questions are left unanswered.[4] He died in medias res,[5] without even having the chance to choose compromise as other Reformers did later in their careers, or to kindle more sparks with them that might have taken the Reformation in a different trajectory. Had he put down his sword and not gone to battle in October 1531, Reformed Eucharistic theology today might have been different.

This chapter will focus on one promising idea of Zwingli which he proposed but did not mature further before his untimely death. Scholars have already noted that the "memorialist" label that is often attached to Zwingli's name does not do justice to the complexity of his Eucharistic views.[6] As far as I am aware, among the major Reformers, he was the only one who made reference to the Jewish festival of the Passover in his understanding of Christ's words at the Last Supper, which all four Gospel accounts locate in the context of the Passover. While this reference was part of his unique and constructive argument in his Eucharistic writings, literature on sacramental theology has not given much weight to it and, instead, commonly focuses on his use of John 6, especially 6:63, "The flesh profits nothing," which was only his negative response to his opponents who advocated a real presence of Christ.[7] Perhaps because he

4. Gordon, "Huldrych Zwingli," 157.

5. Gordon, "Huldrych Zwingli," 168.

6. Gordon, "Huldrych Zwingli," 167; and Opitz, "Ulrich Zwingli," 953.

7. For example, Jacques Courvoisier in his 1961 Annie Kinkead Warfield Lectures on Zwingli, had a subheading entitled "'The Importance of the Sixth Chapter of John" (Courvoisier, Zwingli, 67–69). B. A. Gerrish regarded John 6 as Zwingli's "foremost periscope" (Gerrish, Reformers in Profile, 128–29). John W. Riggs noted how Zwingli, starting with his letter to Matthew Alber, continuing to his major work Commentary on True and False Religion, spent "a good deal of time on John 6" (Riggs, Lord's Supper in the Reformed Tradition, 62–70). According to Thomas Davis, John 6 was indeed Zwingli's concern, although 1 Cor 10–12 was just as important for the later Zwingli (Davis, This Is My Body, 61, 156–59).

first presented his point in a rather theatrical way—he narrated the idea as originated from a dream—it fails to capture the attention of modern commentators.[8] In short, in August 1525, when he had already published his *Commentary on True and False Religion*, Zwingli published an additional, subsidiary essay on the Eucharist.[9] In it, he recalled a dream that he had in April, in which an advisor pointed the text in Exod 12:11, "It is the Lord's Passover," to him, in relation to the interpretation of "This is my body." He concluded that there is indeed a parallel between the two texts, and, because in the first Passover the lamb only signifies the Lord's action of passing-over, therefore at the Last Supper Jesus also only meant that the bread *signifies*, and is not equal to, his body. Hence his denial of a real presence of Christ in the bread and the wine. The use of dreams in one's theological arguments notwithstanding, I feel that, at any rate, Zwingli himself did not carry the attention to the Jewish roots of the Last Supper to its full theological potential. Within six years after his dream and the formal launch of the Zurich Reformation in 1525, he would be dead. Fate did not afford him the chance to develop his argument over a longer period.

This chapter aims to develop further this attention to the history of the Jewish Passover in the Reformed understanding of the Eucharist. While Zwingli was certainly not the first to make the connection between the Eucharist and the Passover,[10] I am not aware of another theologian who interprets Jesus's words "This is my body" at the Last Supper by noticing a close parallel with God's words as he instituted the Passover in Exod 12. I am also not aware of any commentator of Zwingli who further pursues this exegetical lead of his. While it might be only a dream for Zwingli, the allusion to Exodus will prove to be promising and fruitful. This chapter will pick up his lead and continue the investigation. It is divided into three main parts. Part one is the dream itself. It will detail Zwingli's recollection of his dream and, just as importantly, what he himself made of it. As we will see, he made unique historical and christological observations

8. I am only aware of a few exceptions. Renowned Zwinglian scholar Gottfried W. Locher only briefly noted Zwingli's new idea from his dream, see Locher, *Zwingli's Thought*, 221. According to Bruce Gordon, dreams would be taken much more seriously during Zwingli's time than in modern times. Yet Zwingli's opponents mostly interpreted his dream as coming from the demon. This was probably why Luther regarded him as a fanatic. See Gordon, "Huldrych Zwingli's Dream," 302–8.

9. Zwingli, "Subsidiary Essay," in *Huldrych Zwingli: Writings*, vol. 2. All quotes of Zwingli are taken from existing English translations.

10. See the discussion in Hunsinger, *Eucharist and Ecumenism*, 130–32.

about the Eucharist based on it. Part two will dissect the dream. We will expound Zwingli's exegesis and his opponents' criticisms of it. Part three will pursue the dream. I will argue why Zwingli's attention to Exod 12 is promising, and follow his lead by drawing on some possible theological implications that he could have made concerning the Eucharist. In short, he offered an interpretation of Christ's words at the Last Supper *that respects the Jewish roots of the occasion.* He successfully showed what Paul said in 1 Cor 5:7 and also went beyond him, namely not only that but *how* Jesus revealed himself as the new Passover. Unfortunately, in concluding his thoughts, Zwingli abandoned Jewish categories and fell right back to medieval and Platonic categories, as if all that mattered on the first Passover, and centuries of celebration of it, was to decide whether "is" in Christ's words of institution is literal or figurative, and on the relation between sign and reality in medieval Eucharistic debates. Yet so much could be drawn from the Paschal reference of the Eucharist.

The Dream

In his "Subsidiary Essay on the Eucharist" published in August 1525, Zwingli recalled a dream that he had on the night of April 13. In the dream, an advisor told him to respond to the council clerk, likely Joachim am Grüt,[11] who was questioning his views on the Eucharist, with the phrase from Exod 12:11—"It is the Lord's Passover"—in relation to the interpretation of "This is my body." He quoted his advisor from dreamland, "Why do you not answer [the council clerk], sluggard, what is written in Exodus 12:11, 'It is the passover,' that is 'the passing over of the Lord'?"[12] He then immediately leaped out of bed to study the Septuagint. The verse, he then expounded, describes how God instructed Israel to eat the Passover lamb hastily on the fateful night they would leave Egypt, concluding with the phrase, "It is the Lord's Passover." "I wish to go into the matter of the passover somewhat deeply," Zwingli continued.[13] The New Testament, it dawned on him, clearly asserts that the Passover was a foreshadowing of the death of Christ, for example in Hebrews and 1 Cor 5:7. In Matt 26:2, Christ himself predicted that he would die on the Passover. Luke 22 also

---

11. See H. Wayne Pipkin's introduction to "Subsidiary Essay" in *Huldrych Zwingli: Writings,* 2:189.

12. Zwingli, "Subsidiary Essay," in *Huldrych Zwingli: Writings,* 2:209–10.

13. Zwingli, "Subsidiary Essay," in *Huldrych Zwingli: Writings,* 2:210.

makes it explicit that the Last Supper was a Passover meal. Zwingli then concluded, "no passage from the Old Testament ought to be examined more for light upon the force and meaning of Christ's language than this in which the passover of old was instituted."[14] The clue in understanding the Eucharist lies in the relevance of the Passover and, in particular, Exod 12:11. This epiphany, according to him, "scattered all the mist from the eyes of all the candidates in theology who . . . had thus far found something of a stumbling block in the parable matter."[15]

The "parable matter" here refers to Zwingli's more well-known argument which he gave in his earlier *Commentary on True and False Religion*.[16] There he listed a number of parables in Scripture in which "is" only means "signifies." For example, Christ is said to be the cornerstone, the door, the light, the way, the vine, etc. These do not allow a literal reading, Zwingli argued, and neither do Christ's words "This is my body." Thus before his dream, his argument in favor of reading "is" in "This is my body" figuratively was based on these parables. As many commentators have shown, this approach was in fact not Zwingli's originally but was likely borrowed from a letter from Cornelius Hoen.[17] What was original in Zwingli was that he would now compare the Last Supper not only to other parables in Scripture but specifically to the Jewish Passover. Since his dream in 1525, he would base his arguments for his Eucharistic theology on this connection to the Passover.[18]

14. Zwingli, "Subsidiary Essay," in *Huldrych Zwingli: Writings*, 2:211. Later he would write to his German-speaking fellows, "When we ponder and investigate the figurative meaning of Christ's words, there is no text to which we may turn more confidently than that which speaks of the Paschal Lamb: for everything corresponds." Zwingli, "On the Lord's Supper," in *Zwingli and Bullinger*, 225–26.

15. Zwingli, "Subsidiary Essay," in *Huldrych Zwingli: Writings*, 2:210.

16. Zwingli, *Commentary on True and False Religion*, 224–28. See also his Zwingli, "Letter to Matthew Alber," in *Huldrych Zwingli: Writings*, 2:138–39.

17. According to B. A. Gerrish, Hoen borrowed Christ's saying in Matt 24:23 that "If anyone says to you, 'Here [in the bread] is Christ,' do not believe him," and Zwingli published this letter. Gerrish, *Old Protestantism and the New*, 115. See also Pipkin's introduction to Zwingli, "Letter to Matthew Alber," in *Huldrych Zwingli: Writings*, 2:129–30; Bromiley's introduction to Zwingli's "On the Lord's Supper," in *Zwingli and Bullinger*, 179; Locher, *Zwingli's Thought*, 221; Stephens, *Theology of Huldrych Zwingli*, 227–28.

18. E.g., "On the Lord's Supper," which he dedicated to his German-speaking fellows in 1526, in *Zwingli and Bullinger*, 225–28; "Friendly Exegesis," which he wrote to Luther in 1527, in *Huldrych Zwingli: Writings*, 2:353–60; and his "Account of the Faith of Huldrych Zwingli," which he wrote to Emperor Charles V in 1530, in Zwingli, *On Providence*, 52.

It is important to understand what he drew from the dream. First and foremost, the Paschal connection determined his methodology. He saw that the old foreshadows the new, and hence the old and new must be compared. We are to "compare the words about the old lamb with those about the new and everlasting one."[19] "This is my body" is to be compared with, and hence illuminated by, "It is the Lord's Passover." The arrangement of the words is the same, Zwingli noted, "for succession leads to imitation."[20] What Christ did and said at the institution of the Eucharist in the Gospels, God already foreshadowed at the institution of the Passover in Exod 12. For Zwingli, this approach perfectly explains why the disciples at the Last Supper were so calm upon hearing Jesus say, "This is my body." This was because Jesus was not making any perplexing claim. Jews were already accustomed to hearing a similar phrase during a Passover meal.[21]

Zwingli further explained, "By this [Christ] sought to do away with the old festival and institute a new one, substituting for the commemoration of the deliverance of a single people from bondage to Egypt the commemoration of the redemption of the world from the power of the devil and of death."[22] What is important to note here is that Zwingli's method of comparing the old and new testaments prompted him to make a *historical* point about God and a people, rather than mainly drawing metaphysical deductions concerning the bread, or Christ's presence therein, as his opponents mostly did with "This is my body." Christ was doing something in a nation's *history*, not just making a claim about his relation to a loaf of bread. He was reinstituting the Passover anew. In his 1530 "Account of Faith" to Emperor Charles V, after stating the parallel between the Passover and the Eucharist, Zwingli also quickly highlighted the act of God in instituting the new to discontinue the old. For him, it is God's action in history that is crucial.[23]

19. Zwingli, "Subsidiary Essay," in *Huldrych Zwingli: Writings*, 2:211.

20. Zwingli, "Account of the Faith," in *On Providence*, 52. His other example was the foreshadowing of Sarah's impossible pregnancy in the Old Testament with Mary's in the New. As he observed, both women asked, "Is anything impossible to the Lord?" We should therefore compare their words. Zwingli, "Subsidiary Essay," in *Huldrych Zwingli: Writings*, 2:211.

21. Zwingli, "Subsidiary Essay," in *Huldrych Zwingli: Writings*, 2:198, 202, 221. See also Zwingli, "On the Lord's Supper," in *Zwingli and Bullinger*, 228.

22. Zwingli, "Subsidiary Essay," in *Huldrych Zwingli: Writings*, 2:210–11.

23. Zwingli, "Account of the Faith," in *On Providence*, 52. Zwingli's attention to the history of the Passover also prompted him to notice the historical parallel between the

In addition, Zwingli also made a *christological* point, and did so in *Jewish* categories. He saw more than just the institution of two different meals, but that the parallel between the Passover and the Eucharist reveals something about Christ himself. Although he did not expound in fuller details, Zwingli explicitly inferred that "Christ himself is the true passover by which the sanctified are perfected unto eternity, that is, by which believers are freed from the slavery of sin and enter into heaven."[24] Christ did not just institute a new Passover the way God instituted the old, he himself *is* the new, true Passover. This is why he was therefore slain during the very midst of the feast, Zwingli remarked.[25] Later he would write to his German-speaking fellows that "no type of Christ is more precious, more exact or more evident than that of the Paschal Lamb."[26] Zwingli's use of Jewish categories in relation to Christ made him unlike the other prominent voices in the debate, who mostly appealed to traditional and philosophical categories in forming christological questions and arguments, such as the possibility of communication of Christ's divine and human attributes (divine ubiquity *vis-à-vis* local presence), and the characteristics of physical bodies.[27] As I will explain later, these will be some of the points that Zwingli could have advanced and conversed with his opponents more.

As for the Eucharist itself, for Zwingli, the foreshadowing meant that we must learn about the new from the old (he was therefore hardly a supersessionist). He drew several conclusions concerning the Eucharist. First, the old Passover was clearly a commemoration. He stated with certainty, "*no one denies* that the festival which was in old days celebrated in memory of deliverance in the flesh now passed over into our Eucharist."[28] Therefore, especially since 1525, Zwingli's alleged "memorialism" was based on his understanding of the Jewish Passover, of which the Eucharist is a fulfillment.[29] In his major writings since 1525, his emphasis of

---

passing-over of Israel's firstborns in Exodus and the "passing-over" of Barabbas in the Gospels. Zwingli, "On the Lord's Supper," in *Zwingli and Bullinger*, 226.

24. Zwingli, "Subsidiary Essay," in *Huldrych Zwingli: Writings*, 2:210.

25. Zwingli, "Subsidiary Essay," in *Huldrych Zwingli: Writings*, 2:210.

26. Zwingli, "On the Lord's Supper," in *Zwingli and Bullinger*, 225.

27. E.g., Luther, *Confession concerning Christ's Supper*, LW 37:210–32; Calvin, *Inst.* 4.17.16.

28. Zwingli, "Subsidiary Essay," in *Huldrych Zwingli: Writings*, 2:211. Emphasis mine.

29. See the brief note made in Locher, *Zwingli's Thought*, 221.

the commemorative nature of the Eucharist was consistently *within* the context of his discussion of the Passover.[30] It would not do him justice to simply attach the label "memorialist" to him without making reference to his point about the Passover. Second, a related point, the old Passover was a celebration, and hence the Eucharist is as well. The old commemorated and celebrated deliverance of the flesh, and the new now commemorates and celebrates our reconciliation with the most High God.[31]

Third, more than just a similarity in words, Zwingli saw a direct parallel in the form of speech in both "This is my body" and "It is the Lord's Passover." According to the context of Exod 12:11, "It" stands for the Passover lamb slain and eaten. He therefore reasoned that "is" must mean "signifies"—the lamb signified the Lord's saving action of passing over Israelite households while slaughtering Egypt's firstborns. It only symbolized the passing-over of the Lord, and was not itself identical to it. The lamb was eaten first, and salvation took place only later. "Is" is figurative—it could not be understood in any other way, Zwingli concluded.[32] Even when children were taught to ask about the meal, the phrase reappeared in the "standard answer," only now it was "This is the sacrifice of the Lord's Passover" (in Exod 12:26–27).[33] So "This" did not mean the Passover itself, but the sacrifice or symbol of it. In the Eucharist, therefore, the bread could only be a symbol for Christ's death. It signifies his body. The timing of events was important for Zwingli. He emphasized that, in both the old Passover and the new Eucharist, the symbol was instituted *before* the salvific event had been accomplished, to be used as a symbol of commemoration in the coming ages. The symbol of deliverance (lamb, bread) was instituted first, then the actual deliverance would follow (passing-over of the Lord, death of Christ). The lapse in time

30. Zwingli, "Subsidiary Essay," in *Huldrych Zwingli: Writings*, 2:212; Zwingli, "On the Lord's Supper," in *Zwingli and Bullinger*, 225–26; Zwingli, "Friendly Exegesis," in *Huldrych Zwingli: Writings*, 2:359; Zwingli, "Account of the Faith," in *On Providence*, 52.

31. Zwingli, "Subsidiary Essay," in *Huldrych Zwingli: Writings*, 2:212. Modern authors who highlight the importance of the commemorative character of the Eucharist tend to overlook Zwingli's unique argument. See, e.g., Wainwright, *Eucharist and Eschatology*, 60–68; Welker, *What Happens in Holy Communion?*, 127–33; also Lammens, *Tot Zijn Gedachtenis*.

32. Zwingli, "Subsidiary Essay," in *Huldrych Zwingli: Writings*, 2:211–12; also Zwingli, "Account of the Faith," in *On Providence*, 52–53.

33. Zwingli, "Subsidiary Essay," in *Huldrych Zwingli: Writings*, 2:212.

showed that the symbol and the saving event were not the same.[34] Again, from the fact that the disciples at the Last Supper were so calm, hardly confused or raising any questions, Zwingli argued that this showed that they understood Jesus to be speaking figuratively.[35] Thus, both Zwingli's alleged "memorialist" and "symbolist" view of the Eucharist hinged on his mindfulness of the Jewish Passover.

A fourth but related observation is that Zwingli, by construing the Eucharist primarily as a commemoration in a manner similar to the old Passover, naturally brought inquiry into human action to the forefront. It is humans who commemorate. As he said in his *Commentary on True and False Religion*, in a quote which likely brought him the charge of memorialism, "The 'Eucharist,' . . . is nothing but the commemoration by which those who firmly believe that by Christ's death and blood they have become reconciled with the Father *proclaim* this life-bringing death, that is, *preach* it with *praise* and *thanksgiving*."[36] This same quotation nevertheless highlights equally Christian action in and towards the world. Thus, while Zwingli mainly focuses on how elements signify the Lord's body, his attention to Christ's allusion to the Passover commemoration allowed him to pose questions concerning human agency.

In sum, Zwingli's attention to the Passover determined his unique methodology in approaching a theology of the Eucharist. Instead of mainly asking metaphysical questions as his contemporaries did, for example concerning the mode of Christ's presence in the bread and wine, and the relation between sign and the thing signified, he also touched on *historical* questions. In turn, the attention to the Passover also allowed him to make *christological* claims using Jewish categories, i.e., that Jesus is the true Passover. We have also seen how Zwingli uniquely paid attention to the disciples' reactions, i.e., the dynamics *around* the table, during the Last Supper, instead of only Christ's words and the elements on the table that were the main focus of the controversy. While Zwingli was certainly not the first to make the connection between the old Passover and the new Eucharist, his dream in April 1525 prompted him to draw concrete parallels, specifically between Christ's "This is my body" and God's "It is the Lord's Passover."[37] The dream prompted him to robustly ground his

34. Zwingli, "Subsidiary Essay," in *Huldrych Zwingli: Writings*, 2:212.

35. Zwingli, "Subsidiary Essay," in *Huldrych Zwingli: Writings*, 2:198, 202, 221.

36. Zwingli, *Commentary on True and False Religion*, 237.

37. Zwingli already noted the connection to Passover in his *Commentary on True and False Religion* published in March 1525 (*Commentary on True and False Religion*,

theology of the Eucharist on its continuity with the Jewish feast, which for him was commemorative and symbolic. Since 1525, the connection to the Passover would be his major constructive and original argument. Unfortunately, his main conclusion at the end was mostly negating a literal reading of "'This is my body," turning a unique, positive construction into a negative claim. We will see below how his opponents largely rejected his conclusions without addressing his attentiveness to the Passover. In the end, this attentiveness to the Jewish roots of the Eucharist never took root in the history of Reformed theology.

Dissecting the Dream

We have looked at Zwingli's dream and his interpretation of it. Was his dreamed advisor right after all, i.e., that Christ's words at the Last Supper were to be illuminated by the book of Exodus?

The Relevance of the OT to Theology and to the Church

First, a word on methodology. Whether originated from a dream or not, Zwingli's attention to the Passover roots of the Eucharist has proved to be promising. As noted, a trend on the modern theology scene has been the increasing acknowledgment of the importance of the Passover to the doctrine of the Eucharist. As twentieth-century Reformed NT scholar Markus Barth remarked, in understanding the Eucharist, one must never make the whole history of Israel obsolete.[38] By the time Christ instituted the new meal at the Last Supper, Jews had already been celebrating, as well as interpreting, the meaning of the Passover for many centuries. According to the OT, they were even specifically taught from a young age what questions to ask about the Passover, as well as what answers should be given to these questions (Exod 12:26–27; 13:8–10, 14–16). These were, so to speak, standard "FAQs" concerning the Passover that God gave to his people to teach them to reason about the meal in a certain way. The church must not throw this history down the drain. When Christ instituted the Eucharist, he was speaking to twelve Jews (himself also being

233), but not the direct parallel between Christ's words and God's until his dream. He said that the parallel had "escaped [his] mind" at the time (Zwingli, "Subsidiary Essay," in *Huldrych Zwingli: Writings*, 2:214).

38. Barth, *Rediscovering the Lord's Supper*, 18.

a Jew). Even the number twelve speaks volumes about the Jewishness of the occasion. Although Zwingli clearly borrowed neo-Platonist categories in his theology, such as assuming a strong distinction between sensible signs and insensible reality, he, unlike his contemporaries and opponents, acknowledged and respected the Jewish roots of the Eucharist, emphasizing its continuity with the Passover. His theology fully acknowledged the fact that Christ fulfilled, not abolished, Scripture. He allowed this part of Scripture—the Old Testament—to continue to speak to the church. As we have seen, for example, Zwingli paid due attention to the Passover "FAQs" given in Exodus in his arguments.

Zwingli's approach was therefore in stark contrast to his opponents'. Luther and Calvin in their respective treatments of the Eucharist, one may observe, did not acknowledge the Jewish roots of the meal at all. Luther was adamant about taking Christ's words literally, *as is*. He insisted that Christ could not deceive us when he said "This is my body"[39]— something nobody in the debate ever denied. Yet he airlifted Christ's words from their context in the long history of Passover celebrations. Even when he was responding to Zwingli's dream, Luther failed to take note of the importance of the Jewish connection.[40] Overall, he stressed a *contrast* between the OT and NT.[41] Indeed, Luther's construal of the (Jewish) law as the antithesis of the gospel probably did not help the matter.[42] In line with Luther's method, the Lutheran Formula of Concord in fact condemns those who, in interpreting Christ's words at the Last Supper, seek to bring in *other* scriptural passages, presumably including the OT.[43] Unfortunately, even in his later polemic writings, Zwingli himself was mainly preoccupied with the impossibility of understanding "This is my body" literally, and never identified his opponents' (deeper) problem of disregarding of the Jewish roots of the NT while doing theology. Zwingli himself did not identify that his methodology was unique, and the divergence between him and his opponents pertained to more than just exegesis of some passages.

---

39. See, e.g., Luther, *Confession concerning Christ's Supper*, LW 37:308; *Still Stand Firm Against the Fanatics*, LW 37:139–40; LC 5.14.

40. This will be discussed in the next subsection.

41. See, e.g., *Confession concerning Christ's Supper*, LW 37:332.

42. See, e.g., Ap 4.

43. FC 4.25.

In his commentary on the last four books of Moses,[44] Calvin did expound on how the Passover was an OT analogue to the Eucharist, yet his major writings on Eucharistic doctrine manifested little effort to relate back to the Jewish festival. In his latter writings, being a second-generation reformer, he was dominantly concerned with the true union believers have with Christ.[45] Believers are both justified and sanctified in Christ. We do not receive Christ just from afar. But we must have true communion with Christ's body and blood, in order to be saved. In his Eucharistic theology, Calvin was therefore concerned with how this communion is effectively achieved, by the Holy Spirit who lifts the hearts of the faithful to heaven to have real communion with Christ's body and blood. He was then critical of Zwingli's seemingly purely subjective construal of the Eucharist that has little to say about our communion with Christ.[46] In his criticisms of Zwingli, however, Calvin never acknowledged the fact that Zwingli arrived at his conclusion about the subjective character of the Eucharist based on its connection to the Jewish Passover. Calvin had yet to answer how then the Jewish Passover was *not* primarily about commemoration and thanksgiving, or why, even if the Passover was primarily about commemoration and thanksgiving, this had no import on our understanding of the Last Supper, which he understood in his own commentary to be typified by the Passover meal. Ironically, Calvin, in his refutation of Zwingli, as if to return a kind word, acknowledged that he labored more to destroy the evil than to build the good.[47] In fact, Zwingli did build, only that Calvin did not take note. In a later letter to the Lutheran Westphal, Calvin would remark that he did not bother to read Zwingli.[48]

In Catholic thought, theologians such as Peter Lombard and Thomas Aquinas, for example, did link the Eucharist to the Passover. Lombard taught that Christ instituted the Eucharist after a Passover meal "in order to show that the sacraments of the Old Law, among which the sacrifice of the paschal lamb was paramount, were *terminated* at his death, and the sacraments of the New Law were *substituted*, among which the mystery

44. Calvin, *Commentaries on the Four Last Books of Moses*, 1:456–58. See also Parker, *Calvin's Old Testament Commentaries*, 134–38.

45. Mark Garcia has demonstrated how *unio Christi* plays a central role in Calvin's theology. See Garcia, *Life in Christ*.

46. Calvin, *Inst.* 4.17.33; "Short Treatise," *TT* 2:195–96.

47. "Short Treatise," *TT* 2:196.

48. Calvin, "Second Defense to Westphal," *TT* 2:252.

of the Eucharist is chief."[49] Aquinas similarly wrote, "solemnities of the Old Law are *supplanted* by new solemnities . . . the feast of the Passover gave place to the feast of Christ's Passion and Resurrection."[50] Thus, the language is mainly one of the new supplanting the old. This may explain why, when Aquinas drew connections between the two, he did it only in his answers to certain questions, namely the use of unleavened bread and reserving hosts.[51] The connection to the Passover had little import on the Catholic doctrine of the Eucharist as a whole. The doctrine of transubstantiation, fundamentally based on Aristotelian categories of substance and accidents, has little to do with the Jewish Passover meal. Aquinas also strongly asserted that the sacraments under the old law did not confer sanctifying grace, but those under the new do.[52] On the whole, the two laws are to be contrasted rather than compared. The emphasis is discontinuity between the two testaments, rather than continuity as in Zwingli's understanding.[53] Zwingli's contemporary and Catholic counterpart John Eck responded to his dream.[54] As we will see below, he mostly only aimed to correct Zwingli's exegesis of Exod 12, without acknowledging the question of how the Passover should have bearing on our understanding of the Eucharist.

Zwingli in fact did not acknowledge the OT only in his Eucharistic theology. The OT and its interpretation could be said to be at the very heart of his reform. His own conversion from Roman Catholicism was precisely out of the OT sense that an idolatrous people would stand before the judgment of God.[55] He was therefore especially wary of the false worship in the Mass at the time (hence the title of his major work *Commentary on True and False Religion*). His dispute with the Anabaptists was also specifically based on a unity of the two Testaments: that children have always been receiving the covenantal promise of God.[56] He was even

49. Lombard, *Sentences* 4, d. 8, c. 5, n. 1, quoting Rosemann, *Peter Lombard*, 151.

50. *STh* II.I q. 103 a. 3.

51. *STh* II.I q. 74 a. 4 and III q. 83 a. 5, respectively.

52. *STh* III q. 62 a. 6.

53. Although Zwingli also used substitution language in respect to God's action in instituting a new Passover (see Zwingli, "Subsidiary Essay," in *Huldrych Zwingli: Writings*, 2:210–11), his method clearly presupposes a significant continuity between the two testaments.

54. "Refutation of Zwingli by Eck," in Zwingli, *On Providence*, 62–104.

55. Gordon, "Huldrych Zwingli," 163–64.

56. Opitz, "Ulrich Zwingli," 953.

well known for his extensive efforts in promoting the study of the Hebrew Bible, even in its original language, during his lifetime. Most notable was his founding of the *Prophezei* in 1525.[57] This consisted of frequent and public gatherings to read and expound the OT, open to both clergymen and lay people. First, a text in the original Hebrew would be discussed, and then according to the Greek Septuagint, and finally the exegetical results would be translated into the vernacular as bible commentaries, and to be preached to congregations. Zwingli was passionate about making the OT relevant to the church in the present time, not only to doctrinal theologians, but to lay Christians as well. He recalled that, when he first discovered the possible reading of "This is my body" in light of "It is the Lord's Passover," he brought the idea to his congregation *first* and tested its validity by their reaction, before writing about it in a formal essay. For him, "It is the Lord's Passover" was relevant to understanding "This is my body" because members of the church had *actually* found it relevant.[58] He was a Reformer who brought the whole Scripture, Old and New Testaments, into the life and understanding of the church.

Exegesis and Criticisms

Was Zwingli (and his dreamed advisor) right to not only consult the OT but also pinpoint this particular verse, Exod 12:11? Is there indeed a parallel between Christ's words at the Last Supper and God's on the first Passover? Zwingli said that when he first woke from his dream he leaped out of bed to check the Septuagint.[59] He did not lay out the texts for his readers but here is the comparison:

57. Gordon, *Swiss Reformation*, 232–33.

58. Therefore, contrary to the charge of Luther, Zwingli did not think that Exod 12:11 is helpful only because he dreamed it (*Against the Fanatics*, LW 36:346; *Still Stand Firm against the Fanatics*, LW 37:45). In fact, Zwingli never made much of the fact that it was a dream. In his writings, he only ever mentioned once that the connection to Exod 12:11 originated in a dream (only in his "Subsidiary Essay," from August 1525). Even in this essay, he emphasized that his congregation found the insight helpful in understanding the meaning of the Eucharist. In his subsequent writings, he based his arguments in his exegesis, not the fact that it originated from a dream. Cf. Gordon, "Huldrych Zwingli's Dream."

59. Zwingli, "Subsidiary Essay," in *Huldrych Zwingli: Writings*, 2:210. I agree with Zwingli's choice to use the Greek Septuagint text instead of the original Hebrew. At Jesus's time, Jews most commonly read the Septuagint. The original Hebrew gives: *psh hw' lyhwh* (the verb "to be" is implied).

πασχα ἐστὶν κυρίῳ (Exod 12:11)

τοῦτό ἐστιν τὸ σῶμά μου (Matt 26:26; Mark 14:22; Luke 22:19)

Literally, the Septuagint says, "It *is* Passover to the Lord." The Synoptic Gospels quote Jesus as saying, "This *is* my body." For Zwingli, the focus is on the verb "to be," ἐστὶν, present in both.[60] At least they share a similar context: both sentences were said over a meal and explain the meal with the verb "to be." If the old Passover foreshadows the new, it does seem that words said over the former will illuminate the latter.

The two sentences are in fact even more similar than they appear. Exod 12:11 has a dative "*to* the Lord," while the Synoptic Gospels contain a genitive, "*my* body." Nevertheless, to Zwingli's credit (or his dreamed advisor's), the Exod 12:11 phrase is usually interpreted as expressing a "possessive dative." Effectively it means that the Passover *belongs to* the Lord: "It is the Lord's Passover."[61] Hence Zwingli's own formulation, "Est enim Phase, hoc est transitus *Domini*"[62] ("For it is the Passover, which is the passing-over *of* the Lord"). Whether the dative is possessive or not, it seems we can draw a particular conclusion. The dative may be interpreted to mean that the meal (or whatever πασχα refers to) is eaten for the Lord, or is observed for, or in honor of, him. If the dative is possessive or interpreted as a genitive as so many translations do, then it means that God claimed that the meal *belongs to him*, or that it is *his* passing-over, *his* doing. At any rate, in Exod 12:11, God *laid claim to* the meal immediately after he had given instructions to prepare and eat it. This was not unlike Christ's institution of the Eucharist at the Last Supper. Christ laid a claim *to* the meal (not just made a claim *about* the meal) immediately in the context of instructing his disciples to eat. The disciples were to eat as Christ instructed them to, and "this" is *his* body—it is *his*. In both Passover and Eucharist, then, God/Christ defined and laid claim to the meal he instituted. There is indeed a parallel.

Further, we may see how, given the Passover context of the Last Supper, Zwingli was right to focus on a verse like Exod 12:11 in understanding the Eucharist. The formula in the verse " . . . ἐστὶν . . . κυρίῳ" ("It is . . . to the Lord" or "It is the Lord's . . ."), which he held to be a precursor to "This is my body," in fact appears in God's institution of the Passover

---

60. See *Commentary on True and False Religion*, 224–25.

61. This is in fact the understanding of almost all major English translations today.

62. In Latin Vulgate the phrase is "est enim phase id est transitus Domini."

in Exod 12 in a total of *three* verses, not only twice as Zwingli thought.[63] This phrase is far from insignificant in the celebration of the festival. In his instructions to keep the Passover, God said, "It is the Lord's Passover" (12:11); Moses added, "It is [the] Passover sacrifice to the Lord" (12:27); and the biblical narrative also adds, "It is a night to be observed for the Lord . . . this night is for the Lord" (12:42). God repeatedly gave meaning and laid claim to the meal. In fact, the phrase in 12:27 precisely appeared in the very first "FAQ" God gave to Israel: "And when your children say to you, 'What does this rite mean to you?' then you shall say, 'It is [the] Passover sacrifice to the Lord . . .'" (12:26–27). In other words, it was the *first standard phrase* to be given to those who ask about the meaning of the occasion. Zwingli was perhaps drawing attention to the most significant Paschal phrase. If Jews were expecting Jesus to be the new Moses who would deliver them, it would not be surprising that they were expecting to hear a similar definitive phrase in his institution of the new Passover. This is why Zwingli repeatedly pointed to the fact that the (Jewish) disciples showed no sign of being perplexed or needing to ask questions when they heard it in the context of the Passover. "Being Jews," he wrote, "they did not find anything novel in the words, 'This is my body.'"[64]

Yet is Zwingli's conclusion valid at the end, i.e., that "is" is to be interpreted figuratively? It will be helpful now to look at the responses of two of his opponents who critiqued his exegesis. For him, "everything corresponds"[65] when we compare Christ's words over the Eucharist with God's over the Paschal Lamb. "It is the Lord's Passover" (Exod 12:11) was in the immediate context of God's instructions to slay and eat the Passover lamb. So "it" specifically referred to the lamb. The lamb is said to "be" the Lord's Passover. Based on the theological parallel of the institutions of the Passover and the Eucharist, Zwingli concluded that, since the lamb only signifies the Lord's passing-over, so the bread also only signifies Christ's body. John Eck disagreed with him. In his "Refutation of Zwingli," he gave a few arguments.[66] First, he quoted OT texts (such

---

63. Zwingli, "Subsidiary Essay," in *Huldrych Zwingli: Writings*, 2:212. I am including the instance where the verb "to be" is implied (12:27), and is in fact typically translated to be present. The three verses are: "πασχα ἐστὶν κυρίῳ" (12:11), "θυσία τὸ πασχα τοῦτο κυρίῳ" (12:27), and "νυκτὸς προφυλακή ἐστιν τῷ κυρίῳ" (12:42).

64. Zwingli, "On the Lord's Supper," in *Zwingli and Bullinger*, 228. See also Zwingli, "Subsidiary Essay," in *Huldrych Zwingli: Writings*, 2:198, 202, 221.

65. Zwingli, "On the Lord's Supper," in *Zwingli and Bullinger*, 225–26.

66. I will only discuss the arguments which directly targeted Zwingli's exegesis of Exod 12:11. "Refutation of Zwingli by Eck," in Zwingli, *On Providence*, 89–91.

as 2 Chr 35:1) which mention the Passover, and in which the Passover refers to the feast or the festival in general that was kept by the children of Israel, and not specifically to the lamb. So in Exod 12:11, the referent only refers to the feast, and the feast *was* indeed, not only signifying, the Passover. There is no figure of speech. Eck also observed that in Targum, the verse is about the feast being kept unto or before the Lord. Second, Eck argued that, while circumcision also foreshadowed baptism, one never finds any parallel expressions between the proclamations of the two. Nothing demonstrates that the same form of speech must be found in the institutions of the Passover and of the Eucharist.

For Luther, Zwingli was not only a fanatic, but he must have learned about "metaphor-play" from Satan, and prided himself on "empty dreams."[67] Luther charged that, in Exod 12:11, Moses precisely said, "it is the Lord's Passover," and not "it represents the Lord's Passover." Going for another of Zwingli's examples (1 Cor 10:4), Luther pointed out that, in the same way, Paul said, "The rock was Christ," not "The rock represents Christ." We learn that Luther interpreted 1 Cor 10:4 as about the *spiritual* rock, which truly was Christ, and so it was no metaphor.[68] But even if Paul and Moses meant figurative speech, Luther contended, it did not follow that Christ meant it as well at the Last Supper. One must prove the form of speech in each particular instance. As for Exod 12:11, Luther compared it to ordinary sayings such as "Eat meat, it's Sunday; drink water, it's Friday [i.e., fast day]." So the Exodus text is only saying, "Eat in haste, for it is the Lord's Passover."[69] The latter phrase only asserts the time or the circumstance, not referring to the lamb. There is no hint of symbolism or figurative speech.

One may note that Eck and Luther essentially gave the same arguments. First, both purported that Exod 12:11 refers to the *occasion*, instead of the lamb specifically. Therefore there is no figurative speech, because the feast, or the occasion, was indeed truly the Lord's Passover. Second, both men argued that Zwingli had failed to prove that the metaphor in Exod 12:11, if any, or metaphors anywhere else in Scripture, entailed that there is then a metaphor in Christ's words of institution of the

---

67. Luther, *Still Stand Firm against the Fanatics*, LW 37:36–38. Luther very briefly mentioned his arguments again in his *Confession Concerning Christ's Supper*, LW 37:275. Here, again, I will only discuss Luther's arguments which directly targeted Zwingli's exegesis of Exod 12:11.

68. Luther, *Still Stand Firm against the Fanatics*, LW 37:36–38.

69. Luther, *Still Stand Firm against the Fanatics*, LW 37:38.

Eucharist. This second critique, in my opinion, was Zwingli's own fault. He outstandingly paid due attention to the Jewish roots of the Eucharist and even explicated a relevant Exodus text, yet in the end he used it mainly to (very weakly) support a claim about metaphor. Surely, God did not institute the Passover in order to answer a question about a figure of speech, or to determine the medieval debate about the relation between the neo-Platonist categories of *signa* and *res*. Zwingli actually misled his opponents. As a result, his opponents never acknowledged the fact that he drew *other* inferences from his intertextual comparison as well. They did not feel that they had to answer the question, implied by Zwingli's methodology and exegesis, of how the Passover should bear on our understanding of the Eucharist today; if not by teaching us about metaphor, then what should it teach us?

As noted previously, Zwingli in fact made strong historical and christological claims based on the Eucharist's connection to Passover.[70] In a nutshell, Zwingli was arguing that Christ's "This is my body" was in fact a restatement of the key and familiar phrase spoken by God when he instituted the first Jewish Passover, "It is the Lord's Passover." So first, for Zwingli, Christ was instituting the Jewish Passover anew. God was acting in the course of Israel's history. Just as the Passover was explicitly the commemoration and celebration of God's deliverance of his people from bondage, so the Eucharist has to do with commemorating and celebrating of God's deliverance from evil and from death. Second, Christ was not just giving or instituting a new Passover. Zwingli echoed Hebrews in asserting that Christ himself *is* the true Passover, by dying on Passover. Here Zwingli's logic is likely this: if "It is Passover to the Lord" was a precursor to Christ's "This is my body," then effectively Christ was claiming that he was the true Passover to the Lord. Therefore, for Zwingli, Christ's "This is my body" was about God's continuous action in history as well as Christ's claim about himself, as much as about the symbolism of the bread. Unfortunately, neither Eck nor Luther gave responses to the historical and christological inferences, since both were distracted by Zwingli's conclusion about symbolism.

Interestingly, the other of Eck's and Luther's critiques (the first critique listed above) would have helped to develop Zwingli's case further. They argued that "It is the Lord's Passover" refers to the occasion of the Passover rather than to the lamb. "If ['It'] refers to the festival . . ." Zwingli

70. Zwingli, "Subsidiary Essay," in *Huldrych Zwingli: Writings*, 2:209–14. See discussion in previous section.

later boasted to Luther, "then we have won."[71] Given the parallel with the Last Supper, Christ was then claiming that the occasion, i.e., the new Passover, *is* his body. In other words, his body is our salvation. This is fully in line with Zwingli's idea that the meaning of "This is my body" was that Christ himself is the true Passover. In addition, the parallel to Exodus would then imply that "This is my body" possibly has nothing to do with the bread, but more broadly about the occasion! This would actually be a more devastating blow to Eck and Luther than to Zwingli, as they held a realism concerning Christ's presence in the bread based on that phrase.

As a summary, if Christ is the new Passover, then it makes sense that we have to learn from God's institution of the first Passover. Yet Zwingli drew a wrong conclusion from a promising exegesis. His opponents were right that his exegesis of Exod 12:11 in connection to the Eucharist fails to establish the symbolism that he wished to prove. Nevertheless, they neither disproved nor even acknowledged his distinctive attention to the Jewish roots of the Eucharist. They only disproved that the same form of speech must lie behind God's words of institution of the first Passover and behind Christ's words of institution of the Eucharist, not that there is indeed a parallel between the two, nor that Israel's Exodus is relevant to our understanding of the Eucharist today. Unfortunately, Zwingli never successfully convinced his opponents of the vital importance of the Eucharist's parallel with the Passover.

Pursuing the Dream

So much could be developed based on Zwingli's attention to the close parallel between the Passover and the Last Supper. Following his lead, we may gain further textual and doctrinal insights.

Further Textual Observations

First, as explained above, the formula "It is . . . to the Lord" (or "It is the Lord's . . .") in Exod 12:11 was indeed a key phrase in God's institution of the first Passover. It was repeated in three verses (12:11, 27, 42), the second of which appears in the first standard answer given to children who ask about the occasion. Christ was then laying claim to the meal the way

71. Zwingli, "Friendly Exegesis," in *Huldrych Zwingli: Writings*, 2:277.

God did. Second, following Zwingli's lead in identifying parallel phrases between God's institution of the first Passover and Christ's institution of the Eucharist, one may find that, in the former, God indeed also gave elaborate instructions to "take" and to "eat," before laying claim to the meal. Altogether, in Exod 12, the instructions to "take" (vv. 3–5) and to "eat" (vv. 8–9, 11) make up six verses. Again, this is not insignificant. The instructions were then very similar to Matthew's and Mark's accounts.[72] If, as Zwingli argued, "This is my body" echoes "It is the Lord's Passover," then Christ's invitation to "take" and "eat" likely echoes God's same invitation on the first Passover. Third, and finally relating to Zwingli's alleged "memorialism," God explicitly commanded Israel, "Now this day will be a memorial to you, and you shall celebrate it as a feast to the Lord; throughout your generations you are to celebrate it as a permanent ordinance" (12:14). Altogether the passage stresses three times an ordinance to remember (also in 13:3 and 13:9). The Passover is unmistakably for commemoration and celebration. As Zwingli exclaimed, *no one* denies this.[73] In sum, we may see that in the institutions of both the Passover meal and the Eucharist, God/Christ (1) invited his people to "take," (2) to "eat," (3) laid claim to the meal (or the occasion), and (4) decreed that the meal to be kept as commemoration.[74] Christ was truly instituting the Passover anew.

Beautifully, Zwingli's method shows how, at his institution of the Eucharist, Christ was reiterating God's words at the institution of the first Passover meal. He was precisely speaking in God's place. With words parallel to YHWH's, he was claiming to be Israel's God himself. The shock of "This is my body" to Jews was not any metaphysical mystery about the bread (the bread already had a long history with which they were familiar). The shock, if any, would be the pointer to Christ himself, "*my* body." It was the fact that Jesus now laid a claim to the Passover meal, because God and only God made this claim in history. Further, it was now God himself sitting and eating the Passover meal at the same table with his people. In addition, instead of remembering the Exodus event as they were told to for centuries, Israel now was to eat this meal to remember

---

72. See chapter 2 for a more detailed discussion.

73. Zwingli, "Subsidiary Essay," in *Huldrych Zwingli: Writings*, 2:211; see discussion in Locher, *Zwingli's Thought*, 221.

74. Thus each of the Synoptic accounts of the Last Supper highlights different elements of the first Jewish Passover. Matthew highlights (1), (2), and (3); Mark highlights (1) and (3); and Luke highlights (3) and (4).

him. The remembrance is now "of *me.*" Again the accentuation was the pointer to Christ himself.[75] All Israel's history of salvation is now revealed in him—not just in his work and actions, but his very person. He *is* the salvation of his people.[76]

Zwingli's lead is indeed promising. Now with his method, we find that Christ's words over the bread were very well in line with his words over the cup. Biblical scholars agree that when Christ took the cup and said, "This is my blood of the covenant" (Matt 26:28; Mark 14:24; or "This is the new covenant in my blood" in Luke 22:20), he was explicitly hearkening back to Moses's words at Mount Sinai, "Behold the blood of the covenant" (Exod 24:8).[77] In fact in Matthew and Mark, Jesus repeated Moses's phrase almost verbatim. The Septuagint has τὸ αἷμα τῆς διαθήκης (Exod 24:8), while the Greek in Matthew and Mark is τὸ αἷμά μου τῆς διαθήκης. Once again, the shock was a pointer back to Christ himself: the new covenant would no longer be sealed in animal blood as at Sinai, but now with this God-man's own blood. He did not only inaugurate the new covenant: he *is* the new covenant. He is not only God's new covenant with a people, but now the blood is poured out "for *many*" (Matt 26:29; Mark 14:24). In addition, in both Exodus and the Gospels, the words were spoken and blood referenced explicitly in the presence of a group of *twelve*, whether it was twelve pillars at Sinai representing the twelve tribes of Israel (Exod 24:4), or twelve disciples at the Last Supper.[78] The cup at the Last Supper clearly alluded to God's covenant inauguration with Israel at Sinai. So if Jesus reiterated words from Jewish scriptures for the cup, it makes sense that he also did the same for the bread. In my view, Zwingli has successfully identified such an instance. It was a good match: now Christ's words over *both* the bread and the cup spoke of Israel's salvation history in the book of Exodus. The bread and the cup reinstituted *the* two monumental events in Jewish history—Passover and Sinai.[79] In the person of Christ, God ate the Passover meal with his people, and he also

75. Barth, *Rediscovering the Lord's Supper*, 17.

76. While Zwingli identified Exod 12:11 to be the precursor to Christ's "This is my body," I will instead argue that an even more compelling parallel is Exod 12:27, "This is the Passover sacrifice to the Lord." See "The Passover—Old and New" in chapter 2.

77. See Pitre, *Jesus and the Last Supper*, 93–94.

78. Pitre, *Jesus and the Last Supper*, 94–95. See also Ahituv and Paul, "Tribes of Israel," 751–52; and Oded and Freedman, "Tribes, the Twelve," 20:137–40.

79. The allusion to Mount Sinai is also obvious in John's account of the Last Supper, during which Christ gave a new commandment (John 13), as God did at Sinai.

inaugurated a new covenant with them in person. Altogether, the Last Supper as a Passover meal reinstituted the story of Israel's deliverance as in Christ, and as a covenant meal re-inaugurated Israel's covenant at Sinai, now as sealed in his blood. Salvation is in him.

Implications for Doctrine

In light of such close textual parallels with Israel's history—Passover and Sinai, it will be imperative to rethink the categories as well as reframe the questions for a Reformed doctrine of the Eucharist. Traditionally, the questions and disputes have mainly been metaphysical, concerning the mode of Christ's presence in the bread, or in heaven, the characteristics of his human body, and the relationship between visible signs and invisible reality. These are unlikely Jewish questions nor Jewish categories. Metaphysical concerns were hardly implicated in Israel's long history of remembering and celebrating the Passover. These questions and categories were often posed when Christ's phrase "This is my body" had already been airlifted from its Passover and Sinaitic allusion. As noted, Zwingli allowed the OT to continue to inform theology, and his attention to the Passover opened the door for historical and christological questions about the Eucharist *in Jewish categories*. The following shows how Zwingli opened the door for other questions and focuses as well.

Two Rites

The first implication concerns the long tradition in sacramental theology that has always assumed that the Eucharist is a single event. It is commonly assumed in Protestant theology that, as both the bread and the cup are to be equally received by lay believers, they are a single rite, as if one is the solid component regarding Christ's body, one is the liquid component regarding his blood, and whatever interpretation or even mystery applies to one automatically applies to the other.[80] This is an unaccounted for assumption.[81] It also does not explain why the bread must

80. Even Zwingli made this assumption, see Zwingli, "Subsidiary Essay," in *Huldrych Zwingli: Writings*, 2:204.

81. As Alasdair Heron also commented, while the bread and the cup are commonly held to be conceptually denoting the pair body/blood, in the Gospel texts the pair is more likely body/covenant. Heron, *Table and Tradition*, 14.

always come before the cup. Yet we now have seen how the two rites have clear parallels in the history of Israel which were two distinct (although related) events—Passover and Sinai—one a meal accompanying divine deliverance, and one a covenant inauguration, which came after deliverance. So giving the bread and the cup separate treatments in formulating a doctrine of the Eucharist is warranted. According to the account in Luke, for example, the notion of remembrance seems to apply only to the bread but not to the cup.[82]

De-mystifying the Meal

Zwingli's method of acknowledging the historical context of the Last Supper allowed him to de-mystify the Eucharist. He saw *history*, instead of mystery. He paid attention to the Passover meal, the precursor to the Eucharist, in which even young children were expected to take part in historical discourses on the meal. This challenges the long-held theological practice that often classifies the Eucharist as an instance of "sacraments" right at the outset, and treats it according to this genus. "Sacrament" is Latin for the Greek word *mysterion*—a mystery. In the Reformed tradition, according to Calvin, the Eucharistic mystery lies in our spiritual eating of Christ's body and drinking of his blood. Our souls are nourished unto eternal life. Such mystery, for Calvin, is better experienced than explained.[83] Zwingli's turn to the Jewish Passover made him totally unlike Calvin. It illuminates how discourses on a salvific meal were precisely meant to be *explanatory*, even to children. He urges theologians to recover common sense before resorting to mystery.[84] Indeed, the word "sacrament" is in fact neither applied either to baptism or the Eucharist in Scripture, but only to the marital union that reflects the mysterious

---

82. This makes sense since in the OT, it is repeatedly God who remembered his covenant (e.g., Gen 9:15–16; Exod 2:24; 6:5; 32:13; Lev 26:42, 45). Israel was dominantly taught to remember their deliverance from Egypt (Exod 13:3; Deut 5:15; 7:18; 8:2; 9:7; 15:15; 16:3, 12; 24:18, 22). In 1 Cor 11:24–25, however, Paul made the notion of remembrance applicable to both the bread and the cup.

83. Calvin, *Inst.* 4.17.9, 32.

84. G. W. Bromiley, introduction to "On the Lord's Supper," in *Zwingli and Bullinger*, 180–81. This is why Zwingli rejected the idea of physical eating of Christ. For him, there is no need to resort to miracle. See his *Commentary on True and False Religion*, 215; also Zwingli, "Subsidiary Essay," in *Huldrych Zwingli: Writings*, 2:226–27.

union between Christ and the church (Eph 5:31–32).[85] There is little hint from Scripture that the Eucharist is a mystery to be marveled at, or that there is a metaphysical riddle in the meal to be solved. As Markus Barth complained, the use of the notion of "sacrament" has been part of the "cumbersome" and "mysterious" language that has plagued the history of the doctrine of the Eucharist, and should be discontinued.[86] His father the Reformed theologian Karl Barth also agreed with him.[87] Zwingli himself already cast doubts on the term,[88] and rejected resorting to mystery when the meal appeals to ordinary sense, as implied in its history. While salvation is a divine undertaking and hence a mystery, the meal is clearly commanded of believers. The notion of mystery does not do justice to the imperative at all.

The Community

Zwingli took note of what happens *around* the table, not just what is *on* the table. As Peter Leithart complained, traditional Eucharistic theology has mostly conducted its investigation through a "zoom lens," zooming in onto the elements on the table, and hence mostly concerned with Christ's presence in the elements and its benefits to individual believers.[89] As is typical of Western theology, Eucharistic theology has been dominantly about seeing (visible signs) and knowing (invisible reality), instead of *actions* of people. It is time, Leithart contended, that Eucharistic theology uses a wide-angle lens, and gives weight to the faith community along with their culture, history, and dynamics. It is also time that Eucharistic theology listens to ritual studies which approach the Eucharist as a rite, by which people do not only act but their actions have effects.[90] Zwingli

85. Calvin precisely used this Eph 5:32 to buttress his point that the Eucharist is a mystery (*Inst.* 4.17.9).

86. Barth, *Rediscovering the Lord's Supper*, 2.

87. Karl Barth, Preface to *CD* 4/4.

88. Zwingli, *Commentary on True and False Religion*, 179–84.

89. Leithart, "Way Things Really Ought to Be," 159.

90. This latter point was also pressed by Martha Moore-Keish in her work *Do This in Remembrance of Me: A Ritual Approach to Reformed Eucharistic Theology*. In her title, the imperative "Do" is emphasized. Dru Johnson in his *Knowledge by Ritual* similarly argued that Christian sacramental theology has for too long been consumed by the search for signs and symbols, when biblical rituals call for *embodied practice*. While Protestant theology may frown at any emphasis of human action in relation

did precisely that: in contrast to his peers, he was able to zoom out from the table and take heed also of the community's actions around the table in forming a doctrine of the Eucharist. He observed the inter-dynamics of the disciples at the Last Supper. By doing so, he was able to take note of their calmness and lack of questions upon hearing Christ say, "This is my body," and thereby infer that the phrase was not meant to raise any theological riddles. He was willing to see the event through their Jewish lens. He acknowledged that the meal had a history in their community. In addition, he inquired into the effects of the human action of taking part in the Eucharist, i.e., by taking part, a believer expresses thanks and praise, and pledges him or herself to Christ. He was accused of subjectivism, yet his approach was more than just a turn to the inner subject. It was a turn to the concrete, dynamic community. He put doctrine directly in touch with ethics.[91] Zwingli was a forerunner of ritual theory.

In furthering his approach of extending focus to the community around the table, today's Eucharistic theology may also take heed of two things emphasized by the Gospel accounts of the Last Supper that have been neglected by traditional Eucharistic theology. First, all three Synoptic Gospels highlight the presence of the "twelve," which in Jewish scriptures and culture always references the *whole* of God's people.[92] This challenges the long-held assumption that the Eucharist is concerned so much with the *individual* participant as with corporate action. Second,

---

to salvation, here we are focusing on the *social* effects of human (inter)actions, not salvific effects. Even if the Eucharist is not a meritorious work, as a corporate action proclaiming the forgiveness of Christ, it inevitably makes a difference in the community. Barbara Jan Hedges-Goettl helpfully pointed out that Zwingli included liturgical instructions in his final work *A Short and Clear Exposition* that participants of the Eucharist should serve one another, specifically *because* this is how enemies find themselves reconciled. He was aware of the *social* effects of the Eucharist. This liturgical instruction is included in the translation by William John Hinke (in *On Providence*, 288–89), but is however omitted from G. W. Bromiley's translation in *Zwingli and Bullinger* (Hedges-Goettl, "Body Is Missing," 42).

91. Zwingli gave prominence to the *actions* of participants (pledging, praising and thanksgiving). Calvin, in giving prominence instead to the action of God who seals our consciences and assures our weak faith, also acknowledged that sacraments are by which Christians testify their piety towards God (*Inst.* 4.14.1). Nevertheless, Calvin assigned charity as the "third use" of the Eucharist, and it took up less space in his treatment of the Eucharist (mostly in one paragraph in the *Inst.* 4.17.38). Because Calvin still regarded the Eucharist as a divine mystery, the legacy of his theology unfortunately undermines the social significance of human action. See discussion in chapter 5.

92. Pitre, *Jesus and the Last Supper*, 94–95.

all *four* Gospel accounts of the Last Supper highlight the presence of Judas the traitor at the table right at the beginning of the narrative. In fact, in Matthew and Mark, the very first thing that Jesus reportedly said when the disciples sat down for the supper was that there was a traitor in their midst.[93] Thus, ironically, there is at least as much Scriptural emphasis on the "real presence" of Judas at the table as that possibly of the body of Christ in the bread.[94] This may challenge the long-held worry in the Reformed tradition over Luther's *manducatio impiorum*, i.e., whether the "unrighteous" partake of Christ for their judgment if Christ is present in the elements taken. Instead of trying to fence off the "unrighteous" from the true receiving of Christ, focus should be shifted to the undeserving table companions deliberately received *by* Christ, and hence to be received also by the church.

Political Questions

As is clear in Exod 12–13, all annual celebrations of the Passover are meant to draw attention to the fateful event on the very first Passover. It was not just the spiritual salvation of individual souls. That event was *political* in every sense of the word: God struck an oppressive state on behalf of an oppressed people and delivered them. The first Passover meal may even be said to be a rebellion. If Christ chose to institute the Eucharist specifically in the context of the memorial of this political rebellion, it would be intolerable that in developing an understanding of the Eucharist we erase the political factor completely.[95] The allusion to the first Passover and therefore of Israel's suffering also reminds us that sin never only lies in the individual, but is relational, social, even structural, and God avenges such sin. This is in stark contrast to Reformed sacramental theology which has often understood sin as primarily in the soul, for

93. Matt 26:21; Mark 14:18; Luke 22:3; John 13:2. Even Paul explicitly called the night of the Last Supper "the night [Christ] was betrayed" (1 Cor 11:23).

94. Also ironically, while, as Zwingli noticed, the disciples did not react at all to "This is my body," what they *did* react strongly to was the presence of a traitor. The "riddle" of the Eucharist, if any, was not one about metaphysical or miraculous presence, but the presence of a traitor.

95. According to Josephus, the Passover in the first century precisely offered the context for political activism because it was a memorial for deliverance. See *Antiquities* 14.2.1; 17.9.3; 18.2.2, *War* 2.14.3; 4.7.2. According to the Gospel accounts (Matt 26:5; Mark 14:1–2), under Roman rule, the Passover was indeed a politically sensitive time.

example in the form of a weak conscience.[96] Thus, furthering Leithart's suggestion, we should pay attention not only to what goes on around the table or in the room, but also widening our lens to what goes on in the society at large. A Eucharistic theology that pays attention to the history of the Passover would challenge the divorce between doctrinal theology and liberation theology that is typical of traditional Western theology. The meal itself carries a message of liberation, not only of spiritual salvation, but is politically relevant as well.

Conclusion

"No passage from the Old Testament ought to be examined more for light upon the force and meaning of Christ's language than this in which the passover of old was instituted."[97] Zwingli taught us that when Jesus said, "This is my body," he was speaking in the place of God, repeating God's words at the institution of the very first Passover that defined the meal, "It is the Lord's Passover." Instead of presenting a mystery concerning his presence in the bread, he was claiming that his body is the new Passover—he is the salvation of his people. Theology cannot understand the Eucharist without its historical precursor. Most unfortunately, Zwingli himself mainly focused on an unhelpful conclusion based on his promising approach. As a result, his approach never made a more lasting influence. His opponents hardly took note of his allusion to the Passover. Few commentators picked up his unique lead, instead most only focus on his symbolism and memorialism. But we have seen how Zwingli's attentiveness to God's institution of the Passover in Exod 12 and its parallel to the Last Supper has unlocked new questions and focuses concerning the Eucharist. He brought the OT to the life of the church. In a turn away from merely neo-Platonistic and metaphysical concerns, he posed historical and christological questions in Jewish categories. In a turn away from individualistic assumptions and the domination of the Eucharistic elements, he expanded his lens to the concrete community around the table together with their cultural heritage. In a turn away from focusing on seeing and knowing, he inquired the actions and interactions of believers.

96. For example, in Calvin's Eucharistic theology, sacraments are primarily for sealing our consciences and sustaining weak faith (*Inst.* 4.14.1). His discussion of sin in 2.1–2 primarily understood sin as lying in our knowledge and capacities. There is little hint of the *relational* aspect of sin.

97. Zwingli, "Subsidiary Essay," in *Huldrych Zwingli: Writings*, 2:211.

In a tradition that uses mystical language surrounding the Eucharist, he made way for ordinary sense and natural interpretations that respect the heritage of the Jewish people. He noted how God even prepared "FAQs" for the children of Israel!

Apart from de-mystifying Eucharistic theology, Zwingli's exegesis of the Exodus also opened the doors for new exciting approaches. We have seen how the allusion to Exodus reveals that Christ's words over the bread and the cup at the Last Supper beautifully reinstituted the two monumental events in Jewish history—Passover and Sinai. Christ himself *is* the new Passover and new covenant. The reference to the very first Passover also highlights the sociopolitical dimension of sin and salvation. This challenges the tendency in traditional Western theology to over-spiritualize faith, discounting structural sin and the relevance of theology to political liberation. If the first Passover was the precursor to the Eucharist, then Eucharistic theology must not forget that God hears the cries of the oppressed (Exod 3:7–9). Perhaps the allusion to the historical Passover in Eucharistic theology is the much-needed link in the attempt of modern theology to bridge doctrine and liberation. The dreamer from Zurich was truly a forerunner of modern theology.

One last point is worth mentioning. Zwingli's unique attention to the first Passover might have unintentionally shone new light on the controversy as to whether the Last Supper was indeed a Passover meal.[98] Controversy arises because there is an apparent discrepancy concerning the dating of the Last Supper in the four Gospels. In the Synoptic Gospels, the meal is stated to be a Passover meal, specifically "on the first day of Unleavened Bread" (Matt 26:17; Mark 14:12; Luke 22:7). Mark and Luke even added that it was the day the Passover lamb had to be sacrificed. The Last Supper presumably took place after the Passover lamb had been killed. In John 19:14, however, Christ is said to have died the moment when Passover lambs were to be killed (i.e., at twilight on Nisan 14), making the Last Supper impossible to be a regular Passover meal if it was eaten beforehand (lambs were not yet killed). I find that debates on this controversy have often overlooked the important distinction between the *institution* of the Passover meal and the regular, annual Passover meal. In the intertextual parallel closely observed by Zwingli, based on what Christ was saying, Christ's Last Supper was the *institution* of the new Passover meal, akin to God's instructions to Israel via Moses *before* the

98. See a detailed discussion of the controversy in Pitre, *Jesus and the Last Supper*, 251–373.

actual Passover (especially Exod 12:1–27), and therefore must have taken place *before* the date set for all annual Passover celebrations.[99] Zwingli's approach questions the very necessity of the Last Supper to be a "regular" Passover seder in order for the Passover festival to carry immense significance for our understanding of the Lord's Supper. Precisely Christ was not simply hosting a regular seder—he was reinstituting a new Passover. In sum, the fact that Jesus died when Passover lambs were killed makes sense of the fact that Jesus *also* presided over a "Passover" meal before dying, because that was the *institution* of the new Passover meal.[100] Jesus was precisely speaking in YHWH's place, repeating his words, and like him instituting a new meal and laying claim to it before the salvific event was set to take place. If the Last Supper was only a regular Passover meal, it would have been theologically insignificant, because Jesus would have just been any ordinary Jewish household leader. But nobody except God could reinstitute the Passover meal and give meaning to it anew—Jesus is Lord.

99. Zwingli helpfully pointed to the necessary precedence of the institution in time. Zwingli, "Subsidiary Essay," in *Huldrych Zwingli: Writings*, 2:212.

100. Therefore, as we have seen, the Synoptic Gospels clearly quote Jesus as repeating the key words and phrases from Exod 12:1–27.

2

Passover and Sinai

Isaac spoke to his father Abraham . . . "But where is the lamb . . . ?"
—Gen 22:7

Who may ascend onto the hill of the Lord?
And who may stand in his holy place?
—Ps 24:3

HAVING PICKED UP ZWINGLI's lead to pay attention to the Old Testament context of the Lord's Supper, this chapter will then move beyond him in delineating a fuller account of the Supper in light of its connection to the Exodus narrative. Jesus's words of institution at the Last Supper, together with the passion narratives, clearly alluded to the age-old Passover meal, as well as Israel's covenant meal at Sinai. It will be demonstrated that Jesus's instituting and presiding at the Passover and covenant meal enacted and fulfilled the two monumental events of Jewish history—Passover and Sinai. The imperatives to "take" and "eat" in "remembrance," as well as the presentation of the "blood of the covenant" in the presence of the "twelve" were already prefigured in the first Passover and at Sinai. "This is my body" and "This is my blood of the new covenant" were in fact Jesus's rewording of the two climactic phrases said during these two events to make them point to himself. In light of such close parallels, and the fact that Jesus fulfilled Scripture, including the old Passover and the old covenant, we have little excuse to "pass over" the elaborate narrative of the Exodus as handed down to us. It is imperative that we give ears to

44

the detailed narrative of the old Passover and God's covenant made with Israel at Sinai. Indeed, the Exodus is said to be a most influential "master narrative" of the people of God.[1] Our goal is to revive *history*, instead of metaphysics, as the focus of inquiry in a theology of the Supper. The Supper concerns a narrative of the dynamic relationship between a gracious God and his people since the ancient of days, instead of a timeless metaphysics that connects itemized objects to Christ.

In bringing the history of the Jewish Passover to bear on our understanding of the Lord's Supper, this study will not adopt the common approach of comparing the Last Supper to the Jewish Passover seder, as codified in m. Pesaḥ. 10.[2] The problem with this approach is that the seder was in fact established only *after* the year AD 70, when the temple was destroyed.[3] According to Jewish commentary on the *haggadah*, little is known about the customary order of the Passover meal at Jesus's time, *except* what God commanded Israel in the book of Exodus.[4] Precisely, as Zwingli has helpfully led us to reason, we actually need not worry about the post-temple seder because, in the first place, what was most significant about the Last Supper was not that it fit into the order of a regular Passover meal, but that it was the *institution* of a new Passover. Jesus was speaking the words of institution *as God*, not just presiding over the meal as a Jewish household leader. The parallel with the Last Supper is therefore not the Jewish seder, in m. Pesaḥ. 10, but God's instructions to Israel about the Passover meal, in Exod 12.

Similarly, in bringing the history of the Sinaitic covenant to bear on our understanding of the cup, this study will thereby not assume at the outset that the cup of the Last Supper was one of the four cups of wine to be celebrated in the Jewish seder (which was, again, only established after AD 70).[5] Jesus's words over the cup rather clearly hearkened back to Moses's on Mount Sinai, "Behold the blood of the covenant" (Exod 24:8;

---

1. Olson, "Book of Exodus," 27.

2. See, e.g., Jeremias, *Eucharistic Words of Jesus*, 84–88; Heron, *Table and Tradition*, 19–22; Mathison, *Given for You*, 211–14; Feeley-Harnik, *Lord's Table*, 120–27.

3. See discussion in introduction, pp. 1–14.

4. Tabory, *JPS Commentary on the Haggadah*, 3–5.

5. E.g., Jeremias, *Eucharistic Words of Jesus*, 84–88; Heron, *Table and Tradition*, 21–22; Pitre, *Jesus and Jewish Roots of Eucharist*, 149–57; Mathison, *Given for You*, 213. Pitre later in his *Jesus and the Last Supper* (90–129) discussed the Sinaitic narrative more substantially to show that Jesus, the new Moses, saw his own death as a covenant sacrifice.

also Heb 9:20). This study will therefore put Jesus's words in the Sinaitic context, instead of the Passover seder.

This chapter will therefore aim to delve into the detailed narrative of the first Passover as well as Israel's arrival and covenant ceremony at Sinai, and thereby narrate the Last Supper *as part of* that history and tradition. The texts I will focus on will be mainly Exod 12 (institution of the first Passover) and Exod 19–24 (covenant meal at Sinai). I will seek to explicate the Supper in Jewish categories, such as the Passover lamb, blood of the covenant, and significance of the presence of the "twelve." The Passover and covenant narrative should dictate not only answers to the questions concerning the meaning of the Lord's Supper, but also, in the first place, what are the *right* questions to ask. This study offers a new paradigm of questions to ask concerning the Supper, such as the Passover Lamb, and divine-human table fellowship, while rethinking the validity of traditional questions such as the use of the genus of sacraments, and the so-called real presence of Christ (whether in the elements or to each individual). The focus of the Supper is actually less about the conceptual, static pair of body and blood of Christ as related to the bread and cup (whether realistically or only symbolically), but more about two important events in Jewish history. My method also challenges the long-held assumption that the bread and the cup essentially carry the same meaning and therefore what explains one also explains the other. Using Jewish categories, the meal speaks of remembrance of Christ the true Passover, followed by recommitment to him who is the new covenant.

A proper exegesis will be beyond the scope of this project. The following does not intend to be an exhaustive exegesis. I will nevertheless make careful observations from the narrative of the Exodus and make them bear on the new Passover and new covenant. This chapter will aim at a biblical theology of the narrative of Israel's exodus from Egypt and their arrival at Mount Sinai to sacrifice to the Lord. In doing so I will take the text in its final redacted form.[6]

Before delving into the narrative, we must reiterate just how central the Passover context is to the Last Supper. *All* four Gospel accounts narrate the Last Supper specifically as a meal that occurred in the context of the Jewish Passover (Matt 26:17; Mark 14:12; Luke 22:1, 7; John 13:1).[7] All four Gospels gave us the Passover festival as a signpost. Even

6. I agree with Brevard Childs in taking the final redacted form of the text seriously, striving to appreciate its inner coherence. Childs, *Exodus*, 195–97.

7. Here I reference the texts that directly narrate the Last Supper (John 13 rather than John 6).

when the author of the Johannine account chose to omit Jesus's words of institution, the Passover timing of the Last Supper was kept just as explicitly. Presumably the timing is at least as important as the words of institution for our understanding of the Supper, if not more important. The Jews had already been celebrating and interpreting the Passover meal for centuries before Jesus's time. As Markus Barth remarked, in developing a theology of the Lord's Supper, theologians must not make the whole history of Israel obsolete.[8] As will be shown below, the biblical account of the first Passover already contained what Christians are familiar with in the Last Supper accounts, namely the imperatives to take, eat, and remember. In light of this, Eucharistic theologians have little excuse not to pay heed to the narrative of the Jewish Passover. Undoubtedly, controversies have arisen concerning the exact dating of the Last Supper, because of the discrepancies in the Synoptic Gospels on the one hand, and the Johannine account on the other. As argued by Joachim Jeremias, even if we cannot solve the discrepancy between the Gospels, i.e., whether the Last Supper took place on Nisan 14 or Nisan 15, it is no doubt that all four Gospels put the Last Supper in the context of the Passover.[9] Besides, as we have shown, Zwingli's attention to the first Passover in Egypt questions the long-held concern as to whether the Last Supper needed to be a regular Passover meal at all, because precisely Christ was instituting the new Passover meal, not just eating a regular one like every other Jew.

Indeed it is not just that the Last Supper meal, but, as biblical researchers agree, the whole ministry of Christ should be seen in light of the Jewish Passover. John's account can be even read as intentional in employing Paschal language to speak of Jesus: John the Baptist's proclamation "Behold the Lamb of God" (John 1:29), the exact day of Jesus's death as befalling the ancient specified day for the slaughter of Passover lambs (John 19:14), and the mention that Jesus's bones did not break when he died, fulfilling an ancient Passover law (John 19:36; Exod 12:46). In Matthew, it was as if Christ deliberately chose the occasion (Matt 26:2). Paul gave us the apposition "Christ our Passover" (1 Cor 5:7). The book of Revelations presents a marriage banquet of the Lamb (Rev 19:6–9).[10]

---

8. Barth, *Rediscovering the Lord's Supper*, 18.

9. Jeremias, *Eucharistic Words of Jesus*, 41–62.

10. Indeed, even when John's Gospel omits the words of institution, it even more strongly explicates the Passover dimensions of Jesus's passion. See, e.g., Schlund, *Kein Knochen Soll Gebrochen Warden*; Le Déaut, "Paque Juive et Nouveau Testament."

One must take seriously the fact that, when God first instituted the Passover, he repeatedly commanded that the Passover should be observed as "a permanent ordinance" throughout generations (*chukkat olam*, Exod 12:14, 17, 24; also Deut 16:3). The book of Jubilees from the Second Temple period reiterates this decree, that for this ordinance "there is no limit of days, for this is ordained for ever" (49:7-8). We may then note the lack of such emphasis for perpetuity at the institution of the Lord's Supper. By a strong contrast, Jesus's vows of abstinence until the meal is "fulfilled in the kingdom of God" (Luke 22:16, 18; also Matt 26:29; and Mark 14:25), and Paul's liturgical line "until he comes," express the temporary character of the Lord's Supper. The Lord's Supper still awaits final consummation. It is the new Passover meal that fulfilled the old but only temporarily—it will be ultimately consummated only when Christ comes again. Scholars speak of the Passover as a "typology" of all of God's redemption.[11] This typological character of the Passover is displayed most famously and beautifully in a poem in the Palestinian Targum to Exod 12:42. The Passover night is, in this Targum, extended to *four* different nights: the first night when the world was first created, the second night when Abraham nearly sacrificed Isaac to God, the third night when Israel departed Egypt, and the fourth night when the Messiah will finally come again.[12] In other words, in Rabbinic literature, the night of Passover is intertwined with other significant events in the history of salvation. Specifically the Messiah is anticipated to come on the night of the Passover.[13] The redemptive work of God from the beginning to the end is interpreted in light of the Passover. Jesus's redemption was realizing the hope of Israel, one that is attached principally to the event of Exodus.[14] It is in this light that we appreciate how NT language of redemption unequivocally borrows from the typology of the Passover.

---

11. See, e.g., Kugel, *Traditions of the Bible*, 575-77; Le Déaut, "Paque Juive et Nouveau Testament."

12. See the famous work by Le Déaut, *La Nuit Pascale*.

13. Jeremias, *Eucharistic Words of Jesus*, 124.

14. Le Déaut, "Paque Juive et Nouveau Testament," 22.

The Last Supper is significant because it fulfilled the old Passover.[15] Jeremias calls the Supper the "Christian Passover."[16] As such, the meal already had a long history that defined it, before Jesus sat down with his disciples in the upper room. Without understanding the old Passover, one would not understand the new.

The Passover—Old and New

If we take seriously the repeated emphasis in the Gospels that the context of the Last Supper was the Jewish Passover, it is intuitive that we look at Scripture's own presentation of the events of the Passover—the events constituting the institution of the very first Passover. As Zwingli suggested, if we want to understand Jesus's words said over the Last Supper, we should compare those with the words said over the first Passover (in Exod 12). In the following I aim to delve into the narrative of the first Passover, and make it speak to our understanding of the Last Supper. In particular, I will highlight two points. The first is the fact that the narrative of Israel's deliverance out of Egypt intertwines with God's liturgical instructions of the Passover meal. Narrative and liturgy are interwoven together. Second, the main elements of Christ's words of institution at the Last Supper were already contained in God's instructions for the first Passover, including the imperatives to take, eat, and remember, as well as a climactic phrase that begins with "This is . . ." When we refer to the words of institution of the Lord's Supper, strictly they were words of Christ's re-institution of the Passover. It is the first Passover that shines light on how we should understand these words.

15. In this study, the fulfillment of the old Passover and covenant by the life and work of Jesus Christ *in no way* suggests that the old was made obsolete. Quite the opposite: Jesus said that he came not to abolish the law but to fulfill them (Matt 5:17). Such fulfillment is then the antithesis of abolishment. It is rather a confirmation of the old. Jesus's institution of the new Passover and new covenant does *not* abolish the Jewish Passover and God's covenant with Israel sealed at Sinai. In addition, that Jesus fulfilled the Passover also does not deny the fact that the Passover deliverance already functioned as divine promise for similar deliverances in the history of Israel and which had its fulfilment within the OT as well. See, e.g., Ezra 6:19–22.

16. Jeremias, *Eucharistic Words of Jesus*, 19.

Meal and Salvation

One undeniable and profound fact about the first Passover is that the narrative of Israel's deliverance out of Egypt intertwines seamlessly with God's liturgical instructions of the meal and with Israel's eating.[17] The biblical text that recounts Israel's delivery from Egypt in the book of Exodus is very telling. When God had heard the cries of his people enslaved in Egypt, he appeared to Moses and, with Moses and Aaron confronting Pharaoh on behalf of his people, he sent nine plagues one after another to Egypt, ordering Pharaoh to let his people go to the wilderness to worship him (Exod 1–10). When, in chapter 11, Moses was still forewarning Pharaoh that the very last plague was imminent, immediately in the beginning of chapter 12 (v. 1), God told Israel to prepare for a meal. It is as if liturgy has intruded into the narrative of deliverance.[18] God told Israel how to *take* one lamb per household (vv. 3–5) and how to prepare and *eat* it (vv. 8–9, 11). They were given a recipe, so to speak. Israel were also to take the blood of the lamb and put on their doorposts (v. 7). God did not first deliver Israel, and only *then* in retrospect ask them to celebrate and commemorate with a meal. But God first gave Israel the Passover meal, and foretold that his saving actions would take place specifically *in the context* of the meal. The saving event then would unfold only in accordance with, and as part of, this liturgy. In other words, the saving event *is* the liturgy.[19] Indeed the liturgy is also the saving event. Even the manner of eating the Passover meal must be hasty and the dress code was specifically traveling attire: "with your garment belted around your waist, your sandals on your feet, and your staff in your hand; and you shall eat it in a hurry" (vv. 11–12)[20]—God would deliver on his people's behalf any time as they ate. In a way, the meal and the event of Israel's deliverance from Egypt were not separate events, but one.

Immediately after giving instructions for the first Passover meal and promising his mighty deliverance as Israel ate their meal, and before the events actually unfolded, God here also gave instructions for *future* generations of Israel to commemorate the event (vv. 14–20). They would sacrifice and eat a Passover lamb on this day every year, along with

17. See Fretheim, *Exodus*, 136; Olson, "Sacramentality in the Torah," 27–28; Durham, *Exodus*, 155; Kugel, *Traditions of the Bible*, 566.

18. Durham, *Exodus*, 155.

19. Fretheim, *Exodus*, 137.

20. Fretheim, *Exodus*, 155.

unleavened bread and bitter herbs throughout all their generations. Thus God was not only commanding a meal, but a liturgy to be passed down to generations. In other words, with God's command, the participation of all generations of the future was already *included* in this event. Then, the text tells us, Moses reiterated what God said to the people, especially the command to put the blood of the lamb on their doorposts (vv. 21–23), and, just as God did, Moses left instructions to future generations to celebrate as well (vv. 24–27). The Israelites, the text then affirms, did just as God had commanded them (v. 28).

It was only then that God avenged Egypt with his final blow. "Now it came about at midnight that the Lord struck all the firstborn in the land of Egypt, from the firstborn of Pharaoh who sat on his throne to the firstborn of the captive who was in the dungeon, and all the firstborn of cattle" (v. 29). Thus the narrative of destructive plagues on Egypt resumes again only in 12:29, after a detailed account of the liturgy of the Passover meal since 12:1. From vv. 29–42 the saving events took place as God promised in the context of the meal. Israel finally departed Egypt after 430 years of slavery. A more notable detail is their haste in leaving. As the text repeatedly makes clear, they were rushed out of Egypt, so much that they did not even have time to allow their dough to rise (Exod 12:34, 39; Deut 16:3). Thus the unleavened nature of the bread testifies that the people left Egypt in haste and unprepared (the deliverance was therefore entirely God's doing).[21] Again, the particular menu testifies and even embodies the redemptive event. In the same way, liturgy testifies and embodies the redemptive event.

In vv. 43–51, liturgical instructions intrude into the narrative again. Further instructions are given concerning future celebrations, e.g., who can eat the Passover meal in future celebrations. God decreed that gentiles could take part if circumcised. Interestingly, therefore, even gentiles

21. It may be interesting to note that, if leaven typically takes thirty to forty-five minutes to cause bread dough to rise at room temperature, then we are given the clue that when Israel left Egypt, they probably did not even have thirty minutes to spare. The food vividly testifies the almost immediate departure of Jews from Egypt after the Passover meal. As Craig Blomberg noted, in Gen 19:3 unleavened bread was similarly served in the context of fleeing a border hastily when God's judgment befell a region (Blomberg, *Contagious Holiness*, 34–35).

It is only in the New Testament that leaven is associated with sin (e.g., Matt 16:6; 1 Cor 5:7–8). In the Torah, the text is clear that the Passover meal must be unleavened specifically because Israel left Egypt for the wilderness so hastily that they did not even have time to prepare risen doughs, not because leaven itself represented moral corruption. See Sarna, *Exodus*, 58.

are already included in the original divine delivery of the Israelites. Exodus 13 (13:1–16) details the command to consecrate all the firstborn of Israel, the acknowledgment that all firstborn are claimed by God, and the instructions for the future celebrations of the seven-day Festival of Unleavened Bread. Because the first generation who were liberated from Egypt ate unleavened bread, all future generations must also eat accordingly. God even decreed that whoever has possession of leaven during this period will be cut off from God's people. The meal was not just to commemorate the original saving event; it *defines* who participated in that event and who did not.

Finally, in 13:17–22, the narrative resumes again to conclude the event. God led his freed slaves with a pillar of cloud and fire into the wilderness, through a detour away from threats, lest the people became afraid and decided to go back to Egypt. In sum, the liturgical meal and the redemptive event which it commemorates are inseparable. In the first place, the redemptive event as portrayed in the book of Exodus never took place without the meal, i.e., without the accompanying liturgy.[22]

It must be in this light that we read Christ's passion narrative in the four Gospels. The Last Supper is clearly embedded in the passion narrative.[23] Likewise, the event of the cross did not take place without the Last Supper, nor without the institution of the new Passover meal for future generations. The event of the cross unfolded immediately after, and only in light of, Jesus's new interpretation of the elements of the Passover meal. If we acknowledge the context and even typology of the Jewish Passover in reading the Gospel passion narratives, this would mean that the event of the cross cannot be separated from the Last Supper. We would understand Jesus's command to the disciples as well as to

22. In the Passover, the meal is the context of the saving event. This is one of the main reasons why I believe, contrary to the thesis of some scholars, that the Passover and the Christian Eucharist could not have been just a development out of the Hellenistic symposium. Scholars have argued that, just as in the latter, the Jewish Passover involves an elaborate meal with specified table topics. See for example the compilation of essays in Marks and Taussig, *Meals in Early Judaism*. Yet in the case of the Passover, what is talked about is not just table talk. The participants of the Passover meal do not just talk about a past redemptive event, but the meal itself *reenacts* that event, and was prescribed in that event which started the meal in the first place. See also the similarities and contrasts between Greco-Roman symposia and the Jewish Passover meal in LaVerdiere, *Dining in the Kingdom of God*, 16–21; as well as Blomberg, *Contagious Holiness*, 86–92.

23. While the Last Supper was part of a series of other meals, this one meal only was part of the passion narrative. LaVerdiere, *Dining in the Kingdom of God*, 123.

future generations to keep the feast as often as they break bread and drink from the cup as very much part of the redemptive event itself. As will be discussed below and in chapter 4, this has far-reaching implications for our understanding of believers' participation in Christ and in the event of his cross. In short, the various Gospel accounts recount that the meal was not commanded after the saving event, but was part of it. Participation takes the form of concrete obedience to a command given in the event of the cross, not in terms of some mysterious communion with the body and blood sacrificed on the cross that is *extra* to the event itself. The participation of future generations in the event was already commanded and hence included in the event itself. There is no need for future believers to build a metaphysical bridge to the first saving event. That event did not end there and then we have to find a metaphysical or mysterious way to participate in it. Instead, the event itself includes a command that extends to all future generations.

"Take, Eat"

Jesus's command to disciples to take, eat, and to do so as a commemoration, was not new at all. One cannot help but notice the close parallel between Exod 12–13 and the Gospel accounts of the Last Supper: in Exod 12–13 there were elaborate, repeated imperatives to *take* (Exod 12:3–5), to *eat* (12:8–9, 11), and the definition of the Passover as a day for *remembrance* (12:14; 13:3, 9).[24] Jesus's words of institution mirrored closely an ancient divine command, given on this very occasion, to take, eat, and remember. He was precisely speaking as God on the first Passover night.[25] He was reinterpreting the ancient command. His words must

24. The roots for the verbs "to take," λαμβάνω, and "to eat," φάγω, in Septuagint Exod 12 and in Matthew and Mark are the same, respectively.

No doubt, the word "remembrance" (ἀνάμνησιν) used in Luke 22:19 is not the same as in Septuagint Exod 12–13 (μνημόσυνον). Douglas Jones contended that, despite the difference in words, the obvious reference of Jesus's ἀνάμνησιν was the memorial Passover meal. This is not only because Jews had always understood the Passover to be a memorial, but also because the phrase "in remembrance" (εἰς . . . ἀνάμνησιν) likely has its origin in the similar Hebrew phrase *lezikkaron* in Exod 12:14. Jones, "Ἀνάμνησις in the LXX," 188.

25. Thus contrary to Keith Mathison's portrayal, in which Jesus was only taking the role of a *paterfamilias*, the head of the household presiding over a Passover meal (*Given for You*, 210), Jesus was in fact speaking as none other than God himself.

Also, John W. Riggs disregarded the importance of the Passover context of the Last Supper, by only briefly noting that the inner material of Synoptic accounts gives no

therefore be understood in light of that ancient command. The commemorative Jewish Passover also determines how we should understand the kind of remembrance that Jesus had in mind. An astonishing detail of the narrative is that, immediately after God had forewarned Pharaoh of the imminent last plague on Egypt, he gave Israel, through Moses, elaborate instructions to *take* and *eat* the Passover lamb. He did not immediately tell them that he would strike Egypt, nor hurry his people to pack and prepare for their departure, but first came the invitation to take, put blood on their doorposts, and to eat (12:1–11). The imperatives to take and eat were elaborate and repetitive: these include what kind of lamb to take, from where, and when to take it; instructions prescribed with what one should eat the lamb, and the pace with which to eat, and even the proper dress code (vv. 1–11). The foretelling of the strike on the firstborns of Egypt came only after elaborate instructions to take and eat the lamb (v. 12). The command to take and eat the Passover lamb was therefore God's command before his final blow on the oppressive state. One may even say "take, eat" was a battle cry. Because of the command, the people's act of eating the Passover meal was involved in God's retributive action against Pharaoh. He laid a feast for his people in the presence of their enemies (Ps 23:5).

As James Kugel pointed out, the imperative to take and eat the Passover lamb was in fact God's very first collective command to Israel.[26] In addition, commentators note that in God's instructions for the Passover meal, he defined that very month in which Israel would depart Egypt would be the first month of the year (Exod 12:2). The numbering of months would start from the deliverance of slavery. The new calendar and new month signal a new order of life in which God's people are freed from bondage. It was the birth of a new nation.[27]

---

hint that it was Passover meal (Riggs, *Lord's Supper in the Reformed Tradition*, 3n16). But in fact the parallel between the first Passover and Jesus's words of institution at the Last Supper is overwhelming.

26. Kugel, *Traditions of the Bible*, 557, 566.

27. Sarna, *Exodus*, 54; Kugel, *Traditions of the Bible*, 557, 566. According to some scholars, the command to take and eat the Passover Lamb was even the very first day of the (first) month. See Cassuto, *Commentary on the Book of Exodus*, 136; Bloch, *Biblical and Historical Background*, 213. One cannot help but recall that throughout Scripture, there have been similar divine invitations to *eat*: to Adam (Gen 2:16); to Noah (Gen 9:3); here to Israel on the first Passover (Exod 12:1–11); to Peter upon the inclusion of gentiles in the new people (Acts 10:13). Each signals a new era in salvation history.

It is against the backdrop of this first Passover that we ask what Jesus's invitation to "take, eat" means. Jesus's words echoed back to centuries ago when God similarly invited his people to take and eat the lamb. First and foremost, Jesus was speaking in the place of God. Now the one who uttered this invitation does not speak only through a mediating prophet Moses, but himself in person, at the table. Inevitably, Jesus's reiterating of God's words from the first Passover, commanding the people to take and eat, again in remembrance, also signaled to Jews the dawn of a new era as well. If the old "take, eat" on this occasion signaled God's final blow on an oppressive state on behalf of his people, we might see the familiar "take, eat" now signaled that God would strike his final blow to sin and evil. If God commanded future generations of Jews to celebrate the Passover meal, Jesus also similarly commanded future generations of his followers to celebrate. Then, it was God's final blow to Egypt; now, it would be God's final strike on sin and death.

In light of the old Passover, it is also difficult to overlook the shocking fact that the new command to take and eat now no longer applies to a lamb—the central, indispensable item on the Passover table—but only to the bread, i.e., to the side dish (note Exod 12:8). In fact the lamb is missing! A lambless Passover would be inconceivable for Jews. Jesus's new meal should first and foremost prompt questions about the Passover lamb that was supposed to be there but shockingly was not. This will be confirmed by his explicit highlighting of *his* own body and by the fact that now remembrance is of *him* (see discussion below).

"This Is My Body"

As we have seen in the previous chapter, Zwingli identified Exod 12:11, "It is the Lord's Passover," as the historical precursor to Jesus's "This is my body." Instead I will identify another verse as the more likely precursor. Within the texts pertaining to God's instructions and explanations concerning the Passover meal, one of the key phrases was: "It is [the] Passover sacrifice to the Lord" (Exod 12:27). This, I will argue, is the more compelling parallel to Jesus's "This is my body." If so, Jesus was pointing to himself as *the* Passover sacrifice.

First, in the Septuagint (the Greek text widely used by first-century Jews), Exod 12:27 θυσία τὸ πάσχα τοῦτο Κυρίῳ (*"This* is the Passover sacrifice to the Lord") contains exactly the demonstrative pronoun τοῦτο used in Jesus's phrase τοῦτό ἐστιν τὸ σῶμά μου ("This is my body") as recorded in the Synoptics. At the same time, the pronoun τοῦτο does not appear in the other similar phrases in the Septuagint translation of Exod 12–13 (including Zwingli's choice, 12:11, which is only πασχα ἐστὶν κυρίῳ). It is very likely that Jesus's words, "*This* is my body," were alluding to the Greek text of Exod 12:27.

Second, this phrase "This is the Passover sacrifice to the Lord" carries paramount importance in the Passover narrative. It was the *very first phrase* of the standard answer to be given to children who ask about the meaning of the Passover meal. It was the first interpretive phrase commanded of the host of a Passover meal. Moses commanded Israel, "And when your children ask you, 'What do you mean by this rite?' you shall say, '*This is* the Passover sacrifice to the Lord . . .'" (Exod 12:26–27, translated from Greek LXX). What is ironic about this historical allusion is that, amidst the centuries-long controversies concerning the meaning of the Lord's Supper, one might exclaim how convenient it would be if God had given us frequently asked questions (FAQs) about the meaning of the meal. But the truth is that we *were* given such FAQs! These were in the form of "when your child asks you . . ." "you shall answer . . ." (Exod 12:26–27; 13:8–10, 14–16). So as long as we do not disregard the Passover context of the Last Supper, we were indeed already given clues to interpret the meal. It is imperative that we pay attention to the standard answers for the "FAQs" God gave us, the first of which was precisely on the meaning of the meal. If Jesus was reinstituting a new Passover, we expect him to reinterpret these questions and answers.

Third, the phrase "This is the Passover sacrifice to the Lord" references the Passover lamb on the table, the central element of the Passover meal. As such, the phrase is not only important but is the very climax of the meal. And as the first phrase given to a child who asks about the meaning of the meal, it kicks off the whole recounting of the history of the Passover. According to Talmud (b. Pesaḥ. 116b), the verse Exod 12:27 must be recited before anyone is said to be released of their obligation on Passover.[28] Although the Talmud was a later compilation and redaction of earlier Jewish traditions, Jewish commentary acknowledges that it is likely that Second Temple Jews obeyed the commands from Moses, especially the command to answer a child's question with Exod 12:27, from the earliest celebrations of Passover.[29] This also seems to be supported

28. Jeremias, *Eucharistic Words of Jesus*, 56. See also Sandmel, *Judaism and Christian Beginnings*, 213–14.

29. Tabory, in *JPS Commentary to Haggadah*, acknowledges that the Torah does

by Jubilees 49:22. Because the context of the Last Supper was Passover, Jesus was likely expected to utter that phrase. Indeed he did, except that he *rephrased* it.

It is true that, as it has been pointed out even during the Reformation, originally "This is my body" in Aramaic had a different formulation—without the verb "to be" ("This my body," thus making it less likely that the phrase teaches a direct identification between "this" and "my body").[30] Precisely this is the formulation of Exod 12:27 in Septuagint and Hebrew too (although the definite article may be used as a copula).

Lastly, scholars agree that when Christ took the cup and said, "This is my blood of the covenant" (Matt 26:28; Mark 14:24; or "This is the new covenant in my blood" in Luke 22:20), he was explicitly hearkening back to Moses's words at Mount Sinai, "Behold the blood of the covenant," said in the presence of twelve pillars (Exod 24:8).[31] The cup at the Last Supper clearly alluded to God's covenant inauguration with Israel at Sinai. So if Jesus reiterated words from Jewish Scripture for the cup, it makes sense that he also did the same for the bread. Zwingli exactly pointed to the right direction (even though he identified a different verse). Now we have a good match: in our understanding now, Christ's words over both the bread and the cup repeated Moses's words in Israel's salvation history in the book of Exodus. The bread and the cup reinstituted the two monumental events in Jewish history—Passover and Sinai.

For these reasons, I believe that Exod 12:27 is a very likely allusion of "This is my body."[32] If my assessment is correct, a more appropriate

---

not exactly prescribe how to celebrate Passover or what ceremony. But "from what we know about patriarchal societies, it is hard to imagine that the meal in which the family sacrifice was consumed was not accompanied by some verbal elaboration on either the history of the celebration or its significance. This is especially true, as the Torah does prescribe, on several occasions, that the paschal sacrifice should be used as an opportunity to transmit historical traditions to the younger generations. In one case, this prescription appears as a response to a child's question 'What do you mean by this rite?' The answer is 'You shall say, "It is the passover sacrifice to the LORD, because he passed over the houses of the Israelites of Egypt when he smote the Egyptians, but saved our houses"' (Exod. 12:26–27)." Tabory, *JPS Commentary to Haggadah*, 4. Besides, according to Jeremias, Rabbi Gamaliel, whom Talmud cites as teaching that Exod 12:27 must be recited in a Passover meal, was R. Gamaliel I, who was a contemporary of Jesus, not R. Gamaliell II, i.e., not of a later generation. Jeremias, *Eucharistic Words of Jesus*, 56.

30. See, e.g., Anderson, "Language and History in the Reformation," 20–22.

31. Pitre, *Jesus and the Last Supper*, 93–94.

32. There are scholars who propose that Jesus's "This is my body" was alluding

question to ask about the Supper is not what Jesus meant when he said "This is my body," but what Jesus meant when he *rephrased* "This is the Passover sacrifice to the Lord" (recited by Jews for centuries on this occasion) by "This is my body." An immediate, intuitive answer is that he was asserting that *his* body would be the Passover sacrifice to the Lord. Jesus's "This is my body" was likely paraphrasing the old climactic phrase on this occasion, "This is the Passover sacrifice to the Lord," pointing to his own body as the sacrificial Passover lamb.[33] He meant that he himself is the new, true Passover (1 Cor 5:7). The long Jewish tradition of the sacrifice of Passover lambs had been pointing to him.[34] To this we may add the conspicuous absence of a lamb in the new meal, certainly shocking to

---

to a phrase in the seder prescribed in Mishnah: "This is the bread of affliction which our ancestors ate when they came from the land of Egypt" (commonly known as *Ha Lachma Anya*). Jeremias, *Eucharistic Words of Jesus*, 54, 57, 220; Mathison, *Given for You*, 211–12. However, I believe that *Ha Lachma Anya* is an unlikely reference. Such a phrase *"This is* the bread of affliction . . ." is absent in Jewish Scripture. It is only in the post-temple seder that it gained prominence. In fact, the "bread of affliction" in Scripture is *not* the bread on the Passover table on the fateful night (Nisan 15), but is the bread of the seven-day Festival of Unleavened Bread, i.e., the quick, convenient bread that Israel took with them on the road (Deut 16:3). Yet, as we have seen, Jesus's words at the Last Supper *"This is* . . ." directly echoed God's similar phrase in his instructions for the first Passover night (Exod 12:27), not for the seven-day Festival of Unleavened Bread. This may be explained by the fact that the salvation through Jesus no longer involves any geographical journey that would need convenient bread over a period of time.

33. Gustav Dalman, in his search for the Semitic equivalent of the Greek soma in "This is my body," noted that in m. Pesaḥ. 10:3 and Tos. Pes. 10:9, the phrase "*body* of the Passover" (*gupho shellap-pesah*) specifically denotes the body of the lamb during the time of the temple, in distinction from other items on the table. He wrote, "It was evidently usual to differentiate between the lamb as 'body' of the Passover, and the Passover feast. Our Lord might have been influenced by this to point to His body at the distribution of bread, while not bringing it into direct conjunction with the Passover lamb" (Dalman, *Jesus-Jeshua, Studies*, 143). Brant Pitre also noted b. Pesaḥ. 36d, which uses the word "body" (*guph*) eight times to refer to the Passover lamb (Pitre, *Jesus and the Last Supper*, 408).

34. Benjamin B. Warfield also understood the absence of the lamb as indicating that Jesus identified himself with the Passover lamb (Warfield, "Fundamental Significance," 332–38). Brant Pitre's works give a more substantial comparison between the old and new Passover. He also understands Jesus's words of institution to be highlighting himself as the eschatological Passover lamb (*Jesus and the Last Supper*, 405–16). Interestingly, however, Pitre first devoted much ink in elaborating the bread on the Last Supper table as primarily the bread of presence from the old temple (*Jesus and the Last Supper*, 121–29), making the Passover context of the Last Supper less important. Also, he focused on the command to eat the flesh of the Passover lamb, understanding that the allusion means that the body of Christ is to be eaten.

Jews because the lamb had been central in the centuries-old festival. The new meal would have no more lamb on the table. As William H. C. Propp remarked, "we cannot read the Synoptics' Last Supper without finding in the nonmention of the sacrificial victim an implication that Jesus himself is the paschal offering."[35] As B. B. Warfield explained, it is because the typified sacrifice has been fulfilled, ultimately offered once and for all, that the type no longer exists on the table.[36] In other words, Christ's body would be the ultimate lamb to be sacrificed once and for all. "This is my body" meant that Jesus would die as the ultimate Passover Lamb. He was pointing to his imminent death as the final Passover lamb.

Again, Jesus was speaking in the place of God. In addition to the divine invitation to take and eat, he gave a definitive, climactic phrase on the occasion to reinterpret the meal. While in the book of Exodus God spoke only through Moses, and instructed Israel to slaughter and eat lambs, now it is Jesus, God in flesh and blood, who was presiding at the meal, and who now pointed to *his* own body, i.e., himself, as *the* Passover sacrifice to the Lord.

The Lambless Passover (and the Question of Real Presence)

From our approach, Christ's "This is my body" might have little to do with his presence in the bread, whether physical or merely symbolic. It might not even have to do directly with the bread! Even if "this" could refer to the bread, the main point of the phrase does not seem to be to introduce some mysterious or symbolic relationship between Christ's body and the bread. The bread had always been there on the Passover

---

35. Propp, *Exodus 1–18*, 461.

36. Warfield, "Fundamental Significance," 335. Nevertheless, I do not agree with Warfield's construal of the bread and the wine as merely new "symbols" for the new Passover replacing the old symbol, the lamb. Warfield argued that the Lord's Supper is a continued celebration of the Jewish Passover. While the "symbols" are changed, the substance remains the same. In response to him, however, we note that the lamb was never just a "symbol" in the old Passover. Participants in the old meal define themselves as being saved by the Egyptian Passover by sacrificing and eating the lamb. Also, symbolism easily smuggles in Platonistic dichotomy between the visible and invisible (see discussion in next chapter). In addition, such symbolism regards the body and blood of Christ as being eaten *by us*. This ignores the fundamental differences between expiatory sacrifices and communal sacrificial meals (Warfield specifically said that we need not distinguish these two ideas), and distracts our attention from the table fellowship we have with Christ. See discussion in chapter 4.

table, with its long history, as a side dish (Exod 12:8). The main dish had always been the Passover lamb (12:8). God gave elaborate instructions to take and eat the lamb (12:1–11). In fact, pre-70 Mishnah Pesachim (m. Pesaḥ. 1–9) is almost entirely regulations concerning the choosing and sacrifice of Passover lambs to the minutest details. The whole point of the Passover meal was to have the lamb there. In Abraham Bloch's words, it is only "in view of the centrality of the paschal lamb in the observance of Passover, [that] the matzot were to be eaten with the lamb."[37] So one might imagine that the shock to the Jewish disciples of Jesus as depicted in the Gospel accounts of the Passover meal in the upper room was the absence of the lamb. Moreover, another surprise might be that the divinely-mandated and elaborate imperatives to take and eat, and the familiar climactic phrase "This is . . . ," were now uttered not over a lamb (which had been the case in the first Passover), but only over the "next thing" on the Passover table, i.e., the bread. The main shock—and therefore the main point—was the absence of a lamb, which had been the central element on the table for centuries. Now there will be no more lamb. Israel no longer needs to sacrifice lambs year after year. The focus is actually hardly on the bread itself. Any focus on the bread would probably have more to do with the idea that now, *only* the bread is left on the table, than that the bread itself deserved any special attention, because the main dish is unthinkably missing. To Jewish ears, what speaks the loudest is the absence of the lamb.

Is Christ's body present in the bread? Indeed the Passover narrative would challenge whether the traditional question of Christ's real presence is a proper question to ask in the first place. The history of the meal hardly poses the question as to whether the original Egyptian lambs which saved Israel would be present in future Passover meals. The Passover narrative never implies, not even remotely, that Israelites needed to have some mysterious or symbolic communion with the bodily tissue and fluid of the original Egyptian Passover lambs. If "This is my body" was only Christ's rephrasing of an old phrase to point to himself as the true Passover lamb, then there need not be an implied relation between the bread and Christ's body. The question of the real presence of Christ has already airlifted Jesus's utterance, "This is my body," out of its whole Passover context. As Keith Mathison remarked, without the Passover

---

37. Bloch, *Biblical and Historical Background*, 213.

context, "This is my body" could be either literal or figurative.[38] Indeed, without the history of the Passover, *any* interpretation goes.

What question does the Passover context pose instead? Based on our comparison between the old and new Passover "menus," a question prompted by the context would be *But where is the lamb?*—Isaac's burning question to Abraham (Gen 22:7). Indeed there is a long Jewish tradition that understands the sacrifice of the Passover lamb as prefigured by the sacrifice of Isaac, e.g., in Second Temple literature and in the Palestinian Targum to Exod 12:42.[39] Something very important—the lamb—was now unexpectedly missing on the table.[40] The right question is—where is the lamb? And the point is that Christ is the lamb. God himself has provided the lamb (Gen 22:8). This man who is instituting a new meal—he is that lamb. The point is that the bread is not supposed to be the spotlight of a Passover meal, but has moved to the spotlight in the new Passover. We need to ask why, instead of simply taking for granted that the bread should be the focus of inquiry. Our attention to the Passover context thus questions a simple either/or approach to the question of the real presence of Christ. Our study prompts neither a straightforwardly literal or figurative reading to Jesus's famous line at the Last Supper. The bread neither is Jesus's body nor merely signifies Jesus's body. But Jesus *is* the true Passover *lamb*. His body *is* the Passover sacrifice to the Lord. The bread is what is left on the table to celebrate the finally fulfilled—and therefore lambless—Passover.[41]

Sacramental theology has been concerned over the real presence of Christ in the meal partly because of the need to take "This is my body"

38. Mathison, while paying attention to the Passover and Sinaitic contexts of the Last Supper, unfortunately does not truly allow the Exodus narrative to speak and bear on his theology of the Lord's Supper. Like Zwingli, he mainly used the Passover context to prove a figurative interpretation of "This is my body." See Mathison, *Given for You*, 242.

39. E.g., Palestinian Targum to Exod 12:42 (see Le Déaut, *La Nuit Pascale*). Jubilees 17:15; 18:3, 17–19 see Abraham's offering of Isaac as taking place on same day as the Passover. See Kugel, *Traditions of the Bible*, 578; Levenson, *Death and Resurrection of the Beloved Son*, 173–232; Olson, "Sacramentality in the Torah," 28–29.

40. The question of real presence is especially ironic, as the new Passover is precisely about absence (of the lamb) instead of presence. The once central, indispensable Passover lamb is now absent on the table. Even if we focus on the unleavened bread, again its history emphasizes absence (of leaven) instead of presence.

41. I am not ruling out that Jesus could be using the breaking of the bread as a metaphor for his body to be broken on the cross. Yet the Passover context of the Last Supper first and foremost spotlights the absence of the lamb.

very seriously and therefore realistically, and partly because there is a perceived need for a point of contact between the event of the cross (the true sacrifice) and the meal (the thanksgiving meal). The question has been how we participate in Christ's original sacrifice and have a share in its benefits. In chapter 4, we will challenge the assumption that such point of contact must take the form of an organic (or symbolically organic) contact with the body and blood of Christ, instead of a person-to-person table fellowship. We may challenge why such benefits are anything other than a restored table fellowship with Christ. Metaphysical worries in Eucharistic theology have assumed that the redemptive event took place without the meal, and only afterwards the meal was instituted to commemorate, symbolize or make present the redemptive event. But here, when we consider the Passover narrative, there is never any mysterious participation in the original Passover lambs. The Passover meal that the Jews celebrate every year does not need to effect the presence of the original Egyptian lambs, neither does the meal merely symbolize the event of the Exodus. In the first place, the repetition of the meal was already commanded *in* the saving event itself. To repeat the meal *is* to take part in the command of the original event.[42]

All this perfectly aligns with Jesus's shocking command to keep the meal in remembrance "of *me*." Again, the accentuation was the pointer to Christ himself.[43] Our familiarity with the NT instead of the OT might have been the reason we missed this shock. In Exodus, Israel was repeatedly taught to remember God's work in delivering them out of Egypt. But now the remembrance is of this man sitting before the disciples. The Passover is now revealed to be about him. *He* is the new, ultimate Passover.

"Do This in Remembrance of Me"

Finally, a word relating to Zwingli's alleged "memorialism." Just as the elaborate and repeated imperatives to take and eat, God's instructions also repeated the command to keep the feast for remembrance.

> Now this day shall be a memorial to you, and you shall celebrate it as a feast to the Lord; throughout your generations you are to celebrate it as a permanent ordinance. (Exod 12:14)

42. See also "Rethinking 'Participation in Christ'" in chapter 4 , pp. 177–84.

43. Barth, *Rediscovering the Lord's Supper*, 17.

Remember this day in which you departed from Egypt, from the house of slavery; for by a powerful hand the Lord brought you out from this place. . . . (13:3)

And it shall serve as a sign to you on your hand, and as a reminder on your forehead, that the law of the Lord may be in your mouth; for with a powerful hand the Lord brought you out of Egypt. (3:9)

It may be noted that throughout Israel's history, only the Exodus was divinely commanded to be nationally commemorated. Other significant events such as God's call to Abraham, Israel's conquest of Canaan, even the erection of the temple, never received a divinely ordained public holiday.[44] To keep the feast as a memorial is undoubtedly a central command in the Passover festival. As Zwingli exclaimed, no one denies this.[45] The question is what this remembrance pertains to.

The Jewish Passover memorial should inform the kind of remembrance Jesus had in mind when he told his disciples to take and eat in remembrance of him. Critics who opt for a more realist approach to the Supper often accuse Zwingli's memorialism of reducing the Supper and Christ's presence to merely mental recollection.[46] While critics are right in challenging his dualism that tends to demean the material realm, few have noted his explicit references to the Passover commemoration. The Passover commemoration is precisely never simply mental recollection in individuals' minds. It is perceptibly in body and in act.[47] It is never an individual affair but communal (in fact even national).[48] It is never only recollection, but the meal itself reenacts the salvific event of Israel's departure from Egypt, by reinstating the original, historical circumstances of that event. Indeed this is the rationale behind the strict prohibition of leaven during the festival.[49] As Nathan MacDonald argued, in Passover celebrations, food is a "vehicle" to bring Israel back to their journey out of slavery. The food allows people to relive the original event of salvation.

---

44. Kugel, *Traditions of the Bible*, 574. Purim (Esth 9) is a national holiday but was not divinely commanded.

45. Zwingli, "Subsidiary Essay," in *Huldrych Zwingli: Writings*, 2:211.

46. Mathison, *Given for You*, 260. See discussion of the debate in Riggs, *Lord's Supper in Reformed Tradition*, 56.

47. Fretheim, *Exodus*, 147–48.

48. Childs, *Exodus*, 214.

49. Sarna, *Exodus*, 58.

Salvation is reenacted and embodied in the communal Passover meal.[50] The meal allows Israel to enter into the *reality* of the saving event.[51] In the first place, the salvific event did not take place without the meal. The salvific event itself also already included the command for all future generations to keep the meal. The meal therefore involves the participant in the original event, not just reminds her of it. As stated clearly in the instructions, future generations of Israel are to declare during the meal that "it was because of what the Lord did for *me* when *I* came out of Egypt" (Exod 13:8 and Deut 16:3). In other words, all future generations of Israel will be defined as also being saved from Egypt by virtue of their partaking in this meal.[52] As Stephen Wylen put it, "Every Jew is required to look upon himself [*sic*] as if he himself had participated in the exodus from Egypt. This is a significant definition of a Jew aside from the legal, religious, and national definitions."[53] No doubt, a Jew who does not share the experience of the Passover meal is still a Jew, but not in a meaningful sense.[54]

God strictly decreed that those who are able to eat the Passover meal but refrain from doing so will be cut off from his people (Num 9:13). Even those who do not completely remove all leaven during the annual celebration would be cut off as well (Exod 12:15, 19). God's delivered people were to be defined by eating the same menu as their ancestors did on every anniversary of the first Passover night. It is specifically the eating of this communal meal that defines them. As noted by Jewish scholar Joshua Berman, being an Israelite is not defined by prayer or worship or contemplation, but by taking part in meals instituted by God.[55] All these explain why there are strict rules concerning foreigners who wish to take

50. MacDonald, *Not Bread Alone*, 14, also 70–99. For MacDonald, this best explains why the Passover feast is to be ended specifically with people leaving the Sanctuary to stay in tents (Deut 16:7), i.e., to exactly correlate with their ancestors' experience of the exodus.

51. Fretheim, *Exodus*, 139.

52. Likewise, in the Passover seder prescribed in the Mishnah, the language is clear that all subsequent generations should declare that they *themselves*, not just their ancestors, were brought forth from bondage; that God performed miracles for them, not just for their ancestors. The language is that God redeemed *us* (m. Pesaḥ. 10:5).

53. Wylen, *Settings of Silver*, 160.

54. Wylen, *Settings of Silver*, 160.

55. Berman, *Temple*, 137. Again, in Wylen's words, not sharing this experience may still mean one is a Jew, but not part of the community in any meaningful sense. Wylen, *Settings of Silver*, 160.

part in a Passover meal (Exod 12:43–49). Uncircumcised gentiles are strictly forbidden from taking part, because the meal *defines* who is saved by the Lord's Passover.[56] Another way of seeing the defining character of participants is to consider the manner of eating in the annual celebrations. Although this is not prescribed in the Torah but only in the seder that was later developed, all Jews who partake in the Passover meal are to recline at the table (a gesture noted in all four Gospel accounts of the Last Supper, Matt 26:20; Mark 14:18; Luke 22:14; John 13:12), as opposed to having to stand and serve at the table. It is to say that now all Jews, including the poorest, are to eat as free men and women (m. Pesaḥ. 10:1). The meal itself asserts the great reverse in the Jews' status—it is not mere mental recollection.

Again, against this backdrop, we learn what Jesus might likely have meant in saying "do this in remembrance of me" on this particular occasion. Remembrance would hardly only be a mental recollection, especially in light of Jesus's command "do this." Participants actively relive the original event. Remembering means bodily, actively obeying the command to take part in the meal that was inseparable from the event of the cross. As some scholars put it, the language of the Passover means that, just as the current generation of Jews are made to participate in the original Exodus event, so the current generation of believers in Christ is to be made *contemporary* with Christ's act of redemption.[57] Just as it is through reenacting the circumstances of the first Passover that Jews identify themselves with the ancestors who were there during God's acts of redemption, so through reenacting the Last Supper, believers identify themselves with the "twelve" who were there with Christ, in a meal that was part of the passion narrative. Participants define themselves as having a part in the event of the cross by obeying the command to "do this" that was, in the first place, very much part of that event. In Jesus's institution of the meal, it already included the participation of future generations by virtue of their repeating the meal. Now participants allow themselves to be included by this commanded action. "Remembrance" should mean no

56. Surely, there is no reason to forbid a gentile from mentally remembering what happened to Jews in history, that Israel's God has saved them, if the meal was merely about such mental recollection. Yet precisely the meal does not only recall events but defines God's people. Uncircumcised gentiles are therefore strictly forbidden to take part.

57. Keener, *Commentary on Matthew*, 631; referenced in Mathison, *Given for You*, 211–12, 232. Billings, *Remembrance, Communion, and Hope*, 115. See also Thurian, *Eucharist Memorial*, 1:19, 33.

less than such active reliving of history and self-definition of a faith community by obedience of Christ's command.[58] It demarcates those who are saved by Jesus Christ from those who are not. The action asserts that those who take part in the meal have their part in the salvation of Jesus Christ.

The point is that the meal does not just allow mental commemoration, but actively reenacts the Last Supper, which was part of the event of Christ's passion. What we have said so far does not imply that whoever partakes in communion in a church would be a true Christian. Being a part of the community that is reliving the event of the cross does not mean one is a true follower of Christ. But this is not as much of a problem as it first seems—the fact is that even at the very Last Supper in the upper room, one disciple would betray Jesus, and at least one other would deny him (see discussion of sinner-sinner table fellowship in chapter 5). The meal is not some magical spell that metaphysically makes future believers participants in grace. No one participates in grace simply by the action of eating the bread and drinking the wine (i.e., no *ex opere operato*). It is Christ's action to include *sinners*, from Judas the traitor and Peter the denier to future generations of believers, in his passion. Precisely it is sinners, with all their failures, who need to be included in the cross. By his invitation, Christ called us to actively relive the event of the cross through participation in the meal. More importantly, in his passion Christ already included those he saves by commanding them to repeat the meal that took place in his saving act.

Conclusion

"Behold the lamb of God who takes away the sin of the world" (John 1:29). The focus on the Eucharistic table is not some mysterious or symbolic relation between the bread and Jesus's body. Jesus was speaking as God reinstituting the age-old Passover, repeating the words that God did on the very first Passover, inviting his people to take and eat, while pointing to himself as the true, ultimate Passover lamb, who would die for the world. "This is *my* body," he said, echoing familiar words that were uttered for centuries to highlight the Passover lamb. Now the Passover meal would be in remembrance of *him*, no longer of the event of the Exodus. The Lord's Supper is shocking, not because Christ could have been

58. See also Billings, *Remembrance, Communion, and Hope*, 114–16.

present in the bread, but because of his pointers to himself as the lamb, as the ultimate saving event itself, and as the divine agent of salvation. Given the shocking absence of the central item on the table—the lamb—Jesus was revealing that *he* would be the ultimate lamb, to be sacrificed once and for all. The history of the Passover has revealed that, therefore, the focus on the Eucharistic table is hardly on some mystery in the bread. Rather, the ultimate lamb has been sacrificed and risen. In chapter 4 we will also look at how, at the Last Supper, it was now God himself who was sitting and eating the Passover meal at the same table with his people, which was foreshadowed in the Old Testament. All Israel's history of salvation is now revealed in him—not just in his work and actions, but his very person. He is the salvation of his people.

The Covenant—Old and New

After the supper, Christ took the cup and said to his twelve disciples, "This is my blood of the covenant" (Matt 26:28; Mark 14:24; or "This is the new covenant in my blood" in Luke 22:20). These words clearly echoed back to Moses's words at Mount Sinai, "Behold the blood of the covenant," said after erecting *twelve* pillars (Exod 24:8). It is therefore likely that the cup was not one of the cups of wine at a traditional Passover seder, but was instead alluding to a different event in the narrative of the Exodus, namely Israel's arrival and covenant meal with God at Mount Sinai. Even John's account of the Last Supper (John 13) replaces the words of institution of the Supper with the giving of a new commandment, which, too, has a clear Sinaitic allusion. Indeed the story of the Exodus did not end at the Passover. Israel was not only delivered from bondage, but specifically to enter into a life of worship of God. They were departing Egypt *for* Mount Sinai. Therefore, one fundamental approach that this project is adopting is not to assume at the outset that the bread and the cup of the Supper are merely two components of the same rite. For too long, Protestant traditions have always assumed they are a single rite, as if one was the solid component bearing some relation to Christ's body, the other the liquid component bearing some relation to his blood, and whatever interpretation applies to one automatically applies to the other. But this is an unsubstantiated assumption. It also does not explain why the bread *always* comes before the cup. Instead, the bread and the cup clearly have different historical allusions and are therefore possibly two different actions, with different meanings. The two rites have clear parallels in the history of Israel which were two distinct (although related) events—Passover and Sinai—one a meal accompanying divine deliverance, and one a covenant inauguration, which came *after* deliverance. Jesus at the Last Supper reinstituted both events.

A tendency in traditional Eucharistic theology is that it reduces the Lord's Supper to the bread and the cup, presuming them to be standing in some relationship to the body and blood of Christ. One problem with this reduction is that it overlooks that, in the first place, the "blood" in the Last Supper accounts is always unequivocally "blood *of the covenant*," not just blood of Christ.[59] To understand the notion of the blood of the covenant, it is again imperative to look at the book of Exodus, i.e., at the original account of the "blood of the covenant" at Mount Sinai. The covenant at Sinai is said to be the most significant event of Hebrew Bible. It would be the central preoccupation for generations of Jews.[60] Again, the historical context of the cup (the "blood of the covenant") should dictate what we should say, and even what questions we should ask, about a theology of the Supper. The following aims to recount the events at Mount Sinai. In particular, although the biblical passage does not offer an explanation of certain key terms, including "blood of the covenant," it will be helpful to note what happened when the "blood of the covenant" was offered. Again, the question of the presence of sacrificial blood in a covenant meal seems to be off the table. What should be inquired into in a covenant is God's commandment and his call for obedience.

From Egypt to Sinai

When Israelites were slaves in Egypt, God sent Moses and Aaron to command Pharaoh to let his people go *so that* they may worship him. Throughout the many confrontations between Moses and Pharaoh in the book of Exodus, that Israel was to worship God in the wilderness was repeatedly *the* reason given to Pharaoh to release his slaves (Exod 3:18; 4:23; 5:1, 3; 7:16; 8:1, 20, 27; 9:1; 13; 10:3, 25). Even when Pharaoh finally told Israel to leave, he clearly understood that Israel was leaving Egypt *in order to* sacrifice to their God in the wilderness (Exod 12:31–32; see

---

59. As Alasdair Heron also commented, while the bread and the cup are commonly held to be conceptually denoting the pair body/blood, in the Gospel texts the pair is more likely body/covenant. Heron, *Table and Tradition*, 14.

60. Kugel, *Traditions of the Bible*, 634.

also, e.g., 5:17; 8:8, 28; 10:7, 11). The goal of the Exodus was therefore not just deliverance from bondage, but specifically deliverance for life with God. Israel left Egypt *for God*.[61] Thus, Israel's arrival at Mount Sinai to offer sacrifices in the context of establishing a covenant with God was the moment of victory God had over Pharaoh—because Israel did in the end sacrifice to God in the wilderness, as predicted to Pharaoh. Israel now serves God, not Pharaoh. When Israel arrived at the foot of Sinai, God spoke to his people beautifully from the mountain,

> You yourselves have seen what I did to the Egyptians, and how I carried you on eagles' wings, and brought you to myself. Now then, if you will indeed obey my voice and keep my covenant, then you shall be my own possession among all the peoples, for all the earth is mine; and you shall be to me a kingdom of priests and a holy nation. (Exod 19:4–6)

Yet the narrative comes to a screeching halt. Israel, called to be God's "treasured possession," liberated, and finally arrived at the foot of God's mountain to enter into a covenant with him, was now gravely warned not to approach his presence, or even to touch the mountain (Exod 19).[62] It was a matter of life and death. God commanded that boundaries must be made between the people and the mountain. Whoever trespassed would die:

> But you shall set boundaries for the people all around, saying, "Beware that you do not go up on the mountain or touch the border of it; whoever touches the mountain shall certainly be put to death. No hand shall touch him, but he shall certainly be stoned or shot through; whether animal or person, the violator shall not live." (Exod 19:12–13)

The text inevitably invites questions: how could God's people approach him? "Who may ascend onto the hill of the Lord? And who may stand in His holy place?" (Ps 24:3). "Who is able to stand before the Lord, this holy God?" (1 Sam 6:20).[63] The picture is one of awestruck terror.

---

61. Levenson, "Exodus and Liberation." As Brant Pitre put it, "the Passover is ordered to the covenant at Mount Sinai." Pitre, *Jesus and the Last Supper*, 415.

62. They must consecrate themselves for three days before they could come near the presence of God. This was also the interpretation of the author of the NT Letter to the Hebrews (Heb 9:22).

63. Kugel, *Great Shift*, 94. See also discussion in Olson, "Book of Exodus," 34; Sarna, *Exodus*, 105.

"There were thunder and lightning flashes and a thick cloud over the mountain and a very loud trumpet sound, so that all the people who were in the camp trembled." "Mount Sinai was all in smoke because the Lord descended upon it in fire; and its smoke ascended like the smoke of a furnace, and the entire mountain quaked violently" (19:16, 18). The people were so fearful that they asked to only speak to Moses (20:19). Only Moses, possibly along with Aaron, could ascend the mountain and converse with God directly.[64]

Pledge of Obedience

It is in this fearsome context that God gave the Ten Commandments. Many biblical scholars have noted how God's covenant with Israel fits well into the general format of an ancient Near East suzerain-vassal treaty.[65] The suzerain is a sovereign having supremacy over the vassal state. It was likely that the pattern of the covenant, as an agreement, was already familiar among the Jews. An overall pattern can be discerned. First the two parties are named. God called Moses to specifically speak to "the House of Jacob," the "Israelites" (Exod 19:3), to tell them, "I am the Lord your God, who brought you out of the land of Egypt, out of the house of slavery" (20:1). In the future, God would repeatedly refer to himself similarly.[66] The God with whom Israel made a covenant is never an abstract being, but specifically one whose name is YHWH, the one "who brought [Israel] out of the land of Egypt." The covenant with God rules out metaphysical abstraction.

Therefore, secondly, there is a prologue in terms of a preliminary history between the partners, a chronology of events that led to the treaty. God said to Israel, "You yourselves have seen what I did to the Egyptians, and how I carried you on eagles' wings, and brought you to myself"

64. Scholars have noted unresolvable tensions, even within Exod 19, as to who could ascend the mountain. At times the texts are clear that only Moses could ascend, yet 19:24 implies that, after consecration, Aaron could also ascend, and in 19:13b even the whole nation could ascend "when the trumpet sounds a long blast." In chapters 19 and 20, however, it seems that the people were too frightened to come forward even after consecration and hearing the trumpet. See, e.g., Childs, *Exodus*, 340–74; Brettler, "Many Faces of God," 353–67.

65. See Guhrt, "Covenant, Guarantor, Mediator," 1:365–72; Kugel, *Great Shift*, 179–82; Sarna, *Exodus*, 102–3; Levenson, "Exodus and Liberation," 151–54; Berman, *Created Equal*, 28–50.

66. E.g., Lev 19:36; 25:38; 26:13; Num 15:41; Deut 5:6; Isa 43:3.

(19:4). "I . . . brought you out of the land of Egypt, out of the house of slavery" (20:1). The covenantal bond always narrates a concrete, historical reality.

Third, what would follow is a declaration of relationship, and the stipulations for both sides, now enjoined to this new relationship. This is substantial, and will be our main focus. God stated to Israel, "If you obey my voice and keep my covenant, you shall be my treasured possession out of all the peoples. . . . You shall be for me a priestly kingdom and a holy nation" (19:5–6). The Ten Commandments are then laid out, decreeing that Israel must have no other god. The Ten Commandments were given together with other laws, such as those that concern the keeping and freeing of slaves, protection of property, social laws regarding sex and treatment of foreigners, bearing of witness, and the law of Sabbath. These are the conditions by which Israel was to remain in the covenant bond with God. One profound and unexpected feature of such laws is that, contrary to other ancient Near East treaties, the suzerain in this case uniquely showed immense interest in the social and even what the modern world would regard as the private lives of the people of the vassal state.[67] God is not only interested in foreign affairs with other possible suzerains, but internal social affairs immensely too. Loyalty to Israel's God is not only through an exclusive sovereign-vassal relationship, as would be typically required in the ancient world, but also equally through treating one's family and neighbors well. A vertical relationship with God always already encompasses a horizontal dimension. No one can enjoy a divine-human fellowship without a just fellowship with other humans. In addition to this, every individual of the vassal state is equally answerable to the suzerain.[68] Also notable is the reasons given for such laws: "You shall not oppress a stranger, since you yourselves know the feelings of a stranger, for you also were strangers in the land of Egypt" (23:9). It is specifically Israel's memory of past slavery that motivates their protection of the vulnerable and the foreigner.[69]

Lastly, some procedure of formality is in place too. A written contract would be deposited within the temple (25:21). Witnesses to the covenant are typically invoked, although this seems to be lacking in the

67. Sarna, *Exodus*, 102–3.
68. Sarna, *Exodus*, 102–3.
69. Olson, "Book of Exodus," 35.

Sinaitic covenant. Last comes the pronouncement of blessing for adher-
ence and curse for breaching the terms (23:20–33).

The covenant, according to Moses, was specifically made "in accordance with these words" (Exod 24:8), i.e., with God's commandments,
the *terms* of the relationship. It is important to note that, from Israel's
arrival at Sinai (Exod 19) to the sealing of the covenant by a communal
meal with God (Exod 24), they pledged *three times* their obedience to
God's words, once at the beginning and twice nearer the end.

> All the people answered together and said, "All that the Lord has
> spoken we will do!" (Exod 19:8)

> All the people answered with one voice, and said, "All the words
> that the Lord has spoken we will do." (Exod 24:3)

> And they said, "All that the Lord has spoken we will do, and we
> will be obedient!" (Exod 24:7)

It was as if the people's affirmation to obey God's commandments
marks the two ends of the commandments.[70] As such, the pledge of obedience to the terms of the covenant is an indispensable element of its
inauguration. It will be in this light that we ask about the new covenant
sealed by Jesus.

"Blood of the Covenant" and the Covenant Meal

Ultimately, after God had given Moses the law, and Israel had pledged
their obedience, the climax of the story was what followed: Moses erected
an altar and twelve pillars facing it, standing for God and the twelve tribes
of Israel respectively, the two contracting parties. Moses made sacrifices
on the altar. He took half of the blood of the sacrifices and sprinkled
it onto the altar. He read the book of the covenant to the people again.
When the people had for the third time affirmed their obedience to the
commandments, Moses then took the other half of the blood, presented
to the people as the "blood of the covenant," and sprinkled it on them
(Exod 24:4–11).[71] *Only then* were the elders of Israel able to ascend and
approach God's presence. The passage reads:

70. Childs, *Exodus*, 502–3; Olson, "Book of Exodus," 35.

71. It is possible that the blood sprinkled on the people in 24:8 was actually on the
pillars. The altar stood for divine presence, while the twelve pillars stood for the other
contracting party. Sarna, *Exodus*, 151.

So Moses took the blood and sprinkled it on the people, and said, "Behold the blood of the covenant, which the LORD has made with you in accordance with all these words." Then Moses went up with Aaron, Nadab and Abihu, and seventy of the elders of Israel, and they saw the God of Israel; and under His feet there appeared to be a pavement of sapphire, as clear as the sky itself. Yet He did not reach out with His hand against the nobles of the sons of Israel; and they saw God, and they ate and drank. (Exod 24:8–11)

The text does not explain the meaning of the "blood of the covenant."[72] "However," as Brevard Childs noted, "for the Exodus narrative the importance lies with the *effect* of the rite and not with the theory behind it. Israel has accepted the divine offer and entered a covenant with her God."[73] We may note the before and after of the presentation of the "blood of the covenant." Here we see a profound picture. Before, Israel could not approach the presence of God, but could only be at a strict distance (Exod 19). In thunder and earthquake, God commanded that boundaries must be made between the people and the mountain. The people's very lives were threatened if they drew any nearer to the mountain of God. But after sacrifices were made, and God's altar and the people were both in contact with the "blood of the covenant," a community of the people's leaders was invited by God to ascend his mountain and to eat and drink *in his presence.* "He did not reach out with his hand against the nobles of the sons of Israel; and they saw God, and they

72. William Gilders warned against attempting to explain the meaning of blood rituals in the Old Testament, in light of the absence of such explanations in the texts. Scripture seems to be interested instead in how the blood rituals are actually carried out. Nevertheless, according to Gilders, blood seems to have the effect of indexing, forging a bond between God and the people at Sinai. Gilders, *Blood Ritual in the Hebrew Bible*, 2–9, 41–43. Brevard Childs noted that there are different theories for the meaning of the covenant ceremony. For example, in Gen 15, a covenant was sealed by God's passing between pieces of animal flesh offered. Jeremiah 34:18 warns of a fate like the dissected calf as a threat for disobedience. Blood may be seen as a symbol of community of life established between God and the people, or ritual as symbol of purification. Childs, *Exodus*, 505–6. Sarna proposed that the blood likely functions as a cement bond between the covenant parties. Through God's sharing of vital fluid, life of recipient elevated to intimate relationship with God. Sarna, *Exodus*, 152. Gordon Wenham understood the sacrificial blood in terms of purification. By cleansing the unclean, contact with God is made possible. Wenham, *Book of Leviticus*, 26. Keith Mathison agrees with Wenham. As he noted, this point is affirmed by the author of Hebrews (9:22, 26; 10:12). Mathison, *Given for You*, 197.

73. Childs, *Exodus*, 506. My emphasis.

ate and drank" (24:11). God's people now enjoyed his presence, even a joyous meal of food and drink. This is a stark contrast to the fear and distance emphasized in chapter 19. This was the effect of the "blood of the covenant." Mortal humans could dine with the holy and divine. As Dennis Olson put it, "Remarkably, the imagery of a thunderstorm and violent earthquake is replaced by a tranquil outdoor banquet scene on top of Sinai."[74]

Israel did not just survive divine presence. Childs noted that "the text is remarkable for its bluntness: 'They saw the God of Israel.'"[75] Even commentators are quick to tone down the directness of the statement. A more well-known example is Maimonides. For him, the text only implies an intellectual seeing, not with the eye. It is, for Maimonides, similar to Isaiah's vision in Isa 6:1, where the focus is shifted from God to the throne and to God's garment that fills the temple, as well as the accompanying seraphim. Here, it seems, it is the platform under God's feet that is pictured: a "pavement of sapphire."[76] Ibn Ezra also understood the vision in Exod 24 as a prophetic vision, akin to those in 1 Kgs 22:19; Isa 6:1; Ezek 1; Amos 9:1.[77] In fact, the Greek Septuagint simply denies the directness of the people's sight of God in these verses.[78] According to LXX, Israel only saw "the place where the God of Israel stood" (v. 10), and they merely "appeared in the place of God" (v. 11).[79] Indeed, as Childs points out, the book of Exodus itself reminds us that no one can see God and live (33:20). Yet precisely here at Sinai, the emphasis is that the people saw God and lived.[80] JPS Commentary also notes that, in v. 11, the passage does not only reiterate Israel's vision of God but even uses a stronger verb "behold."[81] The question of whether Israel truly saw God, or only indirectly and symbolically, lingers.

Nevertheless, what is clear is that the covenant between God and Israel was sealed by the "blood of the covenant." The God-Israel relationship, specified by the commandments and promises of God, was now

74. Olson, "Book of Exodus," 34.

75. Childs, Exodus, 506.

76. Childs, Exodus, 506–7; see also Sarna, Exodus, 153.

77. Sarna, Exodus, 153.

78. Childs, Exodus, 506–7.

79. "καὶ εἶδον τὸν τόπον, οὗ εἱστήκει ὁ Θεὸς τοῦ 'Ισραήλ" (Exod 24:10) and "καὶ ὤφθησαν ἐν τῷ τόπῳ τοῦ Θεοῦ" (24:11).

80. Childs, Exodus, 507.

81. Chzh ("behold") is used, as opposed to r'h ("see"). Sarna, Exodus, 153.

inaugurated, and was confirmed by a festive communion between the two parties.[82] The fearful distance was overcome and turned to a meal of friendship and joy.[83] In short, the "blood of the covenant" allows divine-human fellowship. *This* was Israel's salvation from Egypt. Repeatedly, Moses's demand to Pharaoh was not only to let the people go, but specifically so that they may worship God in the wilderness (see above). All along this was the goal of their deliverance. Israel's worship at Mount Sinai was therefore the moment of victory God had over Israel's oppressor. Israel now serves God, not Pharaoh.[84] Therefore it is not an overstatement to say that salvation *is* table fellowship with God—eating and drinking in his presence. Israel was saved for real life with God. God did not just save Israel from bondage, but prepared them for table fellowship in his presence.

The Divine Name and Divine Presence

An undeniable message of the narrative is God's commitment to real presence with his people.[85] God had heard the cries of his people oppressed in Egypt. God gave Moses, the chosen leader of the people, his Name such that they may invoke him in their hardship. God's holy name revealed to Moses in the beginning of the Exodus narrative (Exod 3) is related to the verb "to be": I AM WHO I AM, or I WILL BE WHO I WILL BE. A related name of God is also given to Moses, typically written as the tetragrammaton YHWH but pronounced as Adonai ("Lord"). The name both hides and reveals who God is. As Dennis Olson explained, the divine name is unfolded and elaborated at crucial points throughout the Exodus narrative.[86] The name speaks of God's desire to be *with* his people. In the beginning, even in God's first conversation with Moses, God had promised, "I WILL BE with you" (3:12). It was in this context that God gave his name I WILL BE WHO I WILL BE (3:14). When Moses complained of his speech impairment, God promised him, "I WILL BE with your mouth" and, after giving him Aaron to be his partner, again

82. Childs, *Exodus*, 504.

83. Fretheim, *Exodus*, 259.

84. As Levenson pointed out, Rabbis, referencing Lev 25:55, stress that Israel became God's servants on Sinai. Such service or even slavery to God was explicitly an alternative to service or slavery to another human person. "Exodus and Liberation," 156.

85. Fretheim, *Exodus*, 260; Olson, "Book of Exodus," 36–37.

86. Olson, "Book of Exodus," 29, 36–37.

"I WILL BE with your mouth and with [Aaron's] mouth" (Exod 4:12, 15). At the giving of the Ten Commandments, God reiterated his name "I AM the Lord your God, who brought you out of the land of Egypt, out of the house of slavery" (20:2). After establishing the covenantal relationship at Mount Sinai, God commanded Moses to build the tabernacle, God's own dwelling among his people (25:8). God declared, "I will dwell among the sons of Israel and WILL BE their God. 46 And they shall know that I AM the Lord their God who brought them out of the land of Egypt, *so that I might dwell among them*; I AM the Lord their God" (29:45–46). God even decreed Israel to make the ark of the covenant, not only to safekeep the covenant, but also to be his own seat where he will be met ("There I will meet with you . . . ," 25:22). This was a God who desired to be present with his people in the most concrete way. He even made his name known by this desire. The covenant meal in Exod 24 inaugurated this divine-human relationship. Despite their unholiness, the holy God has provided a way to have communion with them.

As is well-known, the relationship between God and Israel after Sinai was not a happily-ever-after. Soon enough Israel would engage in outright idolatry, worshiping a golden calf (Exod 32). God decided to kill his own people, whom he had liberated from slavery. Indeed the burning question is how a holy God could dwell in the midst of a sinful people.[87] Yet, despite this, God listened to Moses's intercession. Moses insisted that God needed to remain "with us" and "in our midst" (33:16). As Olson notes, Moses insisted that God remain true to the expansion of God's name that God had revealed to Moses concerning Israel: "I AM the Lord [YHWH] their God who brought them out of the land of Egypt *that I might dwell among them*."[88] God once again expanded his name, "[I] will proclaim the name of the Lord before you; and I WILL BE gracious to whom I WILL BE gracious, and will show compassion to whom I will show compassion" (33:19). For our purposes, it is important to note God's making of a new Sinai covenant in Exod 34:4–10 after the disaster of Israel's breaking the old Sinai covenant in Exod 32 (32:19). An important expansion and contrast emerges if one compares the revelation of God's name and character in Exod 20 (at Sinai *before* the golden calf rebellion) and the revelation of God's name and character in Exod 34 (at Sinai *after* the golden calf rebellion):[89]

87. Olson, "Book of Exodus," 38.
88. Olson, "Book of Exodus," 38.
89. Olson, "Book of Exodus," 39.

I, the Lord your God, am a jealous God, inflicting the punishment of the fathers on the children, on the third and the fourth generations of those who hate me, but showing favor to thousands, to those who love me and keep my commandments. (20:5–6)

The Lord, the Lord God, compassionate and merciful, slow to anger, and abounding in faithfulness and truth; who keeps faithfulness for thousands, who forgives wrongdoing, violation of His Law, and sin; yet he will by no means leave the guilty unpunished, inflicting the punishment of fathers on the children and on the grandchildren to the third and fourth generations." (34:6–7)

In Exod 20, God is described first of all as "jealous" and punishing. In Exod 34, first and foremost in God's character is that God is "compassionate and merciful, slow to anger, and abounding in faithfulness and truth." The restriction in Exod 20 that God's steadfast love would only be shown to those "who love me and keep my commandments" was dropped in the Exod 34 revision of God's name and character.[90] There was no pledge of obedience by the people as there was at first at Sinai. Presumably, it was in light of the people's utter failure that this prerequisite of obedience cannot be the primary basis for the divine-human covenant to be possible. What was added instead was God's promise to forgive. Obedience to the law remains an expectation, and disobedience and sin still result in consequences, but now only secondarily.[91] It is against this backdrop that we will understand the connection to the forgiveness of sins in Jesus's words at the Last Supper, which was also a new covenant.[92]

The Fulfillment in Christ

In the OT, an ultimate renewal of God's covenant with humankind was already promised:

90. See also Fretheim, *Exodus*, 258.

91. Olson, "Book of Exodus," 39.

92. When God had instructed the building of the tabernacle and Israel had built it, placed the ark of the covenant in it, the final climactic scene of the narrative of Exodus was when God's "glory" is said to cover and fill the tabernacle (Exod 40:34–38). From the call from the burning bush in the beginning to the tabernacle in the end, God proves himself committed to be present among his people. Olson, "Book of Exodus," 40.

> Behold, days are coming . . . when I will make a new covenant
> with the house of Israel and the house of Judah . . . I will put my
> law within them and write it on their heart; and I will be their
> God, and they shall be my people. They will not teach again,
> each one his neighbor and each one his brother, saying, "Know
> the Lord," for they will all know me, from the least of them to the
> greatest of them . . . for I will forgive their wrongdoing, and their
> sin I will no longer remember. (Jer 31:31–34)

Ultimately, Jesus Christ not only fulfilled, but he *is* the new covenant. Just as he pointed to himself, "*my* body," as the ultimate Passover lamb, Jesus now pointed to "*my* blood of the new covenant" (or "the new covenant in *my* blood"). When he said "This is my blood of the new covenant," he was repeating, almost verbatim, Moses's climactic words in the covenant ceremony at Sinai. The Septuagint gives τὸ αἷμα τῆς διαθήκης (Exod 24:8), while the Greek in Matthew and Mark is τὸ αἷμά μου τῆς διαθήκης. Jesus shockingly pointed to his own blood as the blood of the covenant. In addition, the formulation of Exod 24:8 ("Behold the blood of the covenant") in Heb 9:20 became "This is [Τοῦτο] the blood of the covenant." It is possible that the rephrasing reflects an oral tradition, explaining Jesus's use of the definite article Τοῦτο in his allusion to that verse ("This is . . ." instead of "Behold . . .").[93] The historical allusion is clear. Furthermore, the phrase was uttered specifically in the presence of a group of "twelve" (Matt 26:20; Mark 14:17), just as there were twelve pillars specifically "corresponding to the twelve tribes of Israel" (Exod 24:4 NRSV). Luke also uniquely calls the disciples "apostles" in its account of this occasion (Luke 22:14).[94] In other words, as God did at Sinai, Jesus made his covenant with a representative group of the people. While Moses sacrificed animals and used animal blood, Jesus was himself the sacrifice and his own blood sealed the new covenant. Following the Sinaitic narrative, it means that Jesus is the sacrifice that made the divine-human covenant possible. His blood was what allows sinful humanity to enjoy fellowship with God again. In sum, he is not only the sacrificed lamb that liberated the world, but also the one whose blood brought God's forgiveness, and hence restores the broken divine-human relationship. Jesus fulfilled both the Passover and the covenant. "This is my body" and "This is my blood of the new covenant" were in fact Jesus's

93. See discussion in Childs, *Exodus*, 510.

94. LaVerdiere, *Dining in the Kingdom of God*, 133–34.

rewording of the two climactic phrases said during these two events to make them point to himself.

For our purposes, therefore, whether Israel actually saw God at Sinai does not matter as much as the belief that, ultimately, this direct and intimate communion with God would be fulfilled in Jesus Christ, in his divine-human personhood, and also physically by him at his table fellowship with the "twelve" at the Last Supper. God in the person of Christ sat with the "twelve" in a covenant meal, now sealed with Christ's own blood. The number "twelve," which might have hinted to a modern reader that this was some VIP occasion, in fact unambiguously stands for the *whole people* in Jewish culture.[95] "They saw God, and they ate and drank" (Exod 24:11): the remarkable and mysterious table fellowship between God and Israelites hinted at the Sinai event only all the more expresses the longing for this divine-human communion since ancient times. It may be in this context that we appreciate Jesus's saying to his disciples at the beginning of the Last Supper, "I have eagerly desired to eat this Passover *with you . . .*" (Luke 22:15). At the Last Supper, the representatives of the people truly saw God incarnated in flesh and blood, and ate and drank with him in a covenantal meal. If even the Exodus narrative tells us that no one can see God and live (Exod 33:20), now, at the Last Supper, the new people of God saw God and lived. "He did not reach out with his hand against the nobles of the sons of Israel" (24:11). The divine-human table fellowship foreshadowed at Sinai is now realized.[96] A theology of the Supper

---

95. See, e.g., Ahituv and Paul, "Tribes of Israel," in *Oxford Dictionary of the Jewish Religion*, 751–52; Oded and Freedman, "Tribes, the Twelve," in *Encyclopaedia Judaica*, 20:137–40.

In our study, the notion of a "new" people does *not* suggest that the people of the Israel were thereby replaced. Israel remains God's chosen people. The new "twelve" does not replace the old but is now included alongside Israel's "twelve." One must remember John's heavenly vision (in Rev 4:4) of twenty-four thrones with twenty-four elders.

96. No doubt, God repeatedly fulfilled his promises even in the ancient history of Israel. The Old Testament may be read as God's unfailing gracious commitment to his election of Israel. Despite their failures, God has made his presence among them, as promised in the Sinai covenant: he revealed his forgiving character upon Israel's breaking of the first commandment (Exod 34); he went ahead with his plan to have his tabernacle among them in the wilderness even after their idolatry (Exod 25), and later erected his temple in the midst of them (1 Kgs 5–8). Even as they were exiled, God's glorious presence did not leave them as he promised their return (e.g., Ezek 37:26; 43). Now at Jesus's Last Supper, God was present and dined with the "twelve" *in flesh and blood*. In addition, because of Jesus's sacrifice once and for all, God's people would no longer need to offer sacrifices. Hence Jesus pointed to *himself* as the new covenant.

can hardly omit this narrative. At the Last Supper God fulfilled what was anticipated: the ultimate confirmation of a divine-human communion.

From Forgiveness to Faith and Obedience

As we may recall, in the Sinaitic narrative, Israel pledged their obedience *three* times to God in the process, before being allowed to have communion with him. It was an indispensable element of the divine-human covenant. One would expect a similar pledge from the disciples—the human side of the covenant—to take place at a covenant meal with Jesus. Yet such a pledge was absent at the Last Supper. An immediate question to ask about the covenant cup at the Last Supper is this: how is such a covenant possible, given the utter failure of Israel? The absence of consent of obedience from the disciples reminds the reader of the covenant renewal in Exod 34. As Dennis Olson helpfully reminds us, when Israel had hopelessly failed the Sinaitic covenant by creating and worshiping the golden calf, God chose to renew the covenant with them. There in the covenant renewal, precisely the condition of Israel's obedience was dropped. It was declared instead that the Lord is "compassionate and merciful, slow to anger, and abounding in faithfulness and truth; who keeps faithfulness for thousands, who forgives wrongdoing, violation of His Law, and sin . . ." (34:6–7).[97] It was in light of human failure that forgiveness was offered. Human failure never has the final word. Because of *who* God is—God revealed "compassionate and merciful . . ." as part of his Name[98]—the divine-human covenant will not fail, even if we fail. Part of the reason why there was no requirement for disciples to pledge obedience must be that they would fail anyway (and indeed they did soon enough after). Precisely we need Christ to make the ultimate sacrifice to secure forgiveness for us. At the Last Supper, Jesus said that his blood was "poured out for *many* for *forgiveness* of sins" (Matt 26:28). Again, the promise of forgiveness points back to the covenantal renewal in Exod 34, the loud and clear reminder that we cannot fulfill the covenant ourselves, but can only rely on God's forgiveness. Also, now the new covenant is not only for the "House of Jacob," the other party that was named by God at the old covenant, but for many.[99]

97. Olson, "Book of Exodus," 38–39; see also Fretheim, *Exodus*, 528.

98. Olson, "Book of Exodus," 39.

99. This also alludes to Isa 52:13—53:12, in which there is reference of the suffering

Even more importantly, we must say that Jesus Christ did not just make the divine-human covenant possible. He *is* the covenant—on *both* sides. He is God incarnate, *homoousios* with the Father. Yet at the same time as human, he is the obedient Son of Man. He was obedient even unto death (Phil 2)—precisely at the Last Supper, during which this covenant ceremony took place, he was *en route* to the cross. His sacrifice was a sacrifice through perfect obedience.[100] In his life and person, he fulfilled the divine-human covenant on *both* sides. Human failure failed to void the covenant. The covenant fulfilled by him is no longer one that is fallible because of the requirement for human obedience on *our* part, but is infallible. It is on account of Jesus's obedience, not ours. It is ultimate. Christians do not need to look forward to another covenant sacrifice for renewal in the face of our likely failure again, as the anticipation in Jer 31. In retrospect, the covenantal requirement of human obedience at Sinai was in fact never dropped, but was fulfilled by Christ. God did not void it to make another one, but himself fulfilled it. The covenant has already been fulfilled on all sinners' behalf. Jesus is not only the true Passover (*"my* body"), but also the true covenant (*"my* blood").

What is our role to play? Because the covenant has been fulfilled, and the ultimate, once-for-all sin offering has been made for forgiveness, this means we are restored as genuine covenant partners of God once again.[101] We are called to a new life of obedience. The Sinaitic covenant was made "in accordance with all these words," i.e., the commandments God gave. A covenantal relationship is made in accordance with divine commandments. It is true that, in the Synoptic accounts of the Last Supper, the law was neither read out nor referenced at all, as it was solemnly at Mount Sinai.[102] But John's account of the Last Supper specifically includes the giving of a new commandment, even when it omitted the words of institution. This is why the Sinaitic reference is in fact clear in all

---

servant being "poured out," bearing the sins of "many." Mathison, *Given for You*, 214. "Many" is said to be a Semitic expression for "all." Jeremias, "Πολλοί," 536–45.

100. Here I concur with T. F. Torrance who emphasized that it was not only Christ's death but also his *obedience* that fulfilled the covenant. Torrance, *Atonement*, 1–24.

101. The fulfillment of the covenant does not depend on us, but on the perfect obedience of the God-man, who takes away the sins of the world. Yet the covenant includes our renewed role as God's covenant partner, who are to obey him.

102. Presumably, the law given in the OT was not void. Also, in the Gospels Jesus gave many teachings (including sermons on the "Mount," with a clear Sinaitic tone). The Synoptic Gospels might have presupposed these teachings in the new covenant Jesus inaugurated at the Last Supper.

four Gospel accounts. Even in John where the Sinaitic phrase "blood of the covenant" is missing, there Jesus gave a new commandment, as God did at Sinai. A new covenant means that divine commandment is given anew. In John's account, Jesus washed his disciples' feet, including the feet of Judas. Jesus then said, "If I, your Lord and Teacher, have washed your feet, you also ought to wash one another's feet. For I gave you an example, so that you also would do just as I did for you" (John 13:14–15). "I am giving you a new commandment," he continued, "that you love one another; just as I have loved you, that you also love one another" (13:34–35). This is the call to obedience to those who are offered forgiveness and allowed to come to the Lord's table. In this light, drinking the cup of the covenant is an action of participation in the covenant meal, asserting that we are a covenant partner. We may say that, therefore, considering the Sinaitic reference of the Last Supper, Zwingli was right—the Lord's Supper is indeed essentially a human action to pledge allegiance to Christ, or a "testimony" to God's grace.[103] This understanding takes seriously that the Lord's Supper is, apart from a Passover meal, equally a covenant meal, inaugurating a renewed relationship between God and his people. A divine-human covenant, as we have seen from the narrative of Sinai, requires human obedience to God's commandments. While Jesus has fulfilled the covenant, we are once again called to obedience. As at Sinai, where Israelites pledged their obedience and were able to eat and drink in God's presence, now drinking the cup means that we recommit to Christ by obeying his commandments. Note that, again, the new divine commandment given is clearly horizontal, i.e., social, in dimension.

103. Zwingli, *Commentary on True and False Religion*, 180–81; Zwingli, "Account of the Faith," in *On Providence*, 47–48; Zwingli, "Exposition of the Faith," in *Zwingli and Bullinger*, 264–65.

Although Calvin also understood this pledge of giving ourselves to others as part of the uses of the Lord's Supper (*Inst.* 4.17.38), he emphasized the meal as Christ's own pledge of salvation (4.17.1). Unfortunately, he saw the Supper as primarily Christ's offering of his own body and blood for our spiritual nourishment, a "mystery so high and incomprehensible" ("Short Treatise," *TT* 2:166) that is better experienced than explained (*Inst.* 4.17.32). As such, it can hardly be at the same time our action in obedience in response to Christ's commandment to love. To say the least, the two contrasting understandings to the Supper can only be held in tension. It is difficult to reconcile Calvin's formulation with the central role of obedience in a covenantal context. Although ultimately it was only Christ who fulfilled the Sinaitic covenant that requires obedience on the side of the human, we are at the same time called to respond in obedience, precisely because it is a covenant meal. We are truly restored as covenant partners of God.

It should be in this light that we discuss the role of faith in participating in the Lord's Supper. The meal is a *covenant* meal. It is a commitment between two covenant partners. God has chosen to redeem his people, given his commandments, offered forgiveness, and now he is calling his people to a life of obedience again. Taking part in the covenant meal means that we respond to this calling. Faith, therefore, is never separable from deed. Protestant Eucharistic theology has long rejected the Roman Catholic doctrine that a sacrament is effective *ex opere operato*, i.e., that grace is conferred by virtue of the objective fact that the rite is performed. Originally, the notion aims to affirm the objective validity of a sacrament performed irrespective of the moral status of the minister, especially in cases where believers were baptized by ministers belonging to a group alleged to be heretical, and in cases where, during a time of persecution, some ministers had defected from the church but later repented. The notion was, however, developed to be a concern over the importance of faith on the part of the recipient of the sacrament in determining the validity of the sacrament.[104] The Roman Catholic position is always committed to *ex opere operato*. Although later the Catholic Church understood that subjective faith must be present to receive grace, faith still carries less importance than the objective performance of the rite.[105] Reformed theology, however, holding on to *sola fidei*, insists on the vital importance of faith in receiving a sacrament. Calvin, for example, emphasized that sacraments are ineffective in themselves, but we receive Christ's body and blood only in faith (e.g., *Inst.* 4.14.9; 4. 17.5). With the agency of the Holy

104. The Council of Trent condemned all who reject that sacraments confer grace *ex opere operato*. Yet even on this stance, it is held that the recipient of a sacrament must still be in a disposition to receive grace. The phrase used in Trent is *"non ponentibus obicem,"* i.e., those who do not place an obstacle (session 7, On the Sacraments in General, canon 6). Luther's attack on the notion primarily had to do with the idea that the Roman Catholic Mass is held to be a *work* (*opus*, Melanchthon had a similar concern in his defense of the Augsburg Confession). For Lutherans, faith is absolutely necessary and central to receive grace (i.e., remission of sins, etc.). Calvin also firmly rejected the Catholic notion. He affirmed the secret action of the Holy Spirit, not of the objective thing (*Inst.* 4.14.9, 17). For Calvin, it is by the Holy Spirit that sacraments confirm faith by testifying God's grace by an outward sign (14.1, 7). Sacraments profit nothing unless they are received in faith (14.17). See, e.g., Leeming, *Principles of Sacramental Theology*, 5–18; Seeberg, *History of Doctrines*, 2:128–29.

105. It has been denied that the position of Trent allows the reception of grace in the Mass without faith. In addition, the presence of faith was confirmed in Vatican II (*Sacrosanctum Concilium*, 3.59). Believers need to come with the proper dispositions (1.10). See, e.g., Power, *Sacrifice We Offer*, 158–59, 176. Nevertheless, the Eucharist is still held to be a sacrifice of Christ's body and blood (2.47).

Spirit, sacraments confirm faith. Yet Calvin portrayed this faith mostly in subjective terms, in a picture of the Holy Spirit accessing our souls, and us embracing Christ with heart and soul (4.14.8–9). At least in his treatment of the Lord's Supper, he hardly spelled out faith in terms of concrete, embodied, human action.[106] Unfortunately, Reformed theology has always exhibited the tendency to spiritualize faith.[107] But the covenantal context of the Last Supper reminds us that faith is never abstract. Rather it takes the concrete form of obedience to the word of God. Faith without works is dead (Jas 2:26). Indeed, in the Gospel accounts of the Last Supper, the word "faith" is never mentioned, but there is a command to "*do* this." Notably John's account of the Supper devotes substantial ink to the giving of a new commandment to love one another as Christ has loved us. Just when we may think love also sounds abstract, Jesus had just washed his disciples' feet, a lowly service done by a slave at that time.

We may say that a Reformed theology of the Lord's Supper rejects *ex opere operato*, not only because there is no "secret efficacy perpetually inherent in them, by which [sacraments] can of themselves promote or strengthen faith" (*Inst.* 4.14.9), but also because, in the first place, the Supper is not a thing that may or may not have efficacy in relation to some abstract meaning of grace. It is rather a covenant meal between two parties. The covenantal relationship, initiated by God's election, and spelled out in terms of commandments and the gracious offer of forgiveness in spite of human failure, now invites commitment from the believer, i.e., faith. This faith in turn takes the form of concrete action. This commitment is not in the mind but is expressed in embodied, social action. A problem with traditional Reformed theology of the Supper is that, without such a covenantal framework that focuses on the Sinaitic reference of the cup and John's attention to Christ's new commandment, faith is easily made abstract. Overwhelmingly focusing on interpreting John 6 instead of John 13 also distracts us from the new commandment given at the Last Supper and the implied call for obedience. In sum, Christ has already fulfilled the covenant by his perfect obedience. Shedding his blood of the

---

106. One may note Calvin's beginning of his *Institutes* in terms of knowledge of God and knowledge of self, and his definition of faith is construed predominantly in terms of knowledge and certainty (3.2). His well-known third use of the law (2.7.12) unfortunately bears little in his treatment of the Lord's Supper.

107. See also the critique of Calvin's spiritualizing tendency in Grumett, *Material Eucharist*, 281–95; Oliver, "Eucharist before Nature and Culture." See a more detailed discussion in chapter 5.

covenant, he has allowed us to come to the Father. Now that we are offered forgiveness, we are restored as true covenant partners of God, who
are to commit to obey God on our part. We are no longer slaves of sin,
but servants of God. Drinking the cup of the covenant therefore signals
commitment to God. The Supper does not pose a metaphysical question
concerning any relation between the elements and grace, but an *ethical*
question to the believer whether to obey Christ's command.

Drinking the "Blood of the Covenant"?

What do we make of Jesus's "blood of the covenant"? As Moses did at
Sinai, Jesus said the cultic words, "This is my blood of the covenant" (or
"This is the new covenant in my blood"). But a particular sacrificial action highlighted in the old covenant ceremony was absent in the new
ceremony. While Moses sprinkled the sacrificial blood onto the altar
and onto the people, Jesus did *not* put the disciples in physical contact
with his own blood (except telling them to drink the wine in the cup).
Traditional Eucharistic theology has always understood that, when Jesus
uttered "This is my blood" (typically omitting that it is specifically blood
of the covenant), he implied some relationship between his blood and the
cup. Typically in Pauline language, it is presumed that we should have
communion with Jesus's blood (and with his body, 1 Cor 10:16). The
dispute has been whether this communion was meant to be physical, or
merely spiritual, sacramental, or symbolic. Yet we must note the Gospel
accounts of the Last Supper and Christ's passion presented in Scripture.
"My blood of the new covenant" clearly points back to the climactic event
at Sinai in Jewish history. It did not mean that Jesus gave his blood to his
disciples to consume or otherwise.

One important fact that a theology of the Supper must note is that,
in the OT, the consumption of blood was *absolutely* prohibited. A theological account of Christians' "communion" with Christ's blood must
take this very seriously. Unfortunately, traditional Eucharistic theology
seldom makes this observation. It is worth quoting here:

> You shall not eat flesh with its life, that is, its blood. (Gen 9:3–4)

> It is a permanent statute throughout your generations in all your
> dwelling places: you shall not eat any fat or any blood. (Lev 3:17)

And you are not to eat any blood, either of bird or animal, in any of your dwellings. Any person who eats any blood, that person shall also be cut off from his people. (Lev 7:26–27)

And anyone from the house of Israel, or from the strangers who reside among them, who eats any blood, I will set my face against that person who eats the blood, and will cut him off from among his people. For the life of the flesh is in the blood, and I have given it to you on the altar to make atonement for your souls; for it is the blood by reason of the life that makes atonement. . . . No person among you may eat blood, nor may any stranger who resides among you eat blood. . . . For as for the life of all flesh, its blood is identified with its life. Therefore I said to the sons of Israel, "You are not to eat the blood of any flesh, for the life of all flesh is its blood; whoever eats it shall be cut off." (Lev 17:10–14)

Only be sure not to eat the blood, for the blood is the life, and you shall not eat the life with the flesh. (Deut 12:23)

Interestingly, the prohibition seems to be affirmed again in NT (Acts 15:20, 29). There are theologians who have considered the OT prohibition and yet advocate for a realistic consumption of Christ's blood (albeit not necessarily metabolical consumption). Brant Pitre makes the argument that the Torah only prohibits eating animal blood, not human blood.[108] But surely, if eating animal blood is strictly prohibited, how much more offensive and appalling would it be to eat human blood (let alone the Son of God's)? Keith Mathison suggested that it is an "obvious difference" between the old and new covenants, that drinking of blood was prohibited in the old while specifically commanded by Jesus in the new.[109] He explained that this is because the OT was only a foreshadow of the NT. Yet if the OT truly foreshadows the new, we should expect there to be continuity between the two, not exact opposites! We must note that the OT prohibitions specify that it is *because* blood atones that we must not consume it. Therefore, the consumption of Christ's blood, the ultimate sacrificial blood that truly atones for our sins (Heb 10:4), must be all the more unthinkable. It is highly unlikely that the OT absolutely prohibits a certain action (not just regarding it as ritually unclean), yet the NT commands it. Furthermore, if something is prohibited absolutely, there is no reason to do it symbolically (consider, e.g., murder). The OT prohibition seriously challenges the traditional assumption that participants of the

108. Pitre, *Jesus and the Last Supper*, 109.

109. Mathison, *Given for You*, 198.

Lord's Supper must in *some* sense, whether realistically or symbolically, consume Christ's blood.

Focusing on 1 Cor 10, traditional Eucharistic theology has always assumed that there is a need for believers to have realistic communion with the body and blood of Christ. The overwhelming focus on the Bread of Life discourse in John 6 has also played a role (see below). However, it seems that even at the cross, which Protestant Eucharistic theology has always held to be the one true, once-for-all sacrifice, no one other than Jesus himself was in contact with the sacrificial blood. In fact the disciples all fled. We may note here that, in the Gospel accounts, nobody seemed to have even remotely entertained the idea that it would be meaningful to collect and be in contact with Jesus's real blood at the cross (or to deliberately touch his flesh, for that matter). So it is unlikely that being in physical contact with the real body/blood of Jesus was meant to be salvific (even with faith). What is even more unlikely is that we were meant to consume the body/blood of Jesus, in light of the strict prohibition in the OT. The same applies to the time after the resurrection when he was around his disciples. Having physical contact with his blood did not seem to be on anyone's mind. Mary held on to Jesus's body, but Jesus said to her, "Do not cling to me" (John 20:17, ESV).[110] If such physical contact was unnecessary even at the time when his flesh/blood was so easily available, why is it necessary now?

Surely, it is truly Jesus's blood that saves us. Why do we not have to be in contact with it, like the sprinkling of covenantal blood at Mount Sinai (Exod 24)? Again, I want to suggest that Christology provides an answer. Jesus the Son of Man himself is one of us. As a matter of fact he is the true human. He is God while being one of us. And he became sin for our sake (2 Cor 5:21). If sinful humanity needs to be in contact with the blood of the covenant to be cleansed and forgiven, Christ has taken up our sins and has done this for us. In addition, in Jesus the God-man on the cross, *both* God and humanity were already in contact with the blood of the covenant. He *is* himself the new covenant. His very person fulfilled the covenant on both sides. We do not have to be in contact with Jesus's blood because he has taken up our sins on the cross, whereas Moses was only a human mediator and did not bear Israel's sins. He had to apply the blood of the covenant onto the altar and to his fellow Israelites.[111]

110. We may also note that, the disciple who asked to touch Jesus's resurrected body—Thomas—has never been very well received in history either.

111. John Paul Heil has interestingly argued that the Jews' cry before Pilate, "His

The Sinaitic narrative questions the traditional narrow focus on blood instead of specifically blood *of the covenant*, as well as the preoccupation with some form of communion with this blood. The question of the real presence of Christ in the Supper needs to be reassessed as well. This question is often posed in a metaphysical framework that reduces Christ into some *thing* that we need access to in order to be saved. Instead, salvation is a dynamic history between two covenant partners. Also, as we have seen, the presence of God in the OT poses the question of *survival*. Who can ascend the mountain of the Lord (Ps 24:3)? It is God who does not stretch out his hand against us (Exod 24:11). This is hardly a metaphysical concern.[112] The narrative is one in which we are allowed communion with God *because of* the blood of the covenant, not that we need to have communion with this blood in order to be saved. Finally, the question of real presence assumes that what saves us must be somehow (still) there to be accessed. Surely, Christ is risen, ascended to heaven, and has sent his Spirit. Yet the upshot is that after and because of Jesus's sacrifice on the cross, no more sacrifice needs to be made. The whole sacrificial practice is to be ceased. No more blood needs to be there. Just as the fulfillment of the Passover is signified by the absence of any more Passover lambs, the fulfilled covenant is signified by the absence of any more sacrificial blood. In the new Passover, only bread is left to celebrate the fulfilled, lambless Passover; in the new covenant, only wine is left to inaugurate the restored, now bloodless, divine-human fellowship. Thus, it is not only that sacrificial body and blood are not present in the Supper, but *the point is precisely that* there needs to be *no more* sacrificial victim and blood.

---

blood be on us and on our children!" in Matt 27:25 was possibly alluding to the covenant ceremony at Sinai (Exod 24) in which the blood of the covenant had to be sprinkled onto God's people. Thus, far from an anti-Semitic polemic that implicates Jews of Jesus's death, that cry was in fact Matthew's inclusion of Israel even in the new covenant. Heil, "Blood of Jesus in Matthew," 117–24.

112. Borrowing Calvin's language of "wonderful exchange" (*Inst.* 4.17.2), we may say that what is "wonderful" is not that the body and blood of Christ are somehow communicated to us mysteriously, but that sinners are actually allowed to come to the Son of God at all without the threat of death. See discussion of God-sinner table fellowship in chapter 4.

Diagnosing a Problem in the Traditions

We have devoted almost all our expositional effort to the book of Exodus, and to comparing the narrative of Israel's deliverance from Egypt to Sinai with the Last Supper accounts in the four Gospels. What has been intentionally marginalized in this project is the "Bread of Life" discourse in John 6, as well as Paul's well-known Eucharistic text, 1 Cor 10–11. These two texts have been the preoccupation of Eucharistic debates. During the Reformation, Luther, Zwingli and Calvin debated with each other with their own exegesis on John 6, disputing in particular on 6:54–56 ("The one who eats my flesh and drinks my blood has eternal life. . . . For my flesh is true food, and my blood is true drink.") and 6:63 ("the flesh provides no benefit"). As Markus Barth remarked, higher sacramentalists score points with John 6:51–58.[113] Zwingli who is often labeled as a memorialist instead devoted page after page to his exegesis on 6:63, arguing against a realist reading of the text, and that eating Christ's flesh and drinking his blood only means believing in him.[114] Calvin, too, based his discussion on the Lord's Supper in the *Institutes* overwhelmingly on John 6.[115] On the other hand, it may not need to be proven that Paul's liturgical formula in 1 Cor 11:23–26 has been *the* central focus on studies on the Lord's Supper. While it is not within the scope of this project to prove whether John 6 is Eucharistic, we have shown how fruitful it is to take seriously the narrative of the Exodus to which the Gospel accounts

113. Barth, *Rediscovering the Lord's Supper*, 83.

114. E.g., Zwingli, *Commentary to True and False Religion*, 126–28, 200–211; Zwingli, "Letter to Matthew Alber," in *Huldrych Zwingli: Writings*, 2:132–36; Zwingli, "Friendly Exegesis," in *Huldrych Zwingli: Writings*, 2:266–72; Zwingli, "On the Lord's Supper," in *Zwingli and Bullinger*, 199–211. Jacques Courvoisier, in his 1961 Annie Kinkead Warfield Lectures on Zwingli, even had a subheading entitled "The Importance of the Sixth Chapter of John" (Courvoisier, *Zwingli: A Reformed Theologian*, 67–69). B. A. Gerrish regarded John 6 as Zwingli's "foremost periscope" (Gerrish, *Reformers in Profile*, 128–29). John W. Riggs noted how Zwingli spent "a good deal of time on John 6" (Riggs, *Lord's Supper in the Reformed Tradition*, 62–70).

115. The discourse on the Bread of Life is referred to a total of nine times in his chapter on the Lord's Supper in the *Institutes*, when the Gospels' Last Supper accounts hardly received attention. The McNeill-Battles translation in fact adds twelve more John 6 references than the original chapter in Latin where Calvin quoted phrases from John 6 but did not explicitly reference, totaling twenty-one references altogether. What is ironic is that even Calvin himself, who argued firmly for our real nourishment by Christ's body and blood, acknowledged in his commentary on John 6:53 that it is not a Eucharistic text (Calvin, *Commentary on John*, 265; see Gerrish, *Grace and Gratitude*, 129–30).

allude. It is a mistake of traditional Eucharistic theology to allow John 6 and 1 Corinthians to overshadow the Last Supper accounts, in particular allowing John 6 to distract our attention to John 13, and Paul's pastoral rhetoric to distract us from certain historical details in the Gospel accounts.

Many theologians state in their work that the Gospel of John included the Bread of Life discourse in lieu of Jesus's words of institution of the Lord's Supper.[116] This is misleading, as it distracts us from taking seriously John's unique attention to Jesus's act of washing his disciples' feet and of giving a new commandment at the Last Supper. As we have shown above, the divine commandment and the renewed call for obedience is an indispensable element of a renewed covenant. We are truly restored as covenant partners of God. Without John's unique account, the covenant meal would be abstract and contain no specific terms. But we are called to love one another as Christ has loved us, even by washing one another's feet, as he did. John's account of the Last Supper precisely completes the Sinaitic allusion of the Synoptic Gospels. Precisely in the person of Christ, God gave his commandment anew, and with Christ's "blood of the covenant" poured out for us, restored us as covenant partners once again by calling us to obedience to this new commandment. It is not impossible that John omitted the words of institution precisely to highlight this. John 13 highlights not only the divine commandment but the importance of our *obedience*. Ignoring John 13 would easily divorce the doctrine of the Supper from ethics. As will be shown below in chapter 4, this also has strong implications for our understanding of participation in Christ as concrete participation in his *obedience*.

Another fundamental problem of overwhelmingly focusing on John 6 is that it only intensifies a misguided tendency in traditional Eucharistic theology: namely that the Supper is often *itemized*. The focus is often on the static items of the bread and the cup, and their possible relationship with the flesh and blood of Christ, which are equally statically construed. It is as if the Supper was about four nouns: bread, cup, body, blood. This eclipses the dynamic history of the Passover and covenant renewal between God and his people. The focus on the body/blood conceptual pair almost always obscures the fact that, in the Lord's Supper, the blood is

---

116. See Morris, *Gospel according to John*, 311. For theological works, examples include Jeremias, *Eucharistic Words of Jesus*, 90, 107–8, 136, 165; Pitre, *Jesus and the Last Supper*, 5; Mathison, *Given for You*, 217; Stookey, *Eucharist*, 38. Stookey even stated that, in John, the meal in the upper room is "absent altogether," when it is not true.

not just blood but specifically "blood *of the covenant.*" God is doing his work in history. God has fulfilled the Passover by sending his Son to die as the ultimate Lamb, and as the ultimate sacrifice shedding blood once and for all to renew his covenant with sinful humanity. Yet this dynamic history has often been eclipsed by a metaphysical riddle that concerns some mystical or symbolic relationship between *items*, i.e., the bread and cup on the one hand, and Christ's body and blood on the other. The focus on the Bread of Life in John 6 and on the various interpretations of eating Christ's flesh and drinking his blood only reinforces this static outlook.[117]

In fact, an overemphasis on Paul's Eucharistic teaching also has this tendency. Traditional Eucharistic theology almost overwhelmingly focuses and relies on 1 Cor 10–11:

> Is the cup of blessing which we bless not a sharing in the blood of Christ? Is the bread which we break not a sharing in the body of Christ? (10:16)

> For I received from the Lord that which I also delivered to you, that the Lord Jesus, on the night when he was betrayed, took bread; and when he had given thanks, he broke it and said, "This is my body, which is for you; do this in remembrance of me." In the same way he also took the cup after supper, saying, "This cup is the new covenant in my blood; do this, as often as you drink it, in remembrance of me." For as often as you eat this bread and drink the cup, you proclaim the Lord's death until he comes. (11:23–26)

Yet, as some commentators have pointed out, Paul's immediate concern was pastoral, not doctrinal.[118] Paul was specifically addressing pastoral issues within the Corinthian church, namely idolatry (1 Cor 10) and social division (11). His concern was congregational conduct. Indeed he never implied that his account of the Supper was exhaustive. He probably assumed his readers had already read the Jewish Scriptures. He was using rhetoric to make an additional pastoral point. This explains why, in 10:16, he formulated his argument in the form of rhetorical questions,

---

117. In fact, this is also a problem with comparing the Last Supper with the Passover seder. Apart from the fact that the seder postdated the Last Supper, such a move tends to itemize the Eucharist by encouraging a "matching" between the different items on the old Passover table and the new one. It distracts us from noticing the historical narrative.

118. E.g., Barth, *Rediscovering the Lord's Supper*, 30; Leithart, "Signs of the Eschatological Ekklesia," 633.

and why he exhibited some freedom to mention the cup before mentioning the bread.[119] It is important, therefore, to not rely solely on Paul for
a theological account of the Lord's Supper. When theologians use 1 Cor
10–11, a tendency is to ignore the particular social situation to which
Paul was pointing, and airlift the bread-cup verses out of their pastoral
context.

Apart from this, there is also the tendency to ignore the cultural
context of the Last Supper when one relies on Paul's liturgical formula
in 1 Cor 11:23–26. The formula, probably intended for actual liturgical
use across culture and time, eclipses the historical context of the Last
Supper as well as the dynamics between Jesus and his disciples.[120] It does
not mention, first, the Passover context; second, the presence of Judas
the traitor *at the table* (not only that that night was a night of betrayal);
third, Jesus's giving of a new commandment and his example of foot-
washing; and fourth, Jesus's vow of abstinence from "the fruit of the vine"
before the coming of the kingdom (Matt 26:29; Mark 14:25; Luke 22:18).
Without these cultural and deeply dynamic touches, an over-reliance on
1 Corinthians for a theology of the Supper, like an over-reliance on John
6, intensifies the tendency to focus on the items on the table and their
corresponding relations to Christ's body and blood. Again, the outlook
becomes static and ahistorical. It opens the door widely for timeless,
metaphysical questions, instead of historical questions about God's actions in the history of a people and his concrete relationship established
with them, in particular his renewed call to obedience. The overwhelming focus on John 6 and on Paul explains the predominantly metaphysical approach of traditional Eucharist theology.

Conclusion

Jesus's words of institution at the Last Supper precisely echoed back to
the two monumental events in Jewish history—the Passover and Sinaitic
covenant. It is of paramount importance that, when we try to understand
the Last Supper, we consider its historical contexts. Just as God invited
his people to a Passover table to remember his deliverance, and to his

---

119. Barth, *Rediscovering the Lord's Supper*, 31.

120. See also Jeremias's discussion of the influence of liturgical use on 1 Cor 11 that
might have relegated historical details of the Last Supper to the background. Jeremias,
Eucharistic Words of Jesus, 115.

presence for a covenant meal, Jesus invited his people to a new Passover meal and a new covenant meal. As God did in Egypt, Jesus invited his disciples to take, eat, and to do so specifically for remembrance. He presented them with the blood of the covenant. He was speaking as God, reinstituting a new Passover and a new covenant. Precisely, "This is my body" and "This is my blood of the covenant" were Jesus's rewording of the climactic phrases said in these two events to point to *himself.* He was the ultimate Passover lamb that delivered God's people, and as the final sacrifice whose blood was poured out for their forgiveness once and for all. They no longer have to offer any more sacrifice, because God in Christ has offered himself and conquered sin and death, and in person inaugurated a new covenant in his blood. In turn, John's account of the Last Supper (John 13) completes the Sinaitic allusion that the Synoptic Gospels have already painted, by pointing to a new commandment that was given by Jesus. We are truly restored as God's covenant partner, once again called to a life of obedience with God.

We have demonstrated how fruitful it is to consider the narrative of Israel's first Passover as well as their covenant meal with God on Mount Sinai. Different questions concerning the meaning of the Lord's Supper have arisen, for example, questions concerning the missing Passover lamb, what participation and remembrance mean specifically in the Passover context, what the blood of the covenant does, what the number "twelve" means in this occasion, and the exact terms of the new covenant. Traditional questions concerning the Lord's Supper, such as whether Christ's words were meant literally or only figuratively, and whether Christ is truly present in the elements, typically overlook the Jewish context of the Supper. The concern of the real presence of Christ's body and blood in the Supper, even if only spiritually and symbolically, also overlooks the conspicuous *absence* of the redemptive elements, namely the Passover lamb and the blood of the covenant, in the new meal. It is such absence that signals the fulfillment of the historical events. In sum, the meal celebrates and remembers Christ and his passion, as well as re-inaugurates a divine-human covenant relationship. Believers are commanded to remember by reenacting the context of which the saving event took place, and recommit themselves to Christ and his new commandment to love one another.

3

Eating and Drinking without Metaphysics

Food is stuff. It's not ideas. It's not theories.
It's, well, it's food, . . . you put it in your mouth.
—Tim Chester[1]

Keep it concrete, I tell my students.
—Peter Leithart[2]

We have detailed a narrative of God's triumphant redemption of his
people from bondage in Egypt, which is the very backdrop of Christ's
institution of the Eucharist at the Last Supper. Such a narrative of
God's continuing work in history is a stark contrast to what traditional
Eucharistic theologies typically attempt to detail, namely philosophical
explanations of Christ's words and the elements of the Eucharist. While
there is a story about slaves, now we have to move on to a story about
theological giants. While it should be a dynamic story of God's liberation
in history, now we have to move on to timeless philosophical systems
that explain the Eucharist. While the backstory had a strong geopolitical

1. Chester, *Meal with Jesus*, 14. Chester's work for a lay audience calls for a focus
not on theories but on Jesus's table ministry and the mission of the community *around*
the table.

2. Leithart, "Signs of the Eschatological Ekklesia," 631. Leithart argues that sacramental theology is primarily and concretely pastoral theology. See the last chapter for
more discussion.

aspect, now the focus will be predominantly on static elements on the table. As Dru Johnson remarked about Western interpretations of rituals, we often hunger for a rational, timeless system of symbolic meaning, making us overlook historical contexts and embodied participation.[3] As Brevard Childs also noted, "What had been for Israel an unequivocal and straightforward memorial to the deliverance from Egypt became for the Christian church a mysterious and paradoxical sign within God's redemptive history of both the new and the old, of life and of death, of the future and the past."[4] Overall, there is a growing sense of discontinuity from the Jewish tradition. There is also no longer unequivocal warrant for involving children in key roles in the celebration of redemption. In their place we often find metaphysics saved for the more philosophically trained. While the OT should equally interpret the NT, increasingly the OT is interpreted in light of NT.[5]

This chapter will contrast the historical approach with some of the diverse theologies from the history of the doctrine of the Supper. It is divided into several parts. First it will examine the theology of Augustine. In the development of the doctrine of sacraments, Augustine is probably the most widely referenced. His notion that a sacrament is a visible sign of invisible grace is an undergirding framework necessary to understand theologians after him. His neo-Platonism will be demonstrated, and will be shown to be helpful in understanding Eucharistic controversies that unfolded after him. Beginning with Augustine is most warranted. Second, this chapter will narrate the major controversies in the development of Western Eucharistic theology, namely the Radbertus-Ratramnus debate in the ninth century, the Berengarian controversy in the eleventh century, and the Reformation. We will detail the development of the use of Aristotelian philosophy in reaction to neo-Platonism, and see how the several controversies arose out of an attempt to guard against merely symbolic views. While neo-Platonism carries a strong tendency for a symbolic, anti-materialist view of the Eucharist, an Aristotelian approach counteracts this tendency by emphasizing a real presence of the body and blood of Christ in the elements, often even explaining its metaphysics. Just as in the history of intellectual thought Platonism had attracted Aristotle's critique, Augustine's highly Platonic approach to the Supper

---

3. Johnson, *Knowledge by Ritual*, 2–4.

4. Childs, *Exodus*, 212.

5. See Childs, *Exodus*, 212–13.

eventually invited an Aristotelian correction in the development of the doctrine that affirms a real presence of Christ's body and blood. Notably, for example in the official Catholic doctrine of transubstantiation, the Aristotelian notion of substance is used to assert the applicability of a material language to describe Christ's presence as well as explain the kind of change that takes place during consecration.

Such a Platonic *vs.* Aristotelian analysis of the different controversies concerning the Eucharist is different from the common analysis in terms of "Augustinian" *vs.* "Ambrosian" theologies. Ambrose of Milan was a major exponent of real presence, who propounded that the Word of God causes the living body of Christ to be present.[6] As Gary Macy observed, the juxtaposition of "Augustinian" *vs.* "Ambrosian" theologies likely started with Joseph Rupert Geiselmann in the 1920s. Since then, sacramental theologies in the West have often been divided into two camps. On the one hand, there are theologies, dubbed Augustinian, which take a symbolic approach to the Eucharist, stressing the spiritual result of the sacrament. On the other, there are those dubbed "Ambrosian" that stress Christ's real presence in the sacrament.[7] Many followed Geiselmann in this juxtaposition to differentiate theologies leading up to the Reformation: "It is usually presumed, the Tridentine Church adopted the 'Ambrosian' approach to sacraments and the Reformed churches adopted the 'Augustinian' approach."[8] Nevertheless, as Macy noted, this is not an accurate categorization. As we will notice, theologians from both symbolist and realist approaches in fact appeal to both Augustine and Ambrose for authority. What clearly divides the two approaches is their fundamental worldviews. On the one hand symbolists presuppose a neo-Platonic dichotomy between the visible and invisible, the physical sign and signified spiritual reality, with the latter being held as more real. Physical elements are given to us only because of the weakness of our bodily nature. There is in general an emphasis of the mind to "ascend" to the heavenly realm where Christ is present, away from the material world. On the other hand, realists focus on the material realm. They articulate the importance of Christ's physical body and its presence in the material world, which is given great importance. While realists also presuppose Augustine's juxtaposition between sign and signified reality, they

6. Ambrose, *De Sacramentis*, 1.4.16.

7. Macy, "Sacramental Theology," 1680–83.

8. Macy, "Sacramental Theology," 1680.

assert that the elements are not mere signs. On the whole, the outlook is an Aristotelian correction of Platonism.

Third, this chapter aims to lay bare the metaphysical problems entailed in real presence. While the worry over anti-materialism is valid, pro-materialist realist theologies are inevitably dominated by the need to make sense of the presence of a human body in the physical bread and wine. The doctrine of transubstantiation, for example, poses a myriad of metaphysical riddles. As Henry Chadwick put it, these would "rack the brains of the theological teachers and their pupils for generations to come."[9] This chapter will show that, while the realist position is right to correct an anti-materialist tendency to turn the Eucharist into mere symbol, it nevertheless fails *on its own terms*, namely to bring in metaphysics to give a coherent account of the presence of Christ's body and blood. The critical works of Duns Scotus and William Ockham will be helpful here. While presupposing an Aristotelian framework, the orthodox position is required to go beyond Aristotelian metaphysics, indeed any philosophical system, and affirms only a supernatural "body" in the end. Most devastatingly, the "body" of Christ shown to be present in the Eucharist has absolutely no analogy in the natural world. What is emphasized is less a body than an abstract "substance." The "metaphysical baggage," as Michael Dummett worded it,[10] might be what attracted a simpler theory, namely symbolism.

Fourth, this chapter will also consider the alternatives in Luther and Calvin's Eucharistic theologies. Even when Luther affirmed real presence as he rejected transubstantiation and avoided the use of Aristotelian language, he ended up proving an analogy between Christ's presence in the Eucharistic elements with that of an incorporeal substance. Calvin attempted a *via media* between mere symbolism and a metaphysical real presence of Christ in the elements. He instead emphasized our real communion with Christ's body, which is in heaven, and our hearts' ascent there by the Holy Spirit. While Calvin's theology emphasizes the importance of Christ's body, unfortunately it fundamentally operates with neo-Platonist language, which was what attracted an Aristotelian correction in history in the first place. This includes a much accentuated need for souls to ascend to the heavenly realm away from the material world. While Calvin denies that God gives us an empty sign, for him in

9. Chadwick, "Ego Berengarius," 418.
10. Dummett, "Intelligibility of Eucharistic Doctrine," 241.

the Eucharist God truly lifts our hearts away from the physical world to the spiritual world.

Finally the chapter calls theology to rediscover the fundamentally *historical* aspect of the Last Supper, as a third alternative to neo-Platonism and real presence. In ignoring the historical context of the Last Supper, much is lost. Both symbolic and realist positions in fact metaphysicalized the meal, and imported extrabiblical philosophy. Especially the realist position tends to be tied down with the metaphysical make-up of objects, instead of the social, interpersonal world that needs the presence of Christ. Worse, the applicability of metaphysics suggests that the focus is Christ's body as an object, instead of a subject. The conclusion will also diagnose some misassumptions of the realist approach, including the need of a timelessly accessible "body" of Christ, and that Christ's presence purely through the Holy Spirit is a problem.

On the Table: Plato or Aristotle?

Augustine: A Platonic Start

Augustine himself never wrote a treatise devoted to the subject of sacraments. The references to the Eucharist in his writings are rather scattered. Interestingly, Augustine is summoned as witness from opposite camps in the dispute over the presence of Christ in the Lord's Supper.[11] There is a sea of literature on his sacramental theology.[12] For our purpose, we want to highlight the indubitably Platonic character of his sacramental outlook. In his broader understanding of signs and anti-Donatist arguments, he always very carefully distinguished between signs on the one hand, and on the other the reality they signify. His language always conveys a fundamental dichotomy between the outward, physical, visible *versus* the inward, spiritual, invisible. Our attention is taught to go beyond what is *seen* to what is *signified*.

When Augustine wrote about sacraments, he had inherited a fairly established tradition of sacramental understanding, in which the concept of *sacramentum* in fact denoted a wide variety of symbols including

11. Macy, "Sacramental Theology," 1680; Cutrone, "Sacraments," 745.

12. Notably Jackson, "Eucharist"; Cutrone, "Sacraments"; Leithart, "Conjugating the Rites"; Martos, *Doors to the Sacred*; Macy, "Sacramental Theology"; Ayres and Humphries, "Augustine and the West"; Nocent, "Sacraments"; Grappone, "Sacrament."

rituals and events prior to the incarnation.[13] These include, for instance, the flood, the Passover lamb, manna, circumcision, the Sabbath, the temple, feasts.[14] There are symbols in nature as well.[15] Scholars have noted that, within this tradition of diverse uses of *sacramentum*, Augustine's distinct contribution was by offering a more systematic and narrower conception of sacrament as a visible sign for some symbolized invisible reality.[16] It has been argued that, in fact, it was Berengar of Tours (1010–1088) who attributed to Augustine much of what the history of theology holds to be Augustine's definition of sacrament: a visible sign of invisible grace.[17] Berengar clashed with the authorities concerning the question of real presence of Christ's body and blood in the Supper. Taking the side of Ratramnus in the Radbertus-Ratramnus controversy in the ninth century, Berengar denied that the bread and wine consecrated in the Eucharist were actually changed into the body and blood of Christ. His teaching was, however, condemned by the church on more than one occasion. Berengar's position very much hinged on Augustine's understanding of signs to demonstrate that the bread and wine must retain their own, original identity in order to be signs (i.e., sacraments). Berengar attributed to Augustine the definition of a sacrament as a "visible form of invisible grace."[18] As Gary Macy helpfully pointed out, this definition was likely derived from Augustine's *Letter 105* to the Donatists, where Augustine affirmed the validity of baptism performed by immoral priests: "if [the priest] is bad, God produces through him the visible form of the sacrament, but God himself gives the invisible grace" (3.12).[19] As Macy also noted, another commonly adopted definition of sacrament attributed to Augustine likely came from *The City of God*: "A sacrifice, therefore, is a visible sacrament or sacred sign of an invisible sacrifice" (*civ. Dei*

13. Ayres and Humphries, "Augustine and the West," 156; Cutrone, "Sacraments," 741.

14. On manna signifying the Living Bread, see Augustine's *Homilies to John's Gospel* (*Io. eu. tr.*) 26.11–13; on Sabbath and the Passover lamb: *Ep. 55*; Book II in *Teaching Christianity* also discusses various signs in the OT.

15. See Augustine, *Ep. 55*.

16. Ayres and Humphries, "Augustine and the West," 156–57; Grappone, "Sacrament," 447–49.

17. Macy, "Sacramental Theology," 1681. See also Haring, "Berengar's Definitions of *Sacramentum*."

18. Macy, "Sacramental Theology," 1681.

19. All translations of Augustine, unless otherwise stated, are taken from *The Works of Saint Augustine*, edited by Boniface Ramsey.

10.5).[20] This quotation, however, would be rephrased into the definition of "a sacrament [as] the sign of a sacred thing" in the writings of Berengar's opponents during their dispute. Eventually, according to Macy, both these definitions as modified during the Berengarian controversy made their way into Gratian's *Decretum* in the twelfth century under the attribution of Augustine.[21] Eventually, both modified definitions would be widely assumed to be Augustine's own words, and would shape all future discussions on the subject.

We may be able to find a more direct identification of *sacramentum* as a visible sign in his *Answer to Faustus a Manichaean*, which is also frequently referenced by theologians. In it he explained that "people could not be gathered together under the name of any religion, whether true or false, if they were not bound together by some sharing of *visible signs* or sacraments" (*c. Faust* 19.11). Visible signs are, then, necessary for a religious community. More importantly, here we see that *sacramentum* is explicitly used as a synonym for "visible sign."

While the well-known definitions of Augustine are only modifications, they effectively identify and lay bare Augustine's basic Platonic outlook. The visible and invisible are often juxtaposed. As we can see, even in Augustine's own words, there is "visible form" on the one hand, but "invisible grace" on the other; there is "visible sacrifice," and there is "invisible sacrifice." More excerpts from his writings shine light on this Platonic dichotomy foundational to his approach. This dichotomy was already in place in his general discussion of signs from Scripture. A noteworthy text is Augustine's two letters to a Januarius from among his earlier writings. In the second letter, he discussed the *purpose* of "bodily" figures and signs God gave humankind in nature, in commandments, and on the cross. Concerning signs in nature, he said, "if any symbolic likenesses are taken not only from the heavens and the stars, but also from the lower creation for the presentation of the mysteries, the result is a certain eloquence of a teaching conducive to salvation that is suited to turn the affections of the learners from visible things to invisible ones, from bodily things to non-bodily ones, and from temporal things to eternal ones" (*Ep.* 55 7.13). In a nutshell, visible, corporeal signs are meant to direct us to the invisible, incorporeal, eternal. To Augustine, such a direction from the visible to the invisible is the meaning of the "pass-over" lamb, too: "the Holy Spirit,

---

20. Augustine, *St. Augustin's City of God*, 183.

21. Macy, "Sacramental Theology," 1681.

in taking a likeness from visible things for invisible ones and from bodily things for spiritual ones, wanted that passage from one life to another, which is called Pasch" (5.9).

In Augustine's language, signs are meant to point us upward and inward. Concerning the notion of Sabbath as a likeness to our ultimate rest, Augustine said, "All these things . . . that are presented to us in figures pertain somehow to nourishing and fanning the fire of love by which we are carried upward or inward to rest as if by a weight. For they arouse and kindle love more than if they were set forth bare without any likenesses of the sacraments" (*Ep. 55* 11.21). As he explained, it is "a fact that something presented in an allegorical meaning arouses more, delights more, and is appreciated more than if it were said in full openness with the proper terms. I believe that, . . . if [the soul] is confronted with bodily likenesses and brought from there to spiritual realities that are symbolized by those likenesses, it is strengthened by this passage, and is set aflame like the fire in a coal when stirred up, and is carried with a more ardent love toward rest" (*Ep. 55* 11.21). In sum, God makes use of the likeness of bodily signs to point us "from there to spiritual realities that are symbolized."

To Augustine, the physical signs from the Old Testament have ceased. "They were symbols of realities" but more specifically, "they were observed so that their very observance would be a prophecy that Christ was to come" (*c. Faust* 19.11). Because Christ has already come, and he has not destroyed but fulfilled all these symbols, it is most fitting and proper that these symbols have ceased (*c. Faust* 19.13). However, there would still be symbols. These are better symbols, so to speak. These are "greater in power, better in their benefits, easier in their practice, and fewer in number, inasmuch as the righteousness of faith was revealed and the children of God were called to freedom once the yoke of slavery was removed, which was appropriate for a hardhearted people given to the flesh" (*c. Faust* 19.13). These are, specifically "the baptism of Christ, [and] the eucharist of Christ."[22]

---

22. Cf. Augustine's first letter to Januarius (*Ep. 54* 1.1): "Our Lord Jesus Christ . . . bound together the society of the new people by sacraments very few in number, very easy in their observance, and most excellent in what they signify." These few are, according to Augustine, baptism and "the partaking of his body and blood," which are now "observed throughout the whole world." Also *Teaching Christianity*: "the Lord himself and the discipline of the apostles has handed down to us just a few signs instead of many, and these so easy to perform, and so awesome to understand, and so pure and chaste to celebrate, such as the sacrament of baptism, and the celebration of the Lord's body and blood" (*doctr. chr.* 3.9.13).

Concerning the sacrament of the Eucharist specifically, a direct source is a sermon given by Augustine on a Pentecost (*Sermon 272*). Notably, he began his sermon by distinguishing strongly between what we see on one hand, and what is meant and understood on the other. He said, "So what you can see, then, is bread and a cup; that's what even your eyes tell you; but as for what your faith asks to be instructed about, the bread is the body of Christ, the cup the blood of Christ." "The reason these things, brothers and sisters, are called sacraments is that in them one thing is seen, another is to be understood. What can be seen has a bodily appearance, what is to be understood provides spiritual fruit." Thus, we see bread and cup, yet what is to be understood is the body and blood of Christ. As noted by Lewis Ayres and Thomas Humphries, the visible has significance only in relation to what cannot be seen and therefore must be believed in faith.[23]

To Augustine, the categorical dichotomy between sign and reality is fundamental. In *Teaching Christianity*, he wrote, "All teaching is either about things or signs; but things are learned about through signs" (*doctr. chr.* 1, 2.2). Although signs are also things themselves, they signify. "A sign, after all, is a thing, which besides the impression it conveys to the senses, also has the effect of making something else come to mind" (*doctr. chr.* 2, 1.1). For him, because the minds are obsessed with material things, it is more effective for God to give us signification that makes use of the material to lead us to the immaterial.[24] Augustine even warned strongly against confusing figures and reality: "Taking signs for the things signified by them is a matter of slavish weakness" (*doctr. chr.* 3, 9.13). He gave Sabbath and sacrifice as examples. "If, for example, you hear the word 'sabbath,' and all you understand by it is this one of the seven days which recurs week by week; and when you hear the word 'sacrifice,' your thoughts do not go beyond what is usually done with victims from the flock and the fruits of the earth. This, precisely, is the wretched slavery of the spirit, treating signs as things, and thus being unable to lift up the eyes of the mind above bodily creatures, to drink in the eternal light" (*doctr. chr.* 3, 5.9). In short, "Although [*sacramentum*] is to be celebrated in a visible manner, you must understand it in a way that transcends bodily sight" (*en. Ps.* 98.9). Elsewhere he distinguished between sacrament and the virtue (*virtus*) of sacrament: "we at this day receive visible food: but

23. Ayres and Humphries, "Augustine and the West," 159.
24. Ayres and Humphries, "Augustine and the West," 158.

the sacrament is one thing, the virtue of the sacrament another" (*Io. eu. tr.* 26.11).

To Augustine, it is the *word* alone that makes a sacrament a sacrament. In his famous line, word is added to the element, and becomes sacrament. As he explained baptism in his treatise on John 15, "Take away the word, and the water is neither more nor less than water. The word is added to the element, and there results the Sacrament, as if itself also a kind of *visible word*" (*Io. eu. tr.* 80.3).[25] Hence Jesus said, "you are clean through the word which I have spoken unto you" (John 15:3). In water baptism it is the word that cleanses. It is for this reason that, for Augustine, a sacrament is efficacious, not because of the sign, but because of the word. Here lies his refutation of Donatism. The inward *vs.* outward dichotomy implies that the Holy Spirit works internally irrespective of the external sign. In Augustine's words, "the sacrament is one thing, which even Simon Magus could have [in Acts 8:13]; and the operation of the Spirit is another thing" (*On Baptism* 3.16.21).[26] "The water externally presents the sacred sign of grace, and the Spirit internally produces the benefit of grace, removing the bond of sin and reconciling to God the good of nature." Therefore, "one does not have a share in sin through the will of another in the same way as one shares in grace through the unity of the Holy Spirit. For the one Holy Spirit can be in this person and that one, . . . so that through the Holy Spirit grace is common to both" (*Ep. 98* 2). For Augustine, it is important that the power of a sacrament does not lie in the sign but in the word. External signs "take place and pass away; they sound and pass away. Yet the power that works through them remains constant, and the spiritual gift that is signified by them is eternal" (*c. Faust* 19:16).

The physical sign *vs.* spiritual reality dichotomy was also helpful to Augustine (as it would be later to Luther and Calvin) to explain 1 Cor 11:29, the unworthy reception of the body and blood of Christ at the Lord's Supper. "How many do receive at the altar and die, and die indeed by receiving? Whence the apostle says, Eats and drinks judgment to himself. For it was not the mouthful given by the Lord that was the poison to Judas. And yet he took it; and when he took it, the enemy entered into him: not because he received an evil thing, but because he being evil

25. Also c. *Faust* 19.16: "After all, what else are certain bodily sacraments but certain visible words?"

26. Augustine, *Writings against the Manichaeans and against the Donatists*, 443.

received a good thing in an evil way. See ye then, brethren, that you eat the heavenly bread in a spiritual sense" (*Io. eu. tr.* 26.11).

Despite the strong dichotomy's between sign and reality, the sign is held by Augustine to be sacred. Another frequently cited origin of Augustine's definition of sacrament is his *On the Catechising of the Uninstructed*: signs of divine things are visible things, but the invisible things themselves are also honored in them, such that the species is therefore not to be regarded as merely common (*cat. rud.* 26.50). While Augustine warned about venerating signs as signs, he taught about venerating the reality that is referred to by the signs: "Those, you see, who practice or venerate some kind of thing which is a significant sign, unaware of what it signifies, are enslaved under signs, while those who either carry out or venerate useful signs established by God, fully understanding their force and significance, are not in fact venerating what can be seen and passes away, but rather that reality to which all such things are to be referred" (*doctr. chr.* 3, 9.13).

Surveying Augustine's writings on the sacraments, the strong sign *vs.* reality dichotomy, as well as his emphasis of the word, eclipses any instances where he implied that grace or the reality of the sacrament could be conferred by the signs.[27] As Protestant theologians would love to quote him, he even thought that it is possible to receive the reality of the sacrament without the sign: "Why do you prepare your teeth and stomachs? Believe, and you have eaten" (*Io. eu. tr.* 25.12).[28] In sum, one cannot understand Augustine and hence the beginning of the history of sacramental theology without Platonism. In Emmanuel Cutrone's words, "Augustine operates within a platonic worldview which understands the material, visible world to be a manifestation of a deeper inner reality. What is seen and experienced are reflections of a truer world, in such a way that material reality becomes a sign which both reveals and veils the inner world."[29]

27. E.g., in *c. Faustus* 19:13, he said that the new sacraments are "greater in power, better in their benefits"; and *Ep. 98* 9, where he stated that the sacrament of Christ's body is Christ's body, the sacrament of Christ's blood is his blood.

28. Macy, "Sacramental Theology," 1683. Also "Truly to believe in him, this is to eat the living bread. Whoever believes in him, eats him" (*Io. eu. tr.* 26.1).

29. Cutrone, "Sacraments," 741.

Substance: An Aristotelian Correction

Augustine's neo-Platonism would sprout a highly symbolic, even anti-materialist, interpretation of the Eucharist in the history of the doctrine, which would later receive strong counterattacks. "If it's a symbol, to hell with it!"—perhaps it was Flannery O'Connor who best summed up in a line the Catholic orthodox reaction to a merely symbolic approach to the Lord's Supper.[30] This section will highlight the major Eucharistic controversies in the history of theology that are illustrative of the attitudes and reactions of realist theologians towards Platonism (the disregard of Zwingli's symbolism during the Reformation was certainly not a first). Augustine's neo-Platonism is often contrasted with Ambrose of Milan's realist position. Ambrose, in his *On the Mysteries*, contrasted between sacraments of old and new. While the old were only a shadow, the new ones are light. While the ancients only had manna, the church has the excellent flesh of Christ; while they only drank water from rock, the church has blood flowing from Christ, which brings eternal life (8.47–49). The new sacraments are therefore better (8.47). Ambrose stressed a *change* [*mutet, mutare*] that occurs during consecration, which does not occur by the power of nature but by the words of Christ (9.52–54). Christ's words "This is my body" denote the presence of a different thing from that of bread and wine, namely his body and blood. Ambrose also compared this change with the miracle of the Virgin birth. As it was a miracle that he was born of a Virgin, so it is his flesh crucified and buried that is the true sacrament (9.53). In *The Sacraments*, Ambrose said that, when the words of consecration are said, the bread "*becomes*" [*fit*] the body of Christ (4.4.14, also 4.5.23).[31]

Diverse approaches to understanding Christ's presence in the Eucharist have often been categorized into "Augustinian" *vs.* "Ambrosian" approaches, with the former understood to be inclined towards a symbolic understanding and the latter towards a realist approach. Yet, as Gary Macy argued, this is inaccurate. The symbolist-leaning theologians drew from Ambrose for authority, and the realist-leaning theologians quoted Augustine extensively.[32] Instead of an Augustine-Ambrose divide, a more accurate divide is Platonic *vs.* Aristotelian. In reaction to a neo-Platonic dichotomy between the visible sign and invisible reality that is

---

30. O'Connor, *Habit of Being*, 125; quoted in Kugel, *Great Shift*, 101.

31. Ambrose, *De Mysteriis* and *De Sacramentis*.

32. Macy, "Sacramental Theology," 1680.

the tendency in Augustine, characterized by a movement *away* from the material world, theologians have instead stressed the real presence of the body and blood of Christ *in* the physical elements. For them, it is not enough for the Supper to simply function as a symbol (*sacramentum*) for a *res* that is not present. The Plato-Aristotle contrast in the development of sacramental theology may be seen as reflective of the contrast famously depicted in the fresco School of Athens by the Renaissance painter Raphael: while Plato, holding his *Timaeus*, points upward to heaven, Aristotle, holding his *Ethics*, points outward to the world. Just as Platonism invited Aristotle's critique, Augustine's highly Platonic approach to the Supper eventually invited an Aristotelian correction in the development of the doctrine. The following will briefly narrate the major Eucharistic controversies in history in terms of such Platonic dichotomy *vs.* Aristotelian realism. The Catholic Church would settle on the doctrine of transubstantiation, borrowing Aristotelian metaphysics. The substance of bread and wine is said to be converted into the substance of Christ's body and blood upon consecration, while the accidents of the bread and wine remain. Within Catholic orthodoxy, the Aristotelian approach reigns.

Ninth Century: Radbertus vs. Ratramnus

A debate took place at a Benedictine abbey of Corbie during the ninth century that would have ramifications for centuries to come. Paschasius Radbertus was an abbot at the abbey. His famous work *De corpore et sanguine Domini* (*The Lord's Body and Blood*) was possibly the first treatise entirely devoted to the subject of the Lord's Supper by any author.[33] According to what his opponent Ratramnus reported, in their time there was a debate between those who said that the symbol of Christ's body and blood "is performed with a naked manifestation of truth," and those who said that one thing appears to bodily senses, and another thing is beheld by faith.[34] To Radbertus, the bread and wine on the altar *become* Christ's body/blood upon consecration. Christ's body and blood are really present in the elements. While citations are frequent, Radbertus mainly drew from Gregory the Great, although he was indebted to Ambrose, Jerome, and Augustine. To Radbertus, no one may doubt Christ's words at the

33. McCracken, *Early Medieval Theology*, 91.

34. Ratramnus, "Christ's Body and Blood," 118. All translations of Radbertus and Ratramnus are taken from this volume.

Last Supper, and his words to the Jews in John 6, that his flesh is food indeed, his blood truly drink. God's will and power and wisdom are one. Therefore, whatever God wills, he does. With these, Radbertus argued that Christ's true flesh and blood are present in the bread and wine. The body of Christ consumed in the mass is identical to the historical body born of Mary, died, and resurrected. Just as we are regenerated through the water of baptism, so we feed on Christ's body and blood daily to be nourished and strengthened unto eternal life. As the Word's flesh becomes our food, we might be transformed into him. Those who eat his flesh and drink his blood worthily will secure immortality. Because of the resurrection, we may daily eat flesh and blood of Christ while he remains alive and whole, for he can die no more. It is a miracle on par with the Virgin birth and the resurrection. Radbertus argued that, in the same way as the Holy Spirit created true flesh from the Virgin, so out of bread/wine, the same body and blood of Christ is mystically consecrated.[35] Persistently, Radbertus distinguishes between figure and truth. The figure is what is seen outwardly, and the truth is what the Spirit accomplishes invisibly. However, while he makes such distinction, for him a sacrament is *both* figure and truth.

> This which is outwardly sensed is . . . the figure or character but wholly truth and no shadow, because [it is] intrinsically perceived.[36]

It is where the difference between old and new sacraments lies. In the old days the sacraments were figures of Christ, but now we receive his true body and blood, not just foreshadowed. There is both figure and truth. Indeed, the truth is inherent in the figure.[37] Yet, because such a mystery is a spiritual truth, it must be received by faith and not by sight. He urged his readers to discern whether they are in Christ and vice versa, otherwise one cannot eat and drink Christ.[38]

Ratramnus was a priest and monk at the same abbey at Corbie. His famous work, intended for King Charles the Bald and explicitly contrasting Radbertus's position (though without naming him), bears the exact same title *De corpore et sanguine Domini*. The "prince" had inquired about the Eucharistic debate, and specifically whether it is the same body

35. Radbertus, "Lord's Body and Blood," 101, 103.
36. Radbertus, "Lord's Body and Blood," 103.
37. Radbertus, "Lord's Body and Blood," 104–5.
38. Radbertus, "Lord's Body and Blood," 106.

of Christ that is eaten by the faithful and that was born of Mary, crucified, buried and raised again.[39] Ratramnus rejected the idea that the bread and wine, as symbols, are also Christ's body and blood *in truth* (Radbertus's term). To Ratramnus, what was stake was faith itself, which must be of things *unseen*. If the mystery of the body and blood of Christ is to remain a mystery, it means that something must be hidden. Ratramnus strongly and explicitly contrasted between what is corruptible and what is incorruptible, between visible and invisible, outward and inward. For example, the visible elements are subject to corruption, yet the true body and blood of Christ give incorruption. One appears to our outward sense, and the other can only be held by faith.[40] One can be eaten, while for the other, it "would have been a crime if . . . his blood were to be drunk or his flesh to be eaten by his disciples."[41] One nourishes the outer body, while the other purifies souls and gives eternal life. Therefore, the bread and wine are Christ's body and blood only in a figurative sense. "From the point of view of substance [*substantialiter*]," Ratramnus said explicitly, "the bread is not Christ, the vine is not Christ."[42] Instead, as images, they hint at something else. Ratramnus highlighted the neo-Platonist distinctions in the writings of Augustine, Isodore, Jerome, and notably even Ambrose. Directly appealing to Augustine, "the sacraments are one thing and the things of which they are sacraments are another," they are called sacraments precisely because "one thing is seen in them and another is understood."[43] Ratramnus noted how Isodore and Jerome also made a similar distinction: one thing that appears visibly, another is taken invisibly.[44] As for Ambrose, Ratramnus noted how he too said of one thing as "true flesh of Christ" and another thing as "truly . . . the sacrament of his flesh."[45] In short, Ratramnus demonstrated that Ambrose also distinguished between corporeal and spiritual food.

Although Ambrose believed that a real change occurs during consecration, Ratramnus observed that outwardly, appearances do not change

---

39. Ratramnus, "Christ's Body and Blood," 119.
40. See, e.g., Ratramnus, "Christ's Body and Blood," 121, 124, 133, 139–40, 143.
41. Ratramnus, "Christ's Body and Blood," 126; also 124, 131, 137.
42. Ratramnus, "Christ's Body and Blood," 120.
43. Ratramnus, "Christ's Body and Blood," 128, 145.
44. Ratramnus, "Christ's Body and Blood," 131.
45. Ratramnus, "Christ's Body and Blood," 134.

upon consecration. Yet the bread and wine become the sacraments of Christ's body and blood to the minds of believers.

> Since they confess that they are Christ's body and blood and that they could not be such without some change for the better being made, and this change did not take place in a corporeal sense but in a spiritual, it must now be said that this was done figuratively, since under cover of the corporeal bread and of the corporeal wine Christ's spiritual body and spiritual blood do exist.[46]

Given his neo-Platonic framework, the absence of corporeal change means that only a spiritual change is involved. He repeatedly asked his opponents to explain what the sacramental change consists in.[47] Unlike Radbertus who contrasted between old and new sacraments, Ratramnus instead saw continuation between the two in Paul's notion that our ancestors in the OT had the same spiritual food and spiritual drink (1 Cor 10:1–4). Since what they ate corporeally was not the same, while spiritually considered it was the same, it follows that from OT to NT only the figures have changed.[48] Ratramnus concluded that the body eaten in the bread, which spiritually nourishes the soul and gives eternal life, is not Christ's perceptible body, crucified, buried and raised. The sacrament is only a figure. With his emphasis of John 6:63 that it is the spirit that quickens, and his notion that the sacrament is a "memorial" that recalls the past,[49] Ratramnus's work on the whole reads as a ninth-century Zwingli.

There seemed to be little activity from the authorities concerning the disagreement at Corbie, even though Radbertus's views were gaining wide acceptance in the church. There was no movement to condemn Ratramnus during his life time.[50] Yet his book would be caught in heated controversy in the eleventh century during the time of Berengarius of Tours. As a result of the controversy, Radbertus was canonized Saint Paschasius and his views hailed as orthodox.

---

46. Ratramnus, "Christ's Body and Blood," 122–23.

47. Ratramnus, "Christ's Body and Blood," 122, 133.

48. Ratramnus, "Christ's Body and Blood," 125.

49. Ratramnus, "Christ's Body and Blood," 141, 147.

50. For the ensuing history, see, e.g., Macy, *Theologies of the Eucharist*, 21–43; McCracken, *Early Medieval Theology*, 112–17.

Eleventh Century: The Berengarian Controversy

The disagreement at Corbie became a full-blown conflict between symbolic and materialist understandings of the Eucharist in the eleventh century.[51] Berengar of Tours was an archdeacon of Tours, who began to have doubts concerning Radbertus's position. Berengar is said to have addressed a letter to Lanfranc, a prior from Bec, declaring himself opposed to the dominant Radbertus and in favor of Radbertus's opponent (whom he thought to be John Scotus Eriugena, a contemporary of the Corbie writers). Lanfranc attacked his position along with Eriugena's, and brought the matter to the attention of Leo IX. In 1050, just as Berengar's views first became known, he was summoned to councils to answer questions. Both at Rome and at Vercelli that year, his teaching was condemned in absentia by Leo IX. In 1054 at Tours he appeared before the papal legate Hildebrand, the future Gregory VII, who was likely sympathetic to him. He was allowed to simply swear his own oath that the Eucharist was "truly" the body and blood of Christ. This however had little effect in silencing his opponents. He was summoned again to Rome in 1059 by Nicholas II, when he was forced to swear an oath drawn up by his opponent. The controversy would last into the 1080s.

Berengar's main surviving work was his *De Sacra Coena adversus Lanfrancum*.[52] He never confessed to a mere symbolism, but acknowledged that some change takes place in the Eucharist. What he opposed was a *material* change in the elements. The bread and wine, according to him, do not cease to be what they are when they are consecrated— their matter does not change.[53] There is no conversion of substance, but they are made to possess the life-saving potency and effectiveness of the true body and blood of Christ. Thus he actually agreed with Ambrose's

51. For helpful overviews of this controversy, see, e.g., Macy, *Theologies of the Eucharist*, 1–72; Seeberg, *History of Doctrines*, 2:74–79; Somerville, "Case against Berengar of Tours"; Gibson, *Lanfranc of Bec*; Chadwick, "Ego Berengarius"; Radding and Newton, *Theology, Rhetoric, and Politics*, xi–xxxiii, 1–63; Sheedy, *The Eucharistic Controversy of the Eleventh Century*; for a Roman Catholic critique of Berengar, see Montclos, *Lanfranc et Bérenger*; for a Protestant sympathetic account of Berengar, see Macdonald, *Berengar*.

52. It is said to be written after 1063 since it responded to Lanfranc's 1063 treatise. The text was first introduced in Beekenkamp's two volumes, *De avondmaalsleer van Berengarius van Tours* and *De Sacra Coena adversus Lanfrancum*. See Radding and Newton, *Theology, Rhetoric, and Politics*, xvi; Huygens, "À propos de Bérengar et son traité de l'eucharistie"; Wainwright, "Berengar of Tours."

53. Radding and Newton, *Theology, Rhetoric, and Politics*, xvii.

language that the bread and wine are converted through consecration into the true body and blood of Christ.[54] What he qualified in Ambrose, however, was that the elements remain what they are while being made effective. Berengar's first intuitive line of defense was by physical observation: it is obvious that the physical characteristics of the bread and wine remained unchanged after consecration. While God has power to alter natural laws, he does so always only manifestly. Berengar regarded his position as the logical and rational one. Philosophy tells us that if a subject is changed, its qualities cannot remain.[55] Qualities of color, flavor, smell, etc., cannot be separated from their substances.[56] What believers receive cannot be the historical body of Christ. If the body of Christ is now in heaven impassible and incorruptible, then its substance cannot at the same time be produced many times everywhere (as Lanfranc alleged), which would mean there were many such bodies. Also, it would be indignity to think that Christ's flesh is eaten.[57] Christ is therefore present only spiritually.

Berengar's main devotion was to patristics and Scripture.[58] Despite his belief in some Eucharistic change, at the heart of his theology was Augustine, whom he quoted extensively.[59] The elements remain as they are, otherwise they would cease to be *signs*.[60] They remain, while only a spiritual significance is added to them during consecration. At its core, his approach is Augustinian, understanding *sacramentum* to mean *sacrum signum*, and recognizing a fundamental distinction between *signum* and

54. Macdonald, *Berengar*, 316–20.

55. *SCL* 42–43, 91; Macy explained that Berengar assumed that it is either a physical, sensed presence of Christ, or simply a spiritual presence. However, his opponents, yet without more sophisticated metaphysics, affirmed an essential and natural presence of body of Christ while actually not contesting that it is not physical and sensed. Macy, *The Theologies of the Eucharist*, 40, 43.

56. Macdonald, *Berengar*, 304.

57. *SCL* 44–45, 67–68, 159–60; see Macy, *The Theologies of the Eucharist*, 40.

58. Berengar understood that passages in John 6 should not be applied literally to the Supper. He compared 6:58 with Luke 22:36, where Jesus said "the one who has no sword must sell his cloak and buy one." Macdonald, *Berengar*, 302.

59. Radding and Newton, *Theology, Rhetoric, and Politics*, xvi; Chadwick, "Ego Berengarius," 418. Cf. Kilian McDonnell and Charles Edmund Sheedy's assessment that Berengar was more logician than theologian, basing on reason than faith. McDonnell, *John Calvin, Church, and Eucharist*, 55; Sheedy, *Eucharistic Controversy of the Eleventh Century*, 64.

60. Chadwick, "Ego Berengarius," 418.

res. Repeatedly, *sacramentum* is juxtaposed to *res sacramenti.*[61] For him, the bread and wine signify (*significat*) the body and blood of Christ, as, in his language, similitude (*similitudo*), sign (*signum*), figure (*figura*), and pledge (*pignus*).[62] The heavenly body of Christ alone is the *res.* Specifically a sign appears one thing to the senses, but the thing or reality of the sign appears to our *thought.* Thus, the reality of the sacrament comes not into our hands and mouth, but to our minds. Christ's body as incorruptible and impassible is broken and received only in sign.[63] His language bears a neo-Platonic tone: "Eternal salvation is produced in us if we accept with a pure heart the body of Christ, i.e., the reality of the sign while we accept the body of Christ in sign, i.e., in the holy bread of the altar, which has a temporal function."[64] On the whole, Berengar's work constituted a call to return to the understanding of Augustine.[65]

In 1059, in what would be known as a landmark statement in the controversy, Berengar was forced to recant his views and instead swear an oath drafted by his opponents:

> I, Berengarius, unworthy deacon of the Church of St. Maurice at Angers, knowing the true, Catholic, and apostolic Faith, condemn all heresy, . . . attempts to assert that the bread and wine that are placed on the altar are, after the Consecration, only a sacrament [*solomodo sacramentum*] and not the true Body and Blood of Our Lord Jesus Christ and that they are not able to be touched or broken by the hands of the priests or chewed by the teeth of the faithful [*dentibus atteri*] sensibly, but rather only sacramentally [*sensualiter nisi solo in Sacramento*]. I assent to the holy Roman and apostolic See and, concerning the sacraments of the Lord's table, I profess with mouth and heart . . . that the bread and wine that are placed on the altar are, after the Consecration, not only the Sacrament but the true Body and Blood of Our Lord Jesus Christ, and that they are in truth [*in veritate*] sensibly and not only sacramentally touched by the hands of the priests and are broken and chewed by the teeth of the faithful.[66]

61. Macdonald, *Berengar,* 314–15.

62. Seeberg, *History of Doctrines,* 2:75; Radding and Newton, *Theology, Rhetoric, and Politics,* xviii.

63. Radding and Newton, *Theology, Rhetoric, and Politics,* xviii; *SCL* 156.

64. *SCL* 158; translation from Macy, *Theologies of the Eucharist,* 39.

65. Macdonald, *Berengar,* 330.

66. Vaillancourt, *Lanfranc and Guitmund,* 33.

Thus the famous *Ego Berengarius* is the exact opposite of what Berengarius held. It is the true body and blood of Christ in the Eucharist, *sensually*, not only in sign, but in truth, explicitly to be handled and broken by teeth of the faithful. The confession passed into canon law collections.[67] All these never dissuaded Berengar. He wrote in repudiation of his oath and attacked Humbert (the work is lost). His voices likely sparked discussions, and two more councils in 1060s were needed to condemn him again (at Angers and at Lisieux). Although Gregory VII sympathized with him, he was condemned yet again in 1075 at Poitou, and in 1079 at Lent.

Berengar found himself in no shortage of enemies. These included Lanfranc of Bec, Durand of Troanne, Alger of Luttich, Guitmund of Aversa, and Alberic of Monte Cassino. Their common counterattacks asserted, *contra* Berengar, that the Eucharist was the "true body of Christ." They also asserted that God's will is not restricted by nature. But above all, they condemned Berengar for defying the received tradition and authority of the church.[68] Most did not observe that Berengar was also drawing from the Fathers and from Scripture. The counterattack on Berengar was headed by Lanfranc who attempted to show that his interpretations of them were incorrect.[69] In his 1063 *Liber de corpore et sanguine Domini*, Lanfranc refuted Berengar's interpretation of Ambrose. He highlighted instead the importance of distinguishing between the old and new sacraments: while the old sacraments were only a figure, the new ones are the light and truth. More importantly, he introduced a distinction between the earthly substances (which are converted into the essence of Christ, *essentialiter*) and their qualities:

> We believe, therefore, that the earthly substances, which on the table of the Lord are divinely sanctified by the priestly ministry, are ineffably, incomprehensibly, miraculously converted by the workings of heavenly power into the essence of the Lord's body. The species and whatever other certain qualities of the earthly substances themselves, however, are preserved, so that those who see it may not be horrified at the sight of flesh and blood, and believers may have a greater reward for their faith at the sight. It is, nonetheless, the body of the Lord himself existing in

67. Macy, *Theologies of the Eucharist*, 36.
68. Macy, *Theologies of the Eucharist*, 46.
69. Radding and Newton, *Theology, Rhetoric, and Politics*, xx.

heaven at the right side of the Father, immortal, inviolate, whole, uncontaminated, and unharmed.[70]

In terms of essence, the body we receive is the same as the body born of the virgin Mary, etc., but in terms of appearance, it is not.[71] In addition, God's power is above all nature.[72]

Lanfranc did not directly use Aristotelian terminology in his correspondences.[73] In the 1070s, the attack of Berengar was succeeded by Lanfranc's student Guitmund. In his *De Corporis et Sanguinis Christi veritate in Eucharistia*, Guitmund insisted on the transformation of bread and wine into body and blood of Christ and that it happens in the order of reality (not only in a figure). The fact that qualities of the bread and wine remain does not mean that they still remain, since nothing can obstruct the will of God.[74] Guitmund is said to be the first person who used the adverb *substantialiter* to describe the Eucharistic change.[75] He used the word in his treatise twenty-four times.[76] Guitmund provided the Aristotelian substance-accident language of what would become the kernel of the doctrine of transubstantiation: "the substances [*substantiae*] of things are changed, but, on account of horror, the prior taste, color, and the other accidents [*accidentia*], in so far as they pertain to the senses, are retained."[77] Thus, the Synod confession written for Berengar in 1079 at Rome was likely the hand of Guitmund.[78] It read,

70. Translation from Vaillancourt, *Lanfranc and Guitmund*, 66.

71. Vaillancourt, *Lanfranc and Guitmund*, 9–10, 66; Macy, "Eucharist in the High Middle Ages," 373.

72. Radding and Newton, *Theology, Rhetoric, and Politics*, xxiii.

73. Radding and Newton, *Theology, Rhetoric, and Politics*, xxiv; Vaillancourt, *Lanfranc and Guitmund*, 9–10.

74. Radding and Newton, *Theology, Rhetoric, and Politics*, xxv; Vaillancourt, *Lanfranc and Guitmund*, 20.

75. Radding and Newton, *Theology, Rhetoric, and Politics*, xxvi–xxvii; Chadwick, "Ego Berengarius," 432. Radding and Newton argued that the term *substantia* was really borrowed from patristic sources, especially Saint Hilary, since Guitmund drew from him. Thus it is "a remnant of the Arian debates rather than a harbinger of scholastic philosophy" (xxvii). Nevertheless, Chadwick pointed out that Lanfranc's use of *substantia* already had Aristotelian overtones. And Berengar seemed to have understood so, as he protested that it was a misuse of Aristotle ("Ego Berengarius," 427).

76. Vaillancourt, *Lanfranc and Guitmund*, 21.

77. Translation from Vaillancourt, *Lanfranc and Guitmund*, 21.

78. See Chadwick, "Ego Berengarius," 432.

> I Berengarius believe in my heart and confess with my mouth that the bread and wine which are placed upon the altar, through the mystery of the sacred prayer and the words of our Redeemer, are substantially converted [*substantialiter converti*] into our Lord Jesus Christ's very own life-giving flesh, which, after the consecration, is the true body of Christ, born of the Virgin, offered for the salvation of the world, hung upon the cross, that sits at the right hand of the Father; and into the true blood of Christ, which poured forth from his side, not only through the sign and power of the sacrament, but in the reality of nature and the truth of substance.[79]

The language in the 1059 *Ego Berengarius* implying cannibalism was indeed strong. Many thought the statement went too far against Berengar and needed rationalization.[80] Now the adverb *substantialiter* replaced *sensualiter*. Orthodoxy was still eager to unambiguously affirm that consecration brought more than only a spiritual change. Even though there was no more mention of believers handling Christ's body with their hands and teeth, the adverb *substantialiter* was still a bitter compromise by Berengar.

The 1079 Synod at Rome is said to have destroyed all arguments of Berengar. In the subsequent centuries, the "heresy of Berengar" would mean in general a denial of real presence. The near future, at least, belonged to Berengar's opponents.[81] Although he lost, Berengar was never excommunicated, and was allowed to die in union with the church in Tours.

The Dogmatization of Transubstantiation

The church decisively chose the side of Radbertus and Guitmund against Ratramnus and Berengar. The theologies of the latter notably rested on a basic neo-Platonic separation between the earthly and spiritual, sign and reality, what is corruptible and what is not. As noted by Macy, their presupposition was that human beings are made up of inferior bodies and a superior soul. Therefore in the Eucharist, souls receive spiritual

---

79. Translation from Vaillancourt, *Lanfranc and Guitmund*, 34; see also Radding and Newton, *Theology, Rhetoric, and Politics*, xxvii; Somerville, "Case against Berengar," 68–69.

80. Macy, *Theologies of the Eucharist*, 36; Grumett, *Material Eucharist*, 175.

81. Macy, *Theologies of the Eucharist*, 41, 43.

bread while bodies receive the sign of common bread. The reception of the Lord's body can only be a spiritual matter. The Lord is present spiritually, and is received by faith.[82] One might note that their language typically gives expression to the thought of a dichotomy: figure/sign on the one hand, and truth/reality on the other. Against such clear distinction between sign and reality, the church's affirmation of Radbertus was a clear affirmation of a materialist understanding of Christ's Eucharistic presence.[83] The church was anxious to assert that there is more than a spiritual change during consecration, where the elements are said to be changed into the true body and blood of Christ, whether it was expressed as essentially or substantially, instead of there being a sign on the one hand, and the signified reality on the other. While the Augustinian definition of a sacrament as visible form of invisible grace is still upheld as standard, mere symbolism is strictly condemned since 1059.

Guitmund's Aristotelian language would become orthodox. The introduction of Aristotelian categories would develop as theologians discovered its usefulness in explaining the precise mode of presence of Christ.[84] Hugh of St. Victor explained that the appearance of the bread and wine are perceived but their substance is absent, while the substance of Christ's body and blood, the true body hung on the cross and true blood from his side, is not perceived and yet is believed to be present.[85] The substance of bread and wine is changed into the true body and blood of Christ, while the appearance of the former remain, with "substance passing over to substance."[86] Hugh also specified that sacrament contains spiritual grace. Similarly, Peter Lombard expressed the Eucharistic change as a change in substance. The accidents of bread and wine by a miraculous act of God remain without a subject. They neither attach to the substance of the bread and wine, nor the substance of Christ's body and blood. Thus anything that happens to the accidents of the bread and wine, e.g., being eaten, does not affect the substance of Christ (*Sentences* 4.11.1; 4.12.1–3). Lombard took advantage of Aristotelian categories that imply that substance on its own, separated from accidents, is not perceivable by senses, since our sense perception of things in fact only senses

82. Macy, *Theologies of the Eucharist*, 39.

83. Grumett, *Material Eucharist*, 175; Chadwick, "Ego Berengarius," 418.

84. Macy, *Theologies of the Eucharist*, 37.

85. Hugh of St. Victor, *De Sacramentis Christianae Fidei*, 2.8.6–11.

86. Hugh of St. Victor, *On the Sacraments*, 310.

their accidents.[87] The substance of Christ then can be present while its accidents remain in heaven, and is therefore insensible. More importantly, Lombard affirmed that, while a sacrament is a visible sign of grace, it is also the *cause* of the grace it signifies. Therefore, it does not only signify, but sanctifies.[88] Equally influentially, Lombard fixed the number of sacraments to seven.

In the famous 1215 Fourth Lateran Council, the term "transubstantiation" was officially adopted (without giving a formal definition) to describe the change that occurs in a Mass. The bread and wine is said to be "transubstantiated" (*transubstantiatis*, as a past participle) into the body and blood by divine power.[89] It was Aquinas who consolidated a more precise language for articulating transubstantiation that became the standard for Roman Catholicism after the Reformation.[90] Aquinas echoed Lombard that sacraments of the new law do not only signify but are an *instrumental* cause of grace, ruling out the idea that God is the sole agent of grace (*STh* III. q. 62, 64, 79).[91] While God is the principal cause, God employs instrumental efficient causes. Sacraments "effect what they signify," i.e., they are both signs *and* causes of grace (q. 62 a. 1 ad. 1). As such, they have a power proportionate to it to cause grace (q. 62 a. 4). They are even said to impose a divine character on the recipient (q. 63). Christ's power, Aquinas affirmed, can be communicated to the sacraments as his instruments. More specifically, they are ordered to forgive sins (q. 79). Aquinas recalled the condemnation of Berengar's heresy, and affirmed that the Eucharist is more than a figure or sign, but contains the very truth, i.e., the crucified Christ (q. 75 a. 1). Based on the words of Christ, Aquinas reasoned that it is of paramount importance that we have physical contact with Christ.

As to the manner of the Eucharistic change, Aquinas ruled out what the Fourth Lateran Council in fact left open, namely consubstantiation and annihilation. Aquinas ruled out the possibility that the substance of the bread and wine could remain (q. 75 a. 2). First, locomotion of Christ's

87. Macy, "Eucharist in the High Middle Ages," 374–75.

88. *Sacramentum enim proprie dicitur, quod ita signum est gratiae Dei et invisibilis gratiae forma, ut ipsius imaginem gerat et causa existat. Non igitur significandi tantum gratia sacramenta instituta sunt, sed etiam sanctificandi.* Lombard, *Sententiae* 4.1.4.

89. Tanner, *Decrees of the Ecumenical Councils,* 1:230.

90. Macy, "Eucharist in the High Middle Ages," 377.

91. All translations of Aquinas are from *Summa Theologiae,* translated by Fathers of the English Dominican Province, http://www.newadvent.org/summa/index.html.

body is ruled out, because this would imply that Christ's body ceases to exist in heaven and passes through all intermediary spaces, and it is impossible for Christ's body to be locally present in different places at the same time. Therefore, in order to preserve the "truth" of the sacrament, it must be that the substance of the bread and wine is changed into the substance of Christ. Second, the words said by Christ "This is my body" must be true. And thirdly, creaturely substance cannot remain in order to avoid veneration of creatures. In addition, the substance of the bread and wine is not annihilated either (q. 75 a. 3). It must be an exact time when the substance of the bread and wine becomes no more and the substance of Christ begins to be present, otherwise two substances would coexist (which has been ruled out) or there would be a time when no substance is present. Plus, there is no implication by Christ's words that there is an additional divine act of annihilation of the physical elements. Thus the only possibility is that substance of the bread and wine changes into the substance of Christ. "By Divine power . . . the whole substance of the bread is changed into the whole substance of Christ's body, and the whole substance of the wine into the whole substance of Christ's blood" (q. 75 a. 4). Thus, by God's power, only the accidents of the bread and wine remain, which is evident to the senses (q. 75 a. 5).[92] The accidents of bread and wine remain *without* a subject. Because God is the first cause of all substances and accidents, he is able to preserve them without natural causes (q. 77 a. 1). As Marilyn Adams coined it, it is an "absolute whole-being conversion."[93] But, as we shall see, the metaphysics implied by these decisions did not go uncontested.

During the sixteenth-century Reformation, Zwingli's denial of a real presence of Christ, instead seeing the visible elements as only signifying the body and blood of Christ, was met with fueled attacks from all sides, including Luther and other Reformers.[94] Protestant theologians, on the other hand, who upheld that justification is by faith alone, unanimously rejected the idea that the Eucharist is a sacrifice and a work. The Council of Trent in the later sixteenth century, in response to Protestantism, decisively affirmed the efficacy of sacraments, as well as the language

92. As Aquinas explained, God lets Christ be consumed under ordinary food, because it would be horrible to consume human flesh and blood. Additionally, this is to prevent unbelievers from seeing us eat our Lord, and if we eat him only invisibly, this may contribute to our merit of faith.

93. Adams, *Later Medieval Theories*, 90.

94. See chapter 1, and the sections below.

and orthodoxy of Eucharistic real presence and the doctrine of transubstantiation. In the seventh session, the Council condemned those who deny that sacraments of the new law confer grace on those who place no obstacle, "as though they were merely outward signs of grace" (session 7, On the Sacraments in General, canon 6).[95]

Although Trent defined a sacrament along Augustinian lines, i.e., that it is "a symbol of a sacred thing, and is a visible form of an invisible grace" (session 13, Decree on the Eucharist, chapter 3), the Council immediately affirmed that "immediately after the consecration, the veritable Body of our Lord, and His veritable Blood, together with His soul and divinity, are under the species of bread and wine."[96] Thus, under the species of the elements, there is the *whole* Christ:

> The holy Synod teaches, and openly and simply professes, that, in the august sacrament of the holy Eucharist, after the consecration of the bread and wine, our Lord Jesus Christ, true God and man, is truly, really, and substantially contained under the species of those sensible things.[97]

> And because that Christ, our Redeemer, declared that which He offered under the species of bread to be truly His own body, therefore has it ever been a firm belief in the Church of God, and this holy Synod doth now declare it anew, that, by the consecration of the bread and of the wine, a conversion is made of the whole substance of the bread into the substance of the body of Christ our Lord, and of the whole substance of the wine into the substance of His blood; which conversion is, by the holy Catholic Church, suitably and properly called Transubstantiation.[98]

As Adams explained, at the core of the medieval anxiety to refuse mere symbolism and affirm Eucharistic efficacy was the need to distinguish between old sacraments and the new ones instituted by Christ: "What started the whole discussion of sacramental causality was the notion that new-law differ from old-law sacraments . . . in being efficacious signs that 'effect what they figure.'"[99] Whereas the old ones only

95. Similarly, Trent condemned those who deny that sacraments of the new law confer grace *ex opere operato* (session 7, On the Sacraments in General, canon 8).

96. Waterworth, *Council of Trent*, 77–78.

97. Session 13, Decree on the Eucharist, chapter 1. Waterworth, *Council of Trent*, 76.

98. Session 13, Decree on the Eucharist, chapter 4. Waterworth, *Council of Trent*, 78.

99. Adams, *Later Medieval Theories*, 77 (also 42–43, 51). The Council of Trent in fact anathematized those who deny a significant difference exists between old and new sacraments (session 7, On the Sacraments in General, canon 2).

figured the truth, the new ones bring the truth.[100] In reacting against a symbolist interpretations such as that of Ratramnus, Berengar, and the Reformers, the persistent response is to not only affirm but articulate the metaphysics of Christ's real presence in the bread and wine, as well as sacramental causes.[101] In reaction to a neo-Platonic anti-materialist take of the Eucharist, Catholic orthodoxy decided on the Aristotelian language of substance to describe Christ's real presence in the Eucharist, as well as to answer the question "What kind of change?" in relation to the change in consecration.[102] The doctrine of transubstantiation was the verdict of the Roman church in 1215 and again in the late sixteenth century. It is the *substance* of the bread and wine that is changed to the substance of Christ's body and blood, while the *accidents/species* of the bread and wine remain. As Chadwick remarked, one irony of the language of substance was its original intention to, in fact, retune the overcorrection of a crudely cannibalistic understanding of the Eucharist (Guitmund's *substantialiter* as a retuning of Humbert's *sensualiter*).[103] Nevertheless, the doctrine of transubstantiation is now often understood to be a materialist affirmation of Christ's presence, the antithesis of a neo-Platonic anti-materialist take of the Eucharist. The substance language is meant to affirm that Christ's bodily presence in the world can be expressed by language that expresses the material world. It aims to affirm that Christ's bodily presence has analogy in the physical order.[104] Theologians have made this point. Having summarized the history of the Eucharist, David Grumett hailed the concept of substance as necessary to counteract anti-materialist symbolism that implies that the whole material plane is significant only in signifying non-material truths.[105] The Aristotelian category of substance, according to Grumett, best conveys our own material existence, and communicates Christ's presence and activity *in* the world. The belief of a radical Eucharistic change reflects the radical change that

---

100. E.g., Ambrose in his *On the Mysteries*, 47–49; Lanfranc in his *De Corporis et Sanguinis Christi* (Vaillancourt, *Lanfranc and Guitmund*, 82–83); Hugh of St. Victor in his *De Sacramentis*, 2.8.5; Aquinas in *Summa Theologiae*, III q. 62 a. 1, q. 75 a. 1.

101. In reaction to Zwingli, within the Protestant circles Luther and Calvin, along with others, also affirmed a real presence of Christ or a real communion with Christ. See later sections of this chapter.

102. Chadwick, "Ego Berengarius," 426.

103. Chadwick, "Ego Berengarius," 442.

104. Chadwick, "Ego Berengarius," 417.

105. Grumett, *Material Eucharist*, 190.

Christ brings into the world. To Grumett, a symbolist understanding of the Eucharist is "little more than timid theology, by which it is assumed that God is unable to effect any material or spiritual transformation outside the normal run of events."[106] Simon Oliver suggested similarly. To him, it is transubstantiation that upholds the integrity of the world, because nature is transformed in the Eucharist and allowed to participate in divine life.[107] In the words of David Fagerberg, "Transubstantiation affirms that matter is totally suffused with grace."[108]

A Failed Campaign?

Theologians attempted to reconcile Christ's Eucharistic presence with prevailing philosophy of the day. However, the doctrine of transubstantiation is, to say the least, peculiar. The problem is not just the borrowing of extrabiblical categories such as Aristotelian substance and accidents to explain Christ's presence, but that, while the doctrine operates within an Aristotelian framework, in the end it has to resort to highly un-Aristotelian ideas. While it aims at affirming the material realm by explaining real presence with metaphysics that apply to the material world, in the end it constantly has to resort to supernatural power. The problems were already highlighted and criticized by Scotus and Ockham in later medieval times. These have been well captured by Henry Chadwick and Marilyn Adams in their work.[109] In the end, the campaign to salvage materiality failed on its own terms. Here, it will be helpful to rehearse some of the major concerns.

Recall that the official doctrine of transubstantiation dictates that the substance of the bread *changes* into the substance of Christ's body, all the while the bread's accidents remain. It is important that Christ is not just present in or with the bread (i.e., not consubstantiation). Rather, the substance of the bread must be absent on the altar in order to avoid veneration of creatures.[110] Yet this is not by "eviction," so to speak (i.e.,

---

106. Grumett, *Material Eucharist*, 189.

107. Oliver, "Eucharist before Nature and Culture," 345–47.

108. Fagerberg, "Translating Transubstantiation," 12.

109. Chadwick, "Ego Berengarius"; Adams, *Later Medieval Theories*. See also Burr, *Eucharistic Presence and Conversion*.

110. *STh* III q. 75 a. 2. For Duns Scotus, veneration of bread accidents still would count as idolatry, as it is still veneration of creatures. See Adams, *Later Medieval Theories*, 148.

not annihilation), but by one substance being converted to another. First and most obviously, transubstantiation has to posit independently existing accidents (that of the bread). We have a substance-free bread. This is explicitly un-Aristotelian: it is stated in *Categories* (2b6) that, if primary substance is removed, it is impossible for anything (i.e., accidents) to remain.[111] Transubstantiation uses the conceptual distinction of substance and accidents but runs exactly contrary to the definition of accidents, whose very existence depends on inherence in a subject and can only be individuated by their subject.[112] Certainly, the idea is rather counterintuitive as well. This would be akin to the idea that when snow ceases to exist, its whiteness can somehow remain *there*. In the end, the attempted solutions radically departed from Aristotelianism. For example, Scotus had to allow qualities to be capable of independent existence.[113] Ultimately, the explanation by those purporting the theory is to resort to divine omnipotence.[114]

What is involved in transubstantiation is a whole substance being converted into another—matter is converted into new matter, and form is converted into new form, all the while the original accidents remain. Nothing substantial is supposed to be there to persist through the change. Adams calls this "absolute whole being conversion." Aristotle actually does not have the language of such whole-being change.[115] All change must consist of some matter for a natural agent to work on. Furthermore, the form of Christ's body already existed before any consecration of the Eucharist host. The form is also already there in heaven. It is impossible to make it exist anew in the bread as well, *while* maintaining that it is numerically the same as the body in heaven.[116] Aquinas credited the "power of sacrament," namely the power of the words spoken by Christ, for the substantial change that takes place on the altar.[117] Nevertheless, this still poses a serious problem. If we truly partake of Christ, should we not also participate in his soul, his own accidents (in transubstantiation the perceivable accidents are only that of bread)? Aquinas argued that, by

---

111. Chadwick, "Ego Berengarius," 427.

112. Adams, *Later Medieval Theories*, 182–83.

113. Scotus, *Op. Ox.* IV, d. 12, q. 1. See Adams, *Later Medieval Theories*, 198–206.

114. E.g., Adams, *Later Medieval Theories*, 221.

115. Adams, *Later Medieval Theories*, 89–90, 98–99.

116. Adams, *Later Medieval Theories*, 99–101, 143–45.

117. *STh* III q. 76, a.1.

"natural concomitance," all that is Christ's, including his soul and accidents, are also present by virtue of the unity of the person. Yet, as Adams pointed out, in Aquinas's Aristotelian framework, a substance only has one substantial form. For Christ who is divine and human, his soul must be his substantial form. It cannot just be present by concomitance. Giles of Rome attempted to simplify the issue by allowing God to directly work on unquantified matter in its quiddity, even when natural agents can only work on quantified matter.[118] Scotus went further to question the need of substance-to-substance change. For him, one principal objection to Dominican answers to the riddles was not so much substance, but substance *here*.[119] Why did the bread not end up in heaven? After all, Christ did not become bread (a theory called impanation). Thus what happens, for Scotus, is that through the bread Christ's body gains new external relations to place. This change is only external and therefore accidental.

Theologians have to explain how two different substances can be extended in the same circumscribed place at the same time (Christ's body and the bread in the same space), and how a substance is not rendered numerically distinct by multiple place relations at the same time (Christ's body in heaven as well as on many altars). In the Aristotelian conception of place, place contains the thing that is in it. More specifically, the quantitative dimensions of a thing must be commensurate with the surface of the place it is in. A substance is mediated by its dimensive quantity in relation to place. It has been explained that transubstantiation does not violate these common conceptions of things and places, as long as Christ's body is not said to be present on the altar by virtue of its quantitative dimensions. Its quantities (accidents) are there merely by concomitance due to their unity with Christ's body. Christ's body is present under substance, not under dimensive quantity. It therefore coexists and does not compete with the accidents of the bread. It is also not subject to them. Nevertheless, the question remains how such an unquantified body can still be a body in the proper sense. Scotus explained the problems by getting rid of substantial change altogether. To him, the bread simply loses its external place relation with respect to the altar, and Christ's body gains new external place relations with respect to different altars. Thus, Christ's body remains intact in heaven, while simply receiving new, accidental

---

118. See Adams, *Later Medieval Theories*, 100–101.

119. Scotus, *Op. Ox.* IV, d. 10, q. 1; see Adams, *Later Medieval Theories*, 111–14.

external relations.[120] Ockham also agreed that quantity does not mediate substance to a place. Hence, given divine power, a body having multiple locations is metaphysically possible.[121]

Then, how can the human body of Christ, whose dimensions are obviously larger than those of the host on the altar, be said to be present in it? The initial solution is again to emphasize the unquantified character of Christ's body. Scotus complained that Christ's body must be an organic body and hence must be quantified in itself. He instead found it more satisfying to distinguish between two notions of place: intrinsic (or quantitative) position and extrinsic (or categorical) position.[122] The former has to do with the position of different parts of Christ's body relative to one another. The latter has to do with the position of the whole body relative to the place that contains it. Thus, as Scotus held that these two notions are unrelated, to him Christ's body can remain intrinsically quantified and intact (distance of its parts relative to other parts untouched) while it occupies the bread without being commensurate part-to-part with that place. The nominalist Ockham rejects the existence of independent accidents altogether. He distinguishes between two kinds of presence: circumscriptive and definitive. In the former sense, parts of the present body are commensurate with the parts of the space that it occupies. In the latter, the whole of the body is present in every part of the space. It is held that the body of Christ is present on the altar definitively, not circumscriptively, precisely the way an incorporeal substance, e.g., an angel or a soul, is in a place.[123] This also explains why the body on the altar is to be broken, while the body in heaven is held to be glorified and impassible. In fact the body of Christ in the bread is still impassible, as it does not have quantitative dimensions that allow it to be broken into parts. But again, the question is, how is this still a material body in the proper sense? Why do we not resort back to spiritual presence?

How can material rites have causal powers to produce spiritual benefits? This is problematic especially in light of the Aristotelian principle that the cause must be of a more excellent kind than the effect.[124] Aquinas explained this by distinguishing between principal and instrumental

---

120. Scotus, *Op. Ox.* IV, d. 10, q. 1.

121. Ockham, *Quaest. in IV Sent.*, q. 6; see Adams, *Later Medieval Theories*, 159–66.

122. Adams, *Later Medieval Theories*, 119.

123. Ockham, *Quaest. in IV Sent.*, q. 6.

124. Adams, *Later Medieval Theories*, 53.

causes, and between disposing and perfecting causes. In other words, sacraments are only instrumental causes that create the disposition in us for divine grace. However, for Scotus, saying that sacrament produce disposition for grace is just as problematic as saying they produce grace. It is still a supernatural quality. The orthodox view necessitates that God confers supernatural power on sacraments. Yet how does spiritual power, that is unextended, be in extended space? Ultimately, as Scotus and Ockham reasoned, the only option is to posit the divine will—God gives grace to those who participate worthily in the sacraments.[125]

All these are not to mention the interesting issue of timing: words of consecration have to be said over a period of time. How is grace produced, instantly or gradually over a period of time? Even one syllable takes time to be uttered. Is the power to make Christ's body present only in one syllable, and all other syllables are superfluous? Or is the power in each syllable? Compounded with this is the fact that words are conventional signs that assume the hearer's knowledge of the language. It is difficult to regard spoken consecration words as themselves causal.[126] Both Scotus and Ockham, therefore, avoided the problem by simply acknowledging divine will. When the sacrament is participated in a worthy manner, God causes grace in the participant.

What is it that is being eaten? Can Christ's risen body be broken? Remember the doctrine of transubstantiation does not allow the substance of the bread to be there, in order for the church to avoid veneration of creatures. It must be the substance of the body of Christ that is present. If Christ's body is truly present, is it actually torn by our teeth, and eventually mixed with other contents in our digestive system? If not, then at what point does its presence in the accidents of the bread end? This was a serious concern in medieval times, tied to a strict rule to fast for a considerable period of time before one takes the Eucharist.[127] Guitmund's solution was to say that the body of Christ will be separated from other foods, not passed out in waste.[128] This is rather *ad hoc*. A way out is for theologians to say that a body is causally exposed only if its own dimensions are extended in the place. Thus by ruling out Christ's presence as extended presence (i.e., as only through the quantitative dimensions),

---

125. Adams, *Later Medieval Theories*, 54–55, 72–77.

126. Adams, *Later Medieval Theories*, 62.

127. See Augustine's *Ep. 54* 6.8.

128. Chadwick, "Ego Berengarius," 430.

they may protect Christ's body from being exposed to created causes (e.g., crushed by teeth, dissolved by stomach acid). Nevertheless, they would want to uphold, at the same time, that this body of Christ still has causal power on the recipient, *without* being extended. The dilemma is obvious.

Then if physical digestion of Christ's body is to be ruled out, what would be the significance of it being physically present on the altar in the first place? Even if theologians distinguish between different kinds of eating: carnally, sacramentally, and spiritually, the question is why he is not present the same manner in which we eat him.[129] If we only receive Christ's body sacramentally and spiritually, then why cannot Christ just be present sacramentally and spiritually on the altar in the first place? In that case, Aristotelian physics should not be called for.

Finally, what happens to the consecrated bread when it is eaten by participants? We are supposed to have only the accidents of bread present. If we want to avoid seeing Christ's body as being causally acted upon, then what is left is the bread accidents that are present and acted upon. Yet in order to be causally acted on, there needs to be a subject. How can the recipient's digestive system act on pure independent accidents? Does God create new prime matter for the bread accidents?[130]

In sum, one may say that the body of Christ present on altar is not a natural body, and his presence in multiple locations is not by any natural cause. Scotus's corollary was that, because the non-natural presence of Christ has nothing to do with his natural presence while he walked on earth, the Eucharistic change could just as well take place before the incarnation.[131] Indeed we may add that it could take place even *without* the incarnation. In the end, both Scotus and Ockham contended that consubstantiation (that both substances of the bread and Christ's body remain and coexist) requires much simpler metaphysical explications.[132] There is no need to posit independently existing accidents. There is no need to explain the whereto of the bread substance. Consubstantiation was rejected by Aquinas on the consideration that the host is to be venerated, and leaving the substance of the bread there would mean believers venerate a creature. Yet as Scotus noted, accidents of the bread are

129. See Adams, *Later Medieval Theories*, 266.

130. Adams, *Later Medieval Theories*, 268–69.

131. Scotus, *Op. Ox.* IV, d. 10, q. 4; see Adams, *Later Medieval Theories*, 129–30.

132. Adams, *Later Medieval Theories*, 243.

equally creatures.[133] Consubstantiation would not thereby imply idolatry. In the end, Scotus and Ockham gave their nods to the doctrine of transubstantiation only because it was official teaching of the Catholic faith. Even the champion of transubstantiation, Innocent III who affirmed the doctrine, admitted problems with surviving accidents of an absent bread substance, but did not try to solve them.[134]

In the end, Christ's body that is said to be present on the altar is a body in nothing but name. The way to make its presence more intelligible is either by regarding it as unquantified or by regarding its presence as the same as that of an *immaterial* substance such as an angel or soul. What is emphasized throughout the Aristotelian project is either the unquantified character of Christ's body or the immaterial way of his presence. The Aristotelian campaign to salvage the *material* body of Christ in the Supper has failed. Adams concluded that, at the end of the day, theologians had to give philosophically odd accounts of real presence. Making use of an Aristotelian framework, they had to appeal to ideas utterly "unAristotelian" to explain the presence of a body in a place without being extended in it.[135] As Chadwick put it well, the Aristotelian system is meant to be a system for speaking coherently about things in the world. To bring in Aristotelian physics was supposed to suggest that the body of Christ present on the altar, and any change that is involved, had analogy *in the natural world*. Yet it turns out that the presence of the substance of Christ, and the substantial change that is involved, have absolutely no analogy in the natural order.[136] The irony is that "the more Aristotle was called in aid, the less material this actuality became."[137] The list of philosophical obstacles of transubstantiation above is not to imply that they are unsolvable. But as Adams described it, it took nothing less than "*massive* efforts" by theologians to attempt to make philosophical sense of real presence.[138] What is clearly proved is that explaining real presence required Aristotelian theologians to go beyond Aristotelian physics. One

133. Scotus, *Op. Ox.* IV, d. 11, q. 3; see Adams, *Later Medieval Theories*, 148.

134. Chadwick, "Ego Berengarius," 442.

135. Adams, *Later Medieval Theories*, 238; see also Dummett, "Intelligibility of Eucharistic Doctrine," 241–47.

136. Chadwick, "Ego Berengarius," 417. As Guitmund also agreed, the Eucharist has no analogy in natural order. See his *De Corporis et Sanguinis Christi* 1.34 (Vaillancourt, *Lanfranc and Guitmund*, 119–21).

137. Chadwick, "Ego Berengarius," 417.

138. Adams, *Later Medieval Theories*, 255; emphasis mine.

may conclude that the Aristotelian crusade to salvage the body of Christ from mere symbolism has failed precisely *on its own terms.*

Luther's and Calvin's Alternatives

Luther's "Body"

Before giving a theological response, it is necessary to examine Luther's and Calvin's alternatives. Luther rejected the doctrine of transubstantiation and instead subscribed to a view of consubstantiation (even though he never used such terminology). To him, Christ's body and the bread simply coexist. His critique of transubstantiation in fact bears much similarity to Scotus's and Ockham's. Luther blamed the doctrine of transubstantiation for bringing a "Babel of a philosophy."[139] The notion, according to Luther, is neither logically necessary, nor proved by Scriptures or the early Fathers. As later medieval scholars did, Luther charged that the church would have avoided much philosophical trouble if they had allowed real bread to remain. They had to postulate a new substance created by God for the accidents of bread on the altar, all on account of Aristotle, who actually alleged, as Luther quoted him, "It is the nature of an accident to be in something."[140] Luther questioned how there is any difference between transubstantiation and "transaccidentation" in the first place.[141] If there is a danger of idolatry, and we do not want the substance of bread to be the subject in "This my body," the remaining accidents of the bread equally poses the same problems. If it is divine work after all, God can transcend any philosophical hurdle: "The Holy Spirit is greater than Aristotle."[142]

To Luther, it is beyond question that Christ's body and blood are present in the elements. The issue is simple: Christ could not lie. Repeatedly, Luther exclaimed, "we have before us the clear text and the plain words of Christ."[143] "There you hear it, expressed in clear German: he commands you to take his body and blood."[144] "Here stands the text, stat-

---

139. Luther, *Babylonian Captivity of the Church*, LW 36:32.
140. Luther, *Babylonian Captivity*, LW 36:31–32.
141. Luther, *Babylonian Captivity*, LW 36:33.
142. Luther, *Babylonian Captivity*, LW 36:34.
143. Luther, *Against the Fanatics*, LW 36:335.
144. Luther, *Against the Fanatics*, LW 36:348.

ing clearly and lucidly that Christ gives his body to eat."[145] "We have on our side the clear, distinct Scripture which reads, 'Take, eat, this is my body.'"[146] "We must remain content with [the words] and cling to them as the perfectly clear, certain, sure words of God which can never deceive us or allow us to err."[147] "Why it is necessary for Christ's body to be present in the bread. Briefly . . . if it were not so, Christ would be a liar in his words. . . . Since he says here, 'This is my body,' . . . his body must of necessity be present."[148] "My friend, God's Word is God's Word; this point does not require much haggling!"[149] Luther understood the presence of Christ in the Supper as analogous to Christ's two natures, which are present in him both in their entirety: "what is true in regard to Christ is also true in regard to the sacrament."[150] Because the divine coexists with the human Jesus, both intact in their natures, this must be true in the sacrament as well. The incarnation tells us the truth: God does not just set forth spiritual things, but connects the spiritual with what is outward and material.[151] This bread-Christ coexistence is not just his answer to the problem of real presence, but his explanations also have implications on the notion of Christ's "body."

In his later work Luther devoted much time explaining to his opponents how Christ's human body may be present in the Supper.[152] There are two main lines of approach. First, as Ockham did, he differentiated between different kinds of presence. He named three ways in which a thing can exist in a place. First, things can be in a place locally or circumscriptively. The thing and the space it occupies fit and correspond exactly in dimensive measurements. Secondly, things can also exist in a place definitively. The thing and space do not commensurate according

145. Luther, *Still Stand Firm Against the Fanatics*, LW 37:28–29.

146. Luther, *Still Stand Firm Against the Fanatics*, LW 37:33.

147. Luther, *Confession concerning Christ's Supper*, LW 37:308.

148. Luther, *Still Stand Firm Against the Fanatics*, LW 37:139–40.

149. Luther, *Still Stand Firm Against the Fanatics*, LW 37:26.

150. LW 36:35. See also Grumett's use of Christology to understand real presence. Grumett argued that Christ brought salvation precisely through matter, not by changing matter. Christ's human nature was never changed into divine nature, but remains intact. So standard Christology speaks consubstantiation. Supposing that the Eucharist is analogous, Luther strongly affirmed to wholeness of both natures of Christ. Transubstantiation, by contrast, would have been a monophysite Christology, i.e., just one nature. Grumett, *Material Eucharist*, 152, 182–84.

151. Luther, *Still Stand Firm Against the Fanatics*, LW 37:135–36.

152. Luther, *Confession concerning Christ's Supper*, LW 37:214–35.

to dimensions, yet the thing is still obviously present within the place. Examples include spirits and the devil. Lastly, something may be present repletively or supernaturally, i.e., present without relation to a measurable or circumscribed place. This is possible for God alone. Luther also called these three kinds of presence "corporeal," "spiritual," and "supernatural" modes.[153] He concluded that "Christ's body does not have to be present in a given place circumscriptively or corporeally, occupying and filling space in proportion to its size."[154] As a body present to the bread, Christ's body exists in the second mode. Due to God's power, all creatures are permeable to Christ's body. Luther challenged his opponents to prove that this is impossible to God's power. We must note that, however, according to the examples Luther gave, this means that Christ exists in the bread exactly in the way a spirit does. Interestingly, what is proved is *spiritual* presence.

Luther's second line of approach is by way of Christology. To Luther, Christ's two natures are distinct but not separate in the one person that he is. His humanity, while not itself divine but created, is nevertheless united with God as one person. The crux of the matter is Christ's single, indivisible personhood. His person is indivisible such that wherever God is, his humanity is present also. In his words, "wherever Christ is according to his divinity, he is there as a natural, divine person and he is also naturally and personally there. . . . But if he is present naturally and personally wherever he is, then he must be man there, too, since he is not two separate persons but a single person."[155] "Wherever this person is, it is the single, indivisible person, and if you can say, 'Here is God,' then you must also say, 'Christ the man is present too.'"[156] If there was one place in which God is present but not the man Jesus, then the person would have already divided. Therefore, Christ's body enjoys "a far higher, supernatural existence, since he is one person with God."[157] Luther went as far as admitting that Christ's body is present everywhere, even in stones, fire, and water, because God is lord over all things and fills all things. It is only that we may not seek him in these places but only where the Word said so.[158] As

153. Luther, *Confession concerning Christ's Supper, LW* 37:214–17, 222–23.

154. Luther, *Confession concerning Christ's Supper, LW* 37:216.

155. Luther, *Confession concerning Christ's Supper, LW* 37:218; also 229–30.

156. Luther, *Confession concerning Christ's Supper, LW* 37:218.

157. Luther, *Confession concerning Christ's Supper, LW* 37:221.

158. Luther, *Against the Fanatics, LW* 36:342. Later Luther also regarded the "right hand of the Father" as existing everywhere as well, taking the phrase to depict not

this stands, Christ's body is present also supernaturally, according to the third kind of presence that is reserved for God alone.[159] Luther denied confusing the two natures of Christ, stressing that he did not regard the divine as human. "We in turn raise and cry against them for separating the person of Christ as though there were two persons."[160]

However, as Duns Scotus already noted, Christ is not hypostatically united to the bread while his divine nature is to his human nature.[161] The analogy breaks down quickly. We may also stress that the bread is an object. The fact that God is incarnate in a human being is a far cry from implying that the divine would be incarnate in a dead object. While materiality is important, this does not mean that he would be present in a man-made object. This flies against the very logic of the Second Commandment. More importantly, for our purposes we note Luther's emphasis of Christ's body as necessarily *united with the divine*. In fact, at one point, he explained how Christ's flesh can be eaten without being torn by regarding it as *divine* and *incorruptible*.[162] Again, its existence has no analogy in the natural world. Does Lutheran coexistence affirm materiality? We have to resort to spiritual and even divine presence in the end.

Calvin's *via Media*

In 1529 Zwingli and Luther met to form a Protestant alliance against Rome but were unable to reach agreement on the last clause which was on sacraments.[163] While Zwingli insisted on a symbolic interpretation of Christ's words, Luther insisted that Christ's words must be held as they are. Zwingli, sensitive to idolatrous warnings from OT, was wary of ascribing God's saving activity to the created realm. On the whole, his platonic outlook is clear. He stringently distinguished between sign and reality. The bread and wine are seen as outward, material signs and can only signify what is real. To him, what is material can never bear the

some imaginary throne somewhere in space, but the power of God over all, which cannot be circumscribed. Luther, *Still Stand Firm Against the Fanatics*, LW 37:56–57.

159. Luther himself admitted Christ is in fact present according to the supernatural mode. Luther, *Confession concerning Christ's Supper*, LW 37:218.

160. Luther, *Confession concerning Christ's Supper*, LW 37:212.

161. Adams, *Later Medieval Theories*, 66.

162. Luther, *Still Stand Firm Against the Fanatics*, LW 37:130.

163. See Marburg Colloquy, LW 38.

spiritual. "The thing of which I am speaking [the reality of the Lord's Supper] is a spiritual thing, and has nothing to do with bodily things."[164] Most frequently quoted is John 6:63: the physical eating itself profits nothing.[165] God acts upon the inner person, leaving no mediating role for external elements. Zwingli's life efforts were to deny agency to the material sacraments. While Zwingli's dualism completely severed sign from reality, as John W. Riggs noted, it would be Calvin and Bullinger who provided what Zwingli lacked in connecting the sign and reality.[166] Calvin complained that Zwingli endeavored more to bring down evil than build what is good.[167] But Calvin agreed with Zwingli that the body of Christ is only in heaven. In his "Short Treatise," Calvin lamented the unfortunate outcome of Marburg, and saw himself mediating between the two. In his career he would attempt a middle course between Zwingli and Luther, although both sides found fault in him.[168] For our purposes, we will focus on his understanding of signs and how they relate to reality. We will show that, unfortunately, as he attempted a middle course between neo-Platonic dualism and real presence, in the end his theology is guilty of problems from both sides.

Calvin the Realist

Right at the beginning of his section on sacraments in the *Institutes*, he defined a sacrament by directly adopting the Augustinian notion of "a visible sign of a sacred thing," or "a visible form of an invisible grace" (*Inst.* 4.14.1). Yet while also adopting sign-*vs.*-reality language, Calvin devoted his life to defend a true (though not corporeal) communion with Christ that is the effect of the Supper. What drives Calvin's theology is not so much the question of real presence but the fact of our real communion with Christ, because this is necessary if we are to receive benefits from

164. Zwingli, *Commentary on True and False Religion*, 208.

165. E.g., Zwingli, *Commentary on True and False Religion*, 200–212; Zwingli, "Letter to Matthew Alber," in *Huldrych Zwingli: Writings*, 2:132–37; Zwingli, "Friendly Exegesis," in *Huldrych Zwingli: Writings*, 2:268–74 and 320; Zwingli, "Account of the Faith," in *On Providence*, 52; Zwingli, "Exposition of the Christian Faith," in *On Providence*, 285–86.

166. Riggs, *Lord's Supper in the Reformed Tradition*, 110.

167. Calvin, "Short Treatise," *TT* 2:196.

168. Calvin, "Short Treatise," *TT* 2:195–96. See also Rorem, "Consensus Tigurinus," 73; Gerrish, *Grace and Gratitude*, 3.

him.[169] Quoting John 6:55, Calvin affirmed that Christ's flesh is meat indeed, and his blood drink indeed, thus "in order to have our life in Christ our souls must feed on his body and blood as their proper food."[170] "Who does not see that communion of Christ's flesh and blood is necessary for all who aspire to heavenly life?" (4.17.9). This real communion with Christ's body and blood must be certain. "As the blessings of Jesus Christ do not belong to us at all, unless he be previously ours, it is necessary, first of all, that he be given us in the Supper, in order that the things which we have mentioned may be truly accomplished in us. . . . It is necessary, then, that the substance should be conjoined with these, otherwise nothing would be firm or certain."[171] To deny this true communication of Christ as is presented to us at the Supper would be to "render this holy sacrament frivolous and useless."[172]

To Calvin, the sacramental sign must be distinguished from the reality it signified. It is clear: "the breaking of bread is a symbol; it is not the thing itself" (4.17.10). One main reason he gave for rejecting transubstantiation was that it destroys the integrity of the Augustinian visible sign.[173] However, in a way, Calvin sided with Luther that the veracity of Christ is at stake. Christ cannot lie, and therefore the signs cannot be bare, empty signs, but what is figured must be truly given to us. "The bread is given us to figure the body of Jesus Christ, with command to eat it, and it is given us of God, who is certain and immutable truth. If God cannot deceive or lie, it follows that it accomplishes all which it signifies. We must then truly receive in the Supper the body and blood of Jesus Christ."[174] God effects what he promised: "that sacred partaking of his flesh and blood, by which Christ pours his life into us, . . . he also testifies and seals in the Supper—not by presenting a vain and empty sign, but by manifesting there the effectiveness of his Spirit to fulfill what he promises" (4.17.10). "Unless a man means to call God a deceiver, he would

169. See Canlis, *Calvin's Ladder*, 160–61.

170. Calvin, "Short Treatise," *TT* 2:170.

171. Calvin, "Short Treatise," *TT* 2:169.

172. Calvin, "Short Treatise," *TT* 2:170.

173. Calvin, "Short Treatise," *TT* 2:185–86; also *Inst.* 4.17.14. See McDonnell, *John Calvin, Church, and Eucharist*, 231. While his answer to the Lutheran accusation of holding empty signs was his notion of real communion with Christ and the idea that the sign is conjoined to reality, his answer to Roman Catholics was the distinction between sign and reality.

174. Calvin, "Short Treatise," *TT* 2:172.

never dare assert that an empty symbol is set forth by him. Therefore . . . there ought not to be the least doubt that he truly presents and shows his body" (4.17.10). "In his Sacred Supper he bids me take, eat, and drink his body and blood under the symbols of bread and wine. I do not doubt that he himself truly presents them, and that I receive them" (4.17.32).[175] Especially in his later correspondences with Lutherans such as Westphal and Heshusius who accused him of promoting a bare sign, he emphasized our true participation of Christ. In his *Best Method for Obtaining Concord*, he would use words with a certain abandon, such as that we are "substantially fed on the flesh of Christ,"[176] and even implied a legitimate use of Luther's phrases such as "that the body of Christ is given us under the bread, or with the bread."[177]

In his language, the visible sign "is not a bare figure but is combined with the reality and substance."[178] Repeatedly, he said that the sign is *conjoined* [*conioincte*] with the reality.[179] As noted by scholars, Calvin's view of sacramental signs and their relation to signified reality has a clear Chalcedonian overtone, consistent with his Christology.[180] Just as Christ's divine and human natures are distinguished without separation, so the same is held for a sacramental sign and its signified reality. They should be neither separated nor confused. It is a balancing act: "To distinguish, in order to guard against confounding them, is not only good and reasonable, but altogether necessary; but to divide them, so as to make the one exist without the other, is absurd."[181] In his consensus with Bullinger, he also invoked Chalcedonian language. He said, "though we distinguish, as we ought, between the signs and the things signified, yet we do not disjoin the reality from the signs" but we embrace the promises

175. Thus one may note that, in contrast to Catholic understanding, Calvin ascribed effectiveness not to sacramental signs themselves but to God.

176. Calvin, "Best Method of Obtaining Concord," *TT* 2:577.

177. Calvin, "Best Method of Obtaining Concord," *TT* 2:576; also "substantial partaking" in *Inst.* 4.17.19. See McDonnell, *John Calvin, Church, and Eucharist*, 244; Billings, *Calvin, Participation, and Gift*, 95; Rozeboom, "Calvin's Theology and Its Early Reception," 153.

178. Calvin, "Short Treatise," *TT* 2:171.

179. E.g., *CO* 5:439, 440, 441, 452.

180. Rorem, "Consensus Tigurinus," 73; McDonnell, *John Calvin, Church, and Eucharist*, 230; Gerrish, *Old Protestantism and the New*, 111.

181. Calvin, "Short Treatise," *TT* 2:171–72.

and receive Christ spiritually.[182] We may see him taking full advantage of the Chalcedonian distinction and non-separation. It allowed him to maneuver his position while conversing with diverse correspondents. On the one hand, his strong distinction between sign and reality allowed him to reject transubstantiation and consubstantiation, as well as to explain Judas's partaking of the Supper without receiving Christ. On the other, his joining of the sign and reality allows him to distance himself from Zwingli, and answer Lutheran charges of legal fiction and empty sign.

Striking a middle chord between Luther and Zwingli, Calvin (unlike Bullinger) understood that the sacrament actually *does* something. Rather than being a bare sign, he said, it is with good reason that "the bread is called the body, since it not only represents but also presents [*presente*] it to us."[183] "By the showing of the symbol the thing itself is also shown" (4.17.10). A verb that Calvin used frequently was *exhibere*.[184] "[The symbol] not only symbolizes the thing that it has been consecrated to represent as a bare and empty token, but also truly exhibits it, why may its name not rightly belong to the thing?" (4.17.21).[185] Yet, contrary to the Roman Catholic view, it is not that the sacraments themselves are imbued with power. It is the agency of the Spirit alone who works through them. God "does not feed our eyes with a mere appearance only, but leads us to the present reality and effectively performs what it symbolizes" (4.15.14).[186] Nevertheless, a persistent dispute Calvin had with Bullinger was whether sacraments are instruments of God. As Paul Rorem noted, Calvin referred to sacraments as instruments [*instrument*] as early as his "Short Treatise" (1540). He declared, "The bread and the wine are visible signs, which represent to us the body and blood, but that this name and title of body and blood is given to them because they are as it were instruments by which the Lord distributes them to us."[187] The Sup-

---

182. Calvin, "Consensus Tigurinus," *TT* 2:215.

183. Calvin, "Short Treatise," *TT* 2:171–72 (*CO* 5:439).

184. See Tylenda, "Ecumenical Intention of Calvin," 31–32, see also 43n19 about a possible influence from Bucer; Spinks, *Do This in Remembrance of Me*, 280, 289–90.

185. Jesus's referring to "this" as "my body" is akin to Scripture transferring the name of the Holy Spirit to the dove, the visible sign. Calvin identified the metonymy as grounded on the fact that the sign actually presents the reality to us. See especially his commentary on 1 Cor 11:24: *Commentary on the Corinthians*, 376–78; and "Consensus Tigurinus," in *TT* 2:219.

186. Gerrish noted that Calvin added this in 1559. *Grace and Gratitude*, 114.

187. Calvin, "Short Treatise," *TT* 2:171.

per is the "means [*moyen*] of which the Lord leads us to communion with Jesus Christ."[188] Since then, he had been debating with Bullinger about the use of such terminology.[189] He explained in his *Institutes*, "To their other objection—that the glory of God passes down to the creatures, and so much power is attributed to them, and is thus to this extent diminished—our answer is ready: we place no power in creatures. I say only this: God uses means and instruments [*mediis ac instrumentis*] which he himself sees to be expedient, that all things may serve his glory, since he is Lord and Judge of all. . . . He distributes his blessings to us by these instruments" (4.14.12).[190] His terminology was compromised in his consensus with Bullinger in 1549 only in order to form an alliance against military threat.[191] There, *organa* was used instead of *instrumenta*.[192] What was presented was rather a sort of parallelism: it is said that the Lord "truly performs inwardly by his Spirit that which the sacraments figure to our eyes and other senses."[193] In a preface of the consensus, Calvin in fact lamented that more should have been affirmed in the document.[194]

Calvin the Platonist

Nevertheless, while Calvin's theology aimed to be a *via media* between the realist Luther and the symbolist Zwingli, it has a predominantly neo-Platonist language. As many commentators have noted, Calvin's

188. Calvin, "Short Treatise," *TT* 2:166.

189. Rorem, *Calvin and Bullinger*, 7. Rorem, "Consensus Tigurinus," 75. See the correspondences between Calvin and Bullinger in *CO* 7:693–16.

190. Rorem noted that, however, Calvin did not explicitly use the more commonly used phrase "means of grace." *Calvin and Bullinger*, 33.

191. Rorem, *Calvin and Bullinger*, 29. Rorem, "Consensus Tigurinus," 80.

192. Rorem, *Calvin and Bullinger*, 43. Rorem translated *organa* as "implement" instead of "instrument," respecting the different terminology used compared to the Calvin-Bullinger correspondences earlier. However, in the common translation in *Tracts and Treatises* by Henry Beveridge, it is still translated as "instrument." See *TT* 2:216.

193. Consensus Tigurinus, *TT* 2:214.

194. In his later personal letter, Calvin implored Bucer to bear the document "with a sigh." Rorem, "Consensus Tigurinus," 88–89. As Billings also noted, the irony of the compromise is that, after consensus, Calvin all the more emphasized true participation. Billings, *Calvin, Participation, and Gift*, 99. Confessions since the 1550s can be seen as an interplay between Calvin's language of instrumental sign, which offer the spiritual things they signify, and Bullinger's parallelism. See Rozeboom, "Calvin's Theology and Its Early Reception," 157–62.

understanding of sacramental signs is bluntly Platonist.[195] Kilian McDonnell identified that there is a basic structure of two realms: the physical and visible, and the spiritual and invisible.[196] As Julie Canlis noted, Calvin uncritically brought in Augustine's Platonic categories of inward *vs.* outward, invisible *vs.* visible, internal *vs.* external.[197] As Joseph Fitzer also remarked, Calvin was a faithful disciple of Augustine and Augustine was a frank Neo-Platonist.[198] Despite Calvin's affirmation that the sacramental sign is an instrumental sign that is conjoined to the reality it signifies (through the power of the Holy Spirit), it is a Platonic sign nonetheless. To Calvin, a sacramental sign is a sign by virtue of its analogous character.[199] The idea is Platonic in that the material world in general is seen as an image and analogy of spiritual, invisible things. "The earthly sign corresponds to the heavenly thing," according to Calvin (4.17.15). "The signs are bread and wine, which represent for us the invisible food that we receive from the flesh and blood of Christ" (17.1). "From the physical things set forth in the Sacrament we are led by a sort of analogy to spiritual things" (17.3). Because bread and wine nourish, he reasoned, Christ's body and blood must be also for nourishing our souls. As Sue Rozeboom noted, this notion of a sacrament as image and figure was already prominent in Calvin's earliest exposition in 1536, and was never edited out in later *Institutes*. It is foundational to the purpose of sacraments for Calvin.[200] Gerrish also remarked that it is hardly too much to say that Calvin's entire sacramental theology lies in his doctrine of signs.[201]

Given this basic dichotomy of image and reality, Calvin urged that we must not halt at the physical signs, but must lift our minds above to the spiritual, intellectual reality (e.g., 4.14.5). The overall shape of his Eucharistic theology is one of ascent. Calvin agreed with Zwingli that the body of Christ, as a true finite human body, cannot be everywhere but as Scripture tells us is only in heaven until he returns. The Holy Spirit, then, overcomes this spatial separation by lifting our souls and uniting

195. E.g., McDonnell, *John Calvin, Church, and Eucharist*, 33–38; Canlis, *Calvin's Ladder*; Fitzer, "Augustinian Roots of Calvin"; Oliver, "Eucharist before Nature and Culture."

196. McDonnell, *John Calvin, Church, and Eucharist*, 34.

197. Canlis, *Calvin's Ladder*, 165.

198. Fitzer, "Augustinian Roots of Calvin," 90–92.

199. *Inst.* 4.17.1, 3, 10, 14; also Calvin, "Second Defense to Westphal," *TT* 2:250.

200. Rozeboom, "Calvin's Theology and Its Early Reception," 149–50.

201. Gerrish, *Old Protestantism and the New*, 111.

them with the body and blood of Christ (4.17.10). Thus, while Calvin laid his emphasis on our real communion with Christ through the signs, this communion takes place specifically and only in heaven, an invisible realm, not in the sensory world here. "We must always raise our thoughts on high, and *there* seek our Redeemer."[202] "By his descent to earth, he has prepared an ascent to heaven for us" (4.17.2). "It is God's plan . . . to lift us to himself" (17.15) "We are lifted up to heaven with our eyes and minds, to seek Christ *there* in the glory of his Kingdom" (17.18). Calvin quoted Augustine that "visible sacraments were instituted for the sake of carnal men, that by the *steps* of sacraments they may ascend from things discernible by the eyes to those understood" (4.19.15).[203] Those who are assisted by the signs "shall climb . . . step by step from earth to heaven."[204] Even Calvin himself asked, "why do we repeat the word 'ascension' so often?" (4.17.27). Interestingly, to Calvin, visible signs are not empty but through them God truly effects what is signified. Yet what is effected is precisely our minds being drawn *away* from the visible signs. Although Calvin's *via media* assigns certain value to material signs, they have value precisely in lifting our hearts *away from* the physical here and now.

While a real participation with Christ in the Supper can be seen as an antidote to a mere symbolism, this participation is, unfortunately, a participation in the invisible realm. As Fitzer put it well, "The real [for Calvin] is, of course, the heavenly Neo-Platonic really real—not the empirical real of a later age."[205] Reality lies in heaven, the invisible realm, not in the material realm. It is questionable whether such a Platonic participation can be helpful in affirming materiality. Overall, in Calvin's Eucharistic theology there is more than just a sign-reality distinction, but also a clear suspicion of the sensory world. The world of elements are repeatedly described as "corruptible."[206] It is clear that, for Calvin, the emphasis on ascent was for Calvin an antidote to adoration of elements.[207] We are constantly told to fix our mind not on things here, but only to

202. Calvin, "Short Treatise," *TT* 2:187.

203. The phrase is "ladder of sacraments" in the Henry Beveridge's translation of the *Institutes*.

204. Calvin, "Second Defense to Westphal," *TT* 2:250.

205. Fitzer, "Augustinian Roots of Calvin," 95.

206. E.g., Calvin, "Short Treatise," *TT* 2:187, 191, 197–98; *Inst.* 4.17.4, 12, 14, 16, 19, 20.

207. Canlis, *Calvin's Ladder*, 159. See Calvin, "Short Treatise," *TT* 2:193, 197–98.

things above.[208] In a strong anti-materialist tone, the visible sacraments are seen as themselves less than necessary but are only concessions to our weak, bodily nature. The reality of sacraments is "figured to us by visible signs, according as our weakness requires,"[209] "best adapted to our small capacity" (*Inst.* 4.17.1), and, again, "according to our feeble capacity" (17.11). There is a sense that our bodily, sensory nature is unfortunate.[210]

In the end, Calvin's theology fails to deliver what a realist approach aims to materialize: namely to articulate Christ's bodily presence in the *current* natural world, and an affirmation of the material world.[211] Although Calvin affirmed the specificity of Christ's body, what is highlighted is the elevation of our hearts and souls to heaven to be nourished by it. He acknowledged that "the communion which we have with the body of Christ" has little analogy in the natural world: it "is a thing incomprehensible, not only to the eye but to our natural sense."[212] What is stressed is its incorporeal and inward presence to us. As Simon Oliver argued, in Calvin's understanding Christ is not present to and in the natural world. The natural world is at most to mimic our souls' mysterious union with Christ, and does not itself take part in this union. The strong emphasis is instead on our hearts being lifted, as if to escape the natural, corporeal world. Strictly speaking Christ has nothing to do with the current affairs of the world and its future. Unfortunately, a foundation is laid for the spiritualizing of religion, bracketing God out of the secular, political world.[213] One may even add that, under Calvin's framework, both the

208. E.g., *Inst.* 4.14.5; 4.17.29; Calvin, "Short Treatise," *TT* 2:197–98. Consensus Tigurinus, *TT* 2:215, 219; Calvin, "Second Defense to Westphal," *TT* 2:280, 296; Calvin, "Last Admonition," *TT* 2:443; Calvin, "Best Method of Obtaining Concord," *TT* 2:579.

209. Calvin, "Short Treatise," *TT* 2:171–72.

210. Gerrish's understanding is that signs for Calvin are "gracious concessions to our physical nature." Gerrish, *Grace and Gratitude*, 107; see also Canlis, *Calvin's Ladder*, 170; Fitzer, "Augustinian Roots of Calvin," 73. Overall, Calvin's language also includes the need of our souls to be nourished by Christ for immortality, and he used prison language to speak of our souls in our bodies. See McDonnell, *John Calvin, Church, and Eucharist*, 33.

211. Grumett, *Material Eucharist*, 291.

212. Calvin, "Short Treatise," *TT* 2:171.

213. Oliver, "Eucharist before Nature and Culture," 344–47. Oliver argued that transubstantiation instead is able to uphold the integrity of nature by not forcing it to mimic, and by transforming nature, allowing nature to participate in the divine. However, in transubstantiation, nature is no longer itself. It involves nothing less than a mysterious separation between substance and accidents. There is no analogy of such

Second Person and Third Person come to the world only to raise our souls to heaven.

There are many strengths in Calvin's account. He is credited for moving the medieval Eucharistic debate away from a preoccupation with Christ's presence in the Supper to our salvific participation in Christ. Calvin's theology makes it plain that the only bodily presence of Christ is in heaven, avoiding the need for use of metaphysical categories such as substance and accidents. It affirms Christ's body as a localized body with its specificity. The human is thus not abolished. Calvin's understanding of the presence of Christ also does not require creaturely substance to be changed into something it is not.[214] In other words, creaturely nature is allowed to participate *as itself* in the eternal life of Christ.[215] Also, unlike Zwingli's theology which tends to emphasize the past, Calvin's emphasizes a continued, present communion with Christ.[216] Finally, it has also been highlighted that the Reformed emphasis of the Holy Spirit as the sole agent of grace in the Supper is an important move. It is a notable antidote to the traditional and Tridentine stress on *ex opere operato*, which unfortunately stresses a depersonalized causal power of the objective rite itself, as well as a supernatural power ascribed to priests (hence to church structure).[217] The Reformed emphasis of the inward and the spiritual redirected the central concern and reoriented the location of power.

Nevertheless, while Calvin tries to secure an instrumental sacramental sign, avoiding mere symbolism, his theology not only fails to question neo-Platonic dualism, it strongly reinforces it.[218] The overall sign-*vs.*-reality framework that it presupposes is one that fundamentally dichotomizes the visible and physical *versus* the invisible and spiritual, viewing the former negatively, and hailing the latter to be more real. Material nature is seen as outward representations of something more real in *another* realm. Visible things are given to us primarily in light of our

---

change outside the church walls, and this transformation is metaphysical. Salvation calls for more than just metaphysical change.

214. See his own observation in "Short Treatise," *TT* 2:187.

215. Canlis, *Calvin's Ladder*, 161.

216. See discussion in Hedges-Goettl, "Body Is Missing," 53–81.

217. See, e.g., Carvalhaes, *Eucharist and Globalization*, 82–92; Torrance, "Paschal Mystery of Christ," 124.

218. As Torrance noted, Protestantism in general is never able to overcome the neo-Platonist dualism in the fabric of western theology. Torrance, "Paschal Mystery of Christ," 127–31.

feeble, even pitiful, sensory bodies. The persistent emphasis is to move beyond the visible to the invisible. This is hardly affirming the material world.[219] McDonnell concluded that Plato would have recognized Calvin as a true disciple.[220]

The Eucharist as Historical: A Theological Response

Joseph Fitzer has remarked interestingly: whether one chooses a neo-Platonic or Aristotelian interpretation of the Eucharist depends on whether one thinks that Christ's ascension or annunciation, i.e., his departure from or incarnation in the fleshly world, is the archetypal Christian symbol.[221] Theologians are right to react against any neo-Platonic doctrine of the Eucharist that dichotomizes and prioritizes the invisible over the visible, and the spiritual over the material. It is necessary for the church to rethink the long tradition that sees the Eucharistic elements as fundamentally visible "signs" that point to some *other* signified, invisible, spiritual reality. The tendency is anti-materialist symbolism. Even when one emphasizes that God truly effects through the signs a real communion with Christ, as we see in Calvin, the tendency is to juxtapose heaven and earth and turn our backs to the world. Calvin, conscious to avoid idolatry, constantly urged that one must turn one's mind away from the physical elements towards Christ. This is a valid concern. But surely, such "ascent" is already inevitable in the neo-Platonic framework that is presupposed, which assigns little value to the material world. This is not to mention that, in the first place, Platonism is pagan philosophy. The dichotomy between visible things and invisible reality does not appear in scriptural texts that teach the Eucharist. The gospel is a gospel to the created, visible world *here*: peace on *earth*. As the angels best expressed to the disciples at Christ's ascension: "Men of Galilee, why do you stand looking up toward heaven?" (Acts 1:11). This question directs to all neo-Platonist outlooks of the gospel. The church is sent into the world. Even Jesus, who ascended, will return: this Jesus "will come in the same way as

219. Grumett who argued for a deeper connection between the Eucharist and the doctrine of creation and Christ's incarnation, saw that it is necessary for the material order to be transformed by Christ. He argued that Calvin's Eucharistic understanding, characterized by the spiritual ascent, must be balanced by the descent present in the rest of his theology. Grumett, *Material Eucharist*, 284–85.

220. McDonnell, *John Calvin, Church, and Eucharist*, 36.

221. Fitzer, "Augustinian Roots of Calvin," 96.

you saw him go into heaven." The church needs a theology of the Eucharist that does not presuppose neo-Platonic dichotomies, or any need to "ascend" to heavenly realms in disregard of the material world.

However, a realist solution that emphasizes a real presence of Christ's body and blood, especially an Aristotelian correction that employs the notion of substance, fails to establish what it claims, namely a bodily presence of Christ in the physical elements. After much mind-boggling metaphysics, in the end it has to go beyond what is philosophically available and shows only a supernatural presence of Christ. Instead of emphasizing a *human* body that is with us, in the end what it explains and emphasizes is some accident-free *substance*. To quote Chadwick again, "the more Aristotle was called in aid, the less material this actuality became."[222] More devastatingly, the body of Christ that is said to be present has absolutely no analogy with our bodies, or other physical bodies. It is a body in nothing but name. What has resulted in an Aristotelian approach is instead a total dissimilarity between Christ's body and ours. This approach often emphasizes the parallel example of the miracle of Christ's virgin birth. Yet, if that was so, there would have been no need to call in metaphysics in the first place. The Aristotelian approach is right to counteract neo-Platonic anti-materialism, and point to the need to affirm divine presence in, and transformation of, the created material world.[223] The worry that a less emphasized presence of Christ's body in the Supper would devalue the material created world in theology is a valid worry. Yet, unfortunately, the traditional focus on Christ's presence in the elements makes the issue one about material *objects*. Our focus has been turned to objects. The focus is, sadly, on Christ's presence in relation to static dead objects of the bread and wine and the individual believer's contact with these objects. Eucharistic theology then at most affirms Christ's presence in relation to, and transformation of, the objects on the table (in the case of transubstantiation, strictly speaking it only touches the substance and not even the accidents of objects). We only get metaphysical transformation, not the ethical or sociopolitical transformation that is needed in the sinful world.[224] Just as unfortunately, the endeavor to affirm the presence

222. Chadwick, "Ego Berengarius," 417.

223. E.g., in the arguments of Grumett, *Material Eucharist*, and Oliver, "Eucharist before Nature and Culture."

224. The needed transformation is not in the bread or wine, but in the community. We need a social change, not a physical one. See Barth, *Rediscovering the Lord's Supper*, 41; also Segundo, *Sacraments Today*, 14–15, 51.

of Christ's body and fitting it into philosophical systems that apply to all objects in the end only emphasizes Christ's body as an *object*, as opposed to a subject. The preoccupation with Christ's static presence here and now turns our focus away from the interpersonal dynamics of his body in history. As T. F. Torrance pointed out, the notion of real presence envisions Christ's presence in a depersonalized, physio-causal way. Construed spatially apart from a historical sense, it becomes a static, rigid presence. What is lacking is a notion of a dynamic history of the *personal* Christ, as well as an eschatological perspective. Specifically we must speak about the *person* Jesus Christ who was crucified but now risen and glorified.[225] The church needs a theology of the Eucharist that emphasizes the human person Jesus who, as a bodily *subject*, is with us and has full analogy with us. His presence and transformation should concern the world at large, in which we sin and need redemption, not merely the world of objects.

The root of the problem of real presence is threefold. In the first place, it ignores the Jewish Passover and covenant context of the Last Supper, and seeks only a literal interpretation of Christ's words. Ironically, as we have discussed in the last chapter, what is shocking and therefore significant in Christ's institution of the new meal is the *absence* of a lamb in the new Passover as well as *absence* of blood in future celebrations of the covenant. These are absent because the Passover and the covenant have been *fulfilled*. Second, while it is right to reject a mere symbolism and to uphold Christ's physical body and the physical world with uttermost importance, the concern for real presence wrongly assumes that we should be concerned with the body of Christ in its sheer physicality at any point in time and space. Rather, we are concerned with Christ's body as the body of a *fellow human being* who lived in empirical history, who walked on earth, as a Nazarene Jew living under Roman occupation, who ate, slept, preached, touched lepers and attended weddings (even secretly helped!), who died on the cross, rose on the third day and ascended to heaven. We are interested in *this* body of Christ. We need not worry about Christ's body as some thing or "substance" that is supposed to fit (or not fit!) in philosophical systems at times when he is not walking on earth. Precisely as a real human body, Jesus walked the earth only for a finite time, as all other human bodies do. His body does not appear everywhere in any time—such a thing would *not* be a human body. It would have no analogy with the human bodies which Christ redeems. It would

225. Torrance, "Paschal Mystery of Christ," 124–25.

be something utterly peculiar. Our concern is not so much the characteristics of "bodies" as the fact that Christ *is* one of us. Also, Christ's body is important as a human *subject*, not in its objectivity. Christ's body should have analogy not just with objects but with other human beings as cultural, sociopolitical subjects. When we affirm the importance of the material world, it is the dynamic, sociopolitical world in which we live that is important, not the world of objects and their metaphysics. It is in the sociopolitical world that we sin and need salvation. It is Christ's presence in the sociopolitical world—with diverse manifestations of cultures, human interactions, politics—that is important. And he was indeed present to our sociopolitical world in the first century in Palestine. Ironically, it is the belief that Christ's body could be daily present on altars everywhere that would diminish the significance of his incarnation in history—such presence could take place with or without the Son's incarnation *as Jesus of Nazareth*. The question of real presence renders Christ's presence in human history superfluous.

Third, while real presence affirms that the created material world is important, it wrongly rejects spiritual presence. Precisely the empirical world is so important that Christ sent the Holy Spirit to be present to and work in *this* world. If we already have Christ now, why did he send us the Holy Spirit? When we reject theories that see the Supper as merely symbolic and spiritual, the issue is the need to affirm the created physical world, because the Augustinian tradition wrongly assumes a Platonic outlook that disregards the material, sensible world. Yet rejecting this Platonic dichotomy does not mean we diminish the importance of the Holy Spirit. The problem is the philosophy that pits the spiritual against the physical; the problem is *not* the Holy Spirit. The Holy Spirit is not against the material world! He was precisely given to the world! The Aristotelian correction to Platonic dichotomy wrongly infers that Christ, before his return, is present solely through the Holy Spirit is the problem. But there is nothing wrong in holding that Christ is only present through the Holy Spirit—the Third Person of the Trinity—here and now. There is no need to throw the baby (spiritual presence) away with the bathwater (Platonic dichotomy and the debasing of materiality). Christ sent his Spirit in order to be with us. His presence is just as real through his Spirit. Indeed, it is more real than some (unexplainable) metaphysical substance!

For these reasons, it will be helpful for theologians to rethink even the very question of real presence. It is not just that philosophical attempts to make sense of Christ's bodily presence have been futile, but there is much loss. In the focus of what the bread and wine may symbolize or contain, the issue becomes one that concerns things on the table, instead of what God and the people are doing. As Peter Leithart complained, the history of Eucharistic theology has for too long "zoomed in" onto the Eucharistic table, and neglected actions around the table.[226] Indeed, the concern for real presence intensifies this "zooming in," because the miracle is in the elements on the table. The preoccupation with real presence in the elements and how it is possible has distracted theologians from inquiring more about the faith community and what they do in the world. As we will see in the next chapter, we have lost a Christ who dined *with* his people. At the end of the day, Christ's body has become an object to be analyzed, instead of a fellow personal subject as one of us. A real presence would render Christ's presence in human history superfluous. In the first place, as we have shown in the previous chapter, the question arose in disregard of the Passover and covenant context of the Last Supper. In addition to losing a dynamic perspective of the person of Christ, the story of liberation of the oppressed and God's triumphant fulfillment of the Passover are also lost. These have been turned instead into armchair metaphysics. Christ's renewed covenant and call to us to obey his commandments has completely vanished into the background. One must ask: in all the traditional preoccupation with real presence, where is the covenant? Where is the church that is called to be a covenant partner and do Christ's work in the world beyond the Eucharistic table? Furthermore, one must also ask: why did Christ send the Holy Spirit at Pentecost if he is supposedly bodily accessible in the Eucharist? And why do we wait for his physical return? The question of real presence must be reevaluated.[227] Just as after the resurrection the angels questioned the disciples why they kept looking upwards to heaven, Jesus said to Mary, "Do not cling to me . . . but go to my brothers and say to them, 'I am ascending to my Father and your Father, to my God and your God'" (John 20:17, ESV).[228]

226. Leithart, "Way Things Really Ought to Be," 159.

227. In the last chapter we will also look at the sociopolitical implications of real presence. If Christ is said to be present upon consecration by clergy, the notion sees the church as possessor and depository of privileged grace, and the masses are to come to clergy for grace. The result is hierarchy and the tendency is to fence off those we deem "unworthy" from approaching the Lord's table.

228. My concerns over real presence also apply to other theories as long as they do not depart from the traditional preoccupation with Christ's relation to the table elements, for example the notion of transelementation (see, e.g., Hunsinger, *Eucharist and Ecumenism*, 47–92.).

We have examined Luther's notion of real presence. His own explanation of the coexistence between Christ's body and the bread in fact implicates an incorporeal presence. The more he tried to explicate the Eucharistic presence of Christ's body, the more it is shown to be analogous to spiritual presence. Also, Calvin's *via media* unfortunately reinforces the neo-Platonism in Augustine. Physical signs, he insisted, are conjoined to signified reality, but this reality is in heaven, not in the world. Despite Calvin's emphasis on our real communion with Christ in heaven, he strongly juxtaposes heaven and earth, as well as the invisible and the visible, urging a flight from what is material. This was what invited an Aristotelian correction in the first place. Speaking of both neo-Platonic and Aristotelian interpretations of the Eucharist, T. F. Torrance said, "While they may be appreciated for the service they rendered in the past, they cannot be held to be binding on the universal Church as intrinsic extensions of the truth."[229] In fact, neither system is biblical. Biblical accounts of the Last Supper, by contrast, point not to metaphysical concerns, but to history, in particular the history of the Passover and God's covenant with his people. All four Gospel accounts name the Jewish Passover as the context of the Last Supper; all four Gospel accounts also reference either a new covenant or a new commandment.

One alternative to a neo-Platonic anti-materialist symbolism and to an Aristotelian real presence of Christ in the elements is therefore to rediscover a *historical* approach. A theology of the Eucharist must pay heed to the historical context of the Passover and covenant-making. It should avoid extrabiblical categories such as a Platonism or the Aristotelian notion of substance. It must no longer see the Eucharist as fundamentally physical signs that point to something else that is invisible, as if what is invisible is more real. It must also not assume any "Eucharistic supersessionism," eclipsing the old by the new, rendering what God has done in history superfluous. Instead, the Eucharist is God's fulfillment of his continuous work in history. It is the history of the dynamic between two parties—God and his people. It is the story between these two covenant partners detailed in the last chapter.[230] In short, Jesus fulfilled the age-old

229. Torrance, "Paschal Mystery of Christ," 125.

230. Thus my notion of a "historical" approach does not implicate historical Jesus research or critical historical methods that aim to reconstruct the life of Jesus. The "historical" is here contrasted with the "metaphysical" approach that almost all Eucharistic traditions presuppose. What I am challenging are the typical metaphysical and static questions that concern visible signs and the presence of Christ's body and blood

Passover by dying as the ultimate Passover lamb on the cross. The new Passover meal would need no more lamb on the table, but only bread is left to celebrate salvation. Just as God had commanded Israel to keep the meal to remember his saving act in Egypt, now Christ commanded the church to remember *him*. Jesus also fulfilled the covenant by himself living a life of perfect obedience when Israel had failed, and offering himself as the spotless covenant sacrifice. Just as God had led Israel to Mount Sinai to inaugurate a covenant with them, made possible because of the "blood of the covenant" from sacrifices at the altar, now Christ inaugurated a new covenant with his own blood, poured out for many for the forgiveness of sins. There would be no more sacrifices needed or blood to be shed after the sealing of the new covenant, but only wine. Christ's words, "This is my body" and "This is my blood of the covenant" (or "This is the new covenant in my blood"), were in fact his rewording of the climactic phrases said on the old Passover and at the old covenant meal to point to *himself*— "*my* body" and "*my* blood." Just as God had given Israel commandments to live out as a community fit for a covenant partner of God, Christ also gave his disciples a new commandment to love one another. This is a history of God and his people, once estranged as a result of human sin but, because of Christ and his work, they are in fellowship again. Once sinners were driven away from divine presence, but now they may come to the Son's table. Finally, God the Son physically, in flesh and blood, dined with the "twelve"—representative of the new people.

The meal remembers God's acts and celebrates a covenant relationship. It is not some items that signify invisible grace or may change into Christ's body and blood. Just as the Passover lamb on the table every year does not symbolize or change into the first Passover lambs that Jewish ancestors ate in Egypt, but the meal was commanded by God to be kept by each generation of Jews to define them as a delivered people, so the new Passover is not about some signifying items nor some miraculous change in those items. When God first instituted the Passover, in the "FAQs" given to Israel, it is clear that, when the question is posed about the meaning of the meal, the answer does not point to some symbolism,

---

in the elements. Instead I want to pose *dynamic* and *interpersonal* questions that concern what God has been doing in the history of his people. What is emphasized is that God is a *subject* active in history. For a tendency of modern theology to historicize the being of God, see, e.g., McCormack, *Orthodox and Modern*, 10–12; also his introduction to Kapic and McCormack, eds., *Mapping Modern Theology*, 10–20.

nor some miraculous change or presence in the food, but instead narrates *what happened* in the people's history (Exod 12:26–27). The meal *narrates* God's deliverance in the past which is continuous in generations to come.

On this point, Juan Luis Segundo made an interesting observation. When people demanded Jesus for "a sign from heaven," he refused (Matt 16:1–4). Instead, he told them to watch out for *signs of the times,* "refer[ring] them back from heaven to earth."[231] We are to focus on *what happens* in the course of history. Instead of "invariable" and "extraterrestrial" signs, Jesus referred us back to the "variable" and "temporal." In Segundo's words, there would be no "invariable, aseptic, deceitful signs of a celestial grace that does not enter history."[232] In particular, if there was any "sign," as Jesus answered the inquiring John the Baptist, it was that the blind could see, the lame walked, and the poor received good news, etc. (Matt 11:4–5).[233] It is specifically God's liberating work *in history* and *in the community.*

It has been lamented that "lower," spiritualized theologies that emphasize the commemoration of the cross and reject real presence restrict God's work mainly in the past. Such an outlook tends to preclude the possibility of Christ working in the current material realm.[234] But this is not the case. The meal narrates a history that defines the current community and is forward-looking.[235] First, the covenant meal means that forgiven sinners are now reinstated as God's covenant partners once again, receiving a new commandment from Christ to love one another. They are called into the world, to live as a new community. The new covenant relationship, as all relationships do, is a commitment. It defines who we are and looks to the future. In particular, the church is called to love, and do his work in the world. This is related to the second point: Christ sent the Holy Spirit to the church. Christ is not confined to the past, nor to heaven, because he has sent *his* Spirit to be present and to enable the church to work in the present. Spiritual presence *is* Christ's presence on earth before he comes again. The book of Acts reminds us how the early

---

231. Matt 16:1–4; Mark 8:11–13; Luke 11:16; 29–32; 12:54–56. Segundo, *Sacraments Today,* 9. Segundo still saw the Eucharist as a sign that is distinct from its reality. Yet he rejected the idea that it points to some abstract, sacramental realm. Instead, it points to liberative work of God in history.

232. Segundo, *Sacraments Today,* 9.

233. Segundo, *Sacraments Today,* 24, 91.

234. See discussion in Hedges-Goettl, "Body Is Missing."

235. See "The Passover—Old and New" in chapter 2, 49–66.

church, after receiving the Holy Spirit, continued the ministry of Christ on earth, healing and proclaiming the good news. Christ is therefore not absent in the present world at all. In fact, such dynamic presence in relation to the community is more meaningful than metaphysical presence in relation to static objects. The call to the new community to love *directly* transforms the broken sociopolitical world, rather than just metaphysical transformation in dead objects. Third, the meal proclaims the Lord's death until he comes. Precisely we are affirming that Christ's physical body is important here and now—this is why we look to the future and wait for his physical return. Ironically it is the belief that Christ's body is already accessible now that would diminish the significance of his physical return in the future. If we already have him now, why wait?

In sum, instead of metaphysical categories such as sign *vs.* reality, or substance and accidents, it is more helpful to employ the historical categories of past, present, and future. It is also more helpful to see the embodied Christ as an acting subject instead of an object to be analyzed. In the past, God already foreshadowed his salvation in the Passover and the covenant with Israel, now God has sent his Son to fulfill both. Now the world looks forward to the ultimate consummation when he will return to judge and living and the dead, and be physically present with his people again.

It is a historical approach that truly affirms Christ's flesh and blood. It is God's incarnation in history, Jesus of Nazareth in the first century, who has full analogy with our bodies. As Scripture stresses, he could be seen, heard, and touched (1 John 1:1). His body in history would fit any philosophical system that is used to analyze bodies. If no substance can be separated from their accidents or qualities, for example in Aristotelian metaphysics, his body certainly fitted that requirement in the first century in Palestine. If bodies should have their quantitative dimensions commensurate with the dimensions of the space they occupy, his body exactly did in the first century in Palestine. Ironically it is the idea that his body should be accessible to believers timelessly and everywhere (and in heaven) that results in a "body" of Christ that can neither be seen, heard, nor touched, whose presence is analogous to that of an incorporeal substance. Unsurprisingly, such a "body" does not fit into available philosophical systems. In addition, a historical approach fundamentally sees Christ as a person and subject active throughout history. It sees a Trinitarian God accomplishing his redemptive work, with the Son incarnating to be one of us, sacrificing himself and rising to glory in heaven again, and sending the Holy Spirit to continue his presence and work. By contrast, the concern of a real presence in the Eucharist inevitably focuses on his body as an object and its metaphysics. In other words, in Christ we are concerned with a true human body—a free, social subject. Lastly, the anticipation of the future return of Christ's physical body affirms the importance of his materiality. Thus it is not that a historical approach does not value his flesh and blood. It merely questions whether at this stage of history we have direct access to his flesh and blood, when he has sent his Spirit to us and promised to return.

Conclusion

We have shown how the controversies in the history of the doctrine of the Eucharist may be seen as a head-to-head between Platonic and Aristotelian concepts of the meal. A theology of the Eucharist should exercise great caution in presupposing pagan philosophical frameworks. Since Augustine, the neo-Platonistic dichotomy between sign and signified reality always tends towards an anti-materialist interpretation. Yet the Aristotelian correction that aims to establish materiality of the Eucharist unnecessarily juxtaposes old and new sacraments, and fails to deliver what it aims to, namely bodily presence of Christ in the Eucharist. In the end, the "body" it proves has absolutely no analogy with created bodies. The focus also tends to be on the metaphysical make-up of a certain "body," instead of the sociopolitical world that needs the presence of Christ. Although Luther did not employ Aristotelian terminology, his own explanation of real presence proved to be analogous to incorporeal presence. Calvin's attempt to mediate between symbolism and real presence by emphasizing a real communion with Christ's body in heaven fails on both sides: the body with which we have communion can in no way be sensed, and his strong juxtaposing of heaven and earth, and invisible and visible, results in a regress back to neo-Platonism. We have highlighted certain presuppositions behind the concern for real presence. It wrongly assumes that it is a timeless physicality of Christ's body *per se* that we need, and that divine presence through the Holy Spirit is a problem. By contrast, Christ's body is significant because he is an embodied subject, who once walked on earth and has full analogy with every other human body, not as a timeless, insensible object. He ascended to heaven and sent his Spirit to continue his presence on earth. An alternative to symbolism and real presence is to rediscover the historical focus in the scriptural accounts of the Last Supper. Christ *fulfilled* the old Passover and covenant. The meal narrates God's acts of deliverance in Christ, who once and for all died as the ultimate Passover lamb. At the same time, the meal celebrates a new divine-human covenant relationship, which was sealed by Christ's own blood. A historical approach needs not presuppose pagan philosophy but instead respects the Passover and covenant context emphasized by the Gospel accounts. It opens up new perspective and questions, emphasizing Christ as a subject presiding *at* the table, instead of being symbolized or present on the table. Sinners, once driven away from divine presence, are now received *by* Christ at his table. The next chapter will examine this Christ-sinner table fellowship, over and against the traditional presupposition that we receive Christ's body and blood.

4

Eating *With*: God-Sinner Table Fellowship

And [Jesus] said to them, "I have eagerly desired
to eat this Passover *with* you . . ."
—LUKE 22:15

God became man in order that man may, not become God,
but may come *to* God.
—BARTH, *CD* 4/2, 106.

SITUATING THE SUPPER WITHIN historical instead of metaphysical categories compels us to look at it in light of God's dynamic relationship with humankind. The Passover to Sinai narrative invites us to read the Supper in temporal and relational categories, instead of only static, spatial categories. The Supper is an *event*. There is a before and an after of the meal. There was once alienation and enslavement because of human sin. But in history, God has avenged evil, and has spared his people by the Paschal lamb's blood, instructing them to remember this with the Passover meal. With sacrificial blood, he even brought them into his holy presence. God has made possible what was once impossible, namely an intimate fellowship with the unholy human race. This Old Testament narrative had its fulfillment in the person and work of Christ. His body was the ultimate Passover lamb, his blood the ultimate blood of the covenant. The way for sinners to be seated at the divine table is now cleared. Now the Last Supper, with the Son of God sharing the table with the twelve apostles, representatives of God's people, at the Passover and covenant meals, was the realization of this renewed fellowship. It is a homecoming. This chapter aims to present this shocking table fellowship between God and sinners, between the holy and unholy, as a primary aspect of the Supper that, I think, traditional Eucharistic theology has bypassed.[1]

In short, what is radical about the Supper is that we eat *with* Christ. This divine-human table fellowship was once lost but now graciously restored. Yet different Eucharistic traditions almost hardly take note of this table fellowship, but instead focus on the elements and speculate how we somehow *eat* Christ. Whether a tradition agrees with the real presence of Christ in the elements or not, the focus has always been on the elements on the table and their meaning.[2] All sides agree that, in the Supper, there is at least some sense in which Christ is eaten, whether it is physical (Catholic and Lutheran), spiritual (Calvinist), or merely symbolic (Zwinglian). Even Zwingli, who is often labeled a symbolist, later in this life allowed a sacramental and spiritual eating of Christ.[3] In the Reformed tradition, while Calvin rejected any carnal eating of Christ, nevertheless for him, there is a spiritual and real eating of Christ. A case needs be made against such *organic* language in traditional Eucharistic theology, and for recovering a focus on divine-human table fellowship. In other words, the Supper should be first and foremost about us being received *by* Christ at his table, not us receiving Christ. By "organic," I mean primarily that, as traditions have understood, in the Supper, each believer accesses the real or symbolic body and blood of Christ, focusing on the act of receiving and even ingesting of the flesh and blood of Christ, whether it is physical, spiritual, or merely symbolic. Such focus is one on the relation between the ingesting of the bread and wine and the believer's reception of Christ's body and blood (often understood to be for "nourishment" and "growth"). The organic language also extends to the general notion of the flow of some form of life or vital power from Christ to the believer, whether in an imagery of head and members, or

1. Some modern authors who have highlighted the theme of divine-human table fellowship in their treatments of the Lord's Supper do so especially in light of the table fellowship between Christ and sinners in Gospel narratives. These include Cochrane, *Eating and Drinking with Jesus*; Blomberg, *Contagious Holiness*; and Chester, *Meal with Jesus*.

2. Leithart, "Way Things Really Ought to Be," 159.

3. Zwingli, "Exposition of the Faith," in *Zwingli and Bullinger*, 257.

engrafting, or fountain.[4] I am contrasting such organic notions of receiving the body or life of Christ with an interpersonal notion of table fellowship with Christ. Instead of focusing on how we access the body and blood of Christ, *Christ receives us*, his enemies, at his table.

In this chapter I will examine the organic language in the Reformed tradition, in particular Calvin's utilization of it, and the possible motivations for it. I will detail the many dangers of the traditional organic language, including ethical and theological dangers, and how it has unfortunately sidetracked Eucharistic theology from the table fellowship that should be stressed. I will explain the centrality of divine-human table fellowship in the OT Passover and covenant meals, to which the Last Supper alluded. These will be followed by several sessions that serve as clarifications. What needs to be outlined is how we should understand our intimate participation in Christ, if not within an organic framework. Drawing from Reformed commitments, I will explain how our participation in Christ is also to be understood neither organically nor metaphysically but historically. Participation is concrete and relational, as participation in table fellowship and a life of obedience. For this I will draw from insights of Karl Barth as well as OT narratives of the Passover and Sinai. I will then explain a possible understanding of the Supper as a Eucharistic sacrifice, one that speaks of a joyful feast between God and humanity. I will also clarify the nature of the Supper as both divine *and* human action. Lastly I will explain the role of the Holy Spirit, whose presence is Christ's very presence here and now until he comes. Our table fellowship with Christ today is therefore spiritual, without demeaning such a bond, and without having to be lifted to heaven. We eagerly anticipate Christ's physical return.

Christ-Eating in the Reformed Tradition

Calvin stated outright in the chapter on the Lord's Supper in his *Institutes*, "the Lord's body was once for all so sacrificed for us that we may now *feed* [*vescamur*] upon it, and by feeding feel in ourselves the working of that unique sacrifice; and that his blood was once so shed for us in order

---

4. My notion of organic is therefore not akin to what John W. Riggs called metabolic, see Riggs, *The Lord's Supper in the Reformed Tradition*, 15. While Calvin surely does not believe in a metabolic eating of Christ, nevertheless for him the language of eating Christ and being engrafted to Christ for eternal life is organic.

to be our perpetual *drink* [*potus*]" (4.17.1).[5] Feeding and nourishing are almost watchwords for Calvin's Eucharistic theology. Examples abound even within one chapter:

> . . . as bread *nourishes* [*alit*], sustains, and keeps the life of our body, so Christ's body is the only *food* [*cibum*] to invigorate and enliven our soul. (*Inst.* 4.17.3.)

> . . . the chief function of the Sacrament . . . is to seal and confirm that promise by which he testifies that his flesh is *food* [*cibum*] indeed and his blood is *drink* [*potum*], which *feed* [*pascimur*] us unto eternal life. By this he declares himself to be the bread of life, of which he who *eats* will live forever. (4.17.4)

> None but the utterly irreligious deny that Christ is the bread of life by which believers are *nourished* [*nutriantur*] into eternal life. (4.17.5)

> As it is not the seeing but the eating of bread that suffices to be *nourishment* [*alimentum*] for the body, so the soul must truly and deeply become partaker of Christ that it may be quickened to spiritual life by his power. (4.17.5, my revision)

> . . . his flesh is *truly food*, and his blood *truly drink*, and by these *nourishments* [*alimentis*] believers are raised unto eternal life. (4.17.8, my revision; see also 4.17.7)

> To summarize: our souls are *fed* [*pasci*] by the flesh and blood of Christ in the same way that bread and wine keep and sustain physical life. For the analogy of the sign applies only if souls find their *nourishment* [*alimentum*] in Christ—which cannot happen unless Christ truly grows into one with us, and refreshes us by the eating of his flesh and the drinking of his blood. (4.17.10)

> . . . I here embrace without controversy the truth of God in which I may safely rest. He declares his flesh the food of my soul, his blood its drink. I offer my soul to him to be *fed* [*pascendam*] with such nourishment [*alimentis*]. In his Sacred Supper he bids me take, eat, and drink his body and blood under the symbols of bread and wine. I do not doubt that he himself truly presents them, and that I receive them. (4.17.32, my revision)

It comes as no surprise that, in his Eucharistic writings, Calvin drew heavily from John 6. The discourse on the Bread of Life is referred to a

---

5. All quotations of Calvin's *Institutes*, except otherwise noted, are taken from Ford Lewis Battles's translation, edited by John T. McNeill. For Latin, see *CO* 2:1002–33.

total of nine times in his chapter on the Lord's Supper in the *Institutes*,[6] when the Gospels' Last Supper accounts hardly received attention. The Supper as nourishment is in fact also the very starting point of Calvin's 1540 "Short Treatise": the loving God receives us to his household by baptism as children, and nourishes us to life. Yet he does not feed our bodies "with corruptible and transitory provisions," but to feed our souls on "better and more precious diet," which is the Word.[7] "Jesus Christ," Calvin continued, "who alone is our life, is given and administered to us . . . the only provision by which our souls are nourished."[8] His language is bluntest in his commentary on John 6:35. While clarifying that our nourishment by Christ's body is not carnal but by faith alone, Calvin nevertheless affirmed graphically, "we eat Christ."[9] In this "Best Method of Obtaining Concord," Calvin similarly argued that, as long as we remove the absurdity that Christ's physical body goes into the mouth and stomach, then we can affirm that we *substantially* (*substantialiter*) feed on the flesh of Christ, because we are truly united with him, made one with him.[10] Again in his commentary on 1 Cor 11:24, he stated that he did not doubt that Christ's body is really given to us to be wholesome food for our souls.[11]

It is important to acknowledge the motivation behind such organic language. For Calvin, the central concern of his theological corpus is our real union with Christ, on which his Eucharistic theology is layered.[12] The concern, against Roman Catholic polemic (and Osiander), is to show that the Protestant notion of justification *extra nos*, with the strong Reformed distinction between justification and sanctification, is not a legal fiction—it does not consist of only a foreign imputation of righteousness by Christ (see *Inst.* 3.11.11). Calvin's response is that the righteous are reckoned righteous by grasping Christ through faith. It is true that it is not

6. Battles's translation in fact adds twelve more John 6 references than the original chapter in Latin where Calvin quoted phrases from John 6 but did not explicitly reference, totaling twenty-one references altogether.

7. Calvin, "Short Treatise," *TT* 2:165–66.

8. Calvin, "Short Treatise," *TT* 2:166.

9. Calvin, *Commentary on John*, 250.

10. Calvin, "Best Method of Obtaining Concord," *TT* 2:577; for Latin see *CO* 9:521.

11. Calvin, *Commentary on the Corinthians*, 379.

12. See, e.g., McDonnell, *John Calvin, Church, and Eucharist*, 177–205; Billings, *Calvin, Participation, and Gift*, 19, 101–2; Garcia, *Life in Christ*, 2–3, 15, 34, 93–94, 151.

works righteousness (3.11.2). Being clothed in Christ's righteousness, we do appear as righteous in Christ. In addition, to those who ask "whether God leaves as they were by nature those whom he justifies, changing none of their vices," he answered, "as Christ cannot be torn into parts, so these two which we perceive in him together and conjointly are inseparable—namely, righteousness and sanctification. Whomever, therefore, God receives into grace, on them he at the same time bestows the spirit of adoption, by whose power he remakes them to his own image" (3.11.6). By being one with Christ, both justification and sanctification are ours. "We do not, therefore, contemplate him outside ourselves from afar in order that his righteousness may be imputed to us but because we put on Christ and are *engrafted* into his body—in short, because he deigns to make us one with him" (3.11.10). If Christ was outside of us, "all that He has suffered and done for the salvation of the human race remains useless and of no value for us. Therefore, to share with us what He has received from the Father, He had to become ours and to dwell within us" (3.1.1). Thus faith cannot look at Christ at a distance, but must embrace him, becoming one with him, and having his natural body truly communicated to us. Hence Calvin's well-known phrase "wonderful exchange": Christ takes our iniquities and mortality, and Christ's righteousness and immortality become ours (4.17.2).[13] Such an intimate organic language exactly funds Calvin's nourishment language in his treatment of the Supper because, by eating Christ, all that is his may be our own (4.17.2). In short, "Do we therefore eat the body and blood of the Lord?" Calvin affirmed, "I understand so. For as the whole reliance for our salvation depends on him, in order that the obedience which he yielded to the Father may be imputed to us just as if it were ours, it is necessary that he be possessed by us by making himself ours."[14]

Another need for such organic language is to respond to the Lutheran charge that, since Christ is not in the elements of bread and wine, they are therefore empty signs. As Mark Garcia noted, Calvin's response to the charge of fabricated presence was akin to his response to the charge

---

13. Calvin's notion of union with Christ is far more than an interpersonal fellowship, but, for him, Christians are to grow into one body with him. See his interpretation of the *koinonia* in his commentary on 1 Cor 10:16 (*Commentary on the Corinthians*, 335); also Gerrish, *Grace and Gratitude*, 74, 83. J. Todd Billings even argued that Calvin's understanding of union with Christ is very strongly an interpenetration and indwelling. Billings, *Calvin, Participation, and Gift*, 92–95.

14. Catechism of the Church of Geneva (1545), *TT* 2:89.

of legal fiction: we are indeed united to Christ, even though Christ is not physically present in the elements.[15] In fact, in explaining our spiritual eating of Christ for union with him, Calvin did not shy away from substance language: "in bidding us eat, he intimates that it becomes one substance [*substantiam*] with us" (4.17.3), even though elsewhere he was adamant that there is no mingling of substances between Christ and us.[16] During the Reformation, the Eucharistic controversy was a matter of life and death. There was, to say the least, political pressure for the Reformers, at times in the face of Roman forces, to find common ground with the Lutherans. The realist union language would distinguish their position from the symbolism of the more radical Reformers, by emphasizing that believers do have true communion with the body and blood of Christ. Thus we often see their eagerness to emphasize a real nourishment by Christ in their correspondences with their Lutheran counterparts.[17] Examples include many of the main Reformed confessions in the sixteenth century.[18]

No doubt, Calvin rejected any notion of deification in salvation. There is no transfusion of Christ's divine substance or righteousness into us (3.11, also 4.17.32). It is also clear that he rejected outright any carnal ingestion of Christ's body and blood. He devoted considerable time to rejecting the notion of *oral manducation* of Christ's body and blood (e.g.,

15. Garcia, *Life in Christ*, 168–70.

16. *Inst.* 3.11.5, 10, also his Consensus Tigurinus with Bullinger. See discussions of Calvin's ambiguous relationship with substance language in McDonnell, *John Calvin, Church, and Eucharist*, 232; Gerrish, *Grace and Gratitude*, 178–79.

17. See, e.g., Smit, "Calvin on the Sacraments and Church Unity."

18. That the true body and blood of Christ are represented and offered to us with the bread and wine; Christ himself is food for souls unto eternal life; our souls are by faith made to eat and drink Christ's flesh and blood (1534 First Confession of Basel, under the leadership of Oecolampadius). That the body and blood are truly received, and we do indeed eat the body, drink blood of the Lord (1536 First Helvetic Confession, by Bucer and Capito and submitted to Luther). In the Consensus Tigurinus agreed by Calvin and Bullinger (1549) in the wake of the Schmalkaldic War, they affirmed that in sacraments, signs and the things signified are not disjoined, but by promise we do receive Christ and his gifts. Repeatedly the notion of feeding and nourishment to everlasting life with Christ's body and blood appears in Heidelberg Catechism (1563, questions 75–79). That the Lord feeds us with his flesh, gives us his blood to drink, nourish unto eternal life, through the work of Holy Spirit; that spiritual eating of his flesh and drinking of his blood is necessary for salvation, although it is possible apart from the Supper (1564 Second Helvetic Confession, by Bullinger). Calvin's treatise against Heshusius also emphasized that we truly feed on Christ's body and blood ("Clear Explanation of Sound Doctrine," *TT* 2:554).

3.11.10; 4.17.5–6, 33).[19] For Calvin, the eating is not corporeal, as this this would be confusing between signs and the thing signified. As John W. Riggs correctly classified, Calvin's understanding of Christ's presence is non-metabolic.[20] Our partaking of Christ's body and blood, according to Calvin, is not by mouth or digestive system, but by faith (4.17.5–6). There is no physical mixing between Christ's body and ours. By faith, our hearts are lifted to heaven, where he is physically, to feed on his body and blood there. We partake of him purely by faith, and by this bond established by the Holy Spirit. Faith must be present, as the Holy Spirit causes us to truly receive, partake his body and blood. For Calvin, the spiritual nature of this bond is key to avoiding any "gross mingling of Christ with believers," which was Osiander's mistake (3.11.10; 4.17.32).[21]

Nevertheless, this spiritual nourishment is far from figurative speech. As is evident from the quotes above, this feeding of Christ's body and blood is most *real*. Riggs put Calvin in the camp of nonmetabolic realism.[22] For Calvin, the real feeding of Christ's body and blood was precisely the very counter-argument he had against Lutherans who charged that he had turned the sacraments into empty signs. The body and blood of Christ cannot be understood solely by the mind, but actually nourishes the soul to eternal life (4.17.19). His insistence that our communion with Christ's body and blood is real also accounts for his dispute with the Lutheran understanding of *manducatio impiorum* (4.17.40).[23] For Calvin, the unfaithful simply cannot partake in the union with Christ. This is why faith is indispensable. Calvin was also aware of the challenges raised by Zwinglians who held that what he was saying was contrary to reason. He admitted that a notion such as Christ's flesh as penetrating ours is not agreeable to reason, but is a mystery (4.17.9, 24). If the idea of spiritually feeding Christ's body and blood was merely figurative for Calvin, he would not have to insist that it is a mystery, of which he said that it is "too high a mystery either for my mind to comprehend or my words to express; and to speak more plainly I rather feel than understand it" (4.17.32).

---

19. Also *Exposition* to the Consensus Tigurinus, *TT* 2:239–44; "Best Method for Obtaining Concord," *TT* 2:577–78.

20. Riggs, *Lord's Supper in the Reformed Tradition*, 15.

21. See Canlis, "Calvin, Osiander and Participation in God."

22. Riggs, *Lord's Supper in the Reformed Tradition*, 15.

23. See also Garcia, *Life in Christ*, 168.

The idea of the Supper as primarily about nourishment is certainly not new in Reformed writings, but had already stretched a long history. When Aquinas, following Lombard, affixed the total number of sacraments at seven, these seven sacraments were specifically to be understood as analogous to the whole development of a Christian's spiritual life: generation (baptism), growth and strengthening (confirmation), *nourishment* (Eucharist), healing (penance), removal of remaining of sins in dying (unction), reproduction (marriage), empowering to administer sacraments (ordination).[24] This understanding was later dogmatically fixed by Eugene IV at the Florentine Council (1439). On the whole, the idea is that, in the Supper, believers primarily partake of Christ's body and blood. The focus is then *what* each believer ingests, and how (whether physically, spiritually, or symbolically ingesting Christ), instead of *with whom* each believer is eating.[25] Much of the history of Eucharistic theology has assumed that a table fellowship between the Son of God and sinners was not worth theologizing. The Reformers, including both Zwingli and Calvin, left this oversight unchallenged. Calvin, especially, whose theology pivots on a real union between Christ and believers, assumed that such a real union must take the form of some mystical, organic communion with Christ's body and blood. Not only is the Jewish, historical context of the Last Supper ignored, but this has assumed that a fellowship with the person of Christ does not suffice to be real communion.

Problems with Organic Language

The language of nourishment by Christ's body and blood is a dangerous one. The concept of nourishment is individualistic, and the concept of feeding on someone else's flesh and blood can only be abstract, mysterious and therefore ethically impracticable. Worse, focusing on nourishment does not only make us overlook the centrality of Christ-sinner table fellowship, but it *contradicts* this fellowship, as Christ is regarded as an object for our benefits. It is only a slippery slope before we fall into deification, being tempted to say that God became flesh in order to be part of us (not only in order to be with us). This defeats the purpose of his becoming flesh. The dangers also apply to the language of ingrafting.

24. Aquinas, *STh* III q. 65, a. 1.

25. Again, Leithart's complaint is spot-on in his "The Way Things Really Ought to Be."

(1) First, the concept smuggles in the tendency of individualism. Nourishment focuses on the satisfaction and growth of one's own body, and does not necessarily require an "other." Although one person may nourish another with food, nobody can be nourished or satisfied for another. Being nourished is not about being with another. At any rate, it can always take place without others. In Calvin's picture, each believer's *soul* is lifted by the Holy Spirit to feed on the body and blood of Christ in the heavenly realm (4.17.18). Presumably one soul can be lifted and fed with or without others. Even if we want to stress the nourishment of the body of Christ, i.e., communion with Christ, such nourishment still only takes place individual by individual. The idea that the faith community as a corporate whole is nourished by Christ's body and blood can only be a metaphor. Also, here the use of the concept breaks down: ultimately it is the ingesting of food, not the sharing of food nor the act of eating together, that nourishes. The notion of nourishment and spiritual growth has the tendency to draw focus only onto individual need and away from fellowship. And, according to the Platonistic tendencies in Calvin, spiritual feeding of Christ in the heavenly realm is the true reality. This means that our physical eating with others, here and now, is to be held as less real, at most a visible symbol of something else more real.

(2) The idea that believers grow spiritually by partaking and being nourished by Christ's body and blood suggests that something from Christ is passed to us. If as both Catholic and Calvinistic traditions claim the Supper (as a sacrament) confers grace, then grace tends to be seen as something to be imputed from Christ to us, passable from one subject to another. Bullinger effectively named this tendency in Calvin in his correspondences with him before agreeing to the Consensus Tigurinus. In his *Notes*, he rejected the idea that the Supper is an instrument that confers grace. He complained that, for Calvin, the Supper became an implement, a "flow-sluice or canal" through which grace is infused to us.[26] Yet this idea runs counter to the Reformed rejection of the idea that grace is infused in any sense, or some *tertium quid*.[27] The notion that grace is something that could be *conferred* or dispensed to us is in fact inherited from Roman Catholicism. Instead, grace speaks of the divine restoring of a broken relationship, unconditional and unworthy on our part.[28] As

---

26. Quoted in Rorem, "Consensus Tigurinus," 82–83.

27. See Calvin's own commentaries to Rom 5:15 and Gal 3:6.

28. See Barth, *CD* 2/1, 353–54. For Barth, grace is a gift only in so far as God gives himself as the gift, offering himself for fellowship with sinners.

Calvin himself rejected the notion of merit—that we have infused grace in us that merits God's love, the question may be raised as to why, in the Reformed tradition, we need grace to be conferrable at all.

No doubt, Calvin, along with other Reformers, denied that sacraments confer grace *ex opere operato*. From time to time he emphasized that, while God makes use of such means as instruments, grace is conveyed to us only because Christ attested so, not because such elements are tied to such gifts (4.14.17, and Consensus Tigurinus). Also, Calvin responded to Bullinger's challenge by denying he was referring to the Supper as crude channels that enclose grace, explaining that it is instead akin to the human voice that is an instrument of God's saving work.[29] Back in 1536, he gave the analogy that sacraments are like *heralds* that announce gifts, but themselves do not bring them.[30] However, Calvin's nourishment language does carry the tendency that Bullinger named.

If Calvin did not think that the Supper confers grace in the sense of dispensing it to us, he certainly held that eternal life is infused to us as we partake of Christ's body and blood. Calvin commented how everything that pertains to the growth of our souls is to be "compared to food which endure[s] to eternal life."[31] So he often directly identifies this "nourishment" as eternal life. His use of Cyril's analogy of Christ as the fountain of life is well known: "the flesh of Christ is like a rich and inexhaustible fountain, which *transfuses* [*transfundit*] into us the life flowing forth from the Godhead into itself" (4.17.9). "That sacred communion of flesh and blood by which Christ *transfuses* [*transfundit*] his life into us, just as if it penetrated our bones and marrow, he testifies and seals in the Supper" (4.17.10).[32] While there is no transfusion of Christ's flesh and ours, he "diffuses [*diffundere*] his own life into us" (4.17.32).[33] God the Father, for him, is the origin and fountain of life, while Christ as "the Source of life begins to abide in our flesh." He "quickens our very flesh in which he abides, that

29. Rorem, "Consensus Tigurinus," 83.

30. Gerrish, *Grace and Gratitude*, 12. As noted by Gerrish, in Calvin's career, he was in fact ambiguous with respect to his view on the instrumentality of the Supper. In 1539 he wrote that sacraments do not confer grace, while later in 1543, he added that sacraments do not confer grace of themselves.

31. Calvin, *Commentary on John*, 241.

32. I have used Beveridge's translation here. For both 4.17.9 and 4.17.10, Battles translated as saying that Christ "pours" his life to us, whereas the Latin is *transfundit* ("transfuses," CO 2:1008–9). The language is indeed organic. See also 17.18 and 17.32.

33. I have used Beveridge's translation; CO 2:1033.

by partaking of him we may be fed unto immortality" (4.17.8). It was as if incarnation in flesh was not enough: "He is not only life, inasmuch as he is the eternal Word of God who came down to us from heaven, but, by coming down, gave [*diffudisse*] vigour to the flesh which he assumed, that a communication of life to us might thence *emanate* [*promanaret*]" (4.17.8).[34] Calvin also frequently adopted Paul's analogy of the believers as members of the body of Christ (4.17.6, 9, 22, 34, 38).[35] As the head, then, Christ truly adheres to us in body and spirit. The picture is organic and intimate. In this "Best Method of Obtaining Concord," Calvin argued that, our eating of Christ nourishes us in the sense that he infuses his life to us, *just as* life flows from a head to its members.[36] Hence, for Calvin, the idea of feeding Christ is primarily about divine life flowing from Christ to us. As Thomas M. Lindsay explains, for Calvin, the issue of real presence is less in spatial terms than in terms of vital power. The presence of a substance consists in the immediate application of such vital power. So receiving Christ's body consists in receiving its vital force.[37]

Nevertheless, this notion of a flow of eternal life from Christ onto us is problematic. It is worth quoting him again: "inasmuch as he is the eternal Word of God who came down to us from heaven, . . . by coming down, [he] gave [*diffudisse*] vigour to the flesh which he assumed, that a communication of life to us might thence *emanate* [*promanaret*]" (4.17.8); "the flesh of Christ is like a rich and inexhaustible fountain, which *transfuses* [*transfundit*] into us the life flowing forth *from the God-head* into itself" (4.17.9). Calvin explained, borrowing from Cyril, that the flesh of Christ must be what gives us eternal life. Yet it of itself has no power, so it must first be endued with immortality for the purpose of being transmitted to us (4.17.9). Elsewhere Calvin would even say, "from the hidden fountain of the Godhead life was miraculously *infused* [*infusa*] into the body of Christ, that it might flow from thence to us."[38] Taking seriously the imagery of the fountain, the organic infusion of life,

34. I have used Beveridge's translation; *CO* 2:1008.

35. Interestingly, here Calvin also drew from Eph 5:30, which was primarily about mutual submission of husbands and wives, and 1 Cor 6:15, which is about individual bodies. He in fact referenced only once 1 Cor 12:12 which is directly about the faith community as the body of Christ (17.22).

36. Calvin, "Best Method of Obtaining Concord," *TT* 2:574–75.

37. Lindsay, *History of the Reformation*, ii, 59; referenced in Fitzer, "Augustinian Roots of Calvin," 82.

38. Calvin, *Exposition* to Consensus Tigurinus, *TT* 2:238; *CO* 9:31.

for Calvin, is actually twofold: from the Godhead to Christ, and then to us. This concept of a flow of divine life, especially "from the Godhead" to us, to say the least, goes against Reformed theology. It easily slips into deification. Moreover, there is a clear alternative to such organic language. This would be to say that Christ died so that the Father *gives* us eternal life, without there being any transfusion of life or vital force between Christ and us. It is *bestowed*. It is true that Calvin wanted to present the imagery of us being adopted into the household of God as his children. But precisely Calvin's imagery works this way as well: adopted children simply do not feast on the bodies and blood of natural children! They do not receive life from the natural children by transfusion either. Rather, we are made co-heirs and given the same *inheritance* (as the begotten Son, Rom 8:17). This latter understanding makes far more sense even borrowing Calvin's imagery of adoption. Precisely the process of legal adoption is needed because vital connection is lacking. Eternal life does not flow to us organically through ingestion or transfusion.[39] The organic language is redundant at best, and misleading at worst.[40]

In fact, Calvin's idea that divine life flows from the Father as the head of the fountain to the human Christ also runs counter to the Reformed denial of the Lutheran *communicatio idiomatum*.[41] Reformers deny that the divine attribute of omnipresence is communicated to the human body of Christ, such that the body could be present in, with, and under the bread while also in heaven.[42] However, for Calvin, immortal

39. Jonathan Slater points out that, "for Calvin, believers share in what is Christ's according to his human nature rather than his divine nature. The righteousness with which we are clothed in Christ is the righteousness that is proper to his human nature, and this righteousness is not transferred from his divine nature, but is the righteousness of his human obedience" (Slater, "Salvation as Participation," 41). Slater argued that when Calvin referred to divine immortality that is transfused to us, he only meant that the origin of the immortal life is divine, not its essence—we do not receive divine life. Immortal life is a gift from God ("Salvation as Participation," 42, 43, 55). Yet if this was what Calvin meant, this only shows that his analogy of the fountain and language of nourishment are misleading. In a fountain there is something substantial actually flowing continuously between the source and the recipient; and in nourishment (by Christ's body), what is nourishing (Christ) does become part of the eater.

40. Arguing against the notion that the life of a sacrifice is to be transferred to the offerer, Markus Barth helpfully highlighted the fact that, in the OT strict prohibition against consumption of blood, the rationale is explicitly specified to be because *life* is in the blood (Lev 17:14). Barth, *Rediscovering the Lord's Supper*, 93.

41. See McCormack, "What's at Stake?," 104.

42. Thus Keith Mathison is mistaken on this point, arguing that, in Calvin's

life is said to flow as in a fountain from the Godhead to the human body of Christ. If the analogy of the fountain stands between Christ and us, i.e., that immortal life is *transfused* from Christ to us (4.17.9–10), then this transfusion must also occurs "higher up" in the fountain, i.e., between the Father and Son. Indeed this is what he stated in his *Exposition* to the articles of the Consensus Tigurinus.[43] Clearly there would be a communication of a divine attribute (immortality). Indeed this was the language of his notion of "wondrous exchange" too—it is his *immortality* that becomes ours due to the union (4.17.2). As readers of Calvin would agree, for the Reformer, the union we enjoy with Christ is indeed never a communication of essential divine properties between Christ and us. Precisely this was his clash with Osiander's idea that we partake of the "essential righteousness" of Christ by a mixing of substances between the divine Christ and the believer (3.11.5–12). Yet his own organic language betrays him. As Bruce McCormack argued,

> It has to be said that it is hard to understand how a theologian who rejects all mixture of divine and human natures in Christ, who everywhere in his Christology laid emphasis on the thought of "two natures unimpaired after the union" [II.14.1] and who, on that basis, rejected the doctrine of a communication of attributes from the divine nature to the human nature as taught by the Lutherans . . . can now speak of the life flowing forth from the Godhead into Christ's human nature.[44]

The question is, McCormack asked, why would immortal life from the Godhead be infused into the human nature of Christ in the absence of all other divine attributes?[45] In the first place, there is a clear tension between the forensicism in Calvin's doctrine of justification and the organic rhetoric of his Eucharistic theology.[46] Surely, Calvin is right that we

---

theology, "partaking of the flesh and blood of Christ is necessary in Calvin's doctrine because it is how we partake of the divine life of God. . . . Divine life is communicated to Christ's human nature, and when we are united with Christ, it is possible for that divine life to be communicated to us" (Mathison, *Given for You*, 282–83). This would be bluntly contrary to the Reformed rejection of the Lutheran notion of communication of divine attributes.

43. Calvin, *Exposition* to Consensus Tigurinus, *TT* 2:238.

44. McCormack, "What's at Stake?," 104.

45. McCormack, "What's at Stake?," 104.

46. McCormack, "What's at Stake?," 103–6. On this issue, Mark Garcia holds a different view from McCormack. Garcia concluded that Calvin's doctrine of forensic justification is fully consistent with an intimate union with Christ (*Life in Christ*, 85–86).

do not absorb divinity. The union we have with Christ is purely spiritual. So the issue with his language of nourishment/ingrafting/fountain is that it obscures the nature of the gift, by hinting that something essential flows organically from Christ to our possession.[47]

At the outset, if Reformed theology is to be consistent in insisting that divine attributes are not infused to the human Christ in spite of the hypostatic union, then certainly there should not be any infusion of life from Christ to us, when we are not even in any sort of hypostatic union with him. Eternal life is *given* to us, not infused to us.

Zwingli also rightly challenged Calvinists on how the incorporeal spirit could feed on a corporeal body and blood. This is not to mention that eternal life is about the resurrection of the *body*, in which case it should be our body, not our spirit, which has to physically feed on the body of Christ in order to obtain this resurrected life.[48] Calvin's notion of spiritual feeding breaks down precisely where it needs to be useful, i.e., for our growth towards eternal life, which is the resurrection of the body.

(3) The idea that believers spiritually feed on Christ's body and blood makes our communion with Christ mystical. Calvin famously remarked, "it is a secret too lofty for either my mind to comprehend or

---

For Garcia, Christ's justification is made ours by the organic union. Justification, being divine acquittal, belongs only to those who are grafted in Christ through faith by the Holy Spirit. There is thus no union with Christ apart from by faith. Ultimately, Garcia understands righteousness of Christ to be both *extra nos* and *in nobis*, as, he explains, justification without sanctification would be tearing Christ into pieces (98). Our lives are patterned after his death and resurrection, yet only in light of our being engrafted to Christ (129). Thus it seems that, for Garcia, justification is forensic acquittal, yet the *way* it becomes ours is through an organic union with Christ. For Calvin, both justification and sanctification, though distinct, are effects of the union. McCormack agreed that Calvin did refer to justification and sanctification as both resulting from our organic union with Christ, yet precisely justification being both forensic *and* organic pose a tension. Indeed Garcia touched little on the use and implications of Calvin's organic analogies, e.g., Christ as fountain through which his benefits flow to us organically, and the imagery of engrafting is also certainly organic. If by faith we are united with Christ organically, there seems to be no need for a judicial acquittal. In addition, Jared Michelson's criticism of McCormack has also overlooked this point in McCormack ("Covenantal History and Participatory Metaphysics," 392–400). Michelson thinks McCormack was mainly worried that, for Calvin, our (ontologically ambiguous) union with Christ is logically prior to both justification and regeneration. Michelson did not mention that, for McCormack, the more decisive issue is that Calvin's language of the union is *organic*.

47. On this point, Calvin's introducing of the fountain analogy *just* where he was refuting Osiander's notion of essential righteousness is indeed odd (3.11.9).

48. Zwingli, "Account of the Faith," in *On Providence*, 53–54.

my words to declare. And, to speak more plainly, I rather experience than understand it" (4.17.32). The Supper is a "mystery so high and incomprehensible."[49] As such, it is difficult for the Supper to have direct bearing on our Christian life. Our communion with Christ should have implications for ecclesial communion (1 Cor 11:17–34). Calvin himself noted after expounding on how we participate in Christ's body: "Now . . . it is necessary that all of us also be made one body by such participation" (4.17.38). But if our communion with Christ is mystical, how should we model our communal life on such a communion? Despite being a lifelong advocate for ecclesial communion, and in spite of his lifelong pastoral and ecumenical commitments, Calvin nevertheless made the Supper primarily a mystery. For him, charity is the "third" and last use of the Supper, and occupies relatively little space in the whole chapter on the Supper (in 4.17.38 and 40, out of fifty paragraphs). This should not come as any surprise—how can the Supper be our act of charity if it is first and foremost a mystery? As Karl Barth noted in his criticism of traditional sacramental theologies that characterize sacraments as mystery, mystery can only be divine work, and eliminates genuine human action:

> If [a sacrament] were a mystery, if at root God were acting in the place of men [*sic*] and men in the place of God, this ethical significance could be ascribed to it only incidentally, more or less artificially, and fundamentally not at all. Calvin seems to be aware of this ethical meaning. But he could not establish or maintain it seriously.[50]

More specifically, if our communion with Christ consists in his giving his body and blood to others for nourishment, should our communion with one another take a similar form too? This would only be abstract and hardly helpful. How do I also give my body and blood to you? For example, Angel Méndez-Montoya, in his prize-nominated book *The Theology of Food: Eating and the Eucharist*, has insisted on the bluntest notion of believers eating and chewing Christ's flesh. Concerning the ethical application of this realism, he wrote, "As God *becomes* bread from heaven in order to nourish and constitute his own Body, so the members of the ecclesial community are called to nourish one another."[51] Yet precisely here is the tricky part: we do not *become* food and drink for each

49. Calvin, "Short Treatise," *TT* 2:166.

50. Barth, *CD* 4/4, 106.

51. Méndez-Montoya, *Theology of Food*, 150.

other. We can at most *offer* food. Even in the perfect love within the Trinity, we do not learn of the divine Persons becoming food for each other. If, according to Calvin, eternal life is infused to us by our being united to Christ as our head, would such analogy imply that our ecclesial union is a similar infusion too? This would be abstract.[52]

A basic challenge to Calvin's overbearing emphasis of the Supper as first and foremost Christ's offering of himself to be our spiritual food and drink, is how it could also be *our* act of charity. The Supper is said to confer grace, yet obviously we cannot confer grace. We can only be receivers of Christ's own body and blood, not offerers. So Calvin's first and third uses of the Supper actually contradict each other theologically. For something to be our act of charity, it must be that, first, we have to comprehend it; and second, we are able to be offerers too, instead of only takers. But this would mean the Supper cannot be primarily about feeding on Christ (even if only as signs, as Calvin insisted that they were instrumental in conferring grace). The traditional focus on receiving Christ's body and blood cannot be helpful ethically. In charity we should be givers of ourselves, not of someone else. It may be noted that a high view of the Supper, which sees the body and blood of Christ as truly being given for our nourishment, tends to understand that we participate not only in Christ's life, but also specifically in *his* act of giving his body and blood, as if humans can also have a part in this divine giving.[53] Surely, this is beyond what Calvin would allow.

In contrast to such notion of mystical feeding on Christ's body and blood, however, the idea that the Supper is primarily about interpersonal table fellowship is concrete and practical. It has immediate and obvious ethical bearing. We do not become food and drink for one another. Instead, we welcome one another to the table, even strangers and enemies. This is what God is doing: when the unholy is supposed to be driven away from divine presence, God in the person of Christ welcomed sinners back to his table, even washing their feet. According to the fourth Gospel, at the Last Supper Jesus taught his disciples to love one another as he has loved them, namely washing their feet (John 13). The Supper, understood as interpersonal table fellowship and mutual ministry, is directly applicable, hence immediately relevant to ethical and political life.

52. It is important to note that even Paul's chapter on the body of Christ in 1 Cor 12 mainly concerns the diversity of spiritual gifts in the faith community, not any infusion of life or vital power from Christ to us.

53. See Méndez-Montoya, *Theology of Food*, 156.

Vertical God-sinner table fellowship always already includes horizontal sinner-sinner table fellowship (this is beautifully emphasized in Deut 14 and 16). In fact, the practice of table fellowship and ministry is itself the direct antithesis of alienation. It directly addresses and inverts what sin brings—inequality, exploitation, alienation. The destitute and the marginalized are no longer so when included at the Lord's Table.[54] Specifically, the Supper is love by inclusion and feet-washing, even including and washing Judas's feet. It is not some abstract love in the form of allowing others to feed on one's flesh and blood. If such an abstract idea is not how we should love others, then probably it is not how Christ loves us either. He welcomes enemies to his table—concrete and direct.

An underlying problem in the Reformed view is Calvin and Bullinger's disregarding of Zwingli's understanding of the Supper as *human* action (e.g., in Second Helvetic Confession, Consensus Tigurinus). They stressed (explicitly in contrast to Zwingli) that the *sole* subject of action in the Supper is the Holy Spirit. While Calvin understood the divine action to be conferral of grace through the Supper, Bullinger understood it as the divine testimony of the salvation accomplished by Christ.[55] While Calvin, in his "Short Treatise," also acknowledged that the Supper is to incite praise and thanksgiving on our part, and overall he allowed the Supper to be viewed as a (non-expiatory) thanksgiving sacrifice, for him the Supper is still construed as first and foremost the giving of Christ's flesh and blood, and as such its sole agent can only be the Holy Spirit. However, if we understand the Supper as the reconciling table fellowship between the Son of God and sinners, such reconciliation must be a two-way action. Precisely as a *covenant* inauguration meal, the meal reestablishes sinners as God's true covenant partners, i.e., active agents in the divine-human relationship, as well as inter-human relationships. The Supper then is both divine *and* human action. Surely, divine action has priority. It is purely divine grace that justifies and sanctifies human response to it. Divine action puts human response into effect, not vice versa. Yet precisely this divine action demands and affirms instead of overshadows human action.[56] Here Calvin was right that Christ cannot be severed from the Spirit who sanctifies (3.2.8).

---

54. Even the first encounter with gentiles was in the form of inclusive table fellowship, with their food (Acts 10).

55. See Rorem, "Consensus Tigurinus," 76.

56. Here I concur with Barth's affirmation of real human obedience that responds to divine grace. See discussion at the end of this chapter.

(4) Yet the most devastating problem in the language of feeding Christ's body and blood for our nourishment is that it tends to see Christ as a *means* rather than an end. While this is no doubt not intended in Calvin's theology, Christ becomes impersonal. What nourishes is always some *thing* that is useful for personal gain.[57] The picture then presents Christ as what is useful to nourish us for "growth," on the table so to speak, instead of who we have fellowship with at the table. In other words, Christ has become the means for some abstract, private "benefit" for us, e.g., our "growth," instead of him being *the* benefit. In order to emphasize the realness of Christ's effective nourishment of our souls, we find that Calvin constantly had to draw a distinction between the person of Christ on the one hand, and his benefits on the other, and to Calvin it is clear that we receive Christ *in order to* receive these benefits. The order is clear: "*first,* that we might become one body with him; and, secondly, that being made partakers of his substance, we might feel the result of this fact in the participation of all his blessings" (4.17.11). Again, "as the blessings of Jesus Christ do not belong to us at all, unless he be *previously* ours, it is necessary, *first* of all, that he be given us in the Supper, *in order that* the things which we have mentioned [righteousness, eternal life, grace] may be truly accomplished in us."[58] Here Calvin continued to say that "the *reason* for communicating with Jesus Christ is to have part and portion in all the graces which he purchased for us by his death."[59] We are "to possess the whole of Christ crucified, *so as to* enjoy all his blessings" (4.17.33).[60] In his commentary to 1 Cor 11:24, he wrote, "by faith, we embrace Christ, . . . and, *in that way*, come to share effectively in all His benefits. . . . I myself maintain that it is *only after* we obtain Christ himself, that we come to share in the benefits of Christ."[61] And in his 1554 letter to Swiss pastors, "the Lord Jesus Christ, to communicate the gift of salvation which he has purchased for us, must *first* be made ours, and his flesh be our meat and nourishment, seeing that it is from it that we derive life."[62] The picture is clearly that we must obtain Christ *first*, and *by*

---

57. For example, I eat a protein bar for strength and to satisfy my hunger. What nourishes me is not itself an end. I eat it for my own gain, e.g., for strength. At any rate I do *not* have fellowship with the protein bar.

58. Calvin, "Short Treatise," *TT* 2:169.

59. Calvin, "Short Treatise," *TT* 2:170.

60. Here I have used Beveridge's translation.

61. Calvin, *Commentary to the Corinthians*, 246.

62. Calvin, *TT* 2:207–208.

being nourished by his body and blood we draw "benefits." The picture is unfortunately not that God in Christ has cleared the way so that we sinners may be forgiven and come *to him* again. Instead, it seems for Calvin, we make use of the Son of God so that our way to some *other* "benefits" can be cleared. Indeed, such "benefits" play the role of a *tertium quid* in the divine-human relationship. Surely, if we have already obtained the Son of God so intimately, what else do we need? Is he not the prize? The real issue in Calvin is not the instrumentalization of the Supper (as Bullinger worried), but a picture that instrumentalizes *Christ*—this is the more abhorrent problem! Of course, Christ provides and is the means to our salvation, by his obedience, dying and being raised from death, but he himself is not only the means. He is the end, most importantly. Salvation is being reconciled *to him*. We are justified, sanctified, given eternal life, etc., *such that* we can be reconciled to him. He is the end, everything else is only means. True communion is taking the person—especially Christ the Son of God—as an end, not only as means. The greatest problem with Calvin's language of nourishment is that its graphic nature only accentuates Christ as an objectified means for us instead of our end.

This problem of objectification is manifest in Luther as well. As he argued for a true eating of Christ, in his language the body of Christ is explicitly highlighted to be "distributed" as a "common material object," a "common thing."[63] His analogies for Christ's participated body are all dead objects for common use.[64] This is in stark contrast to a theology of the Lord's Supper that emphasizes Christ-sinner table fellowship, which highlights Christ as a full subject, in fact the most gracious Host, and in which reconciliation to God in the person Christ is clearly the end of our salvation.

Again, this problem has ethical repercussions. If we partake in Christ primarily for our own "benefits," it is no wonder that we tend to take our neighbors only as means too. Worse, such teaching even implies that we should do something as ghastly as utilizing others' bodies (and blood!) for our own "benefits." The instrumentality of the Supper, understood in terms of feeding on the body and blood of Christ for benefits, could entail instrumentalizing others' bodies and blood. This is unacceptable even if we insist that only the human Christ, not the divine Christ, is to be a means for us, as this would exactly imply that we can do the same to

---

63. See Luther, *Confession concerning Christ's Supper*, LW 37:355, 356.
64. Luther, *Confession concerning Christ's Supper*, LW 37:353.

other humans.[65] Yet the end should always be the person of Christ, not one's own "benefits." There should not be any benefit outside the fellowship with the person, especially the person of the Son of God, who are to be taken as end.

(5) In the first place, in Christ, God incarnated in human flesh and blood to be *with* us. He dwells among us as one of us. He gave himself to be a human, as a subject among us, not to be an object, or to act as an object, for our use. It is unfortunate that theologians, emphasizing the idea of eating and drinking Christ, have argued that becoming food for us is the goal of the incarnation. Radbertus from the ninth century, for example, suggested a process of the Word being made flesh and then *further* made food for us.[66] For a modern example, Méndez-Montoya argued that the incarnation of the Word is fully realized only in the Word's divine self-offering as flesh and blood for our nourishment.[67] It is as if, apart from the divine incarnation in human flesh, there needs to be an *extra* incarnation in food and nourishment. Therefore, Méndez-Montoya continued, in the Supper, the divine takes the risk of becoming food because of a desire to indwell and abide in the beloved, just as food becomes part of the eater. The desire of the other is translated into the desire to give to the other *as* food to be consumed.[68] Yet this, to say the least, contradicts common sense. We do not desire to become food for our loved ones. Also, God stands in solidarity with humanity fully already by becoming Jesus the Nazareth, why need this extra incarnation to function as an eaten object? More, instead of a furthering of the incarnation of the Word into flesh, it actually defeats the whole purpose of the incarnation, which is to be a fellow human. Being a fellow human precisely means being a full human subject, not an object or means for others. Such objecthood would only kill the fellow-humanity which is the point of the incarnation. Christ gives himself—yes, as a human, not as food. The idea of Christ's body and blood nourishing us can at most be a metaphor.[69]

Worse, if we insist that Christ's body and blood truly feed us (even if only spiritually or sacramentally), it is only a matter of a slippery slope

65. We have mentioned that a mystical union would be too abstract to have ethical bearings; here an instrumentalizing of Christ for our "benefits" would have de-humanizing ethical tendencies.

66. Radbertus, "Lord's Body and Blood," 95–96.

67. Méndez-Montoya, *Theology of Food*, 133.

68. Méndez-Montoya, *Theology of Food*, 144.

69. See Barth, *Rediscovering the Lord's Supper*, 90–91.

before we say that *God* becomes food for us, i.e., that we eat God in some sense. Méndez-Montoya again serves as a good example. He wrote, "God becomes bread from heaven in order to nourish and constitute his own Body."[70] Elsewhere he spoke of "God offering hospitality by becoming food and co-abiding with the other."[71] Not only the human Christ, but God himself in his divinity becomes objectifiable food for our own use. The rationale is that, if abiding with another subject must take the form of feeding on him/her, there is no clear reason why this premise does not apply to our relationship with the divine as well. Of course, this premise does not explain why, if abiding means feeding, why it is not that Christ feeds on us but only vice versa. After all it is not I but Christ who lives (Gal 2:20). But the more fundamental problem lies in the fact that the notion of human participation in the divine by cultic consumption is a pagan concept.[72] In the whole history of Christian doctrine, God simply does not become our food. We don't eat God, period. There is always a tight safeguard in the distinction between the Creator and creature. Unfortunately the seemingly innocent idea of nourishment by Christ's body and blood slips into this paganism easily.[73]

The Lord's Supper as Fellowship with Christ

New Passover and New Covenant

The Passover and Sinai narrative in Scripture, to which the Supper is allusive, hardly hints at the idea that the celebration meals involved are about nourishment (whether physical or spiritual). The Passover meal, for example, precisely deviates from ordinary meals, prompting children's questions: "What is the meaning of this rite?" (Exod 12:26); "Why is this night different than any other night?" (b. Pesaḥ. 115b). The meal,

70. Méndez-Montoya, *Theology of Food*, 150.

71. Méndez-Montoya, *Theology of Food*, 160.

72. See Arthur Cochrane's argument that the notion of sacramental eating of Christ was a relic of Hellenistic Mystery religions. Cochrane, *Eating and Drinking with Jesus*, 129–48. Cochrane remarked that "this time-honored doctrine [of eating and drinking Christ] had to go" (9).

73. One might note that this slippery slope exists in Luther as well. In his understanding of *communicatio idiomatum*, divine attributes are communicable to the human body of Jesus, hence its ubiquity (see, e.g., Luther, *Against the Fanatics*, *LW* 36:336–43). Therefore, there is at least some sense in which, when we eat Christ, it is specifically a divinized body of Christ that we eat.

rather, celebrates a miracle. It was a miracle of deliverance from immense suffering. When celebrating, the food is seldom about nourishment or growth.[74] The covenant meal at Sinai, similarly, celebrates YHWH's victory and inaugurates a divine-human covenant. We have seen that the narrative first documents the supposedly impossible fellowship between YHWH and Israel:

> [The Lord said to Moses,] ". . . You shall set boundaries for the people all around, saying, 'Beware that you do not go up on the mountain or touch the border of it; whoever touches the mountain shall certainly be put to death. No hand shall touch him, but he shall certainly be stoned or shot through; whether animal or person, the violator shall not live.'" (Exod 19:12–13)

The people were prohibited from drawing near to YHWH's presence. The narrative is even filled with thunder and earthquake. But the narrative then climaxes at the exact opposite: a shocking table fellowship between YHWH and his people, which was possible only after the presentation of the blood of the covenant:

> Then Moses and Aaron, Nadab, and Abihu, and seventy of the elders of Israel went up, and they saw the God of Israel. . . . He did not reach out with His hand against the nobles of the sons of Israel; and they saw God, and they ate and drank. (Exod 24:9–11)

The shock is so much that, as we have seen, commentators have tried to tone down the narrative, explaining away the phrase "they saw God."[75] Even if God's people could not see him at the old covenant meal, they at last could at the new one, when God incarnated in flesh and dined with them at the Last Supper. Immediately the meal—a *covenant* meal—highlights fellowship and partnership, not nourishment of individuals. If two warring states have their delegates sit down at a table to dine together and the wronged party declares forgiveness, whether the meal nourishes either party is of minimal importance. Indeed, if the offensive party makes nourishment and growth the central issue (not to mention smuggling in philosophy and metaphysics while doing so), it would only show that

---

74. For this reason, Norman Wirzba argued that feasting and fasting are not opposites but complementary. Wirzba, *Food and Faith*, 137–43.

75. Even the Septuagint toned down the directness of the statement as implying only intellectual beholding of God with the mind, not with the eye. See Childs, *Exodus*, 506.

the undeserved forgiveness and table fellowship has not been registered. God did not stretch out his Hand against his people (explicitly stated in Exod 24:11)—this highlights what was *supposed* to happen, especially in light of the dire warnings against approaching divine presence (Exod 19:12–13). The point of the meal is precisely that parties which were *not* supposed to be together have now come together. This table fellowship is profound. The gracious sovereign host does not then become food on the table for the vassal to consume (not even only symbolically).

In fact the Passover meal also highlights table fellowship between God and his people. In Deuteronomy this message is loud and clear. As dictated in Deuteronomy, it is top priority that Passover feasts must be celebrated at the sanctuary, or only where God had chosen for his name to dwell (Deut 16:1–2, 5–7; see also 12:7; 14:23; 15:19–20). Among Second Temple literature, the command to offer a portion of the Passover lamb on YHWH's altar, and to celebrate Passover only before the Sanctuary, or where YHWH himself appointed, takes up substantial length in the chapter on Passover celebrations in the book of Jubilees (49:16–21). This highlights communion with YHWH as an important aspect of the Passover meal. In Second Temple *haggadah*, the command is very clearly written down (m. Pesaḥ. 5.10). Even after the temple had been destroyed, the Talmud prohibits raising meat on the table, as this would signal that the Passover meat was eaten away from the temple, i.e., not in God's presence, which is inconceivable (b. Pesaḥ. 116b). All these show that Passover remembrance is never simply mental recollection of events, but communal feasting, not only with fellow Jews, but specifically *with* YHWH.[76] This also explains the requirement of eating only in a state of purification.[77] If fellowship with God is indeed the emphasis, then we may appreciate Jesus saying to his disciples, "I have earnestly desired to eat this Passover *with you* before I suffer" (Luke 22:15). God, now in flesh, ate the Passover meal *with* his people. This table fellowship fulfilled the table communion with God foreshadowed in the Passover regulations. God incarnated in flesh and blood in order that he may dwell among his

---

76. Here I disagree with Naphtali Meshel. In his delineation of a "grammar" of sacrifices in the Priestly texts, he reduces the communal feasting of well-being sacrifices (to which the Passover and covenant meals belong) to only an "atomact" of "ingestion." See Meshel, *"Grammar" of Sacrifice*, 237. Because Meshel characterizes communal feasting as "ingestion," in the end he takes it to be on a par with the act of incineration of leftover sacrificial meat, as if the point was merely to eliminate the *materia sacra* (*"Grammar" of Sacrifice*, 159).

77. Milgrom, *Leviticus 1–16*, 223–24.

people as *one* of us, not so that he may become incarnate or symbolized in food and drink to be consumed by us.

I do not deny that food nourishes, and in a world still plagued by hunger in many parts, I am not undermining the importance of nourishment. We are sustained by food, physically and spiritually through community, but *not* for the reason that tradition has assumed. We do not consume our Savior's flesh and blood. I am also not denying the truth of the Bread of Life discourse in John 6, but denying that it be taken literally, and that the Lord's Supper is about believers feeding on Christ's body and blood, eclipsing the interpersonal picture in which Christ is the Gracious Host who receives us and reconciles us sinners to him.[78]

78. I am in agreement with scholars who interpret the Bread of Life discourse in John 6 only metaphorically. For example, Markus Barth, like Zwingli and Augustine, interpreted the Christ-eating language in John 6 as metaphorical. He noted the repeated "I am" discourse in John as symbolic, e.g., "I am" the Good Shepherd, the light of the world, the door, etc. He remarked that any literal interpretation of these passages would be absurd, even "insensitive and dumb." Barth, *Rediscovering the Lord's Supper*, 90. Scholars who rule out a Eucharistic reading of John 6 include: Morris, *Gospel according to John*, 311–15; Carson, *Gospel according to John*, 294–302; cf. Brown, *Gospel according to John*, 284–85, 291–93, 299–300. No doubt, John 6 is rich in imageries and may contain interweaving allusions, including manna, the Eucharist, and faith in Christ. See, e.g., Moloney, *Gospel of John*, 207–25. What I want to rule out is that eating Christ is more than just a metaphor and that it is a primary, overarching focus of the Lord's Supper. At any rate, the fact that Jesus used language that suggests eating of his flesh and drinking of his blood when speaking to a crowd should not distract us from the undeserved *table companionship* which he invited sinners to enjoy with him. One should not ignore the context of the Bread of Life discourse, i.e., a crowd seeing Christ as a provider of unfulfilling food—a parallel of John 4, in which the Samaritan woman saw him as a provider of unfulfilling water, a text we hardly associate with the Lord's Supper. If we base our understanding of the Supper on the Bread of Life discourse, we will have the burden to explain why Jesus indeed gave the invitation to "eat" him to the *whole* crowd that was chasing him for physical food, many of whom were clearly not real followers. In ruling out a realistic reading of the Bread of Life discourse, we are *not* devaluing the material body and blood of Christ. As Zwingli reiterated again and again, the body of Christ is most important, as *slain*, not as eaten (e.g., Zwingli, *Commentary on True and False Religion*, 198–206). My emphasis on fellowship with Christ merely lifts us out of the preoccupation with seeing Christ as an edible *object*, when first and foremost he is a subject and a person.

Rethinking "Participation in Christ"

Calvin's primary concern is our true abiding in Christ, that we are indeed made one with Christ. This is the central, underlying doctrine of his theology:

> That joining together of Head and members, that indwelling of Christ in our hearts—in short, that mystical union—are accorded by us the highest degree of importance, so that Christ, having been made ours, makes us sharers with him in the gifts with which he has been endowed. (*Inst.* 3.11.10)

Calvin strove for a real union with Christ, one that is nevertheless neither ontological (against Osiander) nor merely a forensic imputing of justification (beyond Melanchthon). The Reformers had to answer the charge of justification being merely a "legal fiction." As noted, part of the motivation for the emphasis of an organic language was also a Protestant coalition against the Catholics and to account for a substantial communion with Christ. The question is therefore how we truly participate in Christ, if as argued above we want to rule out an organic language.

So far our biblical exposition fits well with Karl Barth's actualistic approach to the traditional notion of *participatio Christi*. If traditionally, e.g., in Calvin, we must be ingrafted in Christ, becoming one with him, feeding on his body and blood mystically, in order to draw benefits from him, such understanding is static. In the end the picture is impersonal as well. What Barth proposed is a historical and relational instead of metaphysical understanding of participation in Christ.[79] We participate not in some static, metaphysical union with Christ, but in the *history* of Jesus Christ. More specifically, we participate in his life of obedience.

In the first place, for Barth, Christ's own humanity and divinity are not a static union either. Barth favored the Reformed emphasis of *unio hypostatica* over the Lutheran emphasis of Christ's two natures and *communicatio idiomatum*. He complained that classical Christologies concentrate on a *unio*, bearing a static instead of dynamic sense, "with inevitable consequences for the interpretation of *communio* and *communicatio*."[80] Most disastrously, Christology has lost the historicity of Christ,

---

79. See Bruce McCormack's analysis and comparison of Barth's and Eberhard Jüngel's historical-relational construals of participation in Christ. McCormack, "Participation in God, Yes; Deification, No," in *Orthodox and Modern*, 235–60.

80. Barth, *CD* 4/2, 109.

speculating about the penetration of states, instead of the living Jesus Christ.[81] For Barth, Christ is an *event*, a person with a lived history. Jesus Christ is both Son of God and Son of Man, not as a static union of two metaphysical natures, but as a Person, a Subject, a life that is commonly lived by both God and man.[82] His two natures in fact speak of his *events* of humiliation and exaltation, not static states but events of one life.[83] As Barth put it,

> Does not everything depend on our doing justice to the living Jesus Christ? But, at root, what is the life of Jesus Christ but the act in which God becomes very God and very man, positing Himself in this being? What is it but the work of this conjunction?[84]

Barth thus revised the traditional doctrine of *communicatio naturarum*.[85] He defined *communicatio idiomatum* as the impartation of the human essence to the divine, and vice versa, "*as it takes place* in the one Jesus Christ as Son of God and Son of Man."[86] Barth demanded a strict attention to the history of the person, while refusing the natures or attributes of independent ground. "Only the Son of God counts."[87]

Most importantly, even in the person of Christ, his humanity is *not* deified. Even for Christ, exaltation does not take the form of deification. This is of paramount importance for preserving the Chalcedonian definition of the two natures: neither mixture nor change, neither separation nor division.[88] Both natures of Christ are intact fully, even after exaltation. The human remains human, not altered. Neither is there any infusion of grace. Hence for *communicatio gratiarum*, Barth insisted, "there can be no question of a transferred condition, or an infused habit, in this grace addressed to Him."[89] Instead of a status possession, Barth described

81. Neder, *Participation in Christ*, 65.

82. Barth, *CD* 4/2, 36–116.

83. Barth, *CD* 4/2, 106, 110.

84. Barth, *CD* 4/2, 109.

85. For more detailed accounts of Barth's treatment of *communicatio naturarum*, see Neder, "History in Harmony," 148–76; and Sumner, *Karl Barth and the Incarnation*, 128–39.

86. Barth, *CD* 4/2, 73, emphasis mine.

87. Barth, *CD* 4/2, 66.

88. Barth, *CD* 4/2, 80, 109.

89. Barth, *CD* 4/2, 94.

grace as an active "confrontation."[90] Grace is "a divine giving and human receiving. It can be 'had' only in the course of this history."[91] As for *communicatio operationum*, Barth similarly defined it as the "common actualization of divine and human essence *as it takes place* in Jesus Christ."[92] "Again, there can be only a historical thinking. . . . The divine and the human work together. But even in their common working they are not interchangeable."[93] Instead of penetration of states, exaltation speaks of a common life, i.e., a *fellowship* of the human with the divine. One may note that even the language of Christ being seated at the right hand of the Father is surprisingly interpersonal and concrete. There is no metaphysical indwelling. "As the Creator condescended to be a creature, He did not make the creature Creator, but in its unity of existence with His Son He adopted it into *fellowship* [*Gemeinschaft*] with His being as God, Creator and Lord."[94] For Barth, this resonates nothing less than God's own divine name. In accordance with God's name, he wills to be Emmanuel—God with us—and he fulfills this "with."[95] Humanity, as the humanity of Jesus Christ, without ceasing to be human, is placed *at the side* of the Creator (John 1:1).[96]

Instead of a union of static states, Jesus Christ is an event, even a *movement*, in Barth's words.[97] The "union" between Christ and us, is similarly a movement.[98] Our salvation is accomplished in Jesus Christ, "that means the history in which He, the Son of God, becomes and is the Son of Man, going into the far country as the Son of God to come home again as the Son of Man."[99] Our participation in Christ is a dynamic participation in this *history*, not a static, metaphysical participation in another person. Here Barth echoes the spatio-temporal movement that we have argued from the biblical narrative: from far to near, from alienation to fellowship. The history is one of homecoming. What is resulted from the

90. Barth, *CD* 4/2, 87.
91. Barth, *CD* 4/2, 90.
92. Barth, *CD* 4/2, 73, emphasis mine.
93. Barth, *CD* 4/2, 116.
94. Barth, *CD* 4/2, 100.
95. Barth, *CD* 4/2, 100.
96. Barth, *CD* 4/2, 100.
97. E.g., Barth, *CD* 4/2, 110.
98. Barth, *CD* 4/2, 109.
99. Barth, *CD* 4/2, 107.

homecoming is not some metaphysical infusion of life or mystical union between Christ and believers, but specifically *fellowship* between God and sinners restored again. "God became man in order that man may, not become God, but may *come to God*."[100] Again, "God humbles Himself to man, even to the final and most radical depth of becoming man, not to deify man, but to exalt him to perfect *fellowship* with Himself."[101]

This fellowship is not a conceptual word play. More specifically, Barth explained, "Exaltation to what? To that harmony with the divine will, that service of the divine act, that correspondence to the divine grace, that state of thankfulness."[102] The exalted humanity of Christ is not a static state of sinlessness, but active obedience and correspondence to the divine will. If even for Christ, exaltation takes the form of lived obedience, we, being in Christ, are exalted only this way. Thus we "have a share . . . in His fellowship with God, in God's pleasure in Him, but also in His obedience to God, in His movement towards Him."[103] This is how Barth interprets the abiding language in NT. Ultimately Barth interprets Paul's language of "in Christ" to mean "*with* Christ."[104] To be "with Christ" means for the church community's life to be modeled and patterned after Christ's life, death, and resurrection.[105] In sum, to be in Christ is to live a life of obedience, made possible by Christ's exaltation of the human. We do participate in Christ, but not by mythical ingestion or infusion. Rather, we are restored in interpersonal *fellowship* with him, concretely by being freed and restored to obedience to God. Our participation is participation of Christ's life of fellowship with God.

As NT scholar Markus Barth argued, even in Paul, the language of participating in Christ's body and blood is *koinonia* (1 Cor 10:16)—fellowship. It is "strictly interpersonal."[106] This is not to mention that the context in 1 Cor 10 is *pastoral*.[107] Paul was dealing with idolatrous conduct among the Corinthians. This also explains why Paul put the point only by means of rhetorical questions, and the cup is mentioned before the bread

---

100. Barth, *CD* 4/2, 106.

101. Barth, *CD* 4/2, 117.

102. Barth, *CD* 4/2, 92.

103. Barth, *CD* 4/2, 270.

104. Barth, *CD* 4/2, 277.

105. Barth, *CD* 4/2, 277.

106. Barth, *Rediscovering the Lord's Supper*, 37.

107. Barth, *Rediscovering the Lord's Supper*, 30.

(1 Cor 10:16). At any rate, even the rhetorical questions did not imply that the bread is Christ's body or the cup is Christ's blood. Rather, the cup is *koinonia* (fellowship) with Christ's blood, and the bread is *koinonia* (fellowship) with Christ's body. He was saying to the Corinthians that they were in communion with Christ himself.[108] Another pastoral concern in Corinth was that the Supper had become a schism between the haves and have-nots.[109] Taking Paul to mean that the Supper is primarily about some mystical participation by us in the body and blood of Christ is to confuse pastoral rhetoric with doctrine. This misunderstanding is akin to reading, e.g., Ps 113:3, "From the rising of the sun to its setting / the name of the Lord is to be praised," and arguing that the sun revolves around a still earth. This is plainly confusing rhetoric with subject matter. Just as the psalmist was not putting forward a theory concerning the sun's movements, so Paul was not avowing a certain Eucharistic theory (in exclusion of other theories) in his pastoral dealings.

Precisely the Paschal and Sinaitic context of the Supper sheds light on a notion of participation in Christ that is in line with our approach, namely that a real communion with God should take the form of obedience and interpersonal fellowship. To reiterate our findings from the book of Exodus, the Passover meal that commemorates God's liberating action in history does not hint at any mystical participation in the original event. Subsequent generations of Jews do not enter a mystical, organic union with the flesh or blood of the Egyptian Passover lambs. Instead, they obey YHWH's command to keep the feast in a manner very similar to the way their ancestors ate the first Passover meal, as a remembrance of YHWH's deliverance from oppression. In the first place, the command was given in that very event. As instituted by him, while only the first generation who departed Egypt actually partook of the Egyptian Passover lambs, all subsequent generations of Israel nevertheless are *defined* as also being saved from Egypt by virtue of their partaking in this meal that was instituted in that event. This message is most conspicuous when God decreed that those in the future generations who do not participate in the Passover meal, or even who do not exactly follow the menu (i.e., who consume leaven during the time), are cut off from his people (Exod

108. Barth, *Rediscovering the Lord's Supper*, 31.

109. Barth, *Rediscovering the Lord's Supper*, 30. According to Joachim Jeremias, Paul was *not* putting forth a historical account of the Supper, but was repeating a received liturgical phrase, especially one that had already been harmonized for convenient use. Jeremias, *Eucharistic Words of Jesus*, 170, 187.

12:15, 19; Num 9:13).[110] The liturgy of the Passover meal prescribed by scripture (in Exod 13:8 and Deut 16:3) is clear that all subsequent generations are to declare that they *themselves*, not just their ancestors, were brought forth from Egyptian bondage.[111] Participation thus takes the form of obedience to this command as a community. It is not mystical.

By parallel, our union with Christ as set forth in the Lord's Supper does not need to be some mysterious organic partaking of Christ's flesh and blood, but a faithful response to his invitation to partake in the holy Supper he instituted for us, and to live out an interpersonal relationship with him. If there is any "benefit," to use a Reformed terminology, it is this renewed relationship with Christ himself. At the outset, we are not looking for a general, philosophical concept of participation, of which our participation in God or in his salvific work is an instance. Instead, we must notice how God has already instituted what action on our part would *count* as participation in his original salvific event. It is his definition that is decisive. This was precisely the participation of the meal he instituted. Calvin's mistake was to assume that a real, intimate relationship with Christ can only take the form of organic consumption of his flesh and blood, instead of an ethical, interpersonal fellowship with him as a person. At the outset, he sought to develop a mythical account of our union with Christ that is not grounded in the concrete, historical context of the Last Supper.

Also of vital importance is the meal as a *covenant* meal. The Sinaitic narrative tells of a covenant inauguration ceremony. Precisely as such it anticipates future obedience on the part of the people of God. We have seen that an important element in that ceremony was God's laying out of the specific terms and conditions of *keeping* the covenant (Exod 19–23). To obey these commandments includes one in that covenant.[112] So again

110. This cutting off from God's saved people is not necessarily a subsequent penal sentence. Instead, those who do not repeat the meal do not participate in the saving event through the very way instituted by God for future generations to participate in the saving event. They are then not participating in the defining event, and hence not God's people.

111. See also Mishnah: "Therefore it is our duty to thank, praise, laud, glorify, exalt, honor, bless, extol, and adore Him Who performed all these miracles for our ancestors and us; He brought us forth from bondage into freedom, from sorrow into joy, from mourning into festivity, from darkness into great light, and from servitude into redemption" (m. Pesaḥ. 10.5).

112. This may be the primary difference between the Abrahamic covenant on the one hand and the Sinaitic covenant on the other. The latter lays out specific terms

the relationship with God that is called for is an ethical one. Participation takes the form of concrete obedience in everyday life.

In addition, according to the narrative, after the offering of the blood of the covenant, the people of Israel were allowed to dine in the presence of God in a covenant meal (Exod 24). Here, participation in the covenant is more specifically participation in the divine-human *table fellowship*, supposedly impossible because of the vast ontological gap between creator and creature, not to mention between the holy God and sinful humanity. Yet in the life and death of Christ, as God-become-human, he fulfilled the divine-human covenant with its laws. Christ has lived his life of perfect obedience as a Son of Man, even unto death. He did not only pledge obedience as the Israelites did at Sinai upon entering the covenant (and later failed), but actually fulfilled this obedient life. He became sin (2 Cor 5:21), and with his own blood removes all sin, cleanses us and prepares us to have fellowship with God once again (Heb 9:14). As will be explained in the next chapter, we are prepared for fellowship not only with God but with our neighbors once again as well.

In short, Christ *is* the new covenant, maintaining it not only on the side of God but also on the side of humanity. On both sides he fulfills the covenant perfectly. As we are enabled to obey by the power of his Spirit, we are restored as true covenant partners. As we obey, we *participate* in his obedience. This is the sense in which we participate in the blood of Christ. It is not that we must have some mystical communion with his bodily fluid, least of all drink it. But we are now included in this divine-human covenant that is sealed by his pouring of his blood. We are cleansed and freed by his blood such that we are reinstated as true covenant partners who can now keep the covenant *too* (hence the new commandment in John 13). We participate in his obedience by actually obeying on our part. Coming to the Lord's table and drinking the cup *of the covenant*, we are not mystically having communion with his blood, but we recommit ourselves to God with obedient action. Again, participation in Christ is most concrete and non-metaphysical—we are freed to live according to the Word of God, every day. As such, participation in Christ is immediately ethical. We actively come to God with our neighbors. The church embodies the body of Christ, not by individually consuming his body (even only symbolically), but by hosting graciously

---

of obedience by which one abides, and even those outside Abraham's bloodline can choose to be part of it. Indeed the Exodus narrative implies that there were more than just Israelites who departed Egypt when God delivered them (Exod 12:38).

at the table, as he did. Our sanctification is not a further "benefit" that we draw from first being one with Christ's body and blood, but we are sanctified by virtue of being freed for obedience, such that we are restored as true covenant partners of God. The blood that is poured sanctifies and allows us to come to God, not that we already have mystical access to the Son of God and then become sanctified.

Participation in Christ is most concrete, in the form of living an obedient life. The bottom line is that Scripture gives no hint that there was any mystical participation in God by the pre-fall Adam. There was no co-abiding in God metaphysically. The Adam who enjoyed full fellowship with God in Eden also did not draw nourishment from the divine substance of God. God nourished Adam, not with himself, but only with the garden he created (in fact, this was the point of the garden, that Adam may eat from it; Gen 2:16). Thus after the fall, salvation would not come in the form of humanity organically consuming or co-abiding in the Son of God. Rather, salvation would be the restoration of what is lost, namely human obedience, and the original interpersonal fellowship between God and humanity. The human race was once driven away from divine presence. Now, because of the blood of Christ, we are no longer exiles. The antithesis of sin is not eating God or his incarnated body, but returning to God to be able to have fellowship *with* him once again. The table fellowship is this reunion.

Rethinking "Eucharistic Sacrifice"

A counter-argument to our thesis against the language of eating Christ may be that, if Christ is our Passover sacrifice, the Lamb who takes away the sins of the world, then there must be some sense in which we participate by *eating* the Lamb, just as Israelites participate in salvation by eating their Passover lambs. If the Supper is a sacrificial meal, believers participate in the benefits of the sacrifice by feasting on sacrificial meat. There must be, the argument goes, a sense in which we feed on Christ. This is the understanding of Keith Mathison, borrowing from B. B. Warfield, who used the Passover context of the Supper to call for a revival of Calvin's realist Eucharistic theology.[113] Mathison echoed Warfield that it is a "most salient fact" that the Last Supper was a Passover meal, not substituting but continuous with the old Passover. With Warfield, Mathison

113. Mathison, *Given for You*, 168–69.

agrees that, in the new Passover, participation has not changed, but only the symbols have changed: the old lambs represent Christ, now Christ has identified himself with the bread and wine. Thus he describes eating the Supper in terms of our partaking of Christ's body and blood, specifically Christ as the victim on the cross. It is a perpetual sacrificial feast. We continue the festival that testifies our participation in the altar, and claim the benefits of the victim.

Yet this notion of feeding on the sacrifice contradicts the Reformed distinction between propitiatory and eucharistic sacrifices, and the insistence that the Supper belongs only to the latter, not the former. For the Reformers, the only propitiatory sacrifice was the cross, offered and effective once and for all (*Inst.* 4.18.13). For those who embrace the language of Christ nourishing us, we must be one with body and blood of Christ the propitiatory victim to receive life from him. But it is clear that, in the OT, propitiatory sacrifices are *never* to be eaten by those on the behalf of whom the sacrifices are made. Eucharistic sacrifices (peace offerings), which are eaten by the worshippers for celebration, thanksgiving, or vows, are *separate* sacrifices that follow propitiatory sacrifices. These do not involve the same victims. Instead, the communal meals signal that expiation was effective, so that God's people can now come to his presence to eat the eucharistic sacrifice. Thus the language of our feeding on Christ for salvific benefits would in fact make Christ's sacrifice non-propitiatory.[114] If we insist that Christ's body and blood are propitiatory, then they are not eaten by us (whether physically, spiritually or only symbolically). Otherwise we would confuse propitiatory with eucharistic sacrifices. Interestingly, those who embrace the language of Christ nourishing us usually understand that Christ is partaken by us *whole*.[115] Yet again this defies the OT presentation of sacrifices. Peace offerings are never eaten whole by anyone, but are to be shared by all parties, including God (portions to be burned on altar), priests and worshippers and their kin (Lev 3). If traditions want to stress that we were given the

114. As renowned OT scholar Jacob Milgrom stated, "It has generally been denied that the well-being offering [to be eaten by worshippers] served an expiatory function" (Milgrom, *Leviticus 1–16*, 221). In the instructions for well-being offerings, no confession is ever to be made over well-being offering, and the key expiatory term "kipper" is missing. This also explains why a well-being offering victim can be male or female, as it is only used for sharing, whereas expiatory offering victims must be male.

115. E.g., in the Council of Trent (session 13, Decree on the Eucharist, chapter 3), it was stated that Christ is offered whole and entire. Calvin also made this point in his "Clear Explanation" (*TT* 2:516), i.e., that we feed on Christ entire.

whole Christ to partake, then it would have been a burnt offering offered *to us*. It would have meant that we were God, who is the sole recipient of burnt offerings. All this is not to mention that, in OT, consumption of sacrificial blood is absolutely prohibited!

It is not that those who eat an expiatory offering victim will receive expiation from it. Expiatory sacrifices are never eaten by the offerer. Rather, *after* an effective expiatory sacrifice is made, the offerer is allowed to come near to God to share a eucharistic meal with him. It is table fellowship that seals the expiatory sacrifice. The goal of the expiation is precisely such that the sinner may come to God for fellowship again. The root of the Hebrew word for offering *korban* (*qrb*) means *to draw near, to be near.*[116] This reveals the point of offering sacrifices: to come *to* God. This is why in the biblical narratives, we read that sacrifices are typically offered one after another in series, yet they always conclude with peace offerings, in which both God and the offerer receive portions from the sacrifice.[117] This speaks of a communal feast with God. In the renowned Leviticus scholar Jacob Milgrom's words, "The fact that [peace offering] is [usually] last named is significant: it points to a feast at the end of the sacrificial ritual."[118] Expiatory sacrifices always culminate in a final divine-human table fellowship—God's people draw near to God again. This meal speaks of a most joyous communion with God: "the joyous sacrifice par excellence."[119] Thus even if we investigate how sacrifices involve the ingestion of sacrifices, this leads one to the conclusion that ultimately the goal is precisely table fellowship with God, not the consumption of salvific life. There is no question of mystically partaking of the life of God, but only of dining *with* him.[120] This is the case in the old covenant, and also in the new. Christ's body was offered to allow for our fellowship with God, not for consumption of his expiatory life. The consumption of food in the sacrificial meal is the manner of the fellowship. We do not consume divine life, nor have any mystical communion with the expiatory sacrifice.

---

116. See, e.g., Gzella, "קרב," *TDOT* 16:678; Arnold, "קרב," *NIDOTTE* 3:976.

117. Exod 18:12; 20:24; 24:5; 32:6; Lev 9:22; 23:19; Num 6:14; 10:10; 29:39; Deut 27:6–7, and many other examples.

118. Milgrom, *Leviticus 1–16*, 221.

119. Milgrom, *Leviticus 1–16*, 224. There would even be trumpets that signal national celebration (Num 10:10).

120. Milgrom, *Leviticus 1–16*, 221. For a helpful overview of the social and political character of cultic meals in the Pentateuch, see Altmann, *Festive Meals in Ancient Israel.*

Participation in Christ is participation in the obedience and (table) fellowship restored by Christ. The point is reconciliation. The "benefit" we receive from Christ's sacrifice is none other than this restored fellowship with Christ himself. The "benefit" is Christ. No doubt, today we await the final banquet when one day Christ will physically dine *with* his people again. "Behold, I stand at the door and knock. If anyone hears my voice and opens the door, I will come in to him and eat *with* him" (Rev 3:20; also Matt 26:29).

Is Christ not the true Passover Lamb, and do Jews not eat the Passover lamb? Yes. Do we not in this sense eat Christ?[121] However, Christ is the ultimate Passover lamb. He was not only sacrificed once and for all, but was also resurrected from the dead. The point of this ultimate effective sacrifice and the resurrection is precisely that God and humans may come together as covenant partners again, at the table, not such that God becomes our food on the table (real or symbolic). The good news of the new Passover is exactly that we no longer need to sacrifice or eat any lamb. Furthermore, in the OT, the Jews who sacrificed the Passover lambs ate them. Yet did we sacrifice Christ, or did Christ sacrifice himself (John 10:18)? It is God himself, not us, who gave his own Son to be sacrificed (John 3:16).

It Takes Two to Fellowship—
The Supper as Divine and Human Action

We may now tackle the question as to whether the Supper is, as it is for Calvin, an instrument efficacious in conferring grace. It was on this major point that Zurich and Geneva could not reach a lasting agreement, even after the compromised language of Consensus Tigurinus.[122] Zwingli was wearied of ascribing any saving power to the created realm. His concern over idolatry in Catholic practices of the Mass compelled him to staunchly reject any human or created role in salvation. For him, therefore, the Supper does not confer grace. In itself it plays no causal role in grace at all, not even as an "instrument." With this his successor Bullinger agreed. Bullinger would for years engage in debate with Calvin,

---

121. See a similar argument in Warfield, "Fundamental Significance of the Lord's Supper," 332–38; and Pitre, *Jesus and the Last Supper*, 411.

122. The compromise seemed to be sought mainly out of political urgency. See Rorem, "Consensus Tigurinus," 87; Mathison, *Given for You*, 64–68.

who affirmed the Supper as instrumental in conferring grace. For Calvin, the Supper must be instrumental in the conferral of grace, otherwise it would be an empty sign. The visible signs are thus called Christ's body and blood, precisely because "they are as it were instruments by which the Lord distributes them to us."[123] God has ordained sacraments for this purpose. In particular, sacraments confirm our faith (*Inst.* 4.14.11–12). Thus, through our bodies being fed the bread and the wine, Christ also feeds us with our souls with his body and blood. For sure, Calvin also acknowledged that the primary agent of salvation is God. "We place no power in creatures," he said. "I say only this: God uses means and instruments which he himself sees to be expedient, that all things may serve his glory, since he is Lord and Judge of all" (4.14.12). The bread and wine are nothing, except as instruments under which God dispenses blessings to us (4.14.12).

Since, we have shown in chapter 3, the neo-Platonic dualism of sign *vis-à-vis* reality is in fact unnecessary, the Reformed concern over whether the Supper is a mere symbol or an effective sign that confers the signified reality also dissolves. Our historical perspective of the Supper reveals that the concern is not as crucial as it seems. In the first place, in the Reformed tradition, grace is not some abstract, *tertium quid* that may or may not be conferrable by objects. Grace is rather the undeserved *act* on God's part to send his Son to take up sin, to die on the cross for us, and now to include sinners at his table once again. Grace therefore takes the form of God's effective restoration of divine-human fellowship, once lost due to sin. The question then is not whether a static "sign" is effective, but whether divine grace itself is effective in reconciling sinners to him. God invited sinners, and sinners may now actually respond. The Supper as table fellowship is *itself* the concrete act of reconciliation, the undoing of the alienation resulted from sin. If Augustine defined the Supper as a visible word, assuming a visible-*vs.*-invisible dichotomy, our thesis instead emphasizes that the Supper is *acted* word. It is acted word primarily on God's side. At the same time, it is *realized* word—God effectively realizes his word.

In this light, in response to the question whether the Supper is divine action or human action, there is a sense in which the Supper is *both*. It is both divine grace *and* human obedience. As we are cleansed and come to the table, it becomes our active response to God's grace.

123. Calvin, "Short Treatise," *TT* 2:171.

Precisely this is a *covenant* meal. The relationship must be *mutual*. We are effectively reinstated as true covenant partners of God. As such, we are to have full agency and responsibility. On this point, we are once again rallying to Barth (who agreed with Zwingli). In his treatment of baptism, Barth affirmed baptism as a genuine human response to grace, albeit only on the basis of the sanctifying work of the Holy Spirit.[124] Barth ruled out the Lutheran scenario in which the sinner is justified by faith alone and yet left unchanged. For him, this precisely fails to take into account the fact that we *are* restored as covenant partners of God. Grace demands faith *and* actual response. The sinner does not only receive a new external judgement, but is to be inwardly changed as well, so that the sinner may now freely and genuinely respond to God. Surely, it is not human action that puts divine action into effect, but precisely vice versa. Divine action calls for, hence also validates, human ethical response. The visible word is thus *responded* word.

The issue with Calvin's primary use of the Supper as Christ's in- stitution of the sign through which he effects our partaking of Christ's body and blood, is that such an emphasis of mystery undermines human agency and therefore ethical relevance. But because Christ's saving work is effective, we can say that the Supper seals grace, in the sense that it indeed fulfills the restoration of the table fellowship between God and humanity. God's children are called to be home again. We may say that God is gracious through the Supper, i.e., *through table fellowship*. But the idea is not that there is some abstract, impersonal notion of grace or salvific benefits that we need to ask whether the Supper is instrumental in conferring or not, as if the concern was about a causal chain, but that in God and humanity's restored encounter, the wonderful God-sinner fellowship is indeed through concrete table fellowship.

Fellowship with Christ in Heaven?

This work has presupposed at the outset that the Reformed church has been right about the physical presence of Christ now, namely only in heaven, seated at the right hand of the Father. The scriptural support is undeniable: Acts 2, 7; Eph 1; Col 3; Heb 1, 8, 10, 12. Christ's body, being a human body, can only be local. So far our approach has also stressed the

124. Barth, *CD* 4/4, 1–5.

concrete, interpersonal table fellowship with Christ. We eat *with* Christ, not eat him.

Apart from taking seriously the scriptural texts that affirm his physical presence only in heaven, one must also take seriously Christ's own vow of abstinence at the Last Supper:

> I say to you, I shall never again eat it until it is fulfilled in the kingdom of God . . . I say to you, I will not drink of the fruit of the vine from now on until the kingdom of God comes. (Luke 22:16–18; see also Matt 26:29, Mark 14:25)

This strong-worded vow of Christ's appears in all Synoptic Gospels and yet is often overlooked by Eucharistic traditions, which mostly focus on Paul's text in 1 Cor 10–11. The meal is clearly forward-looking, not only for us, but for Christ as well. He looks forward to the day he will eat the meal again, as the Host, not be eaten as food. Thus it is true that, now, we do not eat with him physically. The Lord's Supper as it is commanded to the church is indeed *not* the final consummation of our table fellowship with Christ, the banquet of the Lamb, where God in the person of the Son will physically dine with all his people.

Calvin's emphasis of the *real* communion we now have with Christ's body and blood in fact collapses the eschatological character of the Supper. Christ's avowal of abstinence precisely indicates the unfinished, if not even lacking, character of the meal.[125] Precisely a physical communion with Christ now is wanting. Otherwise there would be no point in waiting for his return. Thus this is not to devalue the bodily at all. We eagerly await his physical return. We declare his death *until* he comes. He is not physically with us now. The more we stress the physical communion we enjoy with Christ now, the less there is a need to wait for his return.[126]

Instead of a physical fellowship, the fellowship we now enjoy with Christ is through the Holy Spirit. On this point, the Reformed tradition is not mistaken. Our communion with Christ is spiritual. Yet it is not that the Spirit lifts us to heaven, *away* from the concrete, communal reality here and now. Rather, as Christ himself made clear, he has sent the Holy

125. Even Calvin's defender Keith Mathison mentioned this point. Mathison, *Given for You*, 214.

126. In fact this waiting speaks to the Reformed notion that Christ is seated at the right hand of the Father, specifically in his office as the High Priest interceding for us. The image of the Yom Kippur is precisely that the people are outside the premise of the sanctuary as the High Priest intercedes for them before the mercy seat (Lev 16). In other words, he is not with them physically.

Spirit *to us* (not to lift us back to him). "I tell you the truth: it is to your advantage that I go away, for if I do not go away, the Advocate will not come to you; but if I go, I will send him to you" (John 16:7). No doubt, before Jesus's physical return, his Spirit is with us as promised by him.

If the Holy Spirit is God, as the Christian doctrine of the Trinity holds, then the spiritual should not be pitted against the bodily. If the Holy Spirit proceeds from Christ, as the Western tradition holds, then the presence of the Holy Spirit *is* Christ's presence. The Spirit is none other than *his* Spirit. To reconcile Matt 28:20, "I am with you always, to the end of the age" on the one hand, and on the other John 16:5–7, "now I am going to him who sent me . . . if I do not go away, the Advocate will not come to you . . . I will send him to you," an obvious solution would be to say that the Spirit's presence *is* Christ's presence with us. This is divine presence in the era between the ascension and parousia. Before he comes again, this is his intended presence. There is no reason to reject this spiritual presence as inadequate, and propose that the Holy Spirit must lift us up to heaven where the body of Christ is, to have the real communion with him *there*. As argued in chapter 3, there is no need to throw away the baby (Holy Spirit's presence) with the bathwater (problems associated with an overly spiritualized framework). Indeed we may ask Calvin: what's wrong with having the Holy Spirit with us *here*? Is Calvin's doctrine implying that the Holy Spirit's presence here and now is not enough?

As explained in chapter 3, the problem with Calvin's understanding of the work of the Holy Spirit, that our hearts are lifted by him to heaven to have communion with Christ's body and blood there, is that it draws attention *away* from the physical reality here and now. The remnant neo-Platonic, dualistic outlook that sees, on the one hand, the invisible and spiritual as real, and on the other, the visible and physical as merely aids for our weak senses, tends to devalue the communal fellowship itself. In Calvin's framework, it is only when our hearts are lifted to heaven away from the real world, so to speak, that we receive what the meal offers. Yet it is hardly a biblical viewpoint that the Holy Spirit lifts us away from the world. Although for Calvin we are lifted away only to have communion with the body and blood of Christ, hence the paramount importance of the physicality of Christ is still affirmed, there is still a Gnostic tendency with respect to how Christians should view the world *here*, where the visible church is. The mystical and otherworldly character of the communion we have with Christ's body and blood in heaven also downplays the ethical aspect of the Supper. Ethics concerns what happens *here* in the world. The indispensably communal aspect of the meal disappears as well: presumably the Holy Spirit can lift our souls up to Christ only individually.

Holding that Christ is present in the Lord's Supper through the Holy Spirit does not erase the uniqueness of the Supper. Although the Holy Spirit is with the church even during times when the Supper is not held, it is the physical Supper that Christ himself has instituted, and his table that we approach. It is in the physical Supper that the community together narrates Christ's passion and anticipate the future physical Banquet of the Lamb.

Our approach does not dismiss the Calvinist anxiety over a real communion with the physical body of Christ. Our salvation is bodily, not just spiritual. We passionately await his physical return. In addition, traditional Eucharistic theology, overlooking the Jewish context of the Last Supper for too long, has overlooked the cultural significance of the physical table fellowship between the Son of God and the *twelve* disciples in that occasion. As argued in chapter 2, the specific number twelve achieves much of what Western Eucharistic theology tries to achieve, namely the individual believer's communion with Christ's body. As argued, in Jewish culture the presence of a group of twelve (far from indicating a group of VIPs!) in fact precisely signifies the *whole* people of God. At the Last Supper, Christ already *physically* ate with the whole people of God. This was indeed physical table fellowship between God incarnate and his people. The Last Supper fulfilled what was already foreshadowed in the OT: that God would himself share the Passover meal with his people, and the people would inaugurate a covenant with him in person. The number twelve means you and I are already included in *that* physical meal with God. As in ancient near East suzerainty treaties, the sovereign makes and seals a pact with a delegated party of the people. This suffices for the pact to be valid to everyone in the vassal state. In sum, although we wait for Christ's physical return now, we have been included in a physical table fellowship with him, and he is with us through his Spirit.

Conclusion

The Lord's Supper embodies a dynamic relationship between two parties: God in the person of Christ, and the people he saved. The two supposedly estranged parties now regather at the table again. It speaks history and even movement, as well as relationship, not metaphysics. Because of sin, the human race was once driven away from his presence. Yet by the death and blood of the Lamb, they may once again return to God, enjoying a renewed fellowship with him. In this sense the Supper, as table fellowship, is not a mere sign. God has undone the consequence of sin. It is a homecoming of God's people to his table. We are once again restored as a covenantal partner in God's presence. Unfortunately traditional Eucharistic theology has long ignored the Jewish context of the Supper, and thereby bypassed this dynamic table fellowship, focusing instead on speculating on the relationship between the static elements and the equally statically-construed body and blood of Christ. We have discussed the dangers of the notion of Christ's body and blood as nourishment in traditional Eucharistic theology, especially Calvin's understanding of organic communion between believers and the body and blood of Christ. We have shown that such a language of eating Christ (even if only spiritually, sacramentally, or symbolically) is abstract, individualistic, ethically impractical, and objectifies Christ. It is also contrary to Reformed commitments, including the denial of *communicatio idiomatum*, and that the Supper is only a thanksgiving not an expiatory sacrifice. We have acknowledged the motivation behind the language of eating Christ, namely to secure a real communion with our savior, especially in light of political pressure to liaise with realist Lutherans. Yet today such political pressure no longer exists. We have also shown how communion with Christ is interpersonal fellowship with him (in particular *table* fellowship). More importantly, we participate in his life of obedience, by obediently coming to his table with our neighbors. Participation in Christ is to be actually *lived*. There is no need for a mysterious, organic penetration that is, in the end, abstract. The Supper as table fellowship is concrete, communal, immediately ethically practicable, and emphasizes the Son of God as end instead of means. This is not to mention that, as we have seen, both the Jewish Passover and Sinaitic covenant meals, to which the Lord's Supper alludes, speak of the wondrous table fellowship between God and his people. The Supper fulfills the God-sinner table fellowship foreshadowed in the old days.

In sum, it is advantageous to abandon organic language in Reformed theology in which we are said to be nourished by Christ's body and blood. In the Supper we do not eat Christ, but eat *with* Christ. We do not receive Christ, but are received *by* Christ at his table. Such non-mysterious table fellowship does not diminish the "wondrous" communion we have with Christ at all (*Inst.* 4.17.2). What is wondrous is the utterly undeserved table fellowship we enjoy with God (as is clear from the shocking Sinaitic narrative). It is wondrous not because of some metaphysical, unexplainable penetration between Christ and us. We come towards the gracious host. The gracious host simply does not become food on the table (even if only symbolically speaking). Such an objectifying and metaphysical move not only has ignored the historical context of the Supper, but would only obscure the undeserved table fellowship we have with Christ.

Today, our communion with Christ is through his Spirit, whom Christ has sent to us here and now in the world, without a need for our hearts to be transported to heaven, a realm construed as more real than the physical world. The Spirit's presence here and now in the world is real divine presence. In the Supper we anticipate Christ's physical return and the final banquet which will consummate God-sinner table fellowship. We will all dine *with* him.

5

Eating *With*:
Sinner-Sinner Table Fellowship

[Jesus said at the Last Supper,] "I am giving you a new commandment, that
you love one another; just as I have loved you,
that you also love one another."
—JOHN 13:34

You prepare a table before me in the presence of my enemies.
—Ps 23:5

IN THIS PROJECT WE have insisted on the necessity of following the verbal
cues of Jesus at the Last Supper which clearly conjured Israel's Exodus
event: the Passover and the Sinaitic covenant. Instead of some visible sign
that bears some mystical or symbolic relationship to the hidden body and
blood of Christ, the Lord's Supper tells, or rather fulfills, a *story*. It is a
story between God and his people, whom he delivered from sin, through
incarnation in the Son who lived a life of obedience to fulfill the law,
who died on the cross and was raised from death. Once, humanity was
driven away from God's presence because of sin. Yet in the person of the
Son, God made possible and himself enjoyed table fellowship with sinful
humanity. This restored table fellowship is the triumphant antithesis of
the exile and banishment that was the result of human sin. This story also
concerns sinners who are estranged from one another. Sin has alienated

not only the human race from God, but also humans from one another. This comes in all forms of oppression, exploitation, racism, sexism, etc. Because of what Christ has done, sinners are called to come together again in remembrance of the Lord who delivered them, and who also commanded them to love one another. The Supper is significant not because of some mystery or symbolism, but because parties that are *not* supposed to come together have nevertheless come together! God's salvation is the exact reversion of alienation. He brings his people back together again to his presence, and they are to be back in fellowship as well. An account of the Supper must detail this sinner-sinner table fellowship.

Unfortunately, traditional Eucharistic theology has been unhelpful in bringing interpersonal dynamics to the forefront of inquiry. Traditional theology engages with issues such as literal *vs.* figurative interpretations of Jesus's words of institution, the connection between the rite and Christ's sacrifice, the metaphysics of the presence of Christ's body and blood, and mechanisms of our participation in him, etc. It is not immediately clear how Christians' interactions at the table and their everyday lives in society should fit into the discourse. In the first place, the theologically untrained find such doctrinal articulations cumbersome, with language such as substance/accidents, sign/reality, even "sacrament," not to mention *ex opere operato*.[1] In Peter Leithart's words, sacramental theology has "again and again" drawn away from concrete situations.[2] On the whole, the Supper seems to have nothing to do with economics and world issues.[3] In addition, liberation theologians complain that current Eucharistic practices of the church fail to express solidarity with the oppressed and marginalized in the church and to address injustice in the society at large.[4] Some theologians even pointed out that sacraments have been used as tools to reinforce unjust hierarchy and abuse.[5] There is undeniably a deep disconnect between traditional doctrinal concerns on the one hand, and ethics and liberation on the other.

1. Barth, *Rediscovering the Lord's Supper*, 2.

2. Leithart, "Signs of the Eschatological Ekklesia," 631.

3. Cochrane, *Eating and Drinking with Jesus*, 8.

4. See, e.g., Segundo, *Sacraments Today*; Balasuriya, *Eucharist and Human Liberation*; Carvalhaes, *Eucharist and Globalization*.

5. See, e.g., Grimes, "Breaking the Body of Christ"; Winner, *Dangers of Christian Practice*; Cavanaugh also argues how a wrong sacramental theology may back ecclesial hierarchy and even supremacy of temporal powers, and thereby legitimizes violence (Cavanaugh, *Torture and Eucharist*, 207–21).

It is time for doctrinal theology to discern, even rethink, some of its own long-held presuppositions that might have driven a wedge between doctrine, and ethics and politics. This chapter first aims to name some deeper, underlying presuppositions in traditional Eucharistic theology that might be factors in marginalizing ethical inquiry, using Reformed theology as an example. In short, (1) a long Augustinian tradition fundamentally dichotomizes the Supper in terms of the physical, visible sign on the one hand, and signified, invisible reality on the other. A tendency of such a dichotomy is to seek the reality of salvation only in the spiritual realm, and not transformation in and of *this* empirical world. What we do physically in this realm ordinarily, i.e., ethics, is pushed to the periphery. (2) If Christ may be physically present in the elements, this miracle inevitably becomes the primary concern. Divine action overshadows questions of human action. A focus on the static elements also overshadows questions of human dynamics. (3) The problem of sin in Western traditions is framed primarily in subjective and noetic terms, instead of fundamentally relational, and sociopolitical terms. It is primarily concerned with the individual soul, its knowing and willing capacities, virtues, and actions. This individualistic and subjective outlook tends to overlook sin that lies deep in our social fabric and even manifests systemically in political structures.

This chapter will show that, in light of the Passover context and the centrality of the covenant, horizontal interhuman relationships are in fact the kernel of the Supper. Ethics is key. Exegetically, traditional Eucharistic theology has overwhelmingly focused on Paul's liturgical formula in 1 Cor 10–11 and Jesus's Bread of Life discourse in John 6, instead of the four Gospel accounts of the Last Supper. In focusing on these two passages, what evades us is the Passover context specified in all four Gospels. What then retreats to the background is the historical *liberation* of Jews that was the very backdrop of the Last Supper. In addition, the two passages are often perceived as presenting to us the conceptual pair body-blood. The perception is that we are to be concerned about the relation between the elements of bread and wine and Christ's flesh and blood. At the core, they invite metaphysical questions. But most devastatingly we tend to only notice "blood" instead of specifically "blood *of the covenant*." As a result, the divine-human covenant retreats to the background, and with it, the ethical terms of the covenant. Furthermore, attention to John 6 almost always distracts theologians from John's own account of the Last Supper, in John 13, in which Jesus washed his disciples' feet and gave a new commandment to love one another. There it was clear that the renewed covenant relationship with God specifically demands right interhuman relationships.

This chapter proposes that we should take seriously Jesus's reference to the new covenant, by rediscovering the centrality of John 13 in our understanding of the Supper. While only Christ fulfilled the covenant, by living a life of perfect obedience, we are nevertheless restored as true covenant partners of God. We are not only made able to eat and drink in his presence, but are called once again to respond to him by obeying his commandments, in particular commandments that govern our social relationships. The *neighbor* should be a focus in a doctrine of the Supper, not some invisible realm of grace, or mystery, or our inner capacities. The covenant is a challenge to us to obey and take up Christ's example to love by serving. The emphasis on this human active response to the Word of God would align with the Reformed emphasis on the Word, and the importance of sanctification, as well as the covenantal basis of reconciliation. In order for the Supper to unequivocally call for human action in the church and even in society, theologians should resist the tendencies to understand it primarily as a sign that signposts invisible grace, or as a mystery.

This chapter will argue that, therefore, contrary to Calvin, the Supper as a covenant meal is hardly some visible, sensory "aid" that assures our minds of some invisible, abstract reality of grace, or of our spiritual nourishment of Christ. Instead, the meal is not meant to be easy: we are to obey Christ's new commandment. We are called to come together with other sinners. It is likely uncomfortable. Even at the Last Supper, as *all four* Gospel accounts highlight, Judas the traitor was present at the table (Matt 26:21; Mark 14:18; Luke 22:3; John 13:2). I will coin this "the real presence of Judas." The Supper precisely highlights the ugly, broken social reality before our eyes. With this, I will also question the Reformed rejection of the Lutheran idea of *manducatio impiorum*. Because the focus has been the receiving of Christ's body and blood and thereby true union with him, there is anxiety then to distinguish between worthy *vs.* unworthy reception. Yet the theological fixing of the category of the *impiorum* to be excluded at the table ignores the precisely unworthy character of God-sinner table fellowship that makes the Supper significant. Parties that are not supposed to come together have nevertheless come together because of Christ. Precisely Christ is able to break down barriers. In recovering the sense of participants being received *by* Christ, instead of them receiving Christ, we emphasize this Gracious Host, not the need to exclude the "unworthy," as if there were some who are "worthy." Unfortunately the creation of such a theological category only further reinforces the tendency to divide and exclude that already plagues our society.

This chapter will conclude with the political dimension of the Supper. In light of the Exodus context of the Last Supper, a doctrine of the Supper *is* already liberation theology—one has only to recall what happened on the first Passover. Christ chose to institute the Supper in his remembrance on the memorial day for liberation. A theology of the Supper must not ignore this context, but must ask about its relevance. The Passover context precisely unveils the political, even structural, character of sin. Sin comes in the form of state oppression, and God liberated his people from such sin as well. The meal remembers how God heard the cries and observed the suffering of the oppressed. It still speaks good news for the marginalized and oppressed.

Discontents with the Reformed Tradition

We should rediscover the resources for an ethics-centered theology of the Supper. Yet the existence of a deep gulf existing between doctrinal concerns and ethics and liberation is likely symptomatic of theology done wrongly in the first place. One must name the roots of the problem. It will be helpful to enlist some underlying philosophical presuppositions responsible for distraction from ethical inquiry.

Augustine's Platonism

Traditional Eucharistic theology has long kept the door wide opened for philosophy including Platonism to frame our understanding of the Eucharist. This must be traced back to Augustine's notion that a sacrament is visible word, specifically as a visible sign of invisible grace.[6] As a result, Eucharistic theology in the West has long operated with a dichotomy between the physical and visible sign on the one hand, and the spiritual and invisible reality on the other. The physical, sensible world, according to this outlook, is at most a "signpost" that points to invisible grace, and therefore value is placed on the latter, not the former. The invisible is

---

6. See, e.g., Augustine's *Ep 105* 3.12; *civ. Dei* 10.5; *c. Faust* 19.11; *cat. rud.* 26.50; also Council of Trent, session 13, Decree on the Eucharist, chapter 3; Calvin, *Inst.* 4.14.1.

the ultimate reality, and the point of the Supper is to contemplate what is signified. The tendency is to view grace as belonging to the invisible realm, detached from the empirical world here and now. Unfortunately, Reformed theology does not only fail to question Augustine's dualistic, Platonic framework, it embraces it, in its strong distinction between the physical sign and the signified reality. In this regard, Zwingli was, at least *prima facie*, more guilty than Calvin. Borrowing Augustine's language, Zwingli defined a sacrament to be a sign of a sacred thing, a visible figure or form of invisible grace.[7] Having envisioned the Supper in such dichotomized terms, he did not allow any connection between the two, except as an "analogy," a signifying.[8] His anti-idolatry efforts precluded him from attaching any salvific value to created physical signs. To him it is explicit that, because only God gives grace, the physical sign does not and cannot offer grace in any sense.[9] The bread only *signifies* the body.

Calvin complained that Zwingli had completely severed the sign from the reality.[10] He himself also started with a clear dichotomy: "the sacred mystery of the Supper consists in two things: physical signs, which, thrust before our eyes, represent to us, according to our feeble capacity, things invisible; and spiritual truth, which is at the same time represented and displayed through the symbols themselves" (*Inst.* 4.17.11). But he sought a middle-ground, Chalcedonian-fashioned distinction-but-not-separation between the sign and the signified (e.g., 4.17.21). He affirmed that, through the signs, God truly realizes a spiritual communion between us and Christ, which for him was the point of the Supper. "That sacred partaking of his flesh and blood, by which Christ pours his life into us, . . . he also testifies and seals in the Supper—not by presenting a vain and empty sign, but by manifesting there the effectiveness of his Spirit to fulfill what he promises" (4.17.10). "Christ is truly shown to us through the symbols of bread and wine, his very body and blood" (17.11). Nevertheless, for Calvin, the physical sign is effective precisely in lifting our hearts away from it to the signified reality. The reality in which our true, spiritual nourishment by Christ's body and blood, and therefore the reality of the Supper, takes place in *heaven*, not on earth. Hence the *sursum corda*. The signs themselves he called the "corruptible elements" (4.17.19,

7. Zwingli, "Account of the Faith," in *On Providence*, 48.

8. Zwingli, "Account of the Faith," in *On Providence*, 48; Zwingli, "Exposition of the Faith," in *Zwingli and Bullinger*, 263.

9. Zwingli, "Account of the Faith," in *On Providence*, 39, 46.

10. Calvin, "Short Treatise," *TT* 2:195.

20).[11] Our hearts and minds must be lifted to heaven. Furthermore, for Calvin, the visible signs are used by God because they are "best adapted to our small capacity" (4.17.1), "according to our feeble capacity" (4.17.11), "as our weakness requires."[12] "The function of the Sacrament is to help the otherwise weak mind of man so that it may rise up to look upon the height of spiritual mysteries" (17.36). Calvin himself had to ask, "But why do we repeat the word 'ascension' so often?" (4.17.27). The rhetoric of the Reformed tradition heavily conveys a strong dichotomy between the physical, corruptible realm with elements given for our weakness on the one hand, and on the other the spiritual realm where Christ is present, and where the reality of the Supper lies.

Yet our social interactions, indeed all our ethical-political actions, take place in *this* physical, visible world. As liberation theologian Juan Luis Segundo contested, once we separate the sacred from the profane, then it is always only the sacred that is given value. Yet love requires deeds in the profane world.[13] It is true that it was necessary for Reformers to have in their hands theological resources to refute the Catholic doctrine of transubstantiation, according to which the elements in the Mass are said to have substantially changed into the body and blood of Christ. Hence the need for Reformed theology to strongly distinguish between the (physical) elements and the (spiritual) reality. They found their resource precisely in Augustine's Platonic dichotomy. Yet in order to avoid idolatry, the tendency is to devalue the physical world in our Eucharistic theology. Most interestingly, for Calvin, because our minds must not be set on the physical "corruptible elements," therefore we must turn to the only alternative, which is the heavenly reality (4.17.12, 19). Indeed, the work of the Holy Spirit is specifically to "lift" our minds and hearts to Christ, who is in heaven, at the right hand of the Father (17.18, 27). "We are lifted up to heaven with our eyes and minds, to seek Christ *there* in the glory of his Kingdom" (17.18). There is, however, no mention in this doctrinal treatment that the Holy Spirit is to edify the church community, or to transform the society, *in this world.* The emphasis is almost always Christ in heaven, not what happens *here.* A Platonic dichotomy between physical sign and signified spiritual reality tends to ignore the social reality of the current world.

11. Also Calvin, "Short Treatise," *TT* 2:187.

12. Calvin, "Short Treatise," *TT* 2:171.

13. Segundo, *Sacraments Today*, 14.

I do not mean that those who hold on to an Augustinian/Platonic worldview in their Eucharistic theology cannot understand the Supper to have ethical implications on the participants' lives. Augustine called his fellow Christians to *be* what they see (i.e., one bread).[14] Nevertheless, the symbolism means that in the Supper, love is only signified by the visible elements. The Supper itself is not an act of love.[15] In his *Institutes*, Calvin called sacraments "exercises of piety," by which we bind ourselves to God, "to purity and holiness of life," and "to pursue piety and innocence" (4.14.19, also 14.1). Nevertheless, this "piety,"[16] as Calvin explained elsewhere in the *Institutes*, is largely our inner, subjective response towards God: "I call 'piety' that reverence joined with love of God which the knowledge of his benefits induces" (1.2.1).[17] Within his treatment of the Supper, Calvin argued that the third use of the Supper is to exhort us to "mutual love" (4.17.38). For him, because we are made one with Christ in heaven, we are also made one body. We should see that we cannot injure our brothers without also injuring Christ, and we cannot love Christ without also loving our brothers. Nevertheless, this paragraph is a short one after thirty-seven paragraphs in a chapter of fifty paragraphs. It is hardly the focus in his doctrine of the Supper. The same observation can be made from this "Short Treatise," where again discussion of brotherly love as the third use of the Supper takes up little space.[18] This may be surprising considering Calvin's life devoted to his fellow Christians and to ecumenical causes. While the intention may not be there, the tendency of a Platonic framework is to prioritize the spiritual, invisible realm over the visible, corruptible, temporal world, and all that happens here in a fleeing manner. Salvation involves ascending to the heavenly realm, and has little to do with transforming the current political *status quo*.[19] One

14. Augustine, *Sermon 57*, session 7; and *Sermon 272*.

15. See Arthur Cochrane's critique below.

16. *Pietatem/pietatis*, CO 2:942.

17. For an account of the pastoral character of Calvin's teachings on piety, see Jones, *Calvin and the Rhetoric of Piety*.

18. Calvin, "Short Treatise," TT 2:174.

19. Martha Moore-Keish defended Calvin by noting that Calvin, in reaction to idolatry in the Mass, wanted to turn our hearts away from the earthly things to heavenly things. The *sursum corda* is just a way to say that the physical elements themselves are not to be worshipped. He was not devaluing the ceremony. See Moore-Keish, *Do This in Remembrance of Me*, 24–26. Nevertheless, Calvin seemed to assume that the available alternatives are the physical elements and the heavenly reality. Moore-Keish noted the third use of the Supper in his "Short Treatise," and quoted from his

might note that there is no "descent" that corresponds to the much accentuated "ascent." Whatever communion accomplished in heaven still needs to be translated into communion "down here." In the Platonic outlook the heavenly realm is always the ultimate reality, the final destination. Our ethical decisions in our mundane life, inside and outside the church, become secondary.

A theology of the Supper that takes ethics seriously must therefore reevaluate the Platonic framework of the Augustinian tradition. If the Supper is to be clearly ethically relevant, we must insist that the visible, sensory realm in which we live is most real. While the concern is indeed not the physical elements of bread and wine in themselves, the physical, social reality of the Supper must be held as important. Theology should be suspicious of any philosophical framework that pits the spiritual and real against the physical, drawing attention to some abstract, invisible notion of grace, instead of how grace transforms the sin-infested temporary world in which we live.[20]

Mystery *vs.* Ethics

It is true that a more realist approach to the Eucharist (represented by Roman Catholic and Lutheran traditions) aims to recover the importance of the *physical* realm by asserting a real, physical presence of Christ's body and blood in the elements. In fact, the Aristotelian language of *substance*

Strassburg liturgy (from 1545), in which he mentioned "brotherly love with [one's] neighbors" (*Do This in Remembrance of Me*, 36–37). Yet this is not emphasized in his doctrine. She acknowledged that Calvin in the end had to emphasize the distance between heaven and earth (24).

Apart from Calvin's stance against the Catholic Mass, Janse also helpfully noted his intra-Protestant confrontations which shaped different periods of his writings. Janse observed that, for example from 1549 onwards, in the course of Calvin's disputes with Westphal who argued for an ontological union with Christ, there was a renewed tendency in Calvin's writings to spiritualize. Janse, "Calvin's Eucharistic Theology," 58–66.

20. This critique also applies to similar dichotomies such as between the visible and invisible church, and Luther's two kingdoms. Commenting on the former, William Cavanaugh pointed out that often such a dichotomy distances the "true" invisible church from the social visible church positioned in a political order. The church then focuses on being a supra-political entity above the much troubled world. While the church may become the eschatological hope of the suffering world, she is also little comfort for them here and now. Cavanaugh, *Torture and Eucharist*, 210–12. In Luther's separation of two kingdoms, again, grace is in a different realm from the earthly realm of politics. See, e.g., Thielicke, *Theological Ethics*, 2:565–98.

in the Catholic doctrine of transubstantiation may be seen as a critique against the Augustinian/Platonic tradition which tends to pit the spiritual against the physical.[21] Nevertheless such a realist, physicalist approach also kills any opportunity to prioritize ethics in a theology of the Eucharist. If Christ's body may be physically present in the elements, then the miracle lying in the elements becomes the primary concern. The result is that the focus of inquiry is predominantly on the static elements of bread and wine, and the mystery that possibly lies *there*, instead of the dynamic interactions between members of the faith community. In other words, we often zoom-in onto what is on the table, instead of the actions of those at the table, and almost never the sociopolitical world at large.[22]

In addition, in theologies where it is believed that a miracle truly takes place in the rite, the problem is not only a matter of priority. The rite would be held as a divine work, and cannot be at the same time our everyday, ethical undertaking. We (at least the laity) cannot be called in our everyday life to act in connection to something that is beyond our comprehension. As Segundo reminded us, the issue is ancient. Historically, in the third to fourth centuries, the need to affirm sacramental validity irrespective of the ethical condition of the minister severed divine efficacy from human efficacy in sacramental theology. Unfortunately divine and human efficacies were juxtaposed as alternatives. The need to affirm the former compromises the latter.[23] According to Segundo, a problem with the traditional preoccupation with the *ex opere operato*, i.e., the objective, efficacious work of the sacramental rite, is that it makes Christians value the rites excessively, overshadowing the point that Christians are *also* to do the work in their own contexts and neighborhoods. The need to labor in history eludes the community.[24]

Building on observations such as that of Henri de Lubac, William Cavanaugh lamented that sacramental realism does not necessarily translate into ecclesial realism—the idea that the church becomes the body of Christ and therefore decides to do his work on earth. The world is often left untouched by a miraculous physical presence of Christ on the altar. As the theology of the Catholic Mass developed, the Church

---

21. See, e.g., Seeberg, *History of Doctrines*, 2:75–79; Fitzer, "Augustinian Roots of Calvin"; Chadwick, "Ego Berengarius"; Adams, *Later Medieval Theories*, 32–33; Grumett, *Material Eucharist*, 166.

22. See Leithart, "Way Things Really Ought to Be."

23. Segundo, *Sacraments Today*, 47.

24. Segundo, *Sacraments Today*, 60.

increasingly focused on objects, not the community's own actions. The Mass is increasingly about the lay congregation watching the spectacle, instead of them seeking to be incorporated with it. Worse, they contemplate the spectacle individually in their minds.[25] The result of upholding a real, holy presence is not edification of the congregation, but distance and awe. Adding to this, real presence often necessitates the special act of consecration, and hence some sort of hierarchical institution in the church, distinguishing those who are authorized, if not empowered, to have intimate access to holy presence from those who are not. The laity is institutionally kept from the divine presence and therefore the vocation to be "efficacious" as well. What is emphasized is instead their inertness, not calling.[26]

Even when Calvin insisted that the physical body and blood of Christ is present only in heaven, he insisted also that our souls are raised to heaven to have a *mystical* communion with him there. This mystical communion is the point of the Supper. The focus is still on a miracle, "something so mysterious and incomprehensible,"[27] it is "a secret too lofty for either my mind to comprehend or my words to declare . . . I rather experience than understand it" (4.17.32). Again, such a miracle only eclipses our responsibilities in our mundane life. One may even point out that, for Calvin, the miracle is in *heaven*, which (at least in lay terms) cannot be further away from the earth and what happens *down here*. Also, as noted in the last chapter, Calvin based our ecclesial union on our union with Christ. Yet our union with Christ is for him a result of our spiritual nourishment by his physical body and blood. It is not immediately clear how we can similarly offer ourselves as mystical, spiritual nourishment for each other too. Yet the most devastating point against Calvin is that, in his theology, "mutual love" among Christians is based on our union with Christ. Not every human being is included. In fact, all unbelievers are explicitly *not* included (preciously because it is a true union with Christ, 4.17.33–34). In his theology there is a category of people who are unworthy to be in communion with Christ. There is a clear limit to the

---

25. Cavanaugh, *Torture and Eucharist*, 213–14. See, e.g., Lubac, *Corpus Mysticum*, 34–39; Beckwith, *Christ's Body*, 36.

26. See the discussion in Segundo, *Sacraments Today*, 56–60. Segundo contested that this ecclesial hierarchy will sadly be translated into hierarchy on other levels of human existence. On this point, see also Luther's criticism of the sacrament of ordination, in *Babylonian Captivity of the Church*, LW 36:112.

27. Calvin, "Short Treatise," TT 2:166.

scope of this "mutual love." The Supper then has little ethical implication outside church doors. Surely, Calvin would not agree to this. But his highly mystical Eucharistic theology makes it inapplicable directly in ordinary and political life. If the Supper is to be a forceful call to human action, the notion of mystery must go. What must be questioned is not only the physical presence of Christ. The Reformed tradition already ruled it out. What should also be questioned is the very question itself. The question does not only fail to respect the Jewish roots of the Last Supper. It also distracts us either to focus on the static objects on the table or in heaven, away from what happens in the community in the ordinary, empirical world.

Perhaps this is why, although Zwingli heavily borrowed Platonic language of sign *vs.* reality, he was able to bring his theology to bear on the communal actions of the participants (albeit only briefly). For him, only the Spirit can give grace. This is God's action alone. Sacraments, therefore cannot in any sense confer or dispense grace. "From this it follows," he said, that a sacrament is a "public testimony of that grace which is previously present to every individual."[28] In eliminating the possibility of divine mystery, and that God works through created elements, Zwingli understood the Supper purely as a human action, and intuitively proceeded to ask ethical questions concerning this human action. For example, as he immediately suggested, to be baptized is to testify that we are to live upright.[29] It is clear that Zwingli also had *communal* action in mind, and not only individual hearts that are nourished by Christ, when the church is made one by Christians doing the same action together.[30]

Sin as Individualistic and Subjective

A fundamental correction that needs to be made to traditional Eucharistic theology is its presuppositions concerning the nature of sin. The Western tradition fundamentally understands humanity by distinguishing it from animals, and has long emphasized human cognitive faculties as what constitute the *imago Dei*. The human soul is said to be the "seat" of the image of God.[31] As a result, sin is construed in terms of what

28. Zwingli, "Account of the Faith," in *On Providence*, 47.

29. Zwingli, "Account of the Faith," in *On Providence*, 48.

30. Zwingli, "Exposition of the Christian Faith," in *Zwingli and Bullinger*, 264–65.

31. E.g., Augustine, *On the Literal Meaning of Genesis*, VI.12; Aquinas, *STh* I. q. 93,

taints the *imago* and obstructs the *soul's* capacity to truly know God. It lies in the corruption of human nature, the loss of free will and the true knowledge of God. The problem of sin is therefore framed primarily in subjective and noetic terms, instead of sociopolitical terms. Even the virtue of justice, for example, which is relational, is understood as the virtue *of an individual*.[32] Eucharistic theology, pertaining to our salvation and therefore layered on our prior understanding of sin, is inevitably tainted with this highly subjective outlook, too. Reformed theology, unfortunately, did not challenge but only reinforced this problem. In reacting against the Catholic notion of *gratia non tollit naturam, sed perficit*, including the idea that human nature remains good in certain aspects even after the fall,[33] Protestantism insists on the total depravity of human nature, specifically depravity not only in the body but also in the soul in its entirety. Such a response, however, even more strongly restricts the discourse within the individual's body-soul makeup, and in the noetic capacities of metaphysical human nature, not extending to social, interpersonal relationships and the political manifestations of sin, nor to how salvation addresses these latter aspects of sin. While Reformed theology emphasizes sanctification as much as justification, it still does so within a subjective framework. The focus of sanctification is still on individual souls and their inner capacities. While it is not the aim of this work to investigate a theology of sin, we will sample some of Calvin's assertions in his treatment of sin to make this point.

Given his historical context, it is inevitable that Calvin's understanding of sin was predominantly framed in natural and intellectual terms.[34] He started his whole *magnum opus* with the *knowledge* of God and

---

a. 2, 6, 7; Calvin, *Inst.* 1.15.3.

32. See, e.g., Aquinas, *STh* II.II q. 58.

33. E.g., Aquinas, *STh* I, q. 1, a. 8, II.I, q. 85, a. 1.

34. Needless to say, Calvin was not the first in this regard. Luther's reformation was strongly associated with disputes on free will *vis-à-vis* "bondage of the will." His anxiety also brought him to affirm a Christian's freedom of conscience from the dread of the law. The gospel, for him, frees the Christian because justification is by faith alone. Whether directly or indirectly, this notion of a free conscience from the law led to the Protestant idea of freedom of conscience from institutional heteronomy of the church and the state. See, e.g., discussion in Scholler, "Martin Luther on Jurisprudence," 270. Yet theologically, the scope and focus of inquiry lie in the individual's will and conscience. For Luther as much as it is for Calvin, the Lord's Supper is for strengthening one's conscience (see *LW* 35:53, 60, 85–86; *LW* 36:350–52; *LW* 37:71). This set the predominantly *subjective* outlook in the Reformed tradition's treatment of sin and salvation.

knowledge of self (*Inst.* 1.1.1). Such a starting point frames the whole corpus of his theology noetically. He locates the *imago Dei* unambiguously in the human soul. "There is no doubt that the proper seat of his image is in the soul," he said (1.15.3). For him, the *imago Dei* must be what distinguishes us from corporeal animals, and therefore lies purely in the faculties of the incorporeal soul. "In order that we may know of what parts this image consists, it is of value to discuss the *faculties* of the soul" (1.15.4). "We do not have a full definition of 'image,'" he continued, "if we do not see more plainly those *faculties* in which man excels" (1.15.4). It is important to note also that Calvin distinguished strongly the soul from the body, the soul being the nobler, immortal part. The soul is to be freed from the "prison house" of the body (1.15.2). Specifically it is the human soul alone that responds to God. This he called the conscience (1.15.2). It responds to God's judgment discerning between good and evil, and is a sign of the soul. Quoting from NT passages, Calvin showed that the essence of the human lies in her soul. "God's image is properly to be sought *within* him, not outside him, indeed, it is an *inner* good of the soul" (1.15.4, emphases mine). Altogether, his outlook of what humanity consists in is largely inward and subjective.

It is not surprising that, for Calvin, the corruption of sin, the tainting of the *imago Dei*, is specifically highlighted to be located in the soul. The fall results in the corruption and deformity of what is unique in humanity. Certainly, as a Reformer he was reacting against Catholic optimism that restricts sin mostly to the corruption of the senses, and the affirmation of the spiritual capacities of fallen human nature.[35] Contrary to such, Calvin insisted on the corruption of the entire human nature (2.1.5, 7), and therefore also of the soul. His definition of original sin is exemplary: "let us define original sin. . . . Original sin . . . seems to be a hereditary depravity and corruption of our nature, diffused into all parts of the *soul*, which first makes us liable to God's wrath, then also brings forth in us those works which Scripture calls 'works of the flesh'" (2.1.8). Referencing Augustine as his authority, he stated that "it is . . . proper to say that man is *naturally* depraved and faulty" (2.1.11). "All parts of the *soul* were possessed by sin after Adam deserted the fountain of righteousness" (2.1.8). Sin "occupie[s] the very citadel of his *mind*, and . . . penetrated to the depths of his *heart*" (2.1.9). In his commentary to Gen 3, Calvin stressed the same point: "depravity was diffused through

---

35. See his refutation of Peter Lombard that sin only corrupts human senses in *Inst.* 2.1.9.

all parts of [the] *soul* as well as [the] body."[36] "Original sin does not reside in one part of the body only, but holds its dominion over the whole
man, and so occupies every part of the *soul*."[37] In short, the emphasis is
inward, that "sin occupies both mind and heart" (2.1.9). What repeatedly
surfaces is the emphasis of knowledge. Even our very knowledge of self is
corrupted. For Calvin, "Paul [in Rom 3:10] teaches that corruption does
not reside in one part only, but pervades the whole *soul*, and each of its
faculties. . . . Original sin . . . seizes upon the very seat of *reason*, and upon
the whole *heart*."[38] Thus, Reformed theologians already note the "noetic"
understanding of sin for Calvin.[39]

As a result, it is hard for Calvin to expound a theology of sin and
salvation fundamentally from a relational, interpersonal perspective. Salvation, therefore for Calvin, is the restoration of our lost inner integrity.
In his theology of sin he devoted comparatively less ink to address social
and political sin. Building his case on Pauline language, he stated that
salvation is our being renewed in Christ's image. Specifically, as expected,
this restoration starts with our *knowledge*, and only then righteousness
and holiness (1.15.4). In his words, God's image must first be "visible in
the light of the *mind*, in the uprightness of the *heart*, and in the soundness
of all the parts" (1.15.4, emphases mine). In fact, Calvin explained that it
is a "principle" that what is renovated in the image of God must have had
the highest place in creation, i.e., *the intellect* (1.15.4). Calvin mentions
alienation from God as a result of sin only very briefly in his treatment
of human nature and sin (1.15.4). At a point he also acknowledged that
it is unfaithfulness and disobedience to God that was the beginning of
the fall (2.1.4). He was aware of the relational aspect of original sin. Yet
immediately, he asserted, it was because of the ancestors' setting aside
truth in favor of falsehood. The focus returned to knowledge again. Calvin acknowledged that the "fruits of sin" were "adulteries, fornications,
thefts, hatreds, murders, carousings" (2.1.8). But soon enough he went
on to again stress that "we are so vitiated and perverted in every part of
our nature," "a contagion imparted by [Adam] resides *in us*" (2.1.8, my
emphasis). For him the heart of the matter is our *inner* nature.[40]

36. Calvin, *Commentaries on Genesis*, 151; emphasis mine.

37. Calvin, *Commentaries to Genesis*, 162; emphasis mine.

38. Calvin, *Commentaries to Genesis*, 155; emphases mine.

39. E.g., Helm, "Calvin, Sensus Divinitatis, and Noetic Effects"; Moroney, *Noetic
Effects of Sin*, 1–26; Vandici, "Calvin and Reformed Epistemology."

40. Thus the problem in Calvin's understanding of sin is not a pessimism *per se*

There was in the first place hardly adequate theological resources even in Reformed theology to identify sin that is embedded in the social fabric of society, beyond the body-soul composition and human nature of an individual. Zwingli's approach to sin was similarly inward-looking. Sin is emphasized to be a "disease" that infects human nature, and more specifically expressed in the (inner) battle between the flesh and the spirit.[41] As noted by scholars, the even stronger inward outlook is in fact characteristic of Reformed theology. Instead of emphasizing power in ecclesial institution and in clergy, Reformed theology emphasizes the experience of God and union with God by the individual heart. The power, instead, lies in the work of the Holy Spirit. The church with its institution and hierarchy is therefore no longer the mediator of grace.[42] Historically the need for the Reformers to repudiate the Mass as expiatory led them to emphasize individual faith in God's promises. However, such an inward emphasis also further reinforces an individualistic, subjective outlook to the problem of sin and salvation.

It is no wonder that Calvin's Eucharistic theology, which concerns redemptive grace for the believer, also takes up a subjective, individualistic framework. If the problem of sin primarily lies in our knowledge, it is no wonder that Calvin's treatment of the Eucharist was predominantly concerned with our lack of assurance, or our weak conscience. Right at the beginning he said that the purpose of sacraments was to be "aids" primarily for assuring our faith and conscience (4.14.1). This manifests in his very definition of a sacrament: "it is an outward sign by which the Lord seals on our consciences the promises of his good will toward us in order to sustain the weakness of our faith; and we in turn attest our piety toward him in the presence of the Lord and of his angels and before men" (4.14.1). Even this "piety," as we recall, is mainly vertical in dimension and expressed noetically: "I call 'piety' that reverence joined with love of God which the knowledge of his benefits induces" (1.2.1).[43] Indeed for

---

with respect to human depravity. His theology in fact affirms individual agency, e.g., in being critical of the political *status quo* and bringing transformations. See Compier, *Calvin's Rhetorical Doctrine of Sin*. The problem highlighted in this section has to do with his individualistic outlook, which emphasizes the individual soul and its capacities.

41. Zwingli, *Commentary on True and False Religion*, 138–53.

42. Carvalhaes, *Eucharist and Globalization*, 98–99; McDonnell, *John Calvin, Church, and Eucharist*, 363–65.

43. As J. Todd Billings noted, for Calvin, *pietas* is the restoration of our *knowledge* and *recognition* that all good things come from God. Billings, *Calvin, Participation, and Gift*, 117–19.

Calvin, a sacrament must always be joined to a preceding divine promise, because the sacrament is what *confirms* the promise, "making it more evident to us," because of our "ignorance" and "weakness" (4.14.3). The concern is that "our faith is slight and feeble unless it be propped on all sides and sustained by every means, it trembles, wavers, totters, and at last gives way" (4.14.3). In short, sacraments are "exercises which make us more certain of the trustworthiness of God's Word" (4.14.6; also 4.17.1). Repeatedly, Calvin held that sacraments were ordained to increase and confirm our faith (4.14.7–11). "The sacraments have effectiveness among us in proportion as we are helped by their ministry sometimes to foster, confirm, and increase the true *knowledge* of Christ *in ourselves*; at other times, to possess him more fully and enjoy his riches" (4.14.16, emphases mine). Even the reason why the Reformed church rejects withholding the cup from laity was because, in our weakness of faith, we need certainty that Christ is our drink no less than our food (4.14.47)!

On this point, Martha Moore-Keish defended Calvin. She argued that Calvin's language of accommodation was not to demean the physical sensory world, but to say that God is truly involved as an actor.[44] This, however, does not overthrow the fact that he assumed a Platonistic framework at the outset. Moore-Keish also argued that, for Calvin, faith as not an individualist and subjective state but an objective work by the Holy Spirit. She quoted Calvin's definition of faith, i.e., it is "a firm and certain knowledge of God's benevolence toward us, founded up the truth of the freely given promise in Christ, both revealed to our minds and sealed upon our hearts through the Holy Spirit" (3.2.7).[45] She noted how Calvin used plural pronouns throughout.[46] While it is right that Calvin understood faith to be an objective work by the Holy Spirit externally on us, it is a work on individual "knowledge," on our "minds" and "hearts." Moore-Keish herself acknowledged that Calvin did not address unjust social structures.[47]

Scholars remarked that a key to understanding Calvin's theology of the Supper is that his concerns were not metaphysical but in fact pastoral. He was concerned with whether his congregation members could have

44. Moore-Keish, *Do This in Remembrance of Me*, 29.

45. Moore-Keish, *Do This in Remembrance of Me*, 33.

46. Moore-Keish, *Do This in Remembrance of Me*, 42.

47. Moore-Keish, *Do This in Remembrance of Me*, 105. See B. A. Gerrish's discussion of Calvin's understanding of faith as knowledge, Gerrish, *Old Protestantism and the New*, 61–65.

a rested conscience in their hearts, that they are indeed free and united with Christ, pardoned by the Father and empowered by Holy Spirit.[48] Yet, we must notice, this pastoral concern is still narrowly subjective. Indeed the language in his Catechism for the church of Geneva was no less subjective. Sacraments are to "seal the promises of God on our *hearts*, and thereby better confirm their truth to us . . . [to] establish our *consciences* in a full *assurance* of salvation . . . to move and affect the *heart*, to enlighten the *mind*, to render the *conscience* sure and tranquil."[49] Overall, sacraments are to make us more certain of God's promises. The problem that the church faced, supposedly, was the lack of certainty in people's hearts. There is hardly any mention of other aspects of sin, e.g., relational and even structural sin.

But our experience of sin today is in stark contrast to this. Precisely if one stresses a pastoral approach to the Supper's concerns, all the more one cannot confine oneself simply to spiritual uncertainties. The reality is much more dire than that. Today we experience sin not only in our minds and hearts, or metaphysically in our nature, but primarily in everyday broken relationships and deep in the very structures of society. Sin is ubiquitous. It is not just in our weak conscience or lack of faith, but pervades our economy, schools, prison system, immigration policies, dictating regimes, foreign wars, etc. Sin always takes the blunt form of economic and political oppression, exploitation, inequality, racism, sexism, abuse. The list goes on. This exposes the obscurity of traditional theology that is dominated by noetic questions. Reformed Eucharistic theology is also shown to be out of touch with reality when it is preoccupied with whether sacraments convey "grace" when a certain individual soul partakes of Christ's body and blood. What "grace" are we talking about in a society plagued by unjust structures such as systemic discrimination and hierarchy? This fundamental problem explains the disgust expressed by liberation theologians who complain that traditional Eucharistic theology fails to address the injustice in society at large. This may even explain why, as some have also pointed out, sacraments may be even used as *tools* to reinforce unjust hierarchy and abuse. When the predominant theological tradition has long restricted our attention to individual souls and noetic assurance, it is not surprising that, in partaking the Supper, we

48. Billings, *Calvin, Participation, and Gift*, 141; also McDonnell, *John Calvin, Church, and Eucharist*, 196–97.

49. Catechism of the Church of Geneva, *TT* 2:84, emphases mine.

have been taught to first focus on our own inward benefits, not mutual relationships or the transformation of society.

Indeed, a long Augustinian tradition that sees contemplation of the divine as the true goal of the human life inevitably frames the problem of sin and salvation in individualistic, noetic terms, instead of social, actualistic terms. The Reformation which challenged ecclesial power structures nevertheless was not successful in moving theological discourse on sin and salvation away from a subjective, noetic emphasis to a more sociopolitical emphasis. The charge of liberation theologians is an opportunity to rethink this underlying framework of Eucharistic theology, and to seek new resources that might assist theology in prioritizing social ills. One must remember the biblical vision of salvation. It is the anticipation of a new Jerusalem (Rev 21:9–27), i.e., the renewal of a *sociopolitical* entity. What is to be redeemed is the social structure of a community, not just individual souls. This is in stark contrast to traditional theology's envisioning of salvation as contemplation of individual souls or our mystical participation in Christ's body and blood.

In sum, a long tradition that emphasizes an invisible realm, a possible mystery, and our inner capacities does not help us turn to the needs of our neighbor, who is visible, ordinary, and outside of us. Against this tradition, theology must assert the reality and importance of the physical realm, salvation that transforms the ordinary, and that sin lies not only in our individual souls, but in the society we, and our ancestors, have fabricated.

Commandments and Obedience

Sin concerns what *people* do and how they *relate* in *this* world. It is hard to deny that sin, as depicted in Scripture, is expressed in terms of human disobedience, in their actions, of God's commands. Sin and salvation therefore deal with this disobedience in real life. Salvation concerns our actions in this life, *not*, in other words, an invisible realm, nor some mystery on the altar or in heaven, nor only our souls and subjective capacities. In order for the Supper to more directly bear on our everyday ethical life, we should be asking questions about what people do and how they relate in this world. Not only the philosophical presuppositions, but the doctrinal questions that we pose in a theology of the Supper might also be fundamentally reevaluated. Apart from embracing Platonic or

Aristotelian philosophical frameworks, exegetically traditional Eucharist theology has always overwhelmingly focused on Paul's liturgical text in 1 Cor 10–11. Catholic-Protestant debates also always turn to Jesus's Bread of Life discourse in John 6, in particular 6:54–56, "Those who eat my flesh and drink my blood have eternal life, . . . for my flesh is true food and my blood is true drink." By focusing on these two passages, what easily evades us is the Passover context of the Last Supper, hence the historical liberation of Jews that was its very backdrop. In addition, the passages are often perceived as presenting the conceptual pair body/blood (or flesh/blood in light of John 6). The perception is that a theology of the Supper is to be concerned about the static elements of bread and wine, and to work out their either symbolic or mysterious relation to Christ's flesh and blood. The outlook is then often static instead of dynamic. At the core, they invite metaphysical questions. But most unfortunately the body/blood conceptual pair makes us focus on "blood" instead of "blood *of the covenant.*" When Jesus instituted the cup, he referenced not only to his blood, but specifically "blood *of the covenant*" (Matt 26:28; Mark 14:24; or "*new covenant* in my blood," Luke 22:20; 1 Cor 11:25). As a result, the divine-human covenant retreats to the background, and with it, the ethical terms of the covenant. John 6 completely lacks any reference to the covenant. Furthermore, attention to John 6 almost always distracts theologians from John's own account of the Last Supper, in John 13, in which Jesus washed his disciples' feet and gave a new commandment to love one another. There it was clear that the renewed covenant relationship with God very specifically demands ethical actions, and that Christ has even set us an example.

Instead of being preoccupied by metaphysical questions about the possible presence of the blood of Christ, and how we may partake of it, we must inquire about the covenant. A more appropriate question to ask concerning the Supper should therefore be *what are the precise contents of this new covenant?* At one point, Calvin specified that a sacrament is a "covenant," which is a "mutual agreement" between God and us (4.14.6, also 14.19). Concerning this covenant, he wrote, "God leagues himself with us, and we pledge ourselves to purity and holiness of life. . . . The Lord promises to cancel and blot out any guilt and penalty contracted by us through our transgression, and reconciles us to himself in his only-begotten Son, so do we, in turn, bind ourselves to him by this profession, to pursue piety and innocence" (4.14.19). As noted, this "piety" for Calvin is concerned with our "vertical" knowledge of God, and is not obviously at all to do with interpersonal, "horizontal" relationships. At any rate, Calvin's theology was bound by the need to present the Supper primarily in Platonistic symbolism, and he completely "passed over" John's account of the Last Supper. The specific contents of the covenant, with its ethical expectations, need to be spelled out and must be the focus of Eucharistic theology.

As we have seen, at Sinai, God entered into a covenant with his people by clearly spelling out his commandments (Exod 19–23). These are meant to be *kept* by the redeemed people (see Exod 19:4–5). These included not only "vertical" decrees that govern an individual's relationship with God, but even more minutely the "horizontal," social relationships to be lived out by the delivered people. In fact, as we have noted, this was what made the Sinaitic covenant unique among similar suzerain treaties from the ancient Near East—the sovereign showed an immense interest in the interpersonal lives of the people of the vassal state. The horizontal dimension of the covenant is therefore the key. These commandments concern just relationships that a redeemed community is commanded to live out *in society*. In the old covenant, God's people were commanded, for example, to allow their workers to take the Sabbath, to treat foreigners well because they were once foreigners too, to bear truthful witness, etc. (Exod 19–23). In short, the divine-human covenant essentially includes commandments, and these command us to *act* in certain ways towards our neighbor. In addition, the Supper is the new Passover meal that celebrates salvation from bondage, which in turns demands that we live a life fit for a freed, reconciled people. The covenant meal presumes the human's part in coming to the table and thereby agreeing to the ethical terms of the covenant.[50]

Precisely, the new covenant came with a new commandment. John's account of the Last Supper specifically includes the giving of a new commandment, even when it omitted the words of institution. Traditional Eucharistic theology has for too long simply noted that John's account lacks the familiar words of institution and some theologians even suggested

50. Segundo, in his critique of traditional Eucharistic theology, did not note the covenantal aspect of the Supper, but he helpfully highlighted Jesus's command to make amends with one's adversaries *before* approaching the altar: "The fact is that the overall context indicates that man's whole destiny depends on just and cordial relations with his neighbor (Matt 5:21–23). This is so true that the necessity of righting these relations takes precedence over the strictly religious function. In other words, the natural causality which directs human relationships is more important than the extraordinary causality which governs cultic worship" (Segundo, *Sacraments Today*, 22–23).

that, therefore, it can be sidestepped.[51] Yet according to John, at the Last Supper, Jesus took the role of a slave by washing his disciples' feet. He then said to them, "If I, your Lord and Teacher, have washed your feet, you also ought to wash one another's feet. For I have set you an example, that you also should do as I have done to you" (John 13:14–15). "I give you a new commandment," he continued, "that you love one another. Just as I have loved you, you also should love one another" (13:34–35). One cannot help but notice that, again, the new commandment is "horizontal" in character. It very bluntly concerns our treatment of one another. In sum, Christ commanded us to *act*. He did so by first setting an example himself. The faith community is *challenged* to act accordingly.[52] John's account did not only not omit the Last Supper, it in fact complements the Synoptic Gospels by spelling out the new commandment that came with the new covenant. Salvation involves not only the forgiveness of sins, but the restoration of us as covenant partners of God who are once again called to obey. Precisely the new covenant meal came with a new commandment: to love one another as Christ has loved us. A theology of the Supper must uphold John 13 as fundamental to our understanding of the Supper.

As we have seen, both Platonic, dualistic as well as Aristotelian, realist approaches to the Supper undermine the ethical nature of the Supper. A recovery of the *covenant* of the Supper, however, allows the Reformed tradition to affirm its fundamental ethical dimension. When seen historically and dynamically as a covenant meal between two parties, instead of metaphysically and statically in terms of some elements that stand in some relationship with Christ's body and blood, the ethical aspect of the Supper is immediately obvious. Therefore, in the first place there is no gap to be bridged between Eucharistic theology and ethics—the Supper *is* a covenant meal. It is a meal that inaugurates and celebrates a covenant

51. Examples include Morris, *Gospel according to John*, 311; Jeremias, *Eucharistic Words of Jesus*, 90, 107–8, 136, 165; Pitre, *Jesus and the Last Supper*, 5; Mathison, *Given for You*, 217; Stookey, *Eucharist*, 38. Segundo may be a rare exception, although his discussion was very brief (*Sacrament Today*, 4–5). He acknowledged the Eucharistic relevance of Jesus's setting an example by washing of disciples' feet in John 13, explaining that, while the Synoptic accounts depict the institution of the Eucharist, John's narrates its fulfillment.

52. Jesus's foot-washing speaks more than just inter-human love but also the divine humility acclaimed in Phil 2:6–11, even taking up the form of a servant, and ultimately laying down his life. See Brown, *Gospel according to John*, 562. Thus a conformity to Christ also calls for a conformity to such self-giving love.

between God and humanity which itself already contains the *ethical* terms of such a relationship. In particular, such terms lay out the *social* expectations of God's people. Instead of us posing doctrinal and philosophical questions, perhaps the cup of the covenant throws the ethical question back at us, namely whether we will to obey Christ's commandment. *We* are being asked the question. The covenant is an ethical issue. We are challenged to act.

This is why it is important that we do not at the outset characterize the meal in terms of a fundamental dichotomy between a physical sign and the signified spiritual reality, because such a picture overlooks the spiritual significance of human action in the *physical* realm that salvation is addressing. Such a picture does not direct us towards the visible neighbor. If we are to take the covenant seriously, with its clear ethical commandments, we must insist that the visible, sensory realm in which we live is most real. The physical, social reality of the Supper must be held with highest importance. It is in this physical realm that the terms of the covenant are to be obeyed. It is not only real—it is the *point* of the Supper. It is the reality of salvation, in fact, because sin is disobedience, and alienates humans from one another, and therefore salvation is in the form of summoning of sinners to obedience again in real life, and a restoration of the lost fellowship. In addition, it is just as important that we do not emphasize a mystery. The notion of a mystery overshadows our everyday human action and responsibility. What needs to be emphasized instead is human action, i.e., *ordinary* human action. Far from a symbol for some invisible reality, or a mystery, the Supper calls for obedient action in visible, ordinary everyday life.

Doubtlessly, the restoration of the covenant relationship between God and us sinners does not hinge on our successful obedience to the word of God (hence the absence of pledging of obedience in the new covenant inauguration, Exod 34:1–27). It is only Christ, not us, who fulfilled the righteousness of the law by his life of perfect obedience. He was obedient even unto death. The new covenant was sealed only in Christ's blood ("new covenant in *my* blood"). With his life and his blood poured out for the forgiveness of many, allowing us to come to God's presence again, our covenant relationship with God can be restored. We are not merely forgiven. What is lost is restored again. Sin is fundamentally disobedience, and therefore salvation is manifested not only in forgiveness, but once again, we are called to obey, specifically by loving one another as he has loved us. Because of the covenant meal, we know that we are indeed restored once again as God's covenant partners. We are now made free to obey again. This is why God's covenant was given anew, with a new commandment.[53]

Because in the covenant we are commanded to obey, to love one another as Christ has loved us, it is not to be understood as easy. We are challenged to act as Christ did. One thing that a theology of the Supper must seriously interrogate is Calvin's idea that the Supper is an "aid" for our faith. At the outset, Calvin characterized a sacrament to be an external "aid" to help to confirm and seal divine promise to the individual mind, to accommodate our weakness senses that are unable to comprehend the reality of the Supper (see 4.14.1, 4). This idea, as we have discussed, presupposes the Platonistic, dichotomized framework in which our physical, sensory realm has much less importance on its own except to direct our focus to what is invisible. What is visible—including our actions and interactions—cannot be the primary focus. This idea also presupposes that what primarily needs to be helped is the individual *mind* in knowing and affirming the promise of God (4.14.3). The Supper is to make us more certain. Repeatedly, Calvin held that sacraments were ordained to increase and confirm our faith (4.14.7–11; also 4.17.1). What is more, this outlook assumes that it is because our faith is weak, and need sensory aids, therefore God gave us these visual aids. The Supper presumably makes it easier for us to have faith by the use of analogous signs. The bread and wine are for us an "analogy to spiritual things," specifically visualizing the giving of Christ's body and shedding of his blood (4.17.3; see also 17.10, 14). Yet if we note and take seriously the covenant and the specific ethical commandment that came with it, the Supper does not make anything easier but is in fact difficult. Christ himself took the role of a slave and washed the feet of his disciples, even his traitor's, and commanded us to take up his example and love one another (he set a very high bar indeed!). It is not meant to be easy, but even uncomfortable, which is why there needs to be a commandment.

Our argument aligns well with recent ritual studies. Many were built on the renowned work of Catherine Bell, who pioneered the turn to focus on the active, embodied, and performative aspect of rituals, over their possible symbolic meanings. The human bodily experience

---

53. Although it is not part of the thesis of this project to demonstrate *how* we are made fully free human agents after the cross, indeed scriptures do not explain *how* the blood of Christ saves, but only *that* it saved us. We can affirm nevertheless *that* we are made free again because of the newly given commandment.

in performing the ritual is crucial.[54] Dru Johnson argued in his book
Knowledge by Ritual that in the Old Testament, knowledge is always by
repeated embodied practice. He complained that "sacramental theology
can suffer from the temptation to over-determine the symbolic nature
of ritual. The function of signs, signals, and symbols has consumed too
much of the discussion."[55] The common error in approaching rites is that
we tend to search for what something *means* and *signifies*, and therefore
the way to decode, instead of being concerned with *action*. Yet rituals are
commanded practice in specific contexts. Johnson therefore argued that
sacramental theology should inquire, not symbols, but what the rituals
are meant to *do*.[56] The question is how practicing what God commanded
change our relationship with God and view of the world.[57] Moore-Keish,
as the title of her book Do *this in Remembrance of Me* (with a highlight
on the first word) suggests, argued that theology of rituals begins with
"doing." She argued that the traditional idea that rituals must point to
a hidden reality beyond themselves need to be counteracted. Borrowing from Roy Rappaport, she noted that in attempting to find more than
what meets the eye, the tendency is to overlook what *does* meet the eye,
namely the people in action.[58] Doctrine and ideas cannot be assessed
without consideration to actual practice. William Gilders's *Blood Ritual
in the Hebrew Bible* also questions the long-held assumption to search
for meanings of sacrificial blood rites, when Scripture is clearly more
concerned with *how* people actually follow instructions and carry out the
rites. We should ask what these actions *do*.[59]

Theologians have noted that, in Paul's liturgical text to the Corinthian church, Paul quickly moved on to what the community is to *do*,

54. See Bell, *Ritual Theory, Ritual Practice*, and Bell, *Ritual: Perspectives and
Dimensions*.

55. Johnson, *Knowledge by Ritual*, xvii.

56. Johnson, *Knowledge by Ritual*, 10.

57. Johnson, *Knowledge by Ritual*, 10–11, 55.

58. Moore-Keish, *Do This in Remembrance of Me*, 90–91. Other studies that argue
for a prioritizing of doing over meaning include Staal, "Meaninglessness of Ritual";
Rappaport, "Obvious Aspects of Ritual," in *Ecology, Meaning, and Religion*, 173–222;
Muir, *Ritual in Early Modern Europe*. My thesis, however, differs from these authors
in that I am not arguing from a general liturgical principle that rites are more about
doing than meaning. In addition, I am concerned with ethics and politics in everyday
life, not just the performing of a ritual.

59. Gilders, *Blood Ritual in the Hebrew Bible*. Once our questions are changed, we
realize that rituals create new relations and statuses of people.

without any concern of some timeless symbolism or sacramental realm. Arthur Cochrane understood the nature of the Supper as an act of proclamation. As such, he argued, it must take the forms of both word and deed, not sign. It is an ethical event. Highlighting 1 Cor 13, Cochrane remarked that

> symbolism and tokenism have been the destruction of genuine Christian fellowship. It is a question of the performance of an ethical act, of a work of love. Only as it is an act of love, and not a "bare sign" of love, is it a proclamation of the Lord's death and of the love of God.[60]

Specifically, a genuine remembrance and worship of Christ calls for loving those for whom Christ cares: the poor and even sinners.[61] Segundo's explication of Paul's Eucharistic text in 1 Cor 11 is illustrative as well. Paul, as Segundo pointed out, did not stop at the liturgy itself, but he quickly went from the Supper to the sharing of the diverse spiritual gifts which God provides for the church (1 Cor 12–13).[62] The end of the Supper was never the possession of some grace. There was also no mention of a mysterious, invisible realm. Instead, "the Church *goes to work* with what God gives."[63] The Lord's table is about the church *doing* work in the real world lying beyond the table. When one receives the Holy Spirit, what one receives are specific ecclesial tasks. Ultimately, the greatest of all is love (13:13). What is given in the Supper is not for possession, but to be concretized in the community and in its assuming full responsibilities.[64] The Reformed tradition is right in emphasizing the work of the Holy Spirit. Yet in Scripture there is hardly any concern of the Spirit uniting us with Christ mysteriously, or lifting us up to heaven at all. Rather, his gifts to the faith community mobilize it to do work in the world.

One may note that, at the outset, traditional Eucharistic theology has not only divorced doctrine from ethics, but also faith from deed. Faith, for example in Calvin's Eucharistic theology, became an individual's subjective affirmation of the promise of God. The soul is seen by him as unfortunately "imprisoned" by the weakness of flesh (see 1.15.2), which therefore needs the accommodating act of God to use physical

---

60. Cochrane, *Eating and Drinking with Jesus*, 82–83.

61. Cochrane, *Eating and Drinking with Jesus*, 90.

62. Segundo, *Sacraments Today*, 44–48.

63. Segundo, *Sacraments Today*, 44.

64. Segundo, *Sacraments Today*, 48.

signs to affirm us. This explains the repetitive mention of the increasing or confirmation of faith. But in the first place, faith is not separable from deed. Faith is human response to God's grace, and is not abstract but has to be expressed concretely (even bodily) in real life. In short, faith is expressed in obedience. While obedience is not required for grace, grace restores our broken covenant relationship with God, which in turns calls for obedience again. We are truly restored as covenant partners of God. A theology that seeks to understand the cup of the covenant should emphasize this call to obedience. Jesus said to his disciples, "*Do* this . . ." Our action as concrete response and obedience to God's commandments is the point.

If the Reformed tradition, following Augustine, insists that sacraments do not stand alone, but must be accompanied by the *Word*,[65] we must uphold the centrality of commandments and therefore of our obedience in response to the Word. Earlier we have asserted that it is helpful to understand the Supper, not as visible word, but as *acted word*—God actually reconciles us to his table. Here, it will be helpful to affirm that it is also *obeyed word*—God actually overcomes disobedience. It is clear that, from Scripture, the Word of God is not concerned about being confirmed by visible, analogous signs (a tradition we inherit from Augustine, not from Scripture). Rather, the Word of God came to us in very concrete commandments and exhortations, to be obeyed in real life. It is unacceptable that the Reformed tradition puts such emphasis on the Word of God, and yet overlooks the significant content of this Word. Lastly, the Reformed emphasis on *sanctification* that is inseparable from justification also calls for considerable weight to be put on the renewed call for obedience in the new covenant. Reformed Eucharistic theology should rediscover the centrality of John's account of the Last Supper, with the emphasis on the new commandment. Our argument calls Reformed theology to be faithful to its own tradition and emphases.

I Believe in the Communion of Sinners

The Undoing of Alienation

Sin concerns what *people* do and how they *relate* in *this* world. Sin, in Scripture, is expressed in terms of disobedience, and results in alienation.

---

65. E.g., Zwingli, "Account of the Faith," in *On Providence*, 48; Calvin, *Inst.* 4.14.4.

Because of disobedience, humanity is driven away from God's presence. Israel in their rebellion was also exiled away from God's promised land. The unholy cannot be in the presence of the holy. At the same time, because of sin, humanity is also estranged from one another. Sin permeates not only their souls but the very social structures that they built. This understanding of sin as fundamentally relational and even structural should provide the framework for what we understand salvation needs to address. Not only divine-human estrangement, but also human-human estrangement, needs to be overcome. If sin is relational, then salvation is reconciliation. If sin brings exclusion in the most concrete way, then salvation also brings inclusion in the most concrete way. If sin permeates our social fabric, salvation as reconciliation should also touch our very social fabric, not only our knowledge of God, or assurance of our consciences. Sin results in divine-human as well as human-human estrangement. Then salvation should involve the overcoming of this estrangement—God bringing his people back to his presence, at the same time bringing estranged humans together as they are brought to Christ. God's institution of table fellowship with humans precisely triumphs over this estrangement resulted by sin. God's people—among whom there are people who have wronged others, and those who have been wronged—are brought together at Christ's table. Precisely it is a covenant meal. God's ancient covenant with his people came with decrees that govern the sociopolitical fabric of the community. The new covenant inaugurated by Christ also came with a new commandment: to love one another as Christ has loved us. The table fellowship is the exact and direct antithesis of alienation. The table fellowship directly *addresses* the problem of alienation.

Again, it is important that we do not at the outset characterize the meal in terms of some fundamental dichotomy between some physical sign and the signified spiritual reality, because such a picture often overlooks the sinful reality in our *social world* that salvation is directly addressing. It does not direct us towards the neighbor. If we are to take the covenant seriously, with its clear ethical commandments, we must insist that the physical, social reality in which we live is most real. It must be held with highest importance. It is in this physical realm that the terms of the covenant are to be obeyed. It is not only real—it is the *point* of the Supper. It is the reality of salvation, in fact, because sin alienates humans from one another, and therefore salvation is in the form of summoning of sinners to come together again in remembrance of salvation that is accomplished by Christ, and a restoration of the lost fellowship. In addition, it is just as important that we do not emphasize a mystery. The notion of a mystery overshadows our everyday human action and responsibility. Especially when the mystery is understood to be a miracle occurring locally, on the altar or in heaven, again the social reality around the table, and in the world at large, is easily ignored. What needs to be emphasized is instead the broken reality in our all too familiar neighborhoods and workplaces. Far from a symbol for some invisible reality, or a mystery, the Supper is rather a *direct* undoing, reversal of alienation, precisely in the physical, ordinary realm of our social world.

In short, a restored relationship with God has to do with one's restored relationship with others. Coming to the table already encompasses our action of fellowship with others.[66] The Supper then has direct and immediate implication on our ethical, social life. There is no distinction between a doctrine of the Supper and ethics. Because the meal is a *covenant* meal with Christ, it restores us as covenant partners of God. The covenant has a specific content. To reiterate, both old and new covenants came with commandments that concern "horizontal" relationships of God's people. We are not only to love and obey God, but also the neighbor as ourselves. In the new commandment, we are taught to love one another as Christ has loved us. The covenant precisely calls for human active response in our social world. The *social reality* of the faith community is the very reality which the Supper addresses. The spiritual, invisible realm of grace should never be pitted against the visible, physical realm. One might even note that the commandments in the old covenant in fact paint a picture of how the society should be *structured*: how strangers are to be treated by locals, and how workers are to be treated by superiors in a society. In addition, the commandments quite regularly reference and the "neighbor." In the new covenant, again, Christ specifically turned our attention to "one another." The covenant has to do directly with our social reality.

---

66. This is true even in the OT sacrificial system. As part of the mandates to keep sacrificial feasts, Israel was commanded to make their servants, the poor, the strangers, Levites who had no land, and orphans and widows among them rejoice as well (Deut 12:12; 16:11, 14; 14:26). The destitute shall "come and eat and be satisfied" (Deut 14:29). For annual tithes, Israel was not allowed to eat the tithes of their herds and produce, or any peace offering, within their gates, but must bring to the Sanctuary, so that the food would be shared with the landless (Lev 12:17–19). See, e.g., MacDonald, *Not Bread Alone*, 82; and Segundo's reminder of Jesus's command to reconcile with an adversary before sacrificing on the altar (*Sacraments Today*, 8, 22–23).

As a matter of fact, in both old and new Passover, the biblical accounts highlight the social reality as the very context of the meal. The meal only took place in light of that context. The old Passover meal was instructed explicitly in the course of a people's struggle against their oppressor. The new Passover also was instructed after Jesus pointed the disciples' attention to the presence of a traitor at the table. *All* four Gospel accounts of the Last Supper highlight *at the very beginning*, either by Jesus himself or the narrator, the presence a traitor at the table (Matt 26:21; Mark 14:18; Luke 22:3; John 13:2). In Matthew and Mark, in fact the very first thing that Jesus reportedly said when they sat down for the Last Supper was that there was a traitor in their midst. Jesus drew attention to the social tension in the room.[67] This should not be taken lightly. We will coin this the "real presence of Judas." The consistent emphasis of a traitor reminds us that the Eucharist is not about partaking Christ individually, but the social reality, often broken, in front of us. Michael Welker remarked that, while the old Passover meal was about solidarity against an external enemy, the Last Supper dealt with an internal enemy.[68] This is helpful in pointing out how both old and new Passover highlight the social reality around which the meal occurred. The reality that the meal specifically addresses is the social reality before our eyes, and how we are to respond. In fact this was precisely what was highlighted by Paul in his first letter to the Corinthians. He was bluntly calling out the "division, discord, and factionalism" that was troubling the congregation at the time.[69] The haves shamed the have-nots by eating without them (1 Cor 11:17–22).

As some theologians have coined it, the Supper is a *counter-politics* (or counter-practice, counter-discipline).[70] For example, Cláudio Carvalhaes drew our attention to the various borders that exist even in the globalizing world, in particular the border crisis in the US, and how the Supper should operate differently, by unsettling prevailing hierarchies and xenophobia. The Lord's table is able to cross, and even dismantle, boundaries where current political institutions and the world at large are

67. As noted by Michael Welker, the presence of Judas at the Last Supper has been "notoriously left out of the picture" by different traditions. Welker, *What Happens in Holy Communion?*, 43.

68. Welker, *What Happens in Holy Communion?*, 46.

69. Leithart, "Signs of the Eschatological Ekklesia," 636.

70. Carvalhaes, *Eucharist and Globalization*, 3; Cavanaugh, *Torture and Eucharist*, 205, 230, 240, 253, 269; Méndez-Montoya, *Theology of Food*, 130–31.

unable to cross: ethnic, sexual, political, and economic. In a world that despises the poor and the "aliens," they are there at the table. This is why, for Carvalhaes, the Supper is never just a symbol, but it is the ordinary folks' interpretation of political power and their social world.[71] He envisions a "borderless border," by which the bordered Eucharistic table invites God's people to negotiate new, expanded borders and imagine a different social world.[72] William Cavanaugh's book *Torture and Eucharist* brought his readers to Chile from 1973 to 1990 under the torturous regime of Augusto Pinochet Ugarte. Cavanaugh demonstrated how the Supper could be for the Catholic Church precisely a counter-politics to the politics of torture of Ugarte's dictatorship. To the Catholic author, the Supper truly realizes the body of Christ in the church. The Chilean church, in the face of the state's torture of bodies, is therefore called to liturgically enact the body of Christ, to continue his body on earth, in particular his self-sacrifice and consequent triumph over sinful powers. The Supper creates a space in which bodies belong to God, not to the state.[73] On this theme, I also recall a sermon by Wang Yi, the high-profile pastor of the persecuted Early Rain Covenant Church in Chengdu, China. He said that when political opponents come together at the Eucharistic table, it is a political event. It is in fact a "higher" politics in the sense that, contrary to the state's political imagination, the gospel demonstrates that harmony between opposite parties is possible without the use of force.[74] While these authors and pastor may hold different doctrinal understandings of the Supper, they share a common approach, namely that they identified (whether explicitly or implicitly) a social ill or a current humanitarian predicament in their context to which the Lord's Supper directly addresses and serves as a counter-practice.

One must not forget that, in John's account, Jesus revealed himself as "Lord and teacher" as he took the role of a slave in washing his disciples' feet (John 13:14). His action highlighted yet completely reversed the oppressive social hierarchy of his day. This should frame the kind of questions we ask.

A theology of the Supper should similarly underscore the sinful social reality that is at stake at a time and place, instead of looking for some

---

71. Carvalhaes, *Eucharist and Globalization*, 89.

72. Carvalhaes, *Eucharist and Globalization*, 12–13, 245–50, 281–84.

73. Cavanaugh, *Torture and Eucharist*, 275.

74. See Yi, "Cross Has Political Significance." Wang was sentenced in December 2019 to nine years in prison for inciting subversion.

invisible realm of grace, or a miracle, or the salvation of individual souls. A theology of the Supper should point to the social reality that needs healing. In both old and new meals, the social context highlighted by Scripture was ugly—there was oppression externally, and then betrayal internally. Carvalhaes put it very well: the Supper is practiced within situations that are "messy, nervous, and uneasy."[75] In Tim Chester's words, "when we eat together, we encounter not some theoretical community, but real people with all their problems and quirks."[76] Precisely, contrary to Calvin's definition of a sacrament (4.14.1), the Supper is not a physical aid for our minds to contemplate spiritual things. In fact it is *difficult*. The commandment to love one another is not easy at all, when one looks at the ugly reality. One may recall that, in the Gospels, Jesus's table ministry was nothing less than shocking to onlookers. As Tim Chester noted, it was always the *guest list* that was the issue whenever Jesus sat at a table.[77] In other words, the concern was never what was in the food, or what the food signified, or any metaphysical issue. People found that eating at the same table as Jesus was uneasy, not because of some incomprehensible mystery or metaphysical riddle, but because of the ugly social reality that they were facing. They found it very uncomfortable, because of how sin deeply permeated their social fabric. They would find, for example, Zacchaeus with Jesus. The point of the Supper is that parties that were *not* able to come together, and *not* supposed to come together, have come together. Theology should highlight this.

At the Last Supper, Jesus interpreted the bread and the cup. But he first turned the disciples' focus to one another by telling them that one of them would be a traitor. In his new commandment, he again turned their focus to "one another." The Supper is a communion of sinners. The point is that sinners have come together, not that they individually contemplate salvation. Our problems today are very different from the time of the Reformation. In reaction to Catholic Eucharistic practice that the congregation is to venerate the host, and the theology that understands the priest to offer Christ on the altar, Reformed theology has insisted that the body of Christ is in heaven, and the elements of bread and wine are therefore physical signs that signify the spiritual reality. The Reformed had a strong reason to emphasize how the physical elements are themselves *not* the signified reality of grace. Yet the tendency is to minimalize the

---

75. Carvalhaes, *Eucharist and Globalization*, 17.

76. Chester, *Meal with Jesus*, 48.

77. Chester, *Meal with Jesus*, 18.

Supper into the items on the table (or tray) and the salvation of our souls. As a result, we have minimalized the Supper, not only turning it into crumbs of cracker and sips of wine or juice, but words and interpersonal interaction are also reduced to a minimum.[78] The Supper is too often about self-reflection and contemplation of spiritual salvation. It becomes an individual matter. It is possible to take communion without knowing who is sitting next to you.[79]

Our point is in line with findings in recent biblical and ritual studies that emphasize the deeply social aspect of food and drink. In particular, food and drink do not only allow socializing, but they have social *effects* on a community. Many scholars built on the grounding work by Mary Douglas.[80] Douglas illustrated how food is so much more than just eating. It is rather a code that conveys messages in social relations. A meal, in her words, is a "structured social event."[81] It marks boundaries and levels of interpersonal intimacy. While we may drink with acquaintances and coworkers, for instance, "meals are for family, close friends, honored guests. The grand operator of the system is the line between intimacy and distance."[82] More importantly, meals do not just symbolize social boundaries, they create them. As explained by Tim Chester, meals change social statuses. When Jesus ate with sinners, he put himself as the same category as they were, and they ceased to be God's enemies.[83] "The marginalized cease to be marginalized when they're included around a meal table. The lonely cease to be lonely. The alien ceases to be alien. Strangers become friends."[84] As the title of Nathan MacDonald's book indicates, even bread

---

78. See complaints in Moore-Keish, *Do This in Remembrance of Me*, 9; Cochrane, *Eating and Drinking with Jesus*, 40; Segundo, *Sacraments Today*, 8.

79. Again, this tendency is present even in Calvin, who insisted that the elements are not mere signs, but by the power of the Holy Spirit, are instrumental in bringing what they signify, namely our spiritual nourishment by the body and blood of Christ. In countering the charge of legal fiction, Calvin insisted that we truly embrace Christ (4.17.6). He therefore held that the very subject matter of the Supper is that our *hearts* are lifted to heaven to have real, albeit spiritual, communion with Christ's body and blood there (4.17.18). Repeatedly, the language of this communion is nourishment—our souls feed on the flesh and blood of Christ (e.g., 4.17.3, 4, 5, 8, 10, 32). Yet it is difficult to understand such lifting of hearts and nourishment of souls except individualistically.

80. Douglas, "Deciphering a Meal," 249–75.

81. Douglas, "Deciphering a Meal," 260.

82. Douglas, "Deciphering a Meal," 256.

83. Chester, *Meal with Jesus*, 41–46.

84. Chester, *Meal with Jesus*, 49.

is not bread alone.[85] For MacDonald, food is deeply social and relational. In the Torah, for example, it was the vehicle for Israelites to remember the saving works of God in the past and his continuing abundance in promised land. Israel's worship of God exactly took the form of joyous communal feasts. In turn, they were to be defined by their inclusion and hospitality in food. Surveying the Old Testament, MacDonald inferred a close link between the table and divine acceptance and judgment. Akin to a royal table, God's table is the site where favor and judgment in fact occur.[86] Craig L. Blomberg also identified the bonding effects of meals in the bible. For example, Joseph's meal with his brothers was the beginning of reconciliation. Specifically, where there was once estrangement, now a new relationship was signaled.[87] Other examples include the royal meal between David and Saul's surviving heir Mephibosheth. Communal meals strengthen kinship ties, promote neighborly solidarity, and establish communion with God. Equally, food can have its negative effects too. For example, diet restrictions set Jews apart from their gentile neighbors.[88] It is in this light that Jesus's eating with outcasts is significant. Jesus did not set himself apart from them, but publicly dined with them. When he mingled with outcasts, they were no longer outcasts.[89]

In sum, as a meal the Supper is a direct counter-practice to alienation. It has *social* effects. The meal does not signify some invisible truth but it includes the supposedly excluded. While we were banished from God's presence, and alienated from one another, Christ sent the Holy Spirit to be among us, and we are also sat at his table with one another. As reminded by Paul Molner, however, we should be cautious of reducing the Lord's Supper to being merely one instance of some general anthropological principle and phenomenon of interhuman table fellowship, rendering Christ's work no longer unique.[90] We are not arguing from a general principle. The point is that a theology of the Supper must not overlook the deeply social aspect of sin and salvation. The Supper directly addresses and reverses alienation in the community. Theologians are to name the social context in which the Supper is practiced and to which

---

85. MacDonald, *Not Bread Alone*, 219.

86. MacDonald, *Not Bread Alone*, 13, 79–83, 194–95.

87. Blomberg, *Contagious Holiness*, 35–36.

88. Blomberg, *Contagious Holiness*, 37; see also Wirzba, *Food and Faith*, 165–78.

89. Blomberg, *Contagious Holiness*, 127.

90. Molnar, *Barth and the Theology*, 70.

it speaks. To Molnar's argument we must also point out that the Supper is the new Passover meal, and by which the redeemed people of God remember Christ's death; it is also the new covenant meal, in which the Son of God himself dined with the representatives of the new people, and in which the people of God received a commandment from Christ anew to love one another. The meal explicitly inaugurates this new relationship. What is effective is not a general principle, nor some visible sign, but Christ's accomplishment of salvation that is being remembered, the work of the Holy Spirit here and now, and human response to the renewed covenant. It was Christ's blood that allowed sinners to come to God in the first place. Now forgiven sinners are called to take up Christ's example in hospitality and service (John 13:14). Instead of turning our minds to some invisible realm, or to some mystery, we should look out for one another, or as Christ has taught us, even look for the "least of these." The Supper is not a timeless principle, but is to be practiced in a social context. A theology of the Supper should be conscious of this context.

Finally, such sinner-sinner table fellowship speaks good news for the marginalized and oppressed also because of its potential effect on sociopolitical relations and even structures. The marginalized and oppressed are not only included at the Lord's table, but, if the church takes seriously the ethical content of the new covenant, those who wronged them are called to face the cross, and submit to Christ. When the *chief* tax collector was included at the table with Christ, and was moved to repent, the oppressive system was probably shaken (Luke 19:1–10). When a theology of the Lord's Supper focuses on the broken social reality, it addresses not only the marginalized and oppressed but also the oppressor. If theology merely turns to the invisible spiritual reality, or to the miracle lying in the elements, or when it is preoccupied with subjective knowledge and capacities, then not surprisingly it fails to address the brokenness in our sociopolitical world. We come to the Lord's table with others in this broken world. This indispensable horizontal dimension of the Supper makes it directly bear on ethics and even politics.

The Real Presence of Judas

The Supper as a covenant meal does not command us to look for some invisible grace, or hidden mystery, or to be concerned with our souls, but to love and serve one another. Who is this "one another"? Who is included and are there some who should be excluded? Again we recall the social tension highlighted by Jesus who pointed out that a traitor was at the table *before* instituting the new Supper. He did so to a point that the disciples were "deeply grieved" (Matt 26:21-22; Mark 14:18-19). If that was not enough, the Gospel narrators of Luke and John even explicitly stated that the devil had already entered Judas (Luke 22:3; John 13:2, again 13:27). John also included a conversation where Jesus, quoting Ps 41:9, lamented that the traitor lifted his heels against him. It is indubitable that Judas was at the scene and was included, not only at the institution of the Supper but also the washing of feet, *despite* being a traitor and having had the devil enter him. He was condemned, but included as one of the "twelve" (Matt 26:20; Mark 14:17; Luke 22:3; Luke also identified the twelve as "apostles," Luke 22:14). As noted by Jeremias, Jesus's announcement of betrayal was early in the development of the narrative, as it is common in all four gospels. In the Synoptics, the announcement was even firmly embedded in the meal.[91] This "real presence of Judas" is especially ironic. When traditional theology has always focused on the question of the real presence of Christ, the presence highlighted at the beginning of all four Last Supper accounts is in fact not the savior's but that of the epitome of sinners. The savior pointed our attention first to our uncomfortable table companionship. The traditional theological oversight might have reflected a socio-ethical oversight.

The Reformed tradition, most unfortunately, has been anxious to rule out the possibility of Judas having truly partaken of Christ at the Last Supper, even though he partook of the bread and cup from Jesus. For this purpose, the strong Augustinian distinction between physical sign and signified reality has been handy. The presence of Judas did not need to take up much discussion in Zwingli, for whom no substantial, but only signified, eating of Christ takes place in the Supper. Nevertheless he still briefly remarked, in his discussion of election and the church, that the apostles only thought Judas belonged to the twelve, but in reality, he was the devil's.[92] Therefore the church is made up of both the elect and reprobate. Zwingli implied that exclusion of Judas from the "twelve" is needed. Compared to Zwingli, Calvin's discussion of Judas in his doctrine of the Supper reflects considerable anxiety on his part. For Calvin, the Supper does not only signify but through it the Holy Spirit actually effects a

---

91. Jeremias, *Eucharistic Words of Jesus*, 97, 100.

92. Zwingli, "Account of the Faith," in *On Providence*, 44.

believer's true union with Christ. The believer spiritually but truly partakes Christ's body and blood. It also results in true knowledge of Christ in us. With this precedent understanding, it is not surprising that Calvin had to exclude nonbelievers, and especially those he deemed "wicked," from the union with Christ. Added to this realist understanding of the Supper, the Reformer fundamentally couple the Supper with baptism under the genus of sacraments. Indeed baptism is baptism *into Christ* (4.14.7). The anxiety is to explain what happens to those who are not in Christ and yet take part in the sacraments.

In the background were two different groups of critics. There were those who argued against any effectiveness of grace in the Supper because the "wicked" also receive it the same way as the faithful (4.14.7). Also in the background was Luther's literal interpretation of words of institution and therefore the idea of *manducatio impiorum* (eating of Christ by the unpious): even the wicked must receive the body and blood with their mouths, although they do it to their destruction.[93] The Luther-Calvin debate focused on Judas's peculiar presence at the Last Supper.

To the former group of critics, Calvin argued with his language of "seals." Just as princes' seals can be ignored or even cursed, they are nevertheless effective and applicable for all. He argued that this is what Paul meant: in the sacraments, Christ is offered to all (4.14.7). The force of a sacrament does not depend on the condition of the person who receives it. "For what God has ordained remains firm and keeps its own nature, however men may vary" (14.16). Calvin quoted from Augustine's commentary on John that, if one only receives "carnally," i.e., only the physical sign, a sacrament does not cease to be spiritual. The Augustinian sign-reality distinction-and-yet-inseparation is crucial here. The sign itself is not the truth. Ultimately grace is conferred by Christ alone, thus we partake in Christ only through the Holy Spirit, only that he does so through outward signs. Thus faith is important. Yet Calvin warned us of the opposite tendency, which is to hold the sign as itself nullified by unbelief. Calvin added that God's truthfulness does not lie in the reception, "but in the constancy of his goodness, in that he is ready to give to the unworthy what they reject, indeed, offers it freely. . . . The flesh and blood of Christ are no less truly given to the unworthy than to God's elect believers." "Among ancient writers Augustine especially has affirmed this article of doctrine, that, by the unfaithfulness or ill will of men, nothing

93. Luther, *LW* 37:86–87, 191, 238; Calvin, *Inst.* 4.17.33.

is taken away from the sacraments, nor is the grace which they symbolize nullified" (17.34).

To Luther's *manducatio impiorum*, on the other hand, Calvin responded by acknowledging the infallibility of God's work, and the true offering of Christ in the Supper, yet he maintained that it is not the whole story. "It is one thing to offer, another to receive, nothing prevents the symbol consecrated by the Lord's Word from being actually what it is called, and from keeping its own force. Yet this does not benefit a wicked or impious man" (14.16). Christ is offered to all; yet the Word is effective in the sacraments not because it is spoken, but because it is believed (14.7). Surely, Calvin agreed, the trustworthiness of God's promises cannot be diminished by human ungratefulness. Yet, again, "it is one thing to be offered, another to be received" (17.33). Here Calvin offered two analogies: while God's truthfulness does not lie in the reception, "at the same time, it is true, however, that, just as rain falling upon a hard rock flows off because no entrance opens into the stone, the wicked by their hardness so repel God's grace that it does not reach them. Besides, to say that Christ may be received without faith is as inappropriate as to say that a seed may germinate in fire" (17.33). "Their own hardness is the hindrance which prevents Christ from coming to them." There are thus two distinctions in play: between offer and reception of grace, and between physical sign and spiritual reality (or between outwardly and inwardly). As Calvin put it, "the antithesis between visible and invisible scatters these clouds" (17.34). For those who lack faith, a sacrament can be received only carnally, i.e., only the physical sign is received, yet "it does not cease to be spiritual, *but* it is not so for you" (14.16). "All those who are devoid of Christ's Spirit can no more eat Christ's flesh than drink wine that has no taste." In other words, "unbelievers communicate only in a visible symbol," not the offered reality of Christ (17.34). Quoting Augustine, he wrote, "he who does not abide in Christ and in whom Christ does not abide, doubtless does not spiritually eat his flesh or drink his blood, although he may carnally and visibly press the sign of the body and blood with his teeth" (17.34). "To profane and impure men nothing is granted but the visible taking of the sign." "Surely," Calvin reasoned, "Christ is too unworthily torn apart if his body, lifeless and powerless, is prostituted to unbelievers" (17.33).

Our concern is with the ethical repercussions of this outlook. The result of a realist (even organic) approach to the Supper, holding that grace is effected in it and the faithful participant receives the body and blood of

Christ in reality, is that we tend to divide the community into two classes of people: the believers who receive Christ on the one hand, and unbelievers and even the "wicked" who cannot on the other. By "the wicked and evildoers," Calvin defined as those who "profess the Christian faith with their lips but deny it by their deeds" (17.34). If the substance of the Supper is a mystical union with Christ, then inevitably some, if not many, will have to be excluded. The Supper would even need to be cautiously fenced. The Supper (unless combined with agape) ceases to be a venue for hospitality to the outsider. For Calvin, the point is not that the unfaithful or the "wicked" simply miss the mystical union, but the language is much stronger: "the unity of the body and blood of Christ, is set forth in the Lord's Supper for some to life, for others to death" (17.34). Needless to say, Paul's charge in his letter to the Corinthians that some receive the Supper not for their benefits but for condemnation (1 Cor 11:27-29) looms large here. To Calvin, the issue is the body of Christ. Concerning the wicked, he explained that "it must not be said that they eat Christ's body, because they must not be reckoned among Christ's members" (17.34). We have noted earlier that Calvin's notion of real union with Christ implied that his notion of "mutual love" in the Supper is applicable only to believer circles. When we hold on to a realist approach, i.e., that in the Supper we indeed receive the body of Christ by faith, it means that we are excluding not only the "wicked and evildoers," but easily also the unbeliever. The Supper then becomes an insider affair. Worse, if we bring in Paul's teaching here, it would imply that, when the unbeliever is received at the Lord's table, the unbeliever would be condemned, instead of receiving grace. What seems to have receded to the background here is what Calvin said earlier, namely that "in the constancy of [God's] goodness, in that he is ready to give to the unworthy what they reject, indeed, offers it freely. . . . The flesh and blood of Christ are no less truly given to the unworthy than to God's elect believers" (17.33). Unfortunately, this self-offering of Christ to "many" (Matt 26:28; Mark 14:24) becomes less the focus when we see the Supper as primarily about a real union with Christ.

A central problem of Calvin's realist construal of the Supper and consequent rejection of *manducatio impiorum* is that it creates the category of the "unworthy" who are to be excluded (presumably meaning that there are others who are "worthy"). Calvin understood the Supper as a *receiving* of Christ, hence the worry over worthy *vs.* unworthy reception. The anxiety to demarcate and exclude is inevitable.[94] In contrast to

94. Luther similarly clearly demarcated between the categories "pure saints and

this, however, our thesis is that we are *received by* Christ. Christ is the Gracious Host at the table, receiving us sinners once again to the presence of God. Although the Supper in part as a new Passover meal and in part as a new covenant meal involves specifically the redeemed people, this redeemed people is *not* an antithesis to the "unworthy." Precisely *all* are unworthy. Tradition has often overlooked our being received *by* Christ, hence the worry over worthy *vs.* unworthy reception. Yet precisely Jesus, as *the* Gracious Host, receives the unworthy. The Supper is shocking, not because God uses the items to signify or effect something, but because sinners who are supposed to be alienated from God are once again restored in table fellowship with him. God is in fellowship with humans again. Parties that are *not* supposed to come together have nevertheless come together, because of Christ. In dogmatically ruling out the so-called "unworthy," i.e., those deemed not supposed to be in communion with us, we have denied the significance of the supposedly impossible table fellowship, turning the Supper into some symbol or mystery.

More authors now argue for the relevance of Jesus's own table ministry to our understanding of the Lord's Supper.[95] Jesus's "partying" was never less than shocking to onlookers, not because of the food, but because of the guest list. The issue was not the guests' lack of faith, but precisely that they were sinners deemed *unworthy* to be with Jesus. All three Synoptic Gospels document Jesus's direct response to the shocked onlookers: "The healthy does not need the doctor, but only the sick. I have not come to call the righteous, but sinners" (Matt 9:12–13; Mark 2:17; Luke 5:31–32). Jesus's specific use of a medical imagery in relation to his table companions implied that it is those who are in a worse shape who will be at the front of the line. At least according to one of Jesus's parables, heaven rejoices for the homecoming of the lost rather than the already "worthy" (Luke 15:7, 10). Indeed the latter are asked to join the homecoming celebration for the former (Luke 15:31–32). Precisely because, even according to Calvin, the efficacy of the Supper is of that of the Holy Spirit *alone*, therefore we cannot decide what a person must or must not receive from the table.

---

worthy recipients" and "unworthy ones, such as Judas, and others," even when he allowed the latter to partake in Christ physically (*LW* 37:353–54). The "unworthy" and "faithless" cannot receive spiritually from the Gracious Lord.

95. E.g., Blomberg, *Contagious Holiness*, 130–63; Cochrane, *Eating and Drinking with Jesus*, 90; Chester, *Meal with Jesus*; LaVerdiere, *Dining in the Kingdom of God*, 21–22.

Seeing the meal as a covenant meal precisely calls for serving one another. It calls for hospitality following Christ's own example. A problem with a realist approach to the Supper such as Calvin's is that it cannot explain the deep disconnect between the church's Eucharistic practice on the one hand, and on the other hand the uncountable moral failures we see in the church. The reality is that an access to Christ's body (whether on the altar or in heaven) does not necessarily bring about moral change. It is only held to be a mystery. Surely, God's call for obedience and hospitality does not necessarily mean people will respond either. Yet, when we pay attention to the covenant and its commandments, the moral demand is acknowledged. The irony is that, when we are captivated by a mystery, we fail to hear the divine command, and to notice Christ's example in serving even his traitor. The way to change must be to start hearing the command to love as Christ has loved, and to take heed of his concrete example.

Calvin also ignored the fact that Paul's rhetoric against those who take part in the Supper "unworthily" was specifically targeting the rich who ate without the poor (1 Cor 11:17-22). He was specifically dealing with class exclusion, not with someone lacking faith or finding themselves in a general state of sin. Paul was rebuking those who deemed the poor as "unworthy" to share a table with as *themselves* unworthy—he did *not* create any prior categories of the "unworthy" or "wicked" based on their state of faith or sinfulness, and dogmatize that those who belong to these labels cannot receive what the Supper offers.[96] Even when the Reformed emphasizes the necessity of faith in coming to the Lord's table, it is quite another thing to dogmatize that all unbelievers and the "wicked" must consequently receive nothing from the Lord's table. Such a belief would only imply that we are not exactly talking about the table of the most Gracious Host.

Calvin quickly ruled out that Judas could have real communion with the Lord, other than receiving the physical signs. Yet in dogmatically ruling out Judas, we have chosen not to inquire why Jesus (and the Gospel narrators) chose to highlight the presence of a traitor in the beginning of the Last Supper. We have also chosen not to inquire why Jesus deliberately included him in the Last Supper and washed his feet. According to Calvin, we should not even ask whether Judas received Christ

---

96. Paul's teaching that everyone must examine oneself and discern the body (1 Cor 11:28-29) was also within the same context of social exclusion, not in a context about personal state of faith.

(*Inst.* 4.17.34). In ruling out Judas, we lose the important fact that Christ was welcoming the one who was hurting him, and the opportunity for this hospitality to the traitor to frame our doctrinal questions. If Judas was such an enemy of God as is portrayed, what does this say about the gospel and our relating to our own enemies? On this point, too, Calvin overlooked that Peter the rock quickly went to deny Christ immediately after the Last Supper too. If Peter failed so miserably, who can be worthy?

Apart from undermining the undeserved table fellowship that Christ has allowed, a realist understanding of the Supper such as Calvin's dogmatically creates two classes of people at the Lord's table: the faithful who receive Christ *versus* the so-called "unworthy" and "wicked" who cannot. This division may be seen as reminiscent of the dogmatic creation of the division between the elect *vs.* the reprobate in Calvin's doctrine of predestination, which could have vast sociopolitical repercussions.[97] Especially, such a theological division is made in our societies where social divisions are already pervasive. We already tend to deem certain kinds of people less worthy and exclude them. Now theology only further justifies and reinforces such labeling and exclusion. The Supper does not only cease to be a venue of hospitality for the outsider, it easily becomes another means of the human tendency to exclude those *we* think are "unworthy." As Carvalhaes argued, the problem is our tendency to unconsciously import existing political, economic, racial, gender borders from the divided world into the church.[98] As Segundo also remarked, "a human life imbued with the prevailing conception of the sacraments prepares us to accept the same mechanisms on other levels of existence."[99] The Roman Catholic belief of a real, miraculous presence of Christ in the elements is closely linked to an ecclesial hierarchy between ordained priests who are empowered for intimate access to the holy presence of Christ on the one hand, and the laity who are kept at a distance on the other. Translated into society, such a fundamental hierarchy also funds other hierarchies, or the legitimacy of some "sacred" elite group, from whom ordinary folks are to acquire blessings.[100]

97. See discussion in, e.g., Du Toit, "No Chosen People."

98. E.g., Carvalhaes, *Eucharist and Globalization*, 17, 31.

99. Segundo, *Sacraments Today*, 56.

100. Segundo, *Sacraments Today*, 56. Segundo's example of such a political parallel between sacrament and real-life is unforgettable. Pius X in his encyclical *Vehementer* wrote, "The Church essentially is an unequal society. That is, it is a society formed by two categories of persons: pastors and flock. . . . As far as the multitude is concerned,

All these have not mentioned that Calvin was self-defeating in his exclusion of Judas from receiving Christ. Calvin's fundamental understanding is that the Supper is a physical sign that affirms our knowledge of our true union with Christ and spiritual nourishment by his body and blood. It assures our conscience. Yet his exclusion of Judas must mean that, contrary to this view, we cannot be assured by the physical sign at all. According to Calvin himself, Judas partook of the physical sign just as everyone else did. The strong sign-reality distinction is the basis of his explanation of Judas's peculiar case. But how do we know we will not suffer the same fate as Judas, i.e., receiving only the sign but not the substance of the Supper? Instead of physical, analogous signs that bear resemblance to some mystical spiritual nourishment, precisely it is the *fact* that Jesus included *even* Judas that assures us. Because *even* Judas was included in the fellowship with Christ, I can have peace.

On the point of inclusion at the Lord's Supper, we have to consider a heartbreaking counterexample given by William Cavanaugh. Under the dictating regime of Ugarte in Chile, there were church members who were involved in torturing. Cavanaugh argued that, for the sake of the ecclesial body which is to be Christ's body, the church should excommunicate these Christians and deny them the Supper. It is by such exclusion that the church stands in solidarity with the suffering and condemns the torturers. It is by such exclusion that the church shows itself to be the body of Christ on earth.[101] I concur with Cavanaugh, for the exact reasons he named. If certain members engage in extreme acts of violence, the integrity of the gospel must be protected by clear borders established at the Lord's table. What I have been questioning in this chapter is rather the preconception that the Supper is about participants receiving Christ, instead of them being received *by* Christ, and allowing metaphysics (in terms of a partaking of Christ) to predetermine who can and who cannot be received by Christ. What is questioned is the doctrinal normalizing of a category of people deemed "unworthy" or "unfit" for the Lord's table. Here Carvalhaes's concept of "borderless borders" is most helpful. His point is that the borders of the Eucharist table, while being necessary, is nevertheless ever re-negotiable and expandable. Grace is the work of the

---

they have no other duty than to let themselves be led" (57). Segundo noted how, in this outlook, the crowd is not even supposed to express themselves, or to be aware of oppression. There is no room for opposition. The "miracle" workers do not have to get close to the feelings, or even the vernacular language, of the people (58).

101. Cavanaugh, *Torture and Eucharist*, 253–64.

Holy Spirit, not of the church. There should therefore be no border at the Lord's table that is timelessly fixed.[102] The point is precisely that Jesus, by his body and blood, is able to break down barriers. God in Christ precisely welcomes the unworthy. The point is that estrangement has been overcome. As Peter Leithart put it, how does a meal show forth the death of Christ on the cross? It is by breaking down barriers that long divided Jews and gentiles. The broken social reality is actually being healed by the gospel. It is "in empirical reality that the church . . . proves that Christ's death was effective in bursting through all barriers that divided human beings from God and one another."[103]

A Political Meal

The last part of this project will highlight the deeply political dimension of the Lord's Supper. We have shown how the Exodus context of the Last Supper which is indispensable for understanding it. That event was political in every sense of the word. God struck an oppressive state on behalf of an oppressed people and delivered them. An equivalent in modern history would be God freeing African slaves by slaying a child in every family in a nation that was involved in the slave trade. It would be an incident of an unspeakable scale and terror. If Christ chose to institute the Eucharist specifically on the memorial of such an event, it would be utterly intolerable if theologians choose to erase that history completely in developing an understanding of the Eucharist. In light of this Exodus context of the Last Supper, a doctrine of the Supper *is* already liberation theology. Instead of pointing to some invisible realm of grace, or some mystery, or our inner capacities, the meal points to the history of liberation of an oppressed people, and their covenant made with their Liberator. Immediately, the political aspect of the Eucharist is brought to the forefront.

As is clear in the book of Exodus (Exod 12–13), all annual celebrations of the Passover are meant to draw attention to the fateful events on the very first Passover. It was precisely an event of liberation. Jews had suffered 430 years in slavery in Egypt. But God called Moses, and said,

> I have certainly seen the oppression of my people who are in
> Egypt, and have heard their outcry because of their taskmasters,

102. Carvalhaes, *Eucharist and Globalization*, 140.

103. Leithart, "Signs of the Eschatological Ekklesia," 636–37.

> for I am aware of their sufferings. So I have come down to rescue
> them from the power of the Egyptians. (Exod 3:7–8)

This was the beginning of the story: God observed, heard and knows the cry of those who are oppressed, and he took action. He sent Moses and Aaron to confront Pharaoh to demand that he let the people go so that they might worship him in the wilderness. After sending nine plagues to the land one after another, Moses warned Pharaoh that the last plague was imminent (Exod 11). It was at this very point that God told Israel to prepare for the Passover meal (12:1), and foretold that he would give his *final blow* to Pharaoh in the context of their eating this meal.

After Moses had warned Pharaoh that the last plague was imminent, the first thing God did was to gather Israel and to tell them to "take" (Exod 12:3–5) and "eat" (12:8–9, 11) the Passover lamb. God commanded them to prepare the Passover meal, in the context of which he would strike his final blow to the oppressive state. In a sense, it was a command to Israel to prepare for a political uprising. The meal was a rebellion of an oppressed people. For an Israelite to eat this meal in Egypt was to conspire against Pharaoh. He laid a feast for his people in the presence of their enemies. God did exactly what he foretold. On that night he slayed every firstborn in the land of Egypt, but spared all Jews. When Pharaoh finally let them leave, they left victoriously, even taking their taskmasters' possessions (12:35–36). God's ultimate triumph over Pharaoh was when Israelites arrived at Mount Sinai to be called to serve only him, and no longer Pharaoh.[104] Because YHWH is Lord, Pharaoh is not. The covenant meal at Mount Sinai was a victory banquet.

As stated in Mishnah (m. Pesaḥ. 10:1, 5), subsequent Passover celebrations declare the free status of every Jew. It is no accident that, as documented by Josephus, many political uprisings by the Jews took place precisely during the Passover. The festival offered the context for political activism because it was a memorial for deliverance.[105] The meal itself sends a blunt message to those in power, that God hears the cry and observes the misery of those suffering, and he has acted on their behalf. The Jewish activisms suggest how God's people may apply the message of the Passover to their own contexts, that they would be redeemed from

---

104. Cassuto, *Commentary on Exodus*, 143.

105. See Josephus, *Ant.* 14.2.1; 17.9.3; 18.2.2; *War* 2.14.3; 4.7.2; also Colautti, *Passover in the Works of Josephus*. Indeed we read from the Gospel accounts of the Last Supper that it was a politically sensitive time (Matt 26:5; Mark 14:1–2).

slavery to the Pharaohs of their own time. The memory of the great re-demption of the past inspires God's people to work for present redemption and gives them hope for messianic redemption in the future.[106] This is also related to the custom of the Passover night specifically as a night of watching for the Lord (Exod 12:42). The tradition interprets that the future deliverance of the Jewish people will take place at this time.[107] The Passover liberation serves as the *type* of all divine redemptive work. Ultimately, tyrannical dominions will end once and for all. God will bring Israel back and the Messiah will rule.[108]

In short, God revolted against the oppressor on behalf of the oppressed and won. It was against this narrative that Jesus instituted a new meal. It should be in this light that we look at the Last Supper and the new Supper. It was against the backdrop of remembering God's instructions to Israel to prepare for the Passover meal that Jesus told his disciples to prepare for a meal. As we have shown, Jesus's words of institution mirrored closely God's ancient divine command given on this very occasion, to "take," "eat," and to remember. He was precisely speaking as God before the first Passover night. It signaled that a whole new beginning is dawning, especially considering that this was why that month became the first of the year (Exod 12:2). If what happened on the first Passover night was the final blow to Israel's oppressor, what happened on the night of the Last Supper would be God's ultimate blow to sin (Matt 26:28). "This is my body"—the Son of God himself dying as the ultimate Passover lamb. There would need be no lamb on the Passover table any more, implying that, on this night, God would strike all sin. Just as the covenant meal at Sinai was a victory banquet, today the new covenant meal also celebrates the accomplished salvation by Christ. The people now serve him, not our oppressive earthly powers. Because Jesus is Lord, Caesar is not.[109]

106. Wylen, *Settings of Silver*, 160.

107. Rosh HaShanah 11b. The liturgical poem "leil Shimurim" for the Passover evening service expresses the hope that footsteps of the messenger Elijah will once again be heard on this night of watching (Machzor Vitry 446). See Bloch, *Biblical and Historical Background*, 238.

108. See, e.g., Kugel, *Traditions of the Bible*, 575–78; Le Déaut, "Paque Juive et Nouveau Testament"; Wylen, *Settings of Silver*, 166.

109. Carvalhaes made the very insightful point that, in the Lord's Supper it is by ascribing power solely to the Holy Spirit, that Reformed Eucharistic doctrine is able to allow the church to maintain a critical distance from human power structures (Carvalhaes, *Eucharist and Globalization*, 89–92). However, ascribing all power to the Holy Spirit was not Calvin's novel idea. It was Zwingli's. See, e.g., Zwingli, "Account of the

The historical context of the Passover precisely offers a very different view of sin from that of traditional theology. Sin does not simply lie in our souls or human nature, manifested in individual wills and actions, but it deeply perpetuates our sociopolitical structures. Sin can come in the form of state oppression, and God avenges such sin as well. Even the manner of eating the meal liturgically asserts their freed status from *political* and *economical* oppression—they now all recline as free men and women, no longer serving at the table (m. Pesaḥ. 10:1; see Matt 26:20; Mark 14:18; Luke 22:14; John 13:12). Precisely because Jesus did not void but fulfilled the Passover, today the Lord's Supper still speaks good news to the oppressed and an imminent judgment to their oppressor. The narrative of liberation is fundamental to our understanding of the Supper.

Some scholars even suggested that the Lord's Supper may be consciously ministered at locations that are politically symbolic—in front of government buildings, courts and prisons.[110] I also recall that, on World Communion Sunday during Hong Kong's Occupy Central movement in 2014, a group of pastors from diverse denominations ministered communion publicly for around five hundred Christians at the protest frontline.[111] The meal does not only embody the unity of the faith community, but it also remembers Jesus's accomplished work in defeating sin and death and therefore declares that Jesus alone is Lord. He is Lord over all earthly powers. The Passover context of the Supper precisely reminds us that God did only work in hearts and minds, or only in domestic and assigned "religious" settings where the meal was partaken, but even in Pharaoh's court as they ate.

God hears the cries of the suffering and the oppressed. A theology of the Supper that takes seriously the Exodus context of the Last Supper would not have left this unsaid. It is good news for the oppressed. God has said, "I have observed the misery of my people . . . I have heard their cry . . . Indeed, I know their sufferings, and I have come down to deliver them" (Exod 3:7–8). As someone who was born and raised in Hong Kong, whose people currently find themselves in endless protests against a totalitarian regime, I find the Passover message of the Lord's Supper especially relevant and precious today.

Faith," in *On Providence*, 46–47; and G. W. Bromiley's introduction to Zwingli's "On the Lord's Supper," in *Zwingli and Bullinger*, 183–84.

110. Cavanaugh, *Torture and Eucharist*, 274; Wright, *Meal Jesus Gave Us*, 81.

111. Chan, "Protestant Community and the Umbrella Movement," 391–92.

Conclusion

Ethics and politics should be at the very forefront of a theology of the Supper. It is not only the restored table fellowship between God and sinners, but also between estranged sinners. Sin comes in the form of disobedience. Yet in Christ God does not only forgive but once again restores us as his covenant partners, who are to obey his commandments. Just as sin brings alienation between God and sinners, and among sinners, his work overcomes this alienation. Estranged parties come together at the Lord's table. Unfortunately, as we have identified, traditional Eucharistic theology has too long been preoccupied by metaphysical questions, specifically by focusing on what is signified, or on some mystery, and has marginalized ethical concerns. In order for the Supper to be ethically and politically relevant, the visible, ordinary neighbor must feature prominently in our theology. The problem in traditional theology is that it turns our focus instead to some invisible realm of grace, or mystery. Traditional theology has also largely overlooked the structural nature of sin. Sin lies not only in our souls but systemically pervades our sociopolitical structures. Salvation must heal not only the soul and human nature, but also our social fabric. We have urged the rediscovery of the centrality of the new *covenant* inaugurated by Christ at the Last Supper, and how it concerns rightful horizontal relationships in society just as much as vertical relationships with God. We have insisted that John 13 is therefore fundamental to our understanding of the Supper, where a new commandment came with the new covenant, and Jesus set us an example. The point of the Supper is our response to Christ's renewed commandment to love one another. A central focus is therefore the social reality of the community, in its brokenness and messiness, instead of metaphysically inquiring about the static elements or what they may signify or contain. Precisely in the covenant and its commandments, we are exhorted to pay heed to "one another" (John 13:14, 34–35). The fact that Jesus highlighted the presence of his traitor at the beginning of the institution of the new Supper must not be ignored. We have also interrogated Calvin's notion that the Supper is a physical sign to affirm weak faith, instead of a most challenging command to us to respond and obey. We have rejected even more strongly the doctrinal fixing of the categories of the "unworthy" and "wicked" who are to be excluded from receiving grace at the table of the most Gracious Host, a view which carries dire political implications. Precisely all are unworthy but are nevertheless received *by* Christ.

In addition to this is the indispensable Passover context of the Last Supper that remembers God's compassion for and action on behalf of the oppressed. The Supper therefore celebrates Christ's ultimate salvation, while also recommits the Christian community in its responsibilities in the renewed covenant. In Segundo's words, Scripture does not stop at the liturgy in 1 Cor 11, but immediately, "the Church *goes to work*" (1 Cor 12–13).[112]

---

112. Segundo, *Sacraments Today*, 44–48.

Conclusion

FOOD—IT IS NOT A timeless idea or theory but about concrete life. A communal meal, especially, resists philosophizing but is about parties living together in concrete situations. For too long, theologians have posed the question of the Lord's Supper as a philosophical riddle that requires the import of extrabiblical philosophical concepts such as visible signs and substance to explain the meal. In line with Western thought, various Eucharistic traditions frame the theology of the Supper primarily in terms of an individual's access to symbols or what is in the symbols, instead of different parties relating and living together. It fails to notice and inquire *who* are at the table. For too long, in the development of the doctrine of the Supper, theologians borrow without question Augustine's neo-Platonist dichotomy between visible sign and signified reality. The resulting tendency is to accentuate an otherworldly, invisible realm of grace, turning away from what happens in the empirical world. Pre-Reformation theology, in attempting to avoid mere symbolism, emphasized the notion of substance. This, however, frames Christ's presence in the Supper primarily in impersonal, metaphysical language, focusing on how the body and blood of Christ may be timelessly accessible, instead of the person of Jesus Christ in history. Traditions fail to inquire what the Supper means *in history*. For too long, while deploying extrabiblical concepts, traditions took little notice of the fact that *all four* Gospel accounts named the Jewish Passover as the context of the Last Supper, and that Jesus explicitly referenced a new covenant and commandment. This thesis calls for a close attention of the narrative of the Exodus in a study of the Lord's Supper, especially God's institution of the first Passover, and Israel's covenant ceremony at Mount Sinai. It has been argued that Jesus's words at the Last Supper should be understood *in light of this history*. Jesus Christ himself—with his body and blood—fulfilled the age-old Passover and the covenant sacrifice typified in the OT. He inaugurated a new covenant with the "twelve." The significance of the Supper lies in the fact that it is now a lambless Passover and bloodless covenant meal—humanity no longer needs any sacrifice to come to divine presence. For too long, the presumed outlook is that, in the Supper, the believer receives the body and blood of Christ (whether realistically, spiritually or symbolically). Yet as we take note of the historical context of the Supper, a way is open to see the Supper as *Christ receiving us*. God in Jesus Christ welcomes sinners back to his holy presence again. When sin has alienated sinners from God, God has restored a concrete fellowship. The significance of the Supper lies in this shocking, undeserved divine-human table fellowship. Although Christ is in heaven interceding for us before his return, he has sent *his* Holy Spirit to be present with us in this world. The Supper is a foretaste of our future physical table fellowship with Christ, which we eagerly anticipate.

This project's attention to history and Jewish categories, such as the Passover and blood of the covenant, has opened the door for a new perspective of the Supper that warrants theological interest—one that sees Christ as receiving sinners at his table, instead of "worthy" believers receiving the body and blood of Christ. The long-held idea that individuals receive the body and blood of Christ (even if only symbolically) has to be reevaluated. Indeed the very question of the real presence of Christ in the elements has to be reevaluated. The traditional outlook encourages individualism. An over-emphasis on the elements invites only impersonal and metaphysical analysis. The preoccupation with the body-blood pair also distracts us from inquiring about historical narrative and the interpersonal covenant. In light of fact that the Supper is a covenant meal, we give weight to the new covenant referenced by Jesus and inquires into its content. It has highlighted Jesus's new commandment in John's account of the Last Supper (John 13) as *fundamental* to our understanding of the Supper. Because of Christ, we are restored as covenant partners of God, and are once again called to obey God's commandment to love one another. Precisely at the Last Supper, Christ himself set an example. As a covenant meal, the Supper doubtlessly calls for a concrete living response from the faith community. The new perspective therefore brings ethical inquiry to the forefront in a theology of the Supper. The meal no longer only concerns the private individual, but the community and its calling in concrete contexts. The emphasis on covenant turns the focus from the inner soul to the visible neighbor. Here, the long-held Augustinian distinction between visible sign and signified reality must also be reassessed. The covenant means that what we do—in the *physical* world—is most real. The Supper, then, is not about some invisible grace. The sociopolitical world in which we live and act *is* the reality. The new perspective that emphasizes Christ's gracious table hospitality means that any distinction between faithful and "unworthy" reception is non-existent. This point highlights the presence of Judas the traitor at the Last Supper that is highlighted, again, by all four Gospel accounts. Finally, a new perspective that points to the Passover narrative points also to the *structural* nature of sin as well as God's liberation of the oppressed. Not only ethics but politics may be brought to the forefront. The Supper speaks to the oppressed in society.

Bibliography

Adams, Marilyn McCord. *Some Later Medieval Theories of the Eucharist: Thomas Aquinas, Giles of Rome, Duns Scotus, and William Ockham.* New York: Oxford University Press, 2010.

Ahituv, Shmuel, and Shalom Paul. "Tribes of Israel." In *Oxford Dictionary of the Jewish Religion*, edited by Adele Berlin and Maxine Grossman, 751–52. New York: Oxford University Press, 2011.

Altmann, Peter. *Festive Meals in Ancient Israel: Deuteronomy's Identity Politics in Their Ancient Near Eastern Context.* New York: de Gruyter, 2011.

Ambrose, *De Mysteriis.* Brepols Library of Latin Texts, Series A.

———. *De Sacramentis.* Brepols Library of Latin Texts, Series A.

Anderson, Judith H. "Language and History in the Reformation: Cranmer, Gardiner, and the Words of Institution." *Renaissance Quarterly* 54 (2001) 20–51.

Aquinas, Thomas. *Summa Theologiae.* Translated by Fathers of the English Dominican Province. http://www.newadvent.org/summa/index.html.

Arnold, Bill T. "קרב." In *New International Dictionary of Old Testament Theology and Exegesis*, edited by Willem A. VanGemeren, 3:976. 5 vols. Grand Rapids: Zondervan, 1997.

Augustine. *St. Augustin: The Writings against the Manichaeans and against the Donatists.* Vol. 4 of *A Select Library of the Nicene and Post-Nicene Fathers of the Christian Church: First Series.* Edited by Philip Schaff. Grand Rapids: Eerdmans, 1956.

———. *St. Augustin's City of God and Christian Doctrine.* Vol. 2 of *A Select Library of the Nicene and Post-Nicene Fathers of the Christian Church: First Series.* Edited by Philip Schaff. Grand Rapids: Eerdmans, 1956.

———. *The Works of Saint Augustine.* Edited by Boniface Ramsey. 50 vols. Hyde Park, NY: New City, 1990–.

Ayres, Lewis, and Thomas Humphries. "Augustine and the West to AD 650." In *The Oxford Handbook of Sacramental Theology*, edited by Hans Boersma and Matthew Levering, 156–69. Oxford: Oxford University Press, 2015.

Balasuriya, Tissa. *The Eucharist and Human Liberation.* Maryknoll: Orbis, 1979.

Barth, Karl. *Church Dogmatics.* 4 vols. in 13 parts. Edited by G. W. Bromiley and T. F. Torrance. Edinburgh: T. & T. Clark, 1956–75.

Barth, Markus. *Das Mahl des Herrn: Gemeinschaft Mit Israel, Mit Christus und Unter den Gästen.* NeuKirchen-Vluyn, Germ.: NeuKirchener Verlag, 1987.

———. *Rediscovering the Lord's Supper: Communion with Israel, with Christ and among the Guests.* Atlanta: John Knox, 1988.

Beckwith, Sarah. *Christ's Body: Identity, Culture and Society in Late Medieval Writings.* New York: Routledge, 1993.

Beekenkamp, W. H. *Berengarii Turonensis De Sacra Coena Adversus Lanfrancum.* Kerkhistorische Studien Behoorende Bij Het Nederlandscharchief Voor Kerkgeschiedenis 2. The Hague: Nijhoff, 1941.

———. *De Avondmaalsleer van Berengarius van Tours.* Kerkhistorische Studiën Behoorende Bij Het Nederlandsch Archief Voor Kerkgeschiedenis 1. The Hague: M. Nijhoff, 1941.

Bell, Catherine M. *Ritual: Perspectives and Dimensions.* New York: Oxford University Press, 1997.

———. *Ritual Theory, Ritual Practice.* New York: Oxford University Press, 1992.

Berman, Joshua. *Created Equal: How the Bible Broke with Ancient Political Thought.* New York: Oxford University Press, 2008.

———. *The Temple: Its Symbolism and Meaning Then and Now.* Northvale, NJ: Aronson, 1995.

Billings, J. Todd. *Calvin, Participation, and the Gift: The Activity of Believers in Union with Christ.* Changing Paradigms in Historical and Systematic Theology. Oxford: Oxford University Press, 2007.

———. *Remembrance, Communion, and Hope: Rediscovering the Gospel at the Lord's Table.* Grand Rapids: Eerdmans, 2018.

———. *Union with Christ: Reframing Theology and Ministry for the Church.* Grand Rapids: Baker Academic, 2011.

Bloch, Abraham P. *The Biblical and Historical Background of Jewish Customs and Ceremonies.* New York: KTAV, 1980.

Blomberg, Craig L. *Contagious Holiness: Jesus' Meals with Sinners.* New Studies in Biblical Theology 19. Downers Grove: InterVarsity, 2005.

Bokser, Baruch M. *The Origins of the Seder: The Passover Rite and Early Rabbinic Judaism.* Berkeley: University of California Press, 1984.

Brettler, Marc Zvi. "The Many Faces of God in Exodus 19." In *Jews, Christians, and the Theology of the Hebrew Scriptures,* edited by Alice Ogden Bellis and Joel S. Kaminsky, 353–67. SBL Symposium Series 8. Atlanta: Society of Biblical Literature, 2000.

Brown, Raymond E., ed. *The Gospel according to John: Introduction, Translation, and Notes.* Anchor Bible 29. 2nd ed. Garden City, NY: Doubleday, 1979.

Burr, David. *Eucharistic Presence and Conversion in Late Thirteenth-Century Franciscan Thought.* Transactions of the American Philosophical Society 74. Philadelphia: American Philosophical Society, 1984.

Calvin, John. *Commentaries on the First Book of Moses Called Genesis.* Translated by John King. Grand Rapids: Eerdmans, 1948.

———. *Commentaries on the Four Last Books of Moses: Arranged in the Form of a Harmony.* Translated by Charles William Bingham. 4 vols. Grand Rapids: Eerdmans, 1950.

———. *Commentary on the Epistle of Paul the Apostle to the Corinthians.* Translated by William Pringle. Calvin's Commentaries 20. Grand Rapids: Baker, 1989.

———. *Commentary on the Gospel according to John.* Translated by William Pringle. Calvin's Commentaries 27. Grand Rapids: Baker, 1989.

———. *Institutes of the Christian Religion.* Edited by John T. McNeill. Translated by Ford Lewis Battles. Philadelphia: Westminster, 1960.

————. *Institutes of the Christian Religion.* Translated by Henry Beveridge. Grand Rapids: Eerdmans, 1970.

————. *Tracts Containing Treatise on the Sacraments.* Vol. 2 of *Catechism of the Church of Geneva* . Translated by Henry Beveridge. Edinburgh: Wentworth, 2009.

Canlis, Julie. "Calvin, Osiander and Participation in God." *International Journal of Systematic Theology* 6 (2004) 169–84.

————. *Calvin's Ladder: A Spiritual Theology of Ascent and Ascension.* Grand Rapids: Eerdmans, 2010.

Carson, D. A. *The Gospel according to John.* Grand Rapids: Eerdmans, 1991.

Carvalhaes, Cláudio. *Eucharist and Globalization: Redrawing the Borders of Eucharistic Hospitality.* Eugene, OR: Pickwick, 2013.

Cassuto, Umberto. *A Commentary on the Book of Exodus.* Jerusalem: Magnes, 1987.

Cavanaugh, William T. *Torture and Eucharist: Theology, Politics, and the Body of Christ.* Challenges in Contemporary Theology. Malden, MA: Blackwell, 1998.

Chadwick, Henry. "Ego Berengarius (For Luise Abramowski)." *Journal of Theological Studies* 40 (1989) 414–45.

Chan, Seguire S. H. "The Protestant Community and the Umbrella Movement in Hong Kong." *Inter-Asia Cultural Studies* 16 (2015) 380–395.

Chester, Tim. *A Meal with Jesus: Discovering Grace, Community, and Mission around the Table.* Wheaton, IL: Crossway, 2011.

Childs, Brevard S. *The Book of Exodus: A Critical, Theological Commentary.* Old Testament Library. Philadelphia: Westminster, 1974.

Ciampa, Roy E., and Brian S. Rosner. *The First Letter to the Corinthians.* Pillar New Testament Commentary. Grand Rapids: Eerdmans, 2010.

Cochrane, Arthur C. *Eating and Drinking with Jesus: An Ethical and Biblical Inquiry.* Philadelphia: Westminster, 1974.

Colautti, Federico M. *Passover in the Works of Josephus.* Supplements to the Journal for the Study of Judaism 75. Leiden: Brill, 2002.

Compier, Don H. *John Calvin's Rhetorical Doctrine of Sin.* Texts and Studies in Religion 86. Lewiston, NY: Mellen, 2001.

Courvoisier, Jaques. *Zwingli: A Reformed Theologian.* Richmond, VA: Wipf & Stock, 1963.

Cutrone, Emmanuel J. "Sacraments." In *Augustine through the Ages: An Encyclopedia,* edited by Allan Fitzgerald, 741–47. Grand Rapids: Eerdmans, 1999.

Dalman, Gustaf. *Jesus-Jeshua, Studies in the Gospels.* New York: KTAV, 1971.

Davis, Thomas J. *This Is My Body: The Presence of Christ in Reformation Thought.* Grand Rapids: Baker Academic, 2008.

Douglas, Mary. "Deciphering a Meal." In *Implicit Meanings: Essays in Anthropology,* 249–75. London: Routledge, 1979.

Dummett, Michael. "The Intelligibility of Eucharistic Doctrine." In *The Rationality of Religious Belief: Essays in Honour of Basil Mitchell,* edited by William J. Abraham and Steven W. Holtzer, 231–62. Oxford: Clarendon, 1987.

Durham, John I. *Exodus.* Word Biblical Commentary 3. Waco, TX: Word, 1987.

Du Toit, André. "No Chosen People: The Myth of the Calvinist Origins of Afrikaner Nationalism and Racial Ideology." *The American Historical Review* 88 (1983) 920–52.

Eberhart, Christian A. *The Sacrifice of Jesus: Understanding Atonement Biblically.* Facets. Minneapolis: Fortress, 2011.

————. *What a Difference a Meal Makes: The Last Supper in the Bible and in the Christian Church*. Translated by Michael Putman. Houston, TX: Lucid, 2016.

European Parliament. *Resolution on the Forced Labour and the Situation of the Uyghurs in the Xinjiang Uyghur Autonomous Region*. December 17, 2020. https://www.europarl.europa.eu/doceo/document/TA-9-2020-0375_EN.html.

————. *Resolution on the Human Rights Situation in Myanmar, Including the Situation of Religious and Ethnic Groups*. October 5, 2021. https://www.europarl.europa.eu/doceo/document/B-9-2021-0504_EN.html.

Fagerberg, David W. "Translating Transubstantiation." *Antiphon* 6 (2001) 9–13.

Farner, Oskar. *Huldrych Zwingli: Seine Verkundigung Und Ihre Ersten Fruchte, 1520–1525*. Zurich, Switz.: Zwingli-Verlag, 1954.

Fee, Gordon D. *The First Epistle to the Corinthians*. New International Commentary on the New Testament. Grand Rapids: Eerdmans, 1987.

Feeley-Harnik, Gillian. *The Lord's Table: Eucharist and Passover in Early Christianity*. Symbol and Culture Series. Philadelphia: University of Pennsylvania Press, 1981.

Fitzer, Joseph. "The Augustinian Roots of Calvin's Eucharistic Thought." *Augustinian Studies* 7 (1976) 69–98.

Fretheim, Terence E. *Exodus*. Interpretation, a Bible Commentary for Teaching and Preaching. Louisville: John Knox, 1991.

Garcia, Mark A. *Life in Christ: Union with Christ and Twofold Grace in Calvin's Theology*. Studies in Christian History and Thought. Milton Keynes, UK: Paternoster, 2008.

Gerrish, B. A. *Grace and Gratitude: The Eucharistic Theology of John Calvin*. Minneapolis: Fortress, 1993.

————. *The Old Protestantism and the New: Essays on the Reformation Heritage*. Chicago: University of Chicago Press, 1982.

————. *Reformers in Profile*. Eugene, OR: Wipf & Stock, 2004.

Gibson, Margaret T. *Lanfranc of Bec*. Oxford: Clarendon, 1978.

Gilders, William K. *Blood Ritual in the Hebrew Bible: Meaning and Power*. Baltimore: The Johns Hopkins University Press, 2004.

Gordon, Bruce. "Huldrych Zwingli." *Expository Times* 126 (2015) 157–68.

————. "Huldrych Zwingli's Dream of the Lord's Supper." In *Crossing Traditions: Essays on the Reformation and Intellectual History in Honour of Irena Backus*, edited by Irena Backus and Maria Cristina Pitassi, 296–310. Studies in Medieval and Reformation Traditions. Leiden: Brill, 2018.

————. *The Swiss Reformation*. New Frontiers in History. Manchester, UK: Manchester University Press, 2002.

Grappone, A. "Sacrament." In *Encyclopedia of Ancient Christianity*, edited by Angelo Di Berardino, 451–55. Downers Grove: IVP Academic, 2014.

Grimes, Katie M. "Breaking the Body of Christ: The Sacraments of Initiation in a Habitat of White Supremacy." *Political Theology* 18 (2017) 22–43.

Grumett, David. *Material Eucharist*. Oxford: Oxford University Press, 2016.

Guhrt, J. "Covenant, Guarantor, Mediator." In *New International Dictionary of NT Theology*, edited by Colin Brown, 1:365–76. Grand Rapids: Zondervan, 1986.

Gzella, Holger. "ברק." In *Theological Dictionary of Old Testament*, edited by G. Johannes Botterweck and Holger Gzella, 16:678. 17 vols. Grand Rapids: Eerdmans, 2018.

Haring, N. M. "Berengar's Definitions of *Sacramentum* and Their Influence on Mediaeval Sacramentology." *Mediaeval Studies* 10 (1948) 109–46.

Hedges-Goettl, Barbara Jan. "The Body Is Missing: Eucharistic Theology of the Presbyterian Church (U.S.A.) in Conversation with Zwingli, Calvin, and Nevin." PhD diss., Garrett-Evangelical Theological Seminary, 2013.

Heil, John Paul. "The Blood of Jesus in Matthew: A Narrative-Critical Perspective." *Perspectives in Religious Studies* 18 (1991) 117–24.

Helm, Paul. "John Calvin, the Sensus Divinitatis, and the Noetic Effects of Sin." *International Journal for Philosophy of Religion* 43 (1998) 87–107.

Heron, Alasdair I. C. *Table and Tradition*. Philadelphia: Westminster, 1983.

Hugh of St. Victor. *On the Sacraments of the Christian Faith (De Sacramentis)*. Translated by Roy J. Deferrari. Eugene, OR: Wipf & Stock, 2007.

Hunsinger, George. *The Eucharist and Ecumenism: Let Us Keep the Feast*. Current Issues in Theology. New York: Cambridge University Press, 2008.

Huygens, R. B. C. "À Propos de Bérengar et Son Traité de l'eucharistie." *Revue Bénédictine* 76 (1966) 133–39.

Jackson, Pamela. "Eucharist." In *Augustine through the Ages: An Encyclopedia*, edited by Allan Fitzgerald, 330–34. Grand Rapids: Eerdmans, 1999.

Jackson, Samuel Macauley. *Huldreich Zwingli: The Reformer of German Switzerland*. 2nd ed. New York: Putnam, 1903.

Janse, Wim. "Calvin's Eucharistic Theology: Three Dogma-Historical Observations." In *Calvinus Sacrarum Literarum Interpres*, edited by Herman J. Selderhuis, 37–69. Göttingen: Vandenhoeck & Ruprecht, 2008.

Jeremias, Joachim. *Die Abendmahlsworte Jesu*. Göttingen: Vandenhoeck & Ruprecht, 1960.

———. *The Eucharistic Words of Jesus*. New York: Scribner, 1966.

———. "Πολλοί." In *TDNT* 6:536–45.

Johnson, Dru. *Knowledge by Ritual: A Biblical Prolegomenon to Sacramental Theology*. Journal of Theological Interpretation Supplements 13. Winona Lake, IN: Eisenbrauns, 2016.

Jones, Douglas. "Ἀνάμνησις in the LXX and the Interpretation of 1 Cor. XI. 25." *Journal of Theological Studies* 6 (1955) 183–91.

Jones, Serene. *Calvin and the Rhetoric of Piety*. Louisville: Westminster John Knox, 1995.

Keener, Craig S. *A Commentary on the Gospel of Matthew*. Grand Rapids: Eerdmans, 1999.

Kugel, James L. *The Great Shift: Encountering God in Biblical Times*. Boston: Houghton Mifflin Harcourt, 2017.

———. *Traditions of the Bible: A Guide to the Bible as It Was at the Start of the Common Era*. Cambridge, MA: Harvard University Press, 1998.

Lammens, G. N. *Tot Zijn Gedachtenis. Het Commemoratieve Aspect van de Avondmaalsviering*. Kampen, Neth.: Kok, 1968.

LaVerdiere, Eugene. *Dining in the Kingdom of God: The Origins of the Eucharist according to Luke*. Chicago: Liturgy Training, 1994.

Le Déaut, Roger. *La Nuit Pascale*. Analecta Biblica 22. Rome: Institut biblique pontifical, 1963.

———. "Paque Juive et Nouveau Testament." In *Studies on the Jewish Background of the New Testament*, edited by Otto Michel et al., 22–43. Assen, Neth.: Van Gorcum, 1969.

Leeming, Bernard. *Principles of Sacramental Theology*. London: Longmans, 1956.

Leithart, Peter J. "Conjugating the Rites: Old and New in Augustine's Theory of Signs." *Calvin Theological Journal* 34 (1999) 136–47.

———. "Signs of the Eschatological Ekklesia: The Sacraments, the Church, and Eschatology." In *The Oxford Handbook of Sacramental Theology*, edited by Hans Boersma and Matthew Levering, 631–44. Oxford: Oxford University Press, 2015.

———. "The Way Things Really Ought to Be: Eucharist, Eschatology, Culture." *Westminster Theological Journal* 59 (1997) 159–76.

Levenson, Jon D. *The Death and Resurrection of the Beloved Son: The Transformation of Child Sacrifice in Judaism and Christianity*. New Haven, CT: Yale University Press, 1993.

———. "Exodus and Liberation." *Horizons in Biblical Theology* 13 (1991) 134–74.

Lindsay, Thomas M. *A History of the Reformation*. International Theological Library. New York: Scribner, 1928.

Locher, Gottfried Wilhelm. *Die Zwinglische Reformation Im Rahmen Der Europäischen Kirchengeschichte*. Göttingen: Vandenhoeck und Ruprecht, 1979.

———. *Zwingli's Thought: New Perspectives*. Studies in the History of Christian Thought 25. Leiden: Brill, 1981.

Lombard, Peter. *Sententiae*. Brepolis Library of Latin Texts, Series A.

Lubac, Henri de. *Corpus Mysticum: Essai Sur L'Eucharistie et l'Église Au Moyen Âge*. Paris: Aubier, 1949.

Luther, Martin. *Luther's Works*. Edited by Jaroslav Pelikan and Hartmut T. Lehmann. 55 vols. American ed. St. Louis, MO: Concordia; Philadelphia: Muhlenberg, 1955–86.

Macdonald, A. J. *Berengar and the Reform of Sacramental Doctrine*. London: Longmans, 1930.

MacDonald, Nathan. *Not Bread Alone: The Uses of Food in the Old Testament*. New York: Oxford University Press, 2008.

Macy, Gary. "Sacramental Theology." In *The Oxford Guide to the Historical Reception of Augustine*, edited by Karla Pollmann and Willemien Otten, 3:1680–83. 3 vols. Oxford: Oxford University Press, 2014.

———. *The Theologies of the Eucharist in the Early Scholastic Period: A Study of the Salvific Function of the Sacrament according to the Theologians, c. 1080–c. 1220*. Oxford: Clarendon, 1984.

———. "Theology of the Eucharist in the High Middle Ages." In *A Companion to the Eucharist in the Middle Ages*, edited by Ian Christopher Levy et al., 365–98. Brill's Companions to the Christian Tradition 26. Leiden: Brill, 2012.

Marcus, Joel. "Passover and Last Supper Revisited." *New Testament Studies* 59 (2013) 303–24.

Marks, Susan, and Hal Taussig, eds. *Meals in Early Judaism: Social Formation at the Table*. New York: Palgrave Macmillan, 2014.

Marshall, I. Howard. *Last Supper and Lord's Supper*. Grand Rapids: Eerdmans, 1981.

Martos, Joseph. *Doors to the Sacred: A Historical Introduction to Sacraments in the Catholic Church*. Revised and updated ed. Liquori, MO: Liquori/Triumph, 2001.

Mathison, Keith A. *Given for You: Reclaiming Calvin's Doctrine of the Lord's Supper*. Phillipsburg, NJ: P&R, 2002.

McCormack, Bruce L. Introduction to *Mapping Modern Theology: A Thematic and Historical Introduction*, edited by Kelly M. Kapic and Bruce L. McCormack, 1–20. Grand Rapids: Baker Academic, 2012.

———. *Orthodox and Modern: Studies in the Theology of Karl Barth*. Grand Rapids: Baker Academic, 2008.

———. "What's at Stake in Current Debates Over Justification? The Crisis of Protestantism in the West." In *Justification: What's at Stake in the Current Debates*, edited by Mark Husbands and Daniel J. Treier. Downers Grove: InterVarsity, 2004.

McCracken, George Englert. *Early Medieval Theology*. Library of Christian Classics 9. Philadelphia: Westminster, 1957.

McDonnell, Kilian. *John Calvin, the Church, and the Eucharist*. Princeton, NJ: Princeton University Press, 1967.

McGuckian, Michael. *The Holy Sacrifice of the Mass: A Search for an Acceptable Notion of Sacrifice*. Chicago: Liturgy Training, 2005.

Méndez-Montoya, Angel F. *Theology of Food: Eating and the Eucharist*. Illuminations—Theory and Religion. Malden, MA: Wiley-Blackwell, 2009.

Meshel, Naphtali S. *The "Grammar" of Sacrifice: A Generativist Study of the Israelite Sacrificial System in the Priestly Writings with a "Grammar" of Σ*. Oxford: Oxford University Press, 2014.

Michelson, Jared. "Covenantal History and Participatory Metaphysics: Formulating a Reformed Response to the Charge of Legal Fiction." *Scottish Journal of Theology* 71 (2018) 391–410.

Milgrom, Jacob, ed. *Leviticus 1–16: A New Translation with Introduction and Commentary*. Anchor Bible 3. New York: Doubleday, 1991.

Molnar, Paul D. *Karl Barth and the Theology of the Lord's Supper: A Systematic Investigation*. Issues in Systematic Theology 1. New York: Lang, 1996.

Moloney, Francis J. *The Gospel of John*. Edited by Daniel J. Harrington. Sacra Pagina Series 4. Collegeville, MN: Liturgical, 1998.

Montclos, Jean de. *Lanfranc et Bérenger: La Controverse Eucharistique Du XIe Siècle*. Leuven: Spicilegium sacrum Lovaniense, 1971.

Moore-Keish, Martha L. *Do This in Remembrance of Me: A Ritual Approach to Reformed Eucharistic Theology*. Grand Rapids: Eerdmans, 2008.

Moroney, Stephen K. *The Noetic Effects of Sin: A Historical and Contemporary Exploration of How Sin Affects Our Thinking*. Lanham, MD: Lexington, 2000.

Morris, Leon. *The Gospel according to John*. Rev. ed. New International Commentary on the New Testament. Grand Rapids: Eerdmans, 1995.

Muir, Edward. *Ritual in Early Modern Europe*. New Approaches to European History 11. New York: Cambridge University Press, 1997.

Neder, Adam. "History in Harmony: Karl Barth on the Hypostatic Union." In *Karl Barth and American Evangelicalism*, edited by Bruce L. McCormack and Clifford B. Anderson, 148–76. Grand Rapids: Eerdmans, 2011.

———. *Participation in Christ: An Entry into Karl Barth's Church Dogmatics*. Columbia Series in Reformed Theology. Louisville: Westminster John Knox, 2009.

Nocent, A. "Sacraments." In *Encyclopedia of Ancient Christianity*, edited by Angelo Di Berardino, 451–55. Downers Grove: IVP Academic, 2014.

O'Connor, Flannery. *The Habit of Being: Letters*. Edited by Sally Fitzgerald. New York: Farrar, Straus & Giroux, 1979.

Oded, Bustanay, and Harry Freedman. "Tribes, the Twelve." In *Encyclopaedia Judaica*, edited by Michael Berenbaum and Fred Skolnik, 20:137–40. 22 vols. Detroit: Macmillan Reference USA, 2007.

Oliver, Simon. "The Eucharist before Nature and Culture." *Modern Theology* 15 (2018) 331–53.

Olson, Dennis T. "The Book of Exodus." In *A Theological Biblical Commentary*, edited by Gail R. O'Day and David L. Petersen, 27–40. Louisville: Westminster John Knox, 2009.

———. "Sacramentality in the Torah." In *The Oxford Handbook of Sacramental Theology*, edited by Hans Boersma and Matthew Levering, 22–36. New York: Oxford University Press, 2015.

Opitz, Peter. "Ulrich Zwingli." *Religion Compass* 2 (2008) 949–60.

———. *Ulrich Zwingli: Prophet, Ketzer, Pionier Des Protestantismus*. Zurich, Switz.: TVZ, Theologischer Verlag, 2015.

Parker, T. H. L. *Calvin's Old Testament Commentaries*. Louisville: Westminster John Knox, 1993.

Pitre, Brant James. *Jesus and the Jewish Roots of the Eucharist: Unlocking the Secrets of the Last Supper*. New York: Doubleday, 2011.

———. *Jesus and the Last Supper*. Grand Rapids: Eerdmans, 2015.

Power, David N. *The Sacrifice We Offer: The Tridentine Dogma and Its Reinterpretation*. New York: Crossroad, 1987.

Propp, William Henry, ed. *Exodus 1–18: A New Translation with Introduction and Commentary*. Anchor Bible 2. New York: Doubleday, 1999.

Radbertus, Paschasius. "The Lord's Body and Blood." In *Early Medieval Theology*, edited by George Englert McCracken, 94–108. Library of Christian Classics 9. Philadelphia: Westminster, 1957.

Radding, Charles, and Francis Newton. *Theology, Rhetoric, and Politics in the Eucharistic Controversy, 1078–1079: Alberic of Monte Cassino against Berengar of Tours*. New York: Columbia University Press, 2003.

Rappaport, Roy A. *Ecology, Meaning, and Religion*. Richmond, CA: North Atlantic, 1979.

Ratramnus. "Christ's Body and Blood." In *Early Medieval Theology*, edited by George Englert McCracken, 118–47. Library of Christian Classics 9. Philadelphia: Westminster, 1957.

Riggs, John W. *The Lord's Supper in the Reformed Tradition: An Essay on the Mystical True Presence*. Columbia Series in Reformed Theology. Louisville: Westminster John Knox, 2015.

Rorem, Paul. *Calvin and Bullinger on the Lord's Supper*. Bramcote, UK: Grove, 1989.

———. "The Consensus Tigurinus (1549): Did Calvin Compromise?" In *Calvinus Sacrae Scripturae Professor: Calvin as Confessor of Holy Scripture*, edited by Wilhelm H. Neuser, 72–90. Grand Rapids: Eerdmans, 1994.

Rosemann, Philipp W. *Peter Lombard*. Great Medieval Thinkers. Oxford: Oxford University Press, 2004.

Rozeboom, Sue A. "Doctrine of the Lord's Supper: Calvin's Theology and Its Early Reception." In *Calvin's Theology and Its Reception: Disputes, Developments, and New Possibilities*, edited by J. Todd Billings and I. John Hesselink, 143–65. Louisville: Westminster John Knox, 2012.

Sandmel, Samuel. *Judaism and Christian Beginnings*. New York: Oxford University Press, 1978.

Sarna, Nahum M. *The JPS Torah Commentary: Exodus*. Philadelphia: Jewish Publication Society, 1991.

Schlund, Christine. *Kein Knochen Soll Gebrochen Warden: Studien zu Bedeutung und Funktion des Pesachfests in Texten des fruehen Judentums und im Johannesevangelium.* Neukirchen-Vluyn, Germ.: Neukirchener Verlag, 2005.

Scholler, Heinrich. "Martin Luther on Jurisprudence—Freedom, Conscience, Law." *Valparaiso University Law Review* 15 (1981) 265–82.

Scotland, Nigel. *The New Passover: Rethinking the Lord's Supper for Today.* Eugene, OR: Cascade, 2016.

Seeberg, Reinhold. *The History of Doctrines.* 2 vols. Grand Rapids: Baker, 1977.

Segundo, Juan Luis. *Sacraments Today.* Vol. 4 of *A Theology for Artisans of a New Humanity.* Maryknoll: Orbis, 1973.

Sheedy, Charles Edmund. *The Eucharistic Controversy of the Eleventh Century.* New York: AMS, 1980.

Slater, Jonathan. "Salvation as Participation in the Humanity of the Mediator in Calvin's Institutes of the Christian Religion: A Reply to Carl Mosser." *Scottish Journal of Theology; Edinburgh* 58 (2005) 39–58.

Smit, Dirk J. "Calvin on the Sacraments and Church Unity." *Die Skriflig* 44 (2010) 246–69.

Somerville, Robert. "The Case against Berengar of Tours, a New Text." *Studi Gregoriani* 9 (1972) 53–75.

Spinks, Bryan D. *Do This in Remembrance of Me: The Eucharist from the Early Church to the Present Day.* SCM Studies in Worship and Liturgy. London: SCM, 2013.

Staal, Frits. "The Meaninglessness of Ritual." *Numen* 26 (1979) 2–22.

Stephens, W. P. *The Theology of Huldrych Zwingli.* Oxford: Clarendon, 1986.

Stookey, Laurence Hull. *Eucharist: Christ's Feast with the Church.* Nashville: Abingdon, 1993.

Sumner, Darren O. *Karl Barth and the Incarnation: Christology and the Humility of God.* London: Bloomsbury, 2014.

Tabory, Joseph. *JPS Commentary on the Haggadah: Historical Introduction, Translation, and Commentary.* Philadelphia: Jewish Publication Society, 2008.

Tanner, Norman P., ed. *Decrees of the Ecumenical Councils.* Washington, DC: Georgetown University Press, 1990.

Thielicke, Helmut. *Theological Ethics.* 3 vols. Translated by John Doberstein. Edited by William H. Lazareth. Grand Rapids: Eerdmans, 1979.

Torrance, Thomas F. *Atonement: The Person and Work of Christ.* Downers Grove: InterVarsity, 2009.

———. "The Paschal Mystery of Christ and the Eucharist." In *Theology in Reconciliation: Essays towards Evangelical and Catholic Unity in East and West,* 106–38. Grand Rapids: Eerdmans, 1976.

Thurian, Max. *The Eucharistic Memorial.* Translated by J. G. Davies. 2 vols. London: Lutterworth, 1960.

Tylenda, Joseph N. "The Ecumenical Intention of Calvin's Early Eucharistic Teaching." In *Reformatio Perennis: Essays on Calvin and the Reformation in Honor of Ford Lewis Battles,* edited by B. A. Gerrish, 27–47. Pittsburgh Theological Monograph Series 32. Pittsburgh, PA: Pickwick, 1981.

Vaillancourt, Mark G. *Lanfranc of Canterbury on the Body and Blood of the Lord and Guitmund of Aversa on the Truth of the Body and Blood of Christ in the Eucharist.* Fathers of the Church. Mediaeval Continuation 10. Washington, DC: Catholic University of America Press, 2009.

Vandici, Gratian. "Reading the Rules of Knowledge in the Story of the Fall: Calvin and Reformed Epistemology on the Noetic Effects of Original Sin." *Journal of Theological Interpretation* 10 (2016) 173–91.

Wainwright, Geoffrey. "Berengar of Tours." In *Encyclopedia of Religion*, edited by Lindsay Jones, 2:837. 2nd ed. Detroit: Macmillan Reference USA, 2005.

———. *Eucharist and Eschatology*. 2nd ed. London: Epworth, 1978.

Warfield, Benjamin B. "The Fundamental Significance of the Lord's Supper." In *Selected Shorter Writings of Benjamin B. Warfield*, edited by John E. Meeter, 1:332–38. 2 vols. Nutley, NJ: Presbyterian & Reformed, 1970.

Waterworth, James, ed. and trans. *The Council of Trent: The Canons and Decrees of the Sacred and Ecumenical Council of Trent*. London: Dolman, 1848.

Welker, Michael. *What Happens in Holy Communion?* Grand Rapids: Eerdmans; 2000.

Wenham, Gordon J. *The Book of Leviticus*. New International Commentary on the Old Testament. Grand Rapids: Eerdmans, 1979.

Winner, Lauren F. *The Dangers of Christian Practice: On Wayward Gifts, Characteristic Damage, and Sin*. New Haven, CT: Yale University Press, 2018.

Wirzba, Norman. *Food and Faith: A Theology of Eating*. New York: Cambridge University Press, 2011.

Wright, N. T. *The Meal Jesus Gave Us*. Rev. ed. Louisville: Westminster John Knox, 2015.

Wylen, Stephen M. *Settings of Silver: An Introduction to Judaism*. 2nd ed. New York: Paulist, 2000.

Yi, Wang. "The Cross Has Political Significance." May 6, 2018. https://www.facebook.com/prayforearlyrain/videos/414678102436800/.

Zwingli, Huldrych. *Commentary on True and False Religion*. Edited by Samuel Macauley Jackson and Clarence Nevin Heller. Durham, NC: Labyrinth, 1981.

———. *Huldrych Zwingli: Writings*. Edited by H. Wayne Pipkin. Translated by Henry Preble. 2 vols. Allison Park, PA: Pickwick, 1984.

———. *On Providence and Other Essays*. Edited by William John Hinke. Durham, NC: Labyrinth, 1983.

Zwingli, Ulrich, and Heinrich Bullinger. *Zwingli and Bullinger*. Edited and translated by G. W. Bromiley. Library of Christian Classics 24. Louisville: Westminster John Knox, 2006.

General Index